Framing Finance

Framing Finance

*The Boundaries of Markets and
Modern Capitalism*

ALEX PREDA

THE UNIVERSITY OF CHICAGO PRESS   CHICAGO AND LONDON

ALEX PREDA is reader in sociology at the University of Edinburgh, United Kingdom.

The University of Chicago Press, Chicago 60637
The University of Chicago Press, Ltd., London
© 2009 by The University of Chicago
All rights reserved. Published 2009
Printed in the United States of America

18 17 16 15 14 13 12 11 10 09   1 2 3 4 5

ISBN-13: 978-0-226-67931-0 (cloth)
ISBN-13: 978-0-226-67932-7 (paper)
ISBN-10: 0-226-67931-4 (cloth)
ISBN-10: 0-226-67932-2 (paper)

Library of Congress Cataloging-in-Publication Data

Preda, Alex, 1960–
    Framing finance : the boundaries of markets and modern capitalism / Alex Preda.
        p. cm.
    Includes bibliographical references and index.
    ISBN-13: 978-0-226-67931-0 (cloth : alk. paper)
    ISBN-13: 978-0-226-67932-7 (pbk. : alk. paper)
    ISBN-10: 0-226-67931-4 (cloth : alk. paper)
    ISBN-10: 0-226-67932-2 (pbk. : alk. paper) 1. Finance—Social aspects. 2. Stock
exchanges—Social aspects. 3. Capitalism—Social aspects. I. Title.
    HG101.P74 2009
    306.3—dc22

                                                                    2008043188

⊗ The paper used in this publication meets the minimum requirements of the American
National Standard for Information Sciences—Permanence of Paper for Printed Library
Materials, ANSI z39.48–1992.

Contents

Acknowledgments

Acknowledgments are about giving credit and acknowledging debts, big and small, short- and long-term. In the present case, debts are mainly of an intellectual nature; but they also are incurred by the debtor having received gifts—of time, conversation, and insight. Gifts bind, and cannot be ever completely returned. Since intellectual debts arise from gifts, one does not want to sever the bond, but to acknowledge it, presenting the book as a small installment against a debt which cannot be written off.

In writing and revising this manuscript, I have indebted myself intellectually and morally to many friends and colleagues. Many of the exchanges I have had over the years have been wonderful occasions for learning and intellectual reflection, as well as for scholarly debates.

My gratitude (and indebtedness) goes first to Karin Knorr Cetina, Barbara Grimpe, Vanessa Dirksen, Stefan Laube, Werner Reichmann, and Leon Wansleben, who read and commented upon the entire manuscript, in a collective meeting which has brought me many intellectual benefits, along with the pleasure of having intense conversations with good friends. If the present book has any qualities, it is because of the intellectual rigor with which they, individually and as a group, have confronted each of its arguments. (If it has none, it is, of course, my entire responsibility.) And, talking about long-term debts, my greatest debt of all is to Karin Knorr Cetina, from whom I have learned so much as a student, colleague, and friend. This debt can never be repaid and it should be mentioned here.

Debts are often incurred within productive intellectual debates, for which two other good friends and conversation partners must be given credit here: Charles Smith and Franck Jovanovic have both helped me sharpen my arguments and ideas, constantly reminding me of the need to anchor them empirically. Many of the central arguments formulated in this book are direct offspring of reflections following debates with Charles and Franck, respectively.

Donald MacKenzie, who is to me an inspiring model of scholarly productivity, has read many chapters of this book, giving precious feedback and constantly encouraging me.

Discussions with Philip Mirowski have steered my interest toward the link between the evolution of financial concepts and that of financial technologies, respectively. Hendrik Vollmer, John Hall, Donna Messner, Michel Callon, Fabian Muniesa, Yuval Millo, and Martha Poon have all read various versions of different chapters and helped me sharpen the argument. Discussions with audiences at Columbia University, the University of Edinburgh, the London School of Economics, École des Mines in Paris, and the Wissenschaftskolleg in Berlin, where I have presented versions of some chapters over the years, have helped me better understand the issues at stake and steer through the maze of data.

Douglas Mitchell and Tim McGovern have provided great support and encouragement in the process of finishing and editing this book. I am particularly grateful to Doug for the interest he has taken in this project from the start, as well as for his perseverance in bringing it to completion. I am also grateful to Ed Scott, Rob Hunt, Dustin Kilgore, and Joan Davies for all their help and effort with bringing the manuscript to book form.

When discussing my moral indebtedness in writing this book, I cannot overlook the generous financial support which has made possible conducting empirical research over nine years. The research underlying the present book started in 1999 with a grant awarded to me by the University of Bielefeld in Germany. A Barra International Fellowship from the Library Company of Philadelphia, a Gilder Lehrman Fellowship at the New York Historical Society, and a further grant awarded by the University of Konstanz have made possible the continuation and expansion of the research which forms the basis of this book.

Some of the chapters in this book build upon articles I have published during my research. Chapter 2 is based on my article from the *British Journal of Sociology* 56, no. 3, pp. 451–71. Chapter 3 is based on my article from the *History of Political Economy* 36, no. 2, pp. 351–86. Chapter 4 is based on my article from *Social Studies of Science* 26, no. 5, pp. 753–82. Finally, chapter 5 is based on my article from the Sociological Review Monograph *Market Devices*. I am grateful to Blackwell Publishing, Duke University Press, and Sage Publications for their permission to use these articles as a basis for the above chapters.

Introduction: Capitalism and the Boundaries of Finance

A Society of Speculators?

If it is true that we live now in an economic age, and that "the new master narrative has abandoned the social for the economic," as Tony Judt (2007, p. 24) has recently put it, then finance is the master of this master narrative. To a large extent, economic identities are nowadays defined by financial markets: many people see themselves as small shareholders, as critical shareholders, as shareholders of ethical businesses, or of venture firms. They may be against grand speculators, or may dream of becoming one someday. Many follow price movements every day, or only now and then, trade online, or go to a trusted broker, watch the news, look at price charts, discuss the market with friends, and so much more. Some are active as day traders, either full time or combining the perceived dullness of a nine-to-five job with the excitement of transactions squeezed in between bouts of office work. These activities have become enmeshed with our daily lives: financial data flash up on screens in public places, market comments incessantly stream through the media, while investments are an appropriate subject for dinner conversations. And if these seem to be just small routines of daily life, then have a look at the recent grand designs for "reinventing Social Security for the 21st century" by reshaping it around individual investment accounts.[1]

Such projects, echoed by similar ones in Western Europe (not to mention Eastern Europe or other parts of the world), aim at creating a "finance society"—including all those who do not have the leisure to stroll the boulevards past electronic stock tickers. Beyond the hotly debated economic (de)merits of such plans, beyond their political motivations, beyond the concrete group interests which may push them to the foreground of the reform agenda, lies the belief that financial markets are the welfare institutions of the future, the belief that financial investments are beneficial for individual well-being and for the welfare of society as whole. Not only that: the future of the entire planet is presented as depending, at least in part, on setting up successfully a market in carbon allowances—financial entities traded in order to entice a reduction in carbon emissions and thus at least slowdown global warming.[2] Financial trading and investments are presented to us as means of securing the future (through taking financial risks) and of widening prosperity. This rhetoric requires a willingness to accept investment activities (and markets with them) as legitimate and highly desirable, to internalize the idea that each of us is an (active or dormant) trader/ investor, that financial investments are the way to safeguard the future, secure social stability, and avoid intergenerational conflicts. To paraphrase André Malraux, according to this rhetoric, the twenty-first century will be the century of finance, or it will not be at all.

And indeed, who would nowadays dream of openly revolting against financial markets, in the way we revolt against mistreating animals or against pollution? There are no mass protests against financial investments, no sit-ins, and no symbolic burning of financial securities. At the same time, it should be said here that the capacity of financial markets to ground policy projects is not taken for granted, and that in many specific instances it is hotly debated. Nevertheless, big financial failures and crises, for instance, which have regularly occurred up to our days, are not seen as menacing the social fabric. Rather, they are attributed to greedy, dishonest, or reckless corporate executives or traders (see the cases of Enron, WorldCom, Bear Stearns, Northern Rock in Britain, or Société Générale in France), or to perverse technological or social effects (the LTCM, the Russian default, the Asian default crises, or the banking crisis of 2008). The interventions and regulations which in many instances follow such crises aim at improving market governance, not at dismantling markets. The movement created in 1998 in Paris, ATTAC ("the international movement for the democratic control of financial markets and their institutions"[3]), has at least until now failed to develop into a sustained, mass-supported, and significant project against financial markets.[4] Nowadays, nobody requests the death penalty for financial speculators, the way representatives in the

Assemblée Nationale did during the French Revolution, and nobody asks for eliminating stock brokers, as some passionate writers did in the eighteenth century. We've come a long way.

Nevertheless, this willingness to accept the legitimacy of financial markets cannot prevent doubts and discomfort from resurfacing in public debates, at least in certain circumstances. At times, events seem to converge in fueling such doubts: the meltdown of the mortgage and credit markets since early 2008, or the discovery that an unsupervised trader had lost his employer $7.6 billion, for instance, has contributed to unsettling, at least for the time being, the public's comfort with how financial markets operate, if not with their legitimacy.

The commonly perceived distinction between an "investor" and a "speculator" may seem to support this broad acceptance: while the former puts his savings in financial securities, but does not actively and constantly intervene in managing their yield, the latter takes an active position in financial transactions, buying and selling constantly. It is speculators who take risks and let themselves go into a frenzy of transactions. This popular perception of recklessness and irrationality (as opposed to the prudence and calculation of the investor) has culminated perhaps in the widespread notion that day traders transact by hitting the computer keys almost at random.[5] According to this distinction, it is the speculator, not the investor, who is morally questionable. Social (and sociological) criticism should be directed against speculators, but not against investors. This sort of argument (which amounts to saying that passivity is morally preferable to activism) treats the distinction between "investing" and "speculating" as a natural one, grounded in the (innate) attitudes of individuals. It is forgotten here that the distinction itself is the outcome of a historical process, shaped by concrete cultural forces.[6]

The notion that financial markets are central to people's lives and their sense of security is relentlessly propagated in countless publications which offer advice, plans, and schemes for financial well-being, assuring readers that it is in their best interest to invest, that numbers of experts will back them up with their knowledge and experience. Computer screens displaying the latest financial data are present in many public places (shop windows, libraries, billboards); perhaps ironically, the computer system displaying messages to participants at the 2007 meeting of the American Sociological Association also integrated an electronic ticker running the latest price data. At my own university, one of the most popular student societies is the investment and trading club. Their weekly meetings regularly pack large lecture halls, and the campus cafes buzz with "sector committees" discussing the latest financial developments.

At the core of this incessant preoccupation with markets and their price dynamics lie the stock exchanges, the institutions generally perceived to form the nuclei of financial markets. Of course, these latter are complex, stratified, and ramified social architectures, comprising heterogeneous actors. Nevertheless, when twenty-year-old students climb the podium of their trading society to report about "the market," when sociologists monitor the flow of price data at their convention, when travelers catch a glimpse of the electronic ticker while on the subway escalator, most will know that all this comes from stock exchanges. When prices euphorically go up, or when they stir a fright by tumbling down, we watch the stock exchange as "the market," as the master in finance's master narrative.

We seem to be living in an endless, diffuse, yet ubiquitous exhortation to trade and invest, and its sense of urgency is hard to match. Invest, or the future will be closed to you! Coming from all directions, this exhortation has taken on a life of its own, so that it is difficult now to point at a single source from which it originates. It has become a membrane which envelops our lives, covering the spaces through which we move and cocooning our projections of the future.

If numbers are anything to judge by, this public rhetoric is matched by the proliferation of financial services and firms. In 2005 in the United States alone, for instance, there were 6,016 firms in the securities industry (compared with 5,248 in 1980), with total revenues of over \$332 billion (US Bureau of Census 2008, table 1192). Rather large number of individuals and families participate in financial investments, in one form or another. In 2001, almost 52% of US families held stocks, directly or indirectly, and the median value of their holdings was \$34,300 (Swedberg 2005, p. 198). At the end of 2006, individuals in the UK owned £239 (ca. \$480) billion worth of shares, an increase of 17% over 2003. Individually held shares represented 12.8% of the total value of UK share holdings, down from 54% in 1963 (Office for National Statistics 2007, pp. 9–10). In 2007 in Germany, the number of direct and indirect shareholders represented over 16% of the population over fourteen, or a total of 10.3 million individuals (Deutsches Aktieninstitut 2007, table 08.3-Zahl-D). Nevertheless, the prominent place of investment discourses in social life cannot be simply attributed to the rise in the number of individuals participating in financial investments.[7] Neither does this mean that contemporary financial markets are dominated by individuals and/ or families. Since the late 1950s, the role of institutional investors has continuously increased (Lowry 1984, p. 23; before World War II, they accounted for only one third of the trading volume). Institutions are now the dominant market participants, although there are considerable differences among them. Along with institutions and individuals, small groups (e.g., hedge funds or investment clubs) are also active and sometimes very important players.

The notion that financial investments enable life projects and ensure the welfare of individuals has been accompanied by an institutional orientation toward financial markets, an orientation attributed to revolutions in the corporate structure (Zorn, Dobbin, Dierkes, and Kwok 2005, p. 270; Fligstein 1990) or to the "financialization" of corporations (Krippner 2004). The corporate revolution designates the growing emphasis put by corporations on shareholder value and on market performance (with concrete consequences for the corporate structure), backed by a rhetoric of market omniscience and infallibility. "Financialization" is another name for the growing role played by investment activities as an autonomous profit center in the corporate structure. On a broader scale, financialization is defined as "changing the social balance of power to the profit of a particular form of capital, the financial capital, and [to the profit] of its actors, its representations, and its institutions" (Bourdieu, Heilbron, and Reynaud 2003, p. 3).

Broadly put, we can identify at least three levels on which the orientation toward financial markets plays a considerable role in defining (economic) identities: (1) that of individual actors, who are told that their economic safety and future depend on their engagement with markets; (2) that of institutional actors, who define their performance as market performance and partly transfer functions and attributes upon financial markets; and (3) that of the whole humanity as a collective, the survival of which is presented as partly depending on the successful creation of new financial entities (like carbon allowances) which should support new forms of ecologically responsible behavior.

If the orientation toward financial markets is perceived as central with respect to social and economic stability, to collective and individual projections of the future, and to understanding "freedom," "choice," "inclusion," and the like, then the following questions arise: How did this orientation emerge and come to play such a central role in our understanding of the social order of capitalism? Is it a new development, something which took shape in recent years,[8] or is it something which developed over a longer period of time? Since public acceptance of stock exchanges as social

institutions is a core component of this orientation, we can start by looking into how this came into being.

The fact that it can provide such a stable foundation to political projects makes us think that it is not a new phenomenon, but rather the result
of a longer cultural development. If this is so, can we track the origins and
the social foundations of this legitimacy? This latter question is essential
for understanding the boundaries between finance and society at large:
without a broad legitimacy (for a definition, see Suchman 1995, p. 574), financial markets could not be perceived as crucial for our projections of the
future. At the same time, the legitimacy of stock exchanges rests on how
the boundaries between them and society at large are drawn. The question of boundaries and legitimacy isn't just one of the public indifferently
noticing (or passively accepting) that there is something called "finance."
It has important implications for how dispersed actions are coordinated
and how uncoordinated actors engage on uncertain paths of action.

Finance and the "Spirit of Capitalism"

One way of dealing with the legitimacy of (financial) markets has been
to treat this as the "spirit of capitalism," a concept which continues to
stir debates among social scientists. While there is a rich and illustrious
sociological lineage that discusses this "spirit," financial markets have not
always been seen as integral to it. Of course, more recent analyses like
those of Luc Boltanski and Eve Chiapello proclaim that "the archetype
[of the capitalist] is the investor who places his money in an enterprise
and expects a financial reward . . . the saver who does not want that his
money sleeps, but breeds" (1999, p. 39). This figure is understood as an
"ensemble of beliefs associated with the capitalist order, which contribute
to justify it and support, by legitimating them, the modes of action and the
dispositions which are coherent with the capitalist order" (Boltanski and
Chiapello 1999, p. 46). However, if we look at the sociological tradition
and its main explanatory schemes dealing with the cultural engine which
drives capitalism, we can see that, while financial markets are not entirely
neglected, they are not always present in these schemes either.

What is the sociologically insightful moment in this blindness toward finance?[9] Can it be attributed to the simple fact that there were not enough
investors around at the time when Karl Marx or Max Weber explored
the spirit of capitalism?[10] This would amount to saying that, not having

seen enough investors, Marx or Weber decided they were not important at all. This argument can be refuted on at least two counts. First, financial markets played a significant role throughout the second half of the nineteenth century. Already in 1850, at the start of the first globalization wave,[11] financial assets represented 39% of all assets owned by individuals in Britain, a proportion which rose to 64% by 1913 (Michie 1999, pp. 71–72). In the period 1870–1914, the number of individual investors rose from 250,000 to 1 million. Moreover, in 1894 Max Weber noticed that ownership of financial securities was relatively widespread in France, the UK, and the US, even among farmers and factory workers, and estimated that at that time in Germany about 1.5–2 million individuals received dividends from investments in financial securities ([1894] 1924, p. 268). It is hard to believe that Max Weber, Karl Marx, or even earlier thinkers like Adam Smith were not aware of the significance of financial markets.

Secondly, we have to take into account the conceptual schemes explaining the collective beliefs which support and justify the capitalist social order. In a restricted sense, this requires an investigation of how classical sociology conceptualizes financial markets in relation to the issue of the "spirit of capitalism." In a larger sense, the question is redirected as follows: what position (if any) do financial markets occupy with respect to the set of beliefs seen as central for the capitalist order?

The possible link between finance and the "spirit of capitalism" thus raises a set of broader issues concerning the relationship between social consciousness and economic action. Marketplace transactions are ultimately individualistic and different from forms of action which aim at attaining a common goal. Profit is an individual goal, the attainment of which may imply cooperation, competition, or even conflict with other actors. The actions of market participants can be similar or based on imitation; nevertheless, their irreducible feature is individuality. Markets are "the negation of collective action" (Taylor 2004, p. 79)[12]. Their order is different from that of the state or of the public sphere. At the same time, economic action is marked by uncertainty; its projected outcome (profit) is anything but guaranteed.

Collective actions (of the kind we encounter in the public and political spheres) can be coordinated by collectively held beliefs and channeled through the same social positions (e.g., like class or group membership).[13] But how can individual, uncertain economic actions coordinate in a flexible fashion—that is, leaving room for contingencies, failures, or retreats, among others?[14] The coordination problem is complicated by the dispersion of individual, uncertain actions: only in rare cases can economic actors directly observe each other. In financial markets, for instance, we encounter a diversity of situations and positions, the coexistence of dispersed grand speculators and small investors, day traders, occasional buyers of bonds, professionals and amateurs, and so on. The problem of coordinating individual, uncertain, dispersed, and diverse actions can be seen as the uncertain coordination of action (Thévenot 1993, p. 276), which manages to articulate both diversity and similarity without guaranteeing outcomes.

The conceptual problem is that economic action, being intrinsically individualistic, is oriented primarily toward oneself, not toward (the benefit of) others. When projecting paths of future action, economic actors are confronted with uncertainties and have to relate to each other. For these purposes, routines are not entirely adequate in and by themselves: due to the individual character of economic action, we cannot conceive them as collective routines or as automatically oriented toward others.[15] But, if we conceive them as individual routines, we would have as many structural positions as there are actors (solipsism). We need therefore to account for how forms of mediation other than routines or direct observation can achieve coordination under conditions of uncertainty. At the same time, these forms should be able to attract new participants to financial activities and define the relationships between financial institutions (like the stock exchange) and the society at large.

Collective beliefs as an explanatory device do not work very well here, not only because they are perilously close to the notion of a collective mind (an entity notoriously difficult to pin down empirically), but also because they cannot explain either the variability of individual actions, nor their uncertain outcomes, while preserving the idea of coordination and variable participation. Instead of searching for an elusive "spirit," perhaps we would do better investigating concrete, material arrangements.[16] Instead of trying to find the Graal of a collective mind, perhaps we should set for ourselves the more modest task of investigating how embodied, talking, adroit, ingenious, industrious actors can coordinate among themselves, albeit in a dispersed and uncertain fashion.

Boundaries and the Uncertain Coordination of Action

There are at least two interrelated ways for the coordination of dispersed actions under uncertainty, ways which emphasize the actors' adroitness and ingeniousness. The first is indirect observation; the second is boundary construction. While direct observation acts as a crucial coordination mechanism for actors concentrated in the same space, or who meet periodically, it cannot work well for actors who only rarely meet, or not at all. Direct observation, of course, cannot be immediate, in the sense that all observation, as a basic cognitive activity, is shaped by mutually shared categories, classifications, and explanatory schemes (e.g., Barnes, Bloor, and Henry 1996, p. 15). In the sociological conceptualization of markets, direct observation is acknowledged as an uncertainty-processing, network-stabilizing device: actors take cues from their reciprocal observations and act accordingly. Network ties influence the observational capabilities of actors, serving as a prism which filters information (Podolny 2001, p. 35). Markets swim in a "sea of discourse" (White 2000, p. 118), which, to a large extent, actually consists of observations. Face-to-face talk and memos allow actors to observe each other, thus building a "quality order" which appears equivalent to Joel Podolny's status order (Podolny 1993, p. 830). In these accounts, forms of direct and indirect observation are not kept separate, although face-to-face talk might shape action in ways different from a memo.

Actors seem to need face-to-face encounters in order to coordinate their actions: periodical conventions, business meetings, golfing trips, and lunches provide many occasions for reciprocal direct observation. There are, however, limits to this form of coordination: dispersed actors do not always meet periodically or, in some cases, do not meet at all. Day traders, for instance, may transact with each other without ever meeting or talking to each other.[17] Therefore, it could be useful to distinguish between direct and indirect observation as coordination devices, since they might have different effects and work in different ways.

Moreover, observation implies (dis)trust, which can be personal or impersonal. In practice, even direct observations have to rely on a combination of personal and impersonal trust. Trust in somebody also means trust in concrete processes and forms of face-to-face interaction, judged as reliable and adequate for coordination. Also, some forms of indirect observation are predicated on a principle of distrust rather than trust. Closed-circuit TV cameras are a case in point. It is important in this respect to distinguish between different kinds of observation, according to who observes whom or what. In the case of closed-circuit TV cameras, or of special interview rooms with one-way mirrors, access to the observers is completely closed off. Detectives do not want to be observed by the interrogated suspects, nor does security staff in a museum want to be conspicuous to visitors (except in cases where visibility is supposed to act as a deterrent). Being inconspicuous or invisible is characteristic to observational forms predicated on the principle of the panopticon. By contrast, there are situations where a group wants to be observed, albeit in controlled ways. The willingness to be observed, to show a face to the world, results from the need for legitimacy, trust, and for attracting interactions or customers. Think of open kitchens in restaurants, for example, put there to build trust. Also, professionals like doctors and lawyers allow external (though controlled), direct (e.g., the examination room, the courtroom), and indirect observation (e.g., publications, documentaries, interviews) for this same reason. Since impersonal trust implies, among other things, reliance on (observational) procedures and processes, it follows that the object of observation cannot be independent of observational procedures.[18] The "lenses" which mediate observation thus shape or "co-constitute" the object being observed. Indirect observation as a coordination mechanism would then require "lenses," or observational arrangements, which provide a common orientation to market actors.

Boundaries can be such lenses. Very often, boundaries have been understood as symbolic and social distinctions among categories such as gender, class, or race (e.g., Lamont and Molnar 2002, p. 168). Usually, boundaries are presumed to be distinct from and even prior to the observational process. They are also often assumed to be set in place after establishing the categories they divide (Abbott 1995, p. 858). Their widespread understanding as categorical distinctions, as well as their association with the idea of border or frontier (e.g., Hannerz 1997, p. 10; Shields 2006, p. 224; Tilly 1998, p. 67; Gal and Irvine 1995), seems to divert the attention from how they are put in place, as well as from their possible features as observational arrangements. Sometimes, boundaries are set to be observed and thus to coordinate dispersed, unrelated actions. At the same time, boundaries can be set not only among groups and categories, but also between a specific group and the society at large. They can be not only "boundaries between," but also "boundaries between and within."

Thinking of the stock exchange, such boundaries would not only have to distinguish groups associated with the stock exchange (brokers, market-makers, traders, and the like) from nonassociated groups, but also to establish the limits of the stock exchange within society. Without this latter, the distinction between associated and nonassociated groups would not be possible.

There is, however, a second meaning of boundaries, centered not on distinction, but on communication: boundaries bridge social worlds and coordinate the activities of heterogeneous groups and individuals (e.g., Star and Griesemer 1989; Star and Bowker 1999; Fleischmann 2006, p. 78). This kind of boundaries is more than discursive distinctions, symbols marking the bodies of social actors, or institutional rules: communicational boundaries can be incorporated in artifacts, theoretical models, and forms of expert knowledge. Artifacts, models, and knowledge can coordinate the action of dispersed actors, who would otherwise have few things in common. They are flexible enough to allow for different takes on them: think of the different uses a telescope can be put to by high school students and by professional astronomers, respectively. Communicational boundaries lend themselves to uncertain outcomes: further courses of action and observational results are not preestablished. Not all high school students using telescopes in a science class are going to be astronomers. Yet telescopes allow various degrees of participation to the same family of activities.

Turning again to the stock exchange, we would need to think whether and how material arrangements (including technology) establish not only distinctions, but also ways of communication and coordination of different groups associated or not associated with the exchange. The work of setting in place such boundaries—observational arrangements or lenses for the uncertain coordination of action—is itself "strategic practical action" (Gieryn 1999, p. 23). It is strategic in at least the following senses: setting up boundaries as observational arrangements can endow a group with control over how certain activities are perceived and valued by the public at large, or by other groups. Moreover, setting up boundaries can endow a group's activities with legitimacy: by allowing controlled observation, the group legitimizes its activities. By legitimizing a group, such boundary work creates group identities and coordinates internal and external exchanges: in short, it generates social entities (Abbott 1995, p. 860) which anchor the group to society at large.

Communicational boundaries do not exclusively imply cooperation or division. Situations can arise where a group's setting up divisional boundaries requires letting outsiders observe and participate in the group's activities in controlled ways. A combination of division and communication along such a boundary can legitimate the group's activities and integrate them into the society at large by allowing various forms of public participation, without presetting their outcomes. An example here is that of children observing what other children are doing in the neighbor's house by peeking through the windows. Let's say that the children in the house could have shut the curtains, but have chosen not to, because they wanted to be observed, albeit in a way which they could control. Or they could have half-shut the curtains, making only certain corners of the room observable from the outside. They leave traces in the room, so that the kids outside can form an idea of what the children inside are doing from these traces. In other words, the children inside have set up both a division (they do not let other children inside) and an observational system, so that their activities can be made sense of by the outside children. They have traced a communicational boundary to the social world outside their house.

Boundaries, Legitimacy, and Access

With respect to the core of financial markets, namely the stock exchange, we can regard its boundaries as akin to those of the house discussed above. Division and closure is accompanied (and legitimated) by controlled systems of observation. Understanding these boundaries (and the legitimacy of the "house of finance") requires understanding systems of observation irreducible to the direct, reciprocal observations of actors on the floor of the exchange, for instance.[19] The problem of (market) boundaries is one of legitimacy too: once we accept a domain of action as legitimate, we can classify it along with other legitimate domains and set up the rules governing it.

Establishing the legitimacy of a domain of activity also means establishing how it can be observed and accessed: what kind of behavior is seen as adequate for legitimate (active or passive) participation? Or, conversely, we could reject a domain as illegitimate, prohibited, and/ or undesirable. In social life, we also encounter situations where society erects observational barriers between itself and certain groups. These barriers are meant to prevent and contain, rather than to facilitate exchanges. They show that such groups, who are not entirely outside society, are not entirely inside it either. They may have ties with the larger society, but the group's legitimacy, its acceptability and respectability, may be contested or left unclear. When the legitimacy of such groups is problematic, or when group activities are illegitimate (or illegal), the issue of barriers to public observation becomes important. In some cases, barriers are made important by an ambiguous legal frame. In other cases, the absence of legal and institutional frames requires such barriers. An example is the early groups of computer hackers. In the 1960s and 1970s, before a legal and institutional frame was put in place, the legitimacy of computer hackers was unclear: were they geniuses or villains? Being a computer hacker was primarily associated with inventiveness and with the ability to solve programming problems, or to restore crashed computers.[20] Yet the term began being associated with accessing computers at a distance, an access which initially was not legally defined. This uncertainty was solved by erecting barriers (e.g., through media stories, books, corporate advertising) that limited the legitimacy of these groups, even before a legal frame was set in place.

In contrast to the situation where a barrier is erected from the outside, a group can set up observational boundaries. These boundaries will determine how the public at large can participate in the group's activities, as well as their legitimacy. Especially if it wants to persuade the public that it is legitimate, or if it wants to attract followers, the group will need an observational arrangement where its activities can be accessed as legitimate. It will need instruments capable of traveling across space and time and of attracting people from the outer social world to the sphere of its activities.

The problem of (market) boundaries, and its two aspects (legitimacy and access), cannot be taken as conceptually distinct from the coordination of dispersed actions. In fact, the only reason for regarding these boundaries as already set in place is our assumption that reciprocal face-to-face observations serve (only) to reduce market-internal uncertainties about price, quality, and quantity. In other words, we assume the coordinating device both to be guaranteed by and to guarantee market boundaries (taken as identical with network boundaries). My argument, however, is that indirect observation is a coordinating device which produces market boundaries. Karin Knorr Cetina (2005, p. 40) makes the point that markets are supported by an observational or "scopic" system (incorporated in the computer screen) which allows dispersed actors to coordinate their actions by observing the outside world together. The notion of scopic systems as coordination devices relies on Alfred Schutz's argument that the world is constituted in the temporal experiences of the subject (Schutz and Luckmann 1974, p. 55) as a flow (and anticipation) of phases of movement (e.g., like when observing a bird's flight). Observational devices (like binoculars) allowing birdwatchers to observe a bird's flight orient the actors to each other and make possible the reciprocal coordination of their actions. (Think of a situation where birdwatchers can recognize each other as such by the devices they use, and coordinate accordingly.) Similarly, dispersed market actors use observational instruments (like computer screens) as coordinating devices.

Back to the example of the house in which children play with toys, while leaving the curtains pulled apart, so that other children can observe them: living in a house with no windows at all would make observation from the outside impossible, but such a house would seem quite weird on a "decent" and "honorable" street. It will also be an undesirable situation for the children inside, if they want the outside kids to participate in their games, even if only by looking. Leaving the door open, so that all children outside can come in and play, can be undesirable too for those inside, since they would run the risk to lose control over the toys. Instead, the children inside might decide to let those outside participate in controlled ways (and thus legitimize their games) with others by controlling what can be seen from the outside and what cannot. Thus, outside children could become participants to the games inside the house, though without becoming its inhabitants. These games include now not only what is going on inside the house, but also the observational arrangements (window, curtains, etc.). It is a game of being observed while playing with toys, not just a mere game of playing with toys. While windows and curtains are constitutive of the boundaries of the house, they are also a way of legitimating what is going inside the house and of controlling participation.

This example sends us rather quickly to the stock exchange and its boundaries to the external world. As in the children's house, we encounter various actors on the stock exchange, taking different positions with respect to each other: brokers, market makers, and the like. These actors and their positions are held in place and (partly) defined by their reciprocal relationships. But this is not enough: they need to define their relationships and their position with respect to the social world too. They need to set up windows and curtains enabling (and controlling at the same time the possibilities for) observation. They need to let actors from this world come in and become players. They need to be accepted by the outside world. They need to present and represent themselves and their interactions to the outside world, to put a face to the world (Goffman 1959; Charaudeau and Maingueneau 2002, p. 259). Stock exchanges cannot dispense with observational boundaries, which are not dissimilar to that used by the children in our story. What do these boundaries consist of? They consist of the observational systems through which the stock exchange (re)presents itself to the society at large, a system through which paths of financial action are opened and actors position themselves with respect to financial activities.

Observational boundaries have a projective character—they open up avenues of future action. They also coordinate dispersed actions under uncertainty. With respect to financial markets, then, the question becomes one of identifying and analyzing the production of the observational apparatus which legitimates them and mediates access to transactions. Observational boundaries are permeable (they let outsiders engage in the activities propagated by the group) and expandable. Expandability means two things: first, such boundaries can reproduce in time and space. Second, they can incorporate an increasing number of ways in which the group's activities are legitimated.[21] Following Marx's argument (outlined in the next chapter), one might say that the expansion of the reproduction modes of capital, as exemplified by the stock exchange, requires an expansion of the reproduction of its legitimacy modes. Permeability and expandability have at least three requirements: (a) that the group's activities are legitimated; (b) that it is legitimate for outsiders to engage in these activities; and (c) that both actual and prospective participants are provided with cognitive and attitudinal instructions for how to enter these activities, together with justifications of success or failure.

Borrowing a concept from Erving Goffman (1974, pp. 82, 156–57), I will call an observational boundary exhibiting the interconnected properties (a)–(c) triply laminated. Goffman (1974, pp. 10–11) employs the notion of frame to analyze the interaction mechanisms used by actors in order to define situations in which they find themselves. It is in this context that he draws our attention to the fact that frames can acquire superimposed representational layers, which endow the situation with new properties, or change the existing ones.[22] If one thinks of the frame of a painting, this not only limits the work of art (which does not expand indefinitely), but also works as an observational instrument: we observe the painting in the frame and through the frame. In many cases, frames are crafted in such a way as to introduce the viewer to the painting, while extending the latter into the world. This, for instance, is true of older religious paintings, whose elaborate frames reproduce ornaments from the churches where they were hung. The same goes for Victorian paintings, with elaborate flowery frames, matching wallpaper motives. A frame, then, akin to the window of the house, not only limits a painting, but is also an observational arrangement connecting it to the outside world and orienting the viewer's gaze.

What is the relationship between barriers and boundaries? Society at large (or parts of it) can erect representational barriers trying to limit (or specify) the legitimacy of a group's activities (or its universality claims). The group, at the same time, generates an expandable boundary which serves to continuously broaden claims of universal legitimacy. What could happen in such cases? One the one hand, the boundary has the crucial properties of lamination and expandability, with the latter not simply meaning expansion in time and space, but the capacity to invent new modes of legitimacy. On the other hand, barriers are mostly local—that is, they contest one aspect (ethical, political, cultural, or economic) of the group's activities.

The above properties make observational boundaries very resistant: points of clash and contestation do arise, but they will have a local character. In other words, when groups active on the stock exchange have put such a boundary in place (or started producing it in a sustained and coherent fashion), it is very hard for external representations to dismantle, demolish, or discredit it entirely. Rather, what will happen is that clashes and contestations arise at certain points: for instance, some financial investments may be contested as ethically problematic or as politically undesirable. Such contestations would be locally contained (see figure 1). Expansion and reproduction take place not in spite of but with these clashes. I call this mode of expansion and reproduction *expansion by manageable dissent.*[23]

A further specification is that observational boundaries leave room for a variety of individual paths of action: they do not predetermine how financial activities have to be accessed, or how each individual makes use of the tools they provide. At the same time, tools of access are also tools for justifying success or failure: the grand speculator and the small investor, the successful day trader and the failed player legitimize their actions with respect to elements of the same boundary.

Observational boundaries enable action at a distance, legitimize financial transactions for a broad public, and allow external actors to penetrate into their sphere. They create modes of financial agency (Taylor 2004, p. 76) and project paths of action without which stock exchanges cannot exist as robust social institutions.

There are at least two additional questions here: where do the boundaries of finance come from? And what do they consist of? With respect to the first question, I do not claim that boundaries come from nowhere, that they are "texts without authors."[24] Based on empirical investigations,

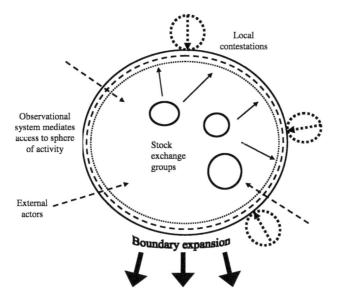

Local
contestations

Observational
system mediates
access to sphere
of activity

Stock
exchange
groups

External
actors

Boundary expansion

FIGURE I. Observational boundaries.

I argue that they are set in place by specific groups who control a domain of activity and are interested in (re)presenting this domain of activity to the outside world as both legitimate *and* accessible.[25] They allow external actors to observe the domain in question, but in ways which these actors do not control.[26] They also allow the domain's actors to observe each other without direct interaction, by providing them with categories of classification and judgment, with frames of perception, and tools of interpretation. Investigating the boundaries of finance, then, would automatically mean investigating the process of social closure of which it is a part.

What do the boundaries of finance consist of? What is to be observed in the first place? We must think here of the central element which makes transactions possible and around which other knowledge features evolve: price. Access to transactions requires first and foremost some form of price observation. A first feature of the boundaries of finance, then, would be the observation of prices without physical copresence. I call this feature *microscopic*, since it works akin to the said instrument, bringing small entities/pieces of information closer to the observer. For instance, prices can be observed flowing at the bottom of a computer screen, or on a Blackberry, without the observer having to be present at every single transaction.

However, observing prices in isolation is not enough. Observations need to be made sense of; they need categories and procedures to compare them, tools for assembling bigger entities out of small bits. We click on the Web site of a financial analysis service, for instance, and we access visually processed assemblages of price data, which are classified along preset categories and interpreted for us. Here's where a second aspect intervenes, bringing together these small entities and allowing for the observation of their relationship. I call this aspect *telescopic*. Analogous to the astronomical instrument, the financial telescope allows the observation of prices in their self-referential context—that is, other prices—from afar.

There is also a third feature: accounting for the place of financial markets in the larger contexts of the economy, society, and the state, and providing categories that may help to make sense of markets and their actors in these contexts. When arguing why a jump in the Dow Jones index is beneficial, economic experts use explanatory templates linking entities like the national economy, employment, incomes, and well-being, interpreting financial events with respect to society. While observing prices and constellations of prices presupposes focus on a specific entity (think of a biologist observing a cell), observing financial markets in their relationship to economic, social, and political entities means looking at several entities at once, entities which may combine in different ways.[27] This aspect is more like a *kaleidoscope*, through which the observer looks at different entities combining in certain patterns. While the microscope and the telescope primarily generate possible paths for financial action, the kaleidoscope primarily represents finance within the larger society.

I take these three interrelated observational modes to be central for the boundaries of finance under modern capitalism. Having stated this, I argue that the analysis of the "spirit of capitalism" should be redirected from collections of abstract beliefs, existing only in the minds of market players, or from an ideology concealing hidden meanings, to the boundaries where modes of public access and participation to financial activities are generated, and to the instruments, techniques, and knowledge forms which enable, constrain, and regulate this access. It is these instruments, techniques, and knowledge forms that allow for the uncertain coordination of dispersed actions and they orient the public and the society at large toward finance. Understanding the spirit of capitalism then implies understanding the concrete processes through which the boundaries of finance emerge.

At a more specific level (and anticipating the overall argument of the book), the notion of boundaries of finance purports to answer a dilemma which can be formulated as follows: the enclosure of stock exchanges, set in place at the start of the nineteenth century, was meant to endow markets with legitimacy. This enclosure, however, together with the social restrictions put on access, cut off possibilities for an outsider acquiring knowledge of financial transactions and actors through in situ observation. This undermines the very limits assumed to be set in place by enclosure, since actors need perspectives, procedures, and definitions in order to be able to access transactions and to differentiate between legitimate institutions. When enclosed, market transactions cannot be directly observed anymore; the knowledge required by the legitimacy and robustness of markets cannot be the result of direct observation. Yet they have to be defined as observable from the outside. Boundaries intervene here as an observational system. These boundaries are not the view from nowhere. They are set in place from within financial markets, by concrete historical actors. They are set in place, along with other boundaries, because these actors acquire authoritative public voices, taking up roles outside the market as educators, writers, and scientists.

The enclosure of the stock exchanges, regarded by many as sealing the birth certificate of modern financial markets, should not be understood as just another modernization story, or reducible to institutional differentiation, or to professionalization. The boundary work implied by such differentiation is irreducible to distinctions between markets, on the one hand, and legal or political institutions, on the other. Empirical evidence points at such distinctions being set in place in a complex process, in which they are inextricably tied to broader aspects concerning legitimacy and the mechanisms for observing transactions. Moreover, in order for boundary work to take place, the groups performing it have to assume legitimate social positions which do not obey principles of social and cultural differentiation. Quite the contrary: such groups have to gain public voices, by becoming writers, scientists, educators, literates, sportsmen, or society gentlemen. Only by being more than what they are professionally—that is, brokers, traders, speculators, or telegraph engineers—can such groups put a collective face to society while closing their activities to direct scrutiny.

This public face includes an observational system which redefines financial knowledge as akin to science and as grounded in observation. This system has at least three interrelated dimensions. The first is the observational system of price data, essential with respect to financial transactions.

It sets up a mode of seeing price data as an appresentation, that is, as perception and representation fused together, of financial transactions. While this allows the close-up observation of data, the second dimension allows the observation of price constellations from afar. Both bring about new skills, new interpretive languages, new professions, and new modes of accessing the market. Finally, the kaleidoscope of finance allows the observation of entities too big, too complex, or too dispersed to be scrutinized from close-up or from afar, like the state or the national economy in their relationship to financial markets. The observation of these entities is made from within; the observers are part of that which is being observed. Therefore, the kaleidoscope of finance includes observations of imagined market actors, providing role models and orientation for the real ones.

Two conflicting elements characterize these boundaries. On the one hand, they are based on the notion of financial knowledge as akin to scientific knowledge, on price observation and analysis. Financial success should be ensured by constant and diligent observation. Everyone can share this success, provided he or she studies the market. On the other hand, the boundaries of finance take over and develop the idea of speculation as driven by a vital force; on this ground, financial markets are seen as fulfilling specific functions, which put stock exchanges at the core of society. This force is not shared by all in equal measure. Charisma, not knowledge, keeps markets in their place. This tension is intrinsic to the boundaries of financial exchanges.

These latter boundaries are not a smooth observational system, without friction and resistances. First, as argued above, they contain an essential tension. Second, they encounter various resistances both from within and from without, like the opposition of some brokers to the introduction of stock tickers, contemporary resistances to market automation (Zaloom 2006, pp. 67–69), or political, religious, and cultural resistances to the dominance of financial markets. Such resistances can take the form of analogies to gambling, or of accusations that financial speculation subverts the productive economy. In essence, these are not new but have been repeated since the eighteenth century. A central asymmetry, which helps explain the boundaries' resilience to these attacks is that, while the former have been able to colonize the genres in which contestations are expressed (i.e., political or religious discourse, or fiction), these genres themselves have not been able to colonize the boundaries of finance as a whole. This sends us to the fundamental property of lamination discussed above (Goffman 1974). Resistances may question one aspect or another, but not the triple

mode of observing financial transactions. In this perspective, the boundaries of finance do not eliminate resistances; they manage them.

The Visibility of Boundaries

Generating observational boundaries means producing devices accessible
to a broad public: they can be manuals, articles, stories, historical narratives, educational novels, newspaper articles, investment journals, securities price lists, analysts' reports. But observational devices can also be
technologies for recording and making visible securities prices. Prices can
be made visible as separated entities or as a continuous flow, as tied to
social events or as self-contained, as unique or as multiple entities, as accessible to all at once or as enabling only a restricted access.

I have argued that boundaries do not come from nowhere. They are not
authorless, but are generated by groups active on or associated with the
activities of the stock exchange: stock brokers (active or retired), grand
speculators, financial journalists, securities analysts, engineers involved in
financial activities. This may seem unusual, if we keep to the cliché that
contemporary stock exchanges are highly differentiated institutions exclusively involved in financial transactions. A closer look at what some
nineteenth century brokers and grand speculators did reveals a wealth of
literary activities, ranging from poetry and novel writing to efforts toward
building rigorous theories of finance. It also reveals deep involvement
with improving technologies for recording, representing, and interpreting
securities prices.

Characteristic of these observational tools is that they are not disconnected from each other: investor manuals teach securities evaluation
methods, which require price data, which are generated by specific recording technologies, while histories of the stock exchange praise the progress made by these technologies; investor biographies evoke the grandeur
of the stock exchange as a social institution, and investor manuals praise
the knowledge and skills of grand investors. Taken together and in their
interdependence they form durable layers, which are resistant to local
contestations.

At the same time, the contestations, the barriers erected in the path of
manuals, advice, praises, and glorious narratives, take the form of pamphlets, critiques, unmasking stories, ethical diatribes, critical novels, sermons, or treatises. Most times, they are not written by persons associated

with or active on stock exchanges, but by outsiders. Since the eighteenth century, we encounter barriers questioning and contesting various aspects of stock exchanges and of investment activities. Yet these barriers do not possess the interconnectedness, the complexity, and the all-enveloping character of observational boundaries. They do not combine heterogeneous literary technologies like those of price-recording and price-interpretation.

There is a third class of devices relevant for investigating boundaries of finance: diaries, letters, self-descriptions, and biographies of market actors. While manuals and how-to books provide instructions and tools for action, this class shows how people involved in financial investments perceive themselves, what rules they adopt, and how they monitor both their behavior and the world of financial transactions. Diaries and letters do not belong to the public domain, in the way investment manuals and stock exchange narratives do. Nevertheless, they uncover an important link between this domain and the private actions of those involved in financial transactions. They show how and to what extent prescribed agency is transposed into concrete, individual actions. Certainly, diaries and letters do not allow generalizations; however, they uncover patterns of self-presentation and representation intrinsic to the figure of the investor.

Overview of the Book

This book is about the observational boundaries mediating the relationship between financial markets and society. It is about how these boundaries crystallized in the period known as the first globalization wave (ca. 1850–1914). Eighteenth-century writers put a lot of effort into erecting representational barriers which could delimit the broader society from the stock exchange and from investment activities. This happened in England and France (which witnessed periods of great financial turbulence), as well as in the young United States. From the mid-nineteenth century on, boundaries were set, which by the dawn of the twentieth century were able to contain criticism, doubts, and ethical questions. These boundaries were set up by authors active as brokers and speculators on the stock exchanges of the time, mainly in New York, London, and Paris, or associated with these institutions. This, for instance, is the case of telegraph engineers, who were deeply involved in the development and implementation of price-recording technologies, but also of some Paris brokers who laid down the founding principles of the random walk hypothesis.

These boundaries could be seen as a relentless process of rationalization, as the constitution of an all-encompassing calculative agency (Callon
2004; Barry and Slater 2002b) which makes financial markets more and
more rational. One of my core arguments, that the boundaries of finance
configure investors/traders as akin to scientists, could reinforce this impression. A possible reaction would be then to argue that the "science of
financial investments" is a false science, that the rationalization process
is an illusion (De Goede 2005), and that all this is just an elaborate setup
for continuing deception. I do not argue here that this science is true or
false (and, in the present context, I do not believe in the relevance of this
question). What I do is show how it was put in place and to what effects.
But I do not analyze the boundaries of finance as a process of relentless
rationalization either, if we understand by that the gradual elimination of
what we call the "irrational," the "emotional," or the "incalculable." As
Max Weber saw, stock exchanges involve a double game, in which rational
and irrational features coexist and feed on each other. And I do not claim
that such boundaries eliminate all fraud, deception, and cheating. Theirs
is a long and glorious history in financial markets. Rather, what I do here
is to show how this system opens up new possibilities and avenues for the
reproduction and proliferation of fraud, deception, and manipulation, in
ways which did not exist before.

I have talked about observational systems and barriers, about the
eighteenth and the nineteenth century. This requires showing two sets of
changes. The first set concerns differences in the genre and character of
data available from the eighteenth and the nineteenth century, respectively. While pamphlets, satires, comedies, and moral diatribes dominate
the eighteenth century, the manual, the handbook, the history of the stock
exchange, and educational biographies and narratives are overwhelmingly
present in the nineteenth century. Of course, archives have lacunae, documents degrade or get lost. Yet it is hard not to notice a striking shift here.
Even more striking, perhaps, is that this shift is encountered in England,
France, and the United States. I relate it to a second set of changes in
the character and organization of exchanges, which can be reconstructed
from primary sources, as well as from secondary analyses. These changes
concern the enclosure of stock exchanges, which limit possibilities for observing and participating in financial transactions, and institute barriers
between the public and brokers.

I examine here both sets, arguing that the first is triggered by the second.
In other words, the character and structure of stock exchanges changed

in the nineteenth century; the boundaries of finance crystallized in this change. I use primary data from the eighteenth and the nineteenth centuries in order to support my argument. The data come from various archives and concern the New York Stock Exchange, the London Stock Exchange, and the Paris Bourse, the three major exchanges of that time. Among the most important archives are the British Library, the Archives of the Bank of England, the Guildhall Library, the New York Historical Society, the New York Public Library, the Library Company of Philadelphia, and the Bibliothèque Nationale of France. These documents consist in pamphlets, diatribes, comedies, handbooks, newspaper articles, journals, memoirs, biographies, narratives of investment activities, histories of the stock exchange, diaries and letters of investors, ledgers and correspondence of brokerage houses, novels, and poems.

Chapter 1 examines the sociological reflection upon the relationship between finance and the "spirit of capitalism." I contrast here Adam Smith's account of financial markets with the ways in which Karl Marx, Max Weber, Werner Sombart, and Joseph Schumpeter saw the place of stock exchanges and investors in the social order. While focusing the analysis on a restricted set of major accounts of the capitalist order, I argue that they have a double character, conceptual and observational. Sociological conceptualizations of finance process observations of stock exchanges and of investors, observations which cannot be entirely separated from the broader representational system which mediates between the stock exchange and the society at large. Therefore such conceptualizations can be seen as a seismograph of the boundary shifts taking place, but also as an effort at comprehending the ties between modern society and one of its major institutions.

I continue by examining changes in the character and organization of three major stock exchanges (New York, London, and Paris), which (perhaps with the exception of the Paris Bourse) are triggered around 1800 but continue until the end of the century. Chapter 2 deals with a rather neglected feature of financial markets: the role of status groups and prestige. I show how, in the eighteenth century, stock brokers lacked one essential thing: prestige and legitimacy. At the turn of the nineteenth century, a process of socio-institutional enclosure begins, which restricts access to brokerage activities and to transactions. Against the lack of a legal frame reinforcing financial transactions, prestige appeared as a means of building trust and legitimacy for stock exchange activities. Along with transaction rituals, rules of good social behavior, dynastic transmission of brokerage privileges, social hierarchies, and the restricted access of outsiders to brokerage activities, another feature of social prestige emerged now on both sides of the Atlantic: the transformation of some brokers into "serious" authors, keen to straighten the public image of stock exchanges and of investment activities. Social closure should not be understood exclusively as professionalization, since it includes (and even sometimes requires) the opposite of the former: namely reaching out into society at large through inventing (or adapting) new activities such as writing.

Chapter 3 examines the emergence and consequences of a vernacular "science of financial investments." While many eighteenth-century writers saw financial knowledge as devilish and destructive (centered upon the bodily and verbal skills required by street transactions), these new authors set out to build a science of investments grounded in observation and calculation. Among the main outcomes of this process were the rationalization of investor behavior and the representation of financial markets as supra-individual, quasi-natural entities, which cannot be controlled by any group. It was this latter notion which allowed the shift to price behavior as the core actor of abstract market models, in the way we know it today. The effort to transform investment knowledge into a science was crowned by the formulation of basic tenets of the random walk hypothesis, which was to dominate the second half of the twentieth century.

While some brokers-cum-authors developed abstract models of price behavior, others were interested in technical devices which could help record or predict price movements. Some were simply interested in using devices to keep outsiders away from price information. These interests met those of telegraph engineers, and so a far-reaching technological shift occurred in the late 1860s: the replacement of pencils and paper by the stock ticker. Chapter 4 examines the context and consequences of the stock ticker. The ticker transformed the character of price data: a continuous flow of data replaced the rather unsystematic price lists. Trust was shifted from idiosyncratic knowledge of transaction partners to a machine which could travel across social contexts. New modes of attention and observation were introduced, which brought individuals together into price monitoring activities, in public places.

Chapter 5 deals with another dimension of the boundaries of finance: the mediation of value judgments by securities analysts. I trace here the emergence of chartists as a specific group in relationship to the new kind of price data generated by the stock ticker. Occasional and unsystematic evaluation of securities has always taken place, and financial information has always been collected, more or less systematically. The new price data, however, boosted efforts to predict future prices movements and, with them, the value of securities. Some brokers left financial transactions and moved into price interpretation. They diligently began selling their intellectual product around: technical analysis was thus born. Using memoirs, letters, journal articles, and manuals, I examine here how a group of former US brokers and statisticians from the East Coast successfully marketed price charts and technical analyses to investors and stock brokers alike. Contrary to the assumption that the growing complexity and mass of financial information required this sort of cognitive intermediation, I show here how intermediaries created a demand for this sort of product.

A device like the ticker, together with the associated interpretations, reinforced and put into practice the requirements formulated by investment manuals. The investor was represented as a kind of scientist. But how could this scientist integrate into the grand tableau of national economies? This required ethical and political reconceptualizations of finance. Chapter 6 deals with the justification of financial markets as "functional." The investor-cum-scientist couldn't be anything but a responsible family father and a good citizen, who contributes to the national welfare by his activities. Accordingly, political economists began legitimizing investment activities as fulfilling economic functions, a discourse which starkly contrasted with the eighteenth-century view of investments as bad passions. Political utopias envisaged a better society based on financial investments. I explore here the functionalist justification of stock exchanges, as well as their transformation into national symbols, inextricably connected with state power.

Chapter 7 examines the double game of what could be superficially seen as relentless increases in efficiency. The notion that financial speculation is endowed with a special force, which justifies its economic functions, is echoed in the tension between thrilling speculation, on the one hand, and the drudgery of everyday capitalist accumulation, on the other hand, as well as in the representation of superhuman speculators.

Chapter 8 investigates how the notion of panic crystallizes in representations of the market and how it affects the hierarchy of speculators. These latter's charismatic features cannot withstand crowd movements like panic. One of the major contradictions at boundaries of markets appears to be that between an individualism grounded in a vitalistic notion of force and the crowd's stampede. I explore here how the notion of (financial) panic, emerging almost simultaneously in economic and psychiatric writings, deals with this contradiction. I also examine how representations of panic—from the media, for instance—are used by market participants to make sense of their own actions. Based on a reconstruction of actual practices, I argue that such representations should be understood as material observational tools, which help dispersed actors see their situations as identical or similar.

With that, I arrive at the conclusion of this book, in which I leave the domain of historical documents in order to explore how these boundaries work in our days. Hopefully by now I could persuade readers that such boundaries are not a mere historical curiosity, but something which is very much with us, and forcefully so. In the light of their historical development, I explore here the proliferation of cognitive intermediations, valuations, interpretations, and predictions of market movements. Returning to the issue of status groups, I ask whether, in an era of automated transactions, securities analysts will play an ever growing role as the prominent status group in financial markets. Recent financial scandals, as well as regulatory measures adopted in the early 2000s, suggest that this is already happening. With regard to the almost total dependence of contemporary financial transactions on sophisticated technological systems, I ask whether new forms of manipulation and deceit constitute the dark side of what we have taken to be rationalization and progress. I also explore a whole series of phenomena which are very much with us, like fascination with charismatic speculators. In an era of global markets, the boundaries of finance play a crucial role in legitimating both universal market expansion and reform projects, like the ones concerning pension systems. Yet to put it in Max Weber's words, we all too often forget here that this is a double game.

And now it's time to begin its story.

CHAPTER ONE

The Boundaries of Finance in the Sociological Tradition

An investigation of the boundaries of finance emerging at about the same time as sociology cannot avoid questioning how the latter saw the former: how do emerging sociological views on the capitalist order deal with financial markets? This question goes beyond the mere exercise in the history of sociological ideas: it concerns both conceptualization (what notions have explanatory force) and observational mode (how shall we see finance in the context of capitalism).[1] It also concerns the nature and character of financial knowledge and its relationship to other forms of social knowledge, as well as to specific social groups.

For many theorists, observation of (economic) knowledge in action meant, among other things, identifying its manifestations on the individual level, its expressions in human types and the related categories of action. It meant finding paradigmatic figures embodying the main principles of finance, figures which constitute the link between this domain and the larger sphere of life and connect individual modes of action to broader social processes. And indeed we encounter in the sociological tradition a continuous preoccupation with the figures generated by the modern order: the expert, the public man, the consumer, the intellectual, the scientist, the writer, the artist—these are only some major examples. Yet the feeling persists that no account of life under capitalism would be complete without taking into account the main figures of economic life, simply because, since the eighteenth century, these figures have been increasingly perceived as the focal point of both society *and* individual lives. In the words of Charles Taylor, "the affirmation of ordinary lives is part of the background to the central place given to the economic in our lives" (2004, p. 74).

At the same time, observing financial knowledge in action means tracing its forms and boundaries within society at large, identifying its intermingling with other forms of knowledge, and its broader implications. To a considerable extent, the sociological tradition distils this knowledge into figures or types, whose positions within society embody the boundaries of social activities.

I will not undertake the Sisyphean enterprise of exploring the whole range of figures enumerated above. Instead, I will focus on a core set of economic figures, on the premise that they belong not only to sociology's conceptual toolbox, but are also relevant with respect to how the boundaries of (or barriers against) finance are set. Among the attempts to define economic life under capitalism by the figures it generates, at least the following are prominent: (1) the manufacturer, (2) the accumulating capitalist, (3) the religious capitalist, and (4) the entrepreneur. Adam Smith's manufacturers, as well as Joseph Schumpeter's and Werner Sombart's entrepreneurs, belong to (1) and (4), respectively.[2] Karl Marx's and Max Weber's respective figures of capitalists are examples of (2) and (3). Their authors saw them not as by-products, but as key with respect to the capitalist order: they are the individual counterpart and the source of the entity called capital. Moreover, these figures do not appear only as contingent on particular (economic or social) developments, but as occupying a central place in their respective conceptual schemes for explaining capitalism. They take specific positions with respect to finance, and these positions are intrinsic to the boundaries of the latter. Be it absolute opposition, continuity, exemplarity, or contiguity, such a position is intrinsic for how finance is understood in relationship to the broader society.

Manufacturer vs. Speculator: Good vs. Bad Passions

In the eighteenth century, "capitalist" was understood by social philosophers, by economic thinkers, and by the educated public as a person who invests money in public debt or in stock, and expects an annuity or a dividend. A capitalist was someone who did not have to work for a living, nor live off land revenue, nor have profits from manufacture or trade. His revenue was derived from the financial securities he owned and traded. At the dawn of the modern era, being a capitalist meant being an investor (DuPlessis 2002, p. 36). Only toward the end of the century did Adam Smith's *Wealth of Nations* give a new, abstract twist to the term "capitalist."

A superficial observer could say that Adam Smith has not depicted a central figure of capitalism, being too busy with the grand tableau of the national economy. Yet Smith's economic landscape is not empty, but populated by a whole array of figures, some of which are of central importance. Increasing the nation's wealth is, in Adam Smith's eyes, the ultimate aim of economic life. While agriculture, trade, and other economic activities may contribute to increases in wealth, manufacture remains the key branch of the economy. Great nations excel in manufacture (Smith [1776] 1991, p. 12); this latter, superior in skills and productivity to agriculture, is the core of the economy. All other economic activities—like banking and trade—are subordinated to increasing the industry of the country (Smith [1776] 1991, p. 258). The manufacturer is skilled and innovative: he has a deep knowledge of production processes and of local conditions, is geared toward permanent improvement, and is interested in long-term development. Of all social types, wrote Smith, the "master manufacturer" plays the central role; the merchant, another important figure, is subordinated to the manufacturer in the social order of wealth. Manufacturers have the best knowledge of their own interest, a self-interest which is the very spirit of capitalism: "During their whole lives (they) are engaged in plans and projects, they have frequently more acuteness of understanding than the country gentlemen. . . . Their superiority over the country gentleman is not so much in their knowledge of the public interest, as in having a better knowledge of their own interest than he has of his" (Smith [1776] 1991, p. 219).

For Smith, then, the manufacturer is superior to all other social characters generated by the capitalist economy. He is at the center of a solar system in which the merchant, the worker, and the country gentleman revolve around him like planets revolving on different orbits around the sun. Some are nearer, and some are farther away, profiting in different degrees from the energy it emanates. How can the centrality of this construct be conceptually grounded in a way consonant with empirical observations? Two concepts support the construct: the first is that of the division of labor and the second that of original sensations, which engender self-interest. Let us begin with the division of labor. While human talents and inclinations are not identical with or equal to each other, they are not naturally unequal either. Nature is responsible for very few, yet crucial, human propensities. If we can identify any natural inclination in human beings, then it is the propensity to exchange. An undifferentiated society would have to be kept small or collapse very quickly. Without the division of labor, the social fabric cannot be made durable (Smith [1776] 1991, pp. 19, 22).

At the same time, with sensations being the basic form of human experience, pain and pleasure emerge out of the natural state of things (Smith [1759] 1966, p. 321). Seeking pleasure and avoiding pain is the primary expression of self-interest and the mark of basic individual rationality. The fulfillment of self-interest cannot take place outside social life or against fellow social beings, and has to combine with the natural propensity to exchange and barter. It follows, then, that self-interest requires social interactions in the production and exchange of goods and commodities. Production and exchange, in their turn, are shaped by the division of labor, which nurtures individual talents and dispositions. While these latter are not unequal by nature, they develop into a hierarchy through the division of labor. Talents and dispositions are brought to the market, the expansion of which means both a deepening of the division of labor and a loosening of traditional ties, rituals, and obligations (Smith [1759] 1966, p. 327; [1776] 1991, p. 24). Growing individualization means at least two things: first, that the talents and dispositions enacted in market exchanges are ranked according to their social importance—that is, to their ability to maintain the differentiated and complex social fabric created by the division of labor. Second, individualization increases the (natural) adaptability and the assimilation capacities of individuals, who need to orient themselves to exemplary characters. This need of orientation, in its turn, generates sentiments and attachment: this is what happens when public life, for instance, produces the character (or figure) of the patriot, whom we view with admiration and take as an example (Smith [1759] 1966, p. 335).

In economic life, at least, exemplary characters are shaped by the talents and dispositions that the division of labor nurtures as most important. Since the manufacturer embodies self-interest at its best, and is central in the system of differentiated labor, it follows that this is the central figure of capitalism. Seen from the viewpoint of the state and of the nation, the manufacturer would appear as embodying the public spirit which Smith opposes to the spirit of system ([1759] 1966, p. 342): unencumbered by ideologies, skilled, practical, self-interested, yet in harmony with fellow citizens.

In this perspective, the central figures of capitalism reinforce the social fabric, since economic actors and the public view them with necessary admiration. As Smith put it, characters produce sentiments ([1759] 1966, p. 335), which, in an individualized society, are very important for social cohesion. Besides being public examples (and fostering imitation), figures structure the economic order of society. They show how self-interest is harmonized with social interests, how wealth is produced and accumulated. The division of labor and self-interest support economic order (and society with it) as a complex, differentiated, yet smoothly running machine.

What place does Adam Smith ascribe to finance in this machine? Where can we find speculation, if at all? Surely, having witnessed much of the eighteenth century's speculative turmoil, Smith could not have neglected it. If capitalism is a system with the manufacturer as its radiant sun, what is the orbit of speculation? To keep within this metaphor, this latter can be found toward the darker regions of Pluto. It appears in the last chapter of the *Wealth of Nations*, which deals with public debt and, not incidentally at all, opens up by discussing bad passions ([1776] 1991, p. 574).

Good passions are social passions, those which reinforce the social fabric by creating attachment to public characters (heroes, or exemplary manufacturers) and to institutions. Bad passions are related to unbalanced expenses, which, while apparently serving the public, grow like tumors on its body. So is public debt, which seems to spring from the abundance of merchants and manufacturers in search of capital. Nations begin then to imitate private persons and cover public needs by borrowing. Yet public borrowing diverts capital from maintaining productive labor and from manufacturing, thus hindering the accumulation of capital ([1776] 1991, pp. 583–84).

This diversion of capital from productive activities leads to loss of knowledge and loss of emotional attachment to economic life and the public sphere. This is even more condemnable than delayed or hindered accumulation of capital, because it endangers the division of labor and with it the social fabric:

> To transfer from the owners of those two great sources of revenue, land and capital stock, from the persons immediately interested in the good condition of every particular portion of land, and in the good management of capital stock, to another set of persons (the creditors of the public, who have no such particular interest), the greater part of the revenue arising from either, must, in the long run, occasion both the neglect of land, and the waste and removal of capital stock. [. . .] But a creditor of the public,[3] considered merely as such, has no interest in the good condition of any particular portion of land, or in the good

management of any particular portion of capital stock. As a creditor of the public he has no knowledge of any such particular portion. He has no inspection of it. He can have no care about it. Its ruin may in some cases be unknown to him, and cannot directly affect him (Smith [1776] 1991, pp. 586–87).

The speculator (who deals in public debt) appears thus as the antipode of the manufacturer: lack of skills, knowledge, and care for productive capital transforms self-interest into selfishness, endangers the harmony of interests, and enfeebles the state. In a conceptual scheme based on the division of labor and on socially ranked, productive talents, the speculator cannot be a figure of capitalism, but rather its nemesis.

This conclusion is reached on the grounds of a postulated similarity between economic life and the public sphere: both need exemplary characters and good passions. These latter are understood as a state of knowledge (skills, dispositions) which orients economic actors toward each other, generating thus emotional attachment and ethical norms of economic behavior. For Smith, there is no substantive difference between political and economic heroes. A prosperous society needs examples of the latter. The imitation of positive examples cannot take place without making visible these figures to all at once. Yet the consequences of bad passions would have to be made visible too, showing what happens when lack of knowledge and care dominate economic action. This situates the speculator outside the boundaries of public life: a speculator cannot relate to other economic figures and to the public but in a negative way. It is rather a barrier which is erected here. The incompatibility between speculators and public life, the lack of harmony between self-interest and public interest make it very difficult to conceive a legitimate way in which financial speculation can be related to the society at large.

Accumulating Capitalist vs. Speculator: From Adam Smith to Marx, via Hegel

Adam Smith saw capitalism as producing exemplary characters (or figures), toward which social actors orient themselves, and who are the outcome of talent-based social rankings. In this perspective, capitalism would be characterized by a restricted number of figures, with the manufacturer at the top of a rather rigid pyramid. How could we then explain the myriad variations in characters, their resemblances and differences, as well as the possible changes from one position to another (e.g., from manufacturer to merchant or, why not, to financial speculator) without resorting to corrosion of character?

Later attempts to solve these problems were indebted to the intellectually mediating moment represented by the social philosophy of Georg Wilhelm Friedrich Hegel. With respect to character and self, Hegel took a more complex stance. First, the constitution of the self cannot be automatically deduced from material activities of production (as those implied by the division of labor), simply because, at a closer examination, these activities appear as extremely complex in terms of the knowledge and skills involved. The self cannot be preprogrammed to execute even simple actions; these, in their turn, are not mere automatisms. Action implies the opening of the self toward the world, an opening which cannot be sudden and immediate: orientation toward the external (that is, social) world is mediated by a complex web of social relationships and representations. An "I" that does not open and orient toward the social world is a negative concept, since it cannot be specified through any kind of knowledge (Hegel [1807] 1986, p. 39). This specification, which constitutes the positive existence of the self ("I am x"), depends on a work of mediation (Hegel [1807] 1986, p. 25): social interactions and representations interpose themselves (mediate) between the self and the external world. Only through this filter (and in a reflexive fashion) can we acquire positive knowledge and move away from a negative, undifferentiated state of mind. Moreover, argues Hegel, this mediation (i.e., the representations and interactions which made the world intelligible) is assimilated (or internalized) in a reflexive process, through which the self moves toward the spirit (or Geist), with this latter concept referring less to phantoms than to a taken-for-granted set of norms of collective life.[4]

The mediating filter (if you pardon the tautology) has at least two major components: ethical norms and property. With respect to ethical norms, the self appears as subject (the "I" is subjected to ethical norms, which mediate relationships with other selves). With respect to property, the self appears as person ("I own," as opposed to "I follow norms").[5] The person "must give herself an external *sphere of freedom*" (Hegel [1821] 1986, p. 102; italics in original), represented by objects, which orient the will of the person. Freedom is manifested in the capacity of the person to detach herself from the object. Ownership of objects is not just a means of fulfilling needs. The actual relationship between the self and objects is determined by freedom of possession, by the free will of the self to depart from the objects (Hegel [1821] 1986, p. 107).[6] If the self can be conceived as person and as subject, it follows that economic consciousness (and transactions) would have to be conceptually grounded in ownership relations and in subjection to ethical norms. Economic life is mediated by legal and ethical institutions, understood not only as sets of rules and norms, but also as systems of representation which legitimate transactions. From the viewpoint of the external observer, then, this system of representations constitutes an observational arrangement which integrates economic activities into social life. The distinction between free will and ethics as one between ownership and norms, drawn by Hegel mainly in his *Philosophy of Right* ([1821] 1986, pp. 102–3), opens the way for two different approaches, each stressing one mediating aspect, and each with far-reaching consequences: Karl Marx's concept of the accumulating capitalist and Max Weber's figure of the religious capitalist can each be seen as echoing it.[7]

In the introduction to the first edition of the *Capital* (reprinted in the second edition), Karl Marx stated that the figure of the capitalist was the "personification of economic categories, bearer of class relationships and interests" ([1872] 2002, p. 37). Relevant here is the fact that in the *Capital*, this figure has two meanings: one is general and determined by the process of accumulation. The other is more specific and related to financial speculation. I start here with the general meaning.

For Marx, capitalism is reducible to two key aspects: the worker selling his labor force to the capitalist, and the capitalist being able to obtain surplus value by paying not for the labor, but for the reproduction of the labor force. Hence, the key relationship of capitalism is that between the capitalist and the worker: while the former accumulates, the latter sells his only possession. For the capitalist, the main type of social action is accumulation; for the worker, it is selling his labor force. Accumulation is a purely economic process, free of any ethical determinations. He who accumulates doesn't need to sell his labor force, and he who has to sell it all the time cannot accumulate. These two kinds of complementary actions are paradigmatic for capitalism and for the relationship between these two figures. Capitalism as a social order depends on the relationship between accumulation and the sale of labor force. Marx's analysis is geared toward deducing the whole laws of capitalism out of this relationship.

The relationships between the accumulating capitalist and the worker are determined by who owns what (capital or labor).[8] Ownership of the means of production, however, is never expressed as a mere relationship between the self and an inanimate thing, but always as a social relationship.

We should not forget here that Marx saw commodities as the "embodiment of abstract human labor," which always has a social character ([1872] 2002, pp. 70, 84). Thus, capitalist social relationships create two main categories of social (and not only economic) life, with a plethora of other, subordinated categories around them.

What place do financial markets occupy here? Again, not a very important one. On a more personal level, Marx was aware that at least some leaders of the German socialist factions were involved in financial speculation, which he spitefully commented on. He wrote the following to Engels about the visit paid to him by the social democrat Ferdinand Lassalle in 1862: "The Jewish nigger Lassalle, who fortunately departs at the end of this week, has happily lost again 5000 talers in a speculation gone wrong. The guy would rather throw away the money than lend it to a friend" (Marx and Engels 1964, p. 257). The background of such vituperative passages (repeated in several letters) was Marx's state of near poverty and his continued financial dependence on friends (mainly Engels), while nineteenth-century "limousine socialists" (if one allows such a historically incongruent term) happily engaged in speculation.

Marx's theoretical attention to this topic increased considerably from the first to the third (posthumously published) volume of the *Capital*. He starts by seeing financial speculation as characteristic to a primitive phase in the accumulation of capital ([1872] 2002, p. 698)[9]. Speculation produces a class of leisurely persons who live from dividends, do not work, and divert capital from productive activities. What brings about "paper speculators and stock exchange wolves" is public debt ([1872] 2002, pp. 698–99); in time, these characters become autonomous and participate in the concentration of capital by expropriating other capitalists ([1872] 2002, pp. 704–6). Thus, on the one hand speculation participates in concentration processes, contributing to the general logic of capital. On the other hand, it transfers capital away from productive tasks. By doing this, individuals engaged in financial speculation undermine ownership relationship, and with that the system of characters (or figures) on which the capitalist order is based.

Still, Marx's position becomes more complex; the author is not very sure anymore about the fringe character of speculation. Noticing the increase in financial transactions on the (London) stock exchange, Marx asks himself if this is a mere consequence of industrial overproduction or a special phenomenon ([1894] 1964, p. 493). Corporate bonds appear to be "paper duplicates of destroyed capital" (i.e., taken away from industrial production and used in financial transactions). Brokers and investors take them as tradable commodities, and therefore as real capital. Financial securities are "nominal representatives of a non-existing capital," but their exchange can be seen as accumulation of capital and as representing the expansion of the reproduction of capital ([1894] 1964, p. 494). These very financial securities could be seen as illusory, as duplicates and as imaginary wealth, yet their mere existence expresses a very real process, called by Marx "an artificial system of violent expansion of the reproductive process" ([1894] 1964, p. 507), characterized by the autonomous movement of the credit capital (*Leihkapital*).

After a period of accumulation, the sphere of industrial production becomes too narrow (i.e., there is too much capital out there that cannot be employed in production or in related commercial processes). Consequently, capital migrates outside this sphere; it can do so because it is abstract, expressed in the universal form of money. In its new form of credit capital, it can partly serve production needs and contribute to the accumulation of industrial capital. However, credit capital is abstract and plastic, and can take many shapes (Marx [1894] 1964, p. 521). Part of it becomes autonomous and begins attracting individual savings into its sphere (Marx [1894] 1964, p. 524), a process in which these latter are alienated from their initial intention. The expansion of autonomous credit capital is thus tied to increased wealth and generates a mass of "money capitalists" and of financial securities.

Generally speaking, then, the whole process can be summarized as follows: capital expands its sphere primarily by expanding (i.e., by multiplicating) its modes of reproduction. In this expansion, at least a part of the credit capital becomes autonomous and does not serve any productive (or industrial) purposes anymore. However, it is exactly this part which is significant with respect to the multiplication of the modes of reproduction: the autonomous part of credit capital engulfs and transforms savings (something which industrial, productive capital could only difficultly achieve). This movement (partly) substitutes financial speculation for the exploitation of labor force as the original source of capital accumulation. Financial speculation also replaces the "direct violence" which alienates the products of work (Marx [1894] 1964, p. 495). Consequently, speculators do not appear anymore as an atavistic phenomenon, characteristic for the age of primitive accumulation, but as a very direct, important consequence of capitalist development. Capital multiplies its forms of reproduction; this process requires that more and more money (like savings) and more and more individual savers are attracted into its sphere. Autonomous credit capital, detached from production processes, and exemplified by financial markets and transactions, works best here. Without financial markets and without investors, this expansion of the modes of reproduction would be seriously hampered.

Consequently, financial speculation emerges as one of the most important expressions of mature capitalism (if not the most important). Going back to the distinction between person and subject, and to Marx's concern with the person (as expressed in the ownership of capital),[10] we can infer from the above arguments that, in advanced capitalism, the transformation of savers into speculators/investors becomes crucial. This is so because the manifold expansion of the reproduction of capital requires the continuous transformation of persons into capitalists,[11] a transformation which works very well within the domain of autonomous credit capital (as embodied by financial markets). This is where savings are metamorphosed into capital and where ordinary people are metamorphosed into capitalists. Financial markets, which treat representations of capital as real, tradable capital, are a unique interface between ordinary individuals and institutions, on the one hand, and the central category of the capitalist order, on the other hand: abstract, continuously metamorphosing money.

Several aspects should be emphasized here: the first is that speculation shifts places, from a fringe, atavistic position in the first volume, to prominence in the third volume of *Capital*. This echoes a shift in the way capital is conceptualized: from the accumulation of capital (with its counterpart, the accumulating capitalist) to the reproduction of capital. The second aspect is given by the later Marx's position that ownership and exchange are not to be understood as in rigid opposition. As Hegel saw it, freedom to own also means freedom to alienate the owned object. Ownership and exchange are two sides of the same process. Object(s) do not have an absolute, natural "reality." Rather, they are real insofar they are defined and constituted in a web of social relationships and institutions. Representations of capital (i.e., financial securities in Marx's terms) are not less real capital than factory chimneys and assembly lines. They are real insofar they play a crucial role in transforming savings into capital. With that, they fulfil a double role: as a medium of transformation and as capital.

The consequence is that an autonomous, expanding reproduction of capital requires autonomous mediating devices. Such devices are representations of capital, intrinsic to the reproductive process itself. Being autonomous, they are divorced from the ethical sphere and do not distinguish between good and bad passions. Instead they represent a "pure" work of transformation by giving practical hints and tips and by showing the social legitimacy (and desirability) of financial investments. We are now far from Smith's notion that the imaginary of economic life should stress care and emotional attachment to production processes. The reproduction of capital into society at large necessitates then a boundary which legitimates financial markets in the eyes of the public and with respect to other social institutions (e.g., charities, universities), a boundary which provides this public with avenues and tools for participation.

If we accept this line of reasoning, then the next steps would be to investigate how this boundary works; which are the social institutions that support it; how are representations of capital constituted; and what are the requirements put on individuals in this transformation process, from an average person to a speculator? Karl Marx did not go into these questions, but Max Weber did, at least in part and in a specific fashion. Yet Weber is perhaps better known for his treatment of the religious capitalist rather than of the investor, a subject to which I now turn.

The Religious Capitalist and the Speculator:
Max Weber's Hegelian Legacy

At the first sight, Max Weber didn't pay much attention to financial speculation either. Some of his best-known works are concerned (though not exclusively) with another figure, namely that of the religious capitalist. Yet the rapidly expanding economy of the German Reich after the Franco-Prussian war of 1870 included outbursts of frenzied financial speculation. These didn't go unnoticed, and in 1894 Max Weber felt compelled to write two articles about the stock exchange, initially published in a series called *The Göttingen Workers' Library*, edited by Friedrich Naumann.[12] In 1924, these two articles were reprinted under the title "The Stock Exchange" in the *Collected Essays on Sociology and Social Policy*, edited by Marianne Weber after the death of her husband. Weber took much care to stress that they were exclusively meant for a nonspecialist, financially uneducated (and implicitly nonacademic) readership. He saw himself as motivated by the socially broad, yet not entirely informed public criticism of the stock exchange in Germany (Weber [1894] 1924, p. 256). This is not to say that these articles are entirely devoid of any theoretical insight. Nevertheless, confronted with Weber's emphasis on their popularizing character, we cannot ignore the question of the relationship between them, on the one hand, and his academic works, on the other hand. How then does Weber's explicitly more ambitious treatment of the figures of capitalism fit together with the treatment received by speculation?

An appropriate strategy for examining these questions would be to go back to the Hegelian distinction between person and subject and see how Weber's conceptual scheme accommodates it. The explanation of the emergence and rise of generic capitalism is not the aim of the *Protestant Ethic and the Spirit of Capitalism*. Rather, what counts for Weber is a particular, and particularly successful, brand, namely Western capitalism. This is characterized by the rational organization of formally free labor (Weber [1920] 1988, p. 7) with all that this entails: separation between the household and the firm, rational accounting, separation between labor and capital, and so on. This rational organization cannot be guided by irrational speculation However, financial speculation itself can become rationalized when it is penetrated by the modes of calculation specific to the capitalist enterprise.

From this perspective, financial markets are just one among the many economic institutions which are brought into the rationalizing stream of capitalism, and the speculator is just one variety of capitalists (Weber [1920] 1988, p. 9). The persisting question here is what makes people shift from irrational chance-taking and adventure-seeking to the rational organization of enterprises. This decisive factor cannot be given by the ownership of the means of production, since the organization of this ownership is the outcome, not the source, of a rationalization process. It is rather norms of behavior and collective belief which explain successful capitalist rationalization. But where do they come from? More importantly, perhaps, once we start looking for norms and beliefs, we have crossed to the other side of the Hegelian distinction: we are now looking for subjects, not persons.

And since the norms of rational capitalism have to be both universal and universally enforceable, the place to look for them is religion. It follows, then, that the constitution of the religious subject determines that of the economic person: the economic order becomes subjected to (and integrated in) a larger moral order. While Marx's capitalist accumulation is anything but ethical, Max Weber saw the capitalist as a religiously motivated man: his drive toward redemption justifies getting rich as a self-contained aim. But redemption is uncertain and all that is left is hope, which is supported by a constant strive toward accumulating riches. Accumulation, however, has to obey certain rules: the virtuous capitalist accumulates by his own ingenuity, frugality, sustained work, and constant preoccupation with economic processes. Religious ascesis forbids accumulation by speculation (Weber [1920] 1988, p. 191). Continuous work and profit through production (Weber [1920] 1988, p. 175) are the legitimate means of religious salvation.

In this account, a tension persists between the rational capitalist and the speculator: while accumulation can be religiously motivated and investing can be rationally organized, it is hard to ground speculation in religious norms. Walter Benjamin's ([1972] 1999, pp. 427, 497) impression that speculation is an awkward activity, grounded in observation, in hours spent on the street, lacking identification with proper work and accumulation, seems to apply here. The speculator can be then explained either as an atavistic manifestation (a remnant of adventure capitalism) or through the increased separation of economic action from religion. At least in *The Protestant Ethic and the Spirit of Capitalism*, Weber seems to adopt both explanations ([1920] 1988, p. 11). However, it becomes difficult to explain on these grounds how individuals become speculators: if there is a process of relentless capitalist rationalization, how are individuals driven toward atavistic capitalist activities, which do not entirely fit a normative model of accumulative behavior?

The picture gets more complicated when we take into account Weber's position from *Economy and Society*, where he acknowledges that the spirit of capitalism has a double nature: one the one hand, "professional, bureaucratized everyday capitalism" is grounded in relentless rationalization. On the other hand, however, we encounter a radically different, "grandiose predatory capitalism" with a specific spirit, which is mainly manifested in the financial speculators active on the stock exchange (Weber [1921] 1972, p. 659). The grand speculators whose daring exploits and "coups" fascinate the public are the manifestation of a charismatic authority not entirely compatible with the rational, ethical constraints imposed by Puritanism upon profit-seeking (Weber [1921] 1972, p. 378).

This authority emerges in part from the specific forms of interaction in financial markets. Financial transactions do not rely on rational, intersubjectively verifiable proofs (like written contracts or bookkeeping), but rather on personal trust and on the subjective belief in the validity of unwritten rules of conduct (Weber [1921] 1972, pp. 192–93). This trust in tacit rules is the "archetype of all rational social action through market exchange" and the basis of a process of "community-building through money use" (Vergemeinschaftung kraft Geldgebrauchs), opposed to socialization through rationally agreed norms (Weber [1921] 1972, p. 382). One consequence of this is that traditions and charismatic authority play an important role. Seen from the outside, this reliance on tradition and personal authority, in an institution perceived as the pinnacle of modern capitalist order, reinforces the public's fascination with it.

Transactions on the stock exchange (including the much maligned short selling and options trading) can be defined through their economic functions: the stock exchange centralizes information, hedges the risk of price volatility (derivatives), processes economic uncertainties, and brings together demand and supply (Weber [1894] 1924, pp. 261, 308–9). As a social institution, and as the product of a historical development, however, the stock exchange cannot be reduced to a set of three or four economic functions (see also Abolafia 1996; Baker 1984). Understanding its centrality in the capitalist order means taking into account aspects which may appear as peripheral, as devoid of any economic function, or even as apparently undermining these functions.

The stock exchange is an institution with enormous power, which cannot but include political aspects (Weber [1894] 1924, p. 316). Since it unites two major forms of power (economic and political), the stock exchange serves not only the interests of the national economy, but also state interests: "for economic policy stock exchanges cannot be but an instrument of power in the economic struggle" (Weber [1894] 1924, p. 321). Eliminating them from the economic and political life of a state (as some of Weber's contemporaries were suggesting) would be equivalent to unilateral disarmament, and therefore unthinkable. All the "naïve apostles of economic peace" who ask for dismantling the stock exchange put the nation at a peril.

Clearly, tremendous power and centrality in economic, political, and social life cannot come only from a set of limited economic functions. This would imply a kind of reductionism which was most strange to Weber. Where do they come from, then? In order to answer this question, Weber goes back to the main figure generated by the stock exchange: the speculator. The stock exchange can only work by attracting external wealth into its circuit. Those who invest their fortune in financial securities (like bonds) expect not only profit; they also secure the right to receive a tribute from society, or from parts of it. The investment process is a tributary arrangement, by which (initially wealthy) investors secure tribute rights from other social institutions and from non-investors (Weber [1894] 1924,

p. 266). Financial securities thus appear as "guarantees of tributary rights" which tax the totality of taxpayers (Weber [1894] 1924, p. 272).[13] Speculators receive tribute from taxpayers, but they also pay tribute: a web of reciprocal obligations emerges, which increases the complexity and the solidarity of modern societies. We can formulate it the other way around, too: the increased complexity of modern societies is grounded in the increased reciprocal dependency of its members. This dependency, however, goes beyond the personal reciprocal obligations of premodern societies. In a complex yet individualized society, reciprocal but impersonal obligations are maintained in part by "expressing and circulating an ever increasing part of the national economy as tributary rights" (Weber [1894] 1924, p. 274).

Consequently, the speculator becomes a central economic figure of advanced capitalist societies.[14] The stock exchange does not simply fulfill economic functions: by processing wealth into reciprocal obligations, it makes social actors reciprocally dependent. The logic, then, is one through which more and more individuals are attracted into the sphere of financial investments and transformed into investors. This process does not mean social homogenization, equal wealth for everyone, fixed paths of investment, or increased social inclusion. Quite the contrary: the speculative society is a stratified, unequal one.

The process through which wealth is transformed into tributary rights is partly equivalent to Marx's transformation of savings into capital, but it also has the connotation of a power relationship. The relationships between those who speculate and the rest of society, between those who do it more and those who do it less, will always be relationships of power and subordination. As long as only the wealthy have access to financial transactions, the stock exchange works in a reasonably rational fashion, argues Weber. Wealthy investors can pay for the knowledge, expertise, and advice required for complex decisions. They have a high stake in maintaining their social prestige, and would therefore fulfill their unwritten contracts. Weber ([1894] 1924, pp. 279, 285) admired "the plutocratic organization" of the London Stock Exchange and the "monopoly of the rich" which it built together with the New York Stock Exchange because these monopolies also implied a system of honor which compelled financial actors to fulfill their promises.[15] Open social access to financial investments and the mingling of social categories at the stock exchange weakens this system and leads to psychological excesses, or "fever symptoms" (Weber [1894] 1924, p. 320).

In opposition to wealthy speculators, smaller ones do not have the resources to buy knowledge and expertise and are less rational and prone to psychological excesses such as panics. Moreover, they are not bound by any honor system and subvert any educational (i.e., rationalization) efforts the stock exchange might undertake: "the small speculator impedes on the emergence of a class of investors which should be homogeneous in its socially exemplary character, education and position, capable to produce honor tribunals, respected, and having the necessary energy for educational measures" (Weber [1894] 1924, p. 286). But, since transforming wealth into tributary rights is the dominant social logic of financial transactions, and because the stock exchange has such a tremendous economic, political, and social power, its opening to small-scale speculators is inevitable: "the temptation of the domestic public to gamble on the stock exchange and the subsequent losses must be seen as part of the war costs in the nations' wrestling for economic domination" (Weber [1894] 1924, p. 320).[16]

Summarizing these arguments, the "spirit of capitalism" has a double nature: on the one hand, it is that of the religious capitalist, grounded in ethical norms governing capital accumulation, and manifested in a relentless rationalization of economic processes. On the other hand, the spirit of capitalism is that of the investor, generated by the relentless transformation of wealth into tributary rights, which in their turn are required for maintaining the social fabric of highly individualized and complex societies. This spirit is not grounded in a relentless rationalization of the stock exchange: the logic of financial transactions hinders the completion of this process. At the same time, the stock exchange cannot be a center of power (economic, political, and social) if it does not continuously expand and engulf more and more social actors within its sphere. Social cohesion cannot be maintained if reciprocal tributary obligations are not expanded. Therefore, the spirit of speculation is neither a homogenous one (like that of the accumulating capitalist), nor entirely rational: it includes the charismatic attraction exercised by grand speculators, "fever symptoms," and ignorance, all mixed up with rational knowledge and information.

Similar to Marx, Weber sees the transformation of wealth into tributary rights as central with respect to the differentiation and solidarity of a complex society. Yet there are some contradictions at work here, between the social stratification triggered by this transformation, on the one hand, and the necessity of broad access to financial transactions, on the other. The upper class of rich speculators, supposed to educate the public by the power of example, is hindered in its social mission by the economically uneducated and psychologically labile crowds of small investors.

Both stratification and broad access, as conflicting consequences of this transformation, require mechanisms of mediation between the stock exchange and the society at large. These mechanisms should impose norms of "honorable" behavior and transmit solid economic knowledge to potential investors. Solid knowledge and honorable behavior would make investors into responsible financial subjects and integrate them into the process of relentless capitalist rationalization. Open access to financial investments, however, undermines group monopoly over what is considered "solid economic knowledge" and "honorable" behavior. Economic knowledge itself becomes stratified; "impure," vernacular elements are intrinsic to these mechanisms of mediation.

Several aspects should be emphasized here. First, the logic of these arguments is one of social and institutional differentiation, according to which the ethical norms and the cognitive elements governing financial behavior and decisions cannot come from outside financial markets, but have to be internally generated. Second, this requires boundary work: the effort of outlining legitimate paths of access to financial activities. This boundary work should create attitudes and transmit knowledge to potential financial actors. Third, in a manner reminiscent of Adam Smith's argument, this boundary work should contain charismatic elements—that is, show examples to be followed and characters to be emulated. Fourth, because of the intrinsic irrationality of these elements and because of the broad access to financial investments, there is no way of distinguishing a priori between "good" and "bad" examples.

The Entrepreneur and the Speculator: Good vs. Bad rebels

The preoccupation with the "spirit of capitalism" seems to have been rather widespread in the German intellectual milieu in the early decades of the twentieth century; Weber's own writings partly incorporate and partly emerge as a reaction to what other intellectuals had to say about this "spirit." Werner Sombart was certainly among them, and his *The Bourgeois* (1920) gives the problem a particular spin. Trained as an economic historian, Sombart starts his argument by noticing that capital accumulation was not the dominant means of acquiring wealth in the early modern era. Robbery, privateering, and treasure hunting were quite popular

enterprises at that time (Sombart 1920, pp. 47–51). These potentially rewarding yet high-risk activities required daring, innovative, energetic participants, qualities which were later channeled into project making. This
implied selling (not always ripe) ideas to a broader public, a process in
which the projector's powers of persuasion played a crucial role (Sombart
1920, p. 57). Trading projects on financial markets combined these powers
of persuasion with gambling fury in the figure of the projector, or entrepreneur (Sombart 1920, pp. 61, 66).

While project making or entrepreneurship also require organizational
talent and planning capacities, talent for persuasion is key: after all, the
public must be convinced to part with their money on the basis of the simple promise that an idea will yield profit in the future.[17] Speculators thus
appear as a "special type of the capitalist entrepreneur," with a "gambling
fury" intrinsic to the spirit of capitalism (Sombart 1920, pp. 115, 120). The
constant use of persuasion transforms it from an external constraint upon
hearers into an autonomous, internalized force: that is, speculators themselves come to believe what they say without much, if any, critical thinking;
in this process, hope replaces fear of loss as the main projective mechanism of economic action (Sombart 1920, p. 121). In this account, financial
speculation emerges not as an epiphenomenon, but as a central feature of
modern capitalism, channeling human energies and ideas into more legitimate domains of action. The rhetorical power to convince and impress the
public, to make promises and awaken hopes, mediates between markets
and society and is essential with respect to the former's legitimacy.

Entrepreneurship as the "cultural complement of the capitalist economy" was taken over by Joseph Schumpeter (1943, p. 121), who sought to
investigate it within the context of Weberian rationalization. Rationalization processes have several consequences: the first is that they reinforce
individualization, which in turn requires the creation of human types to
match the categories of economic action. The second consequence is that
rationalization promotes standardization and routines. This process runs
counter to that of individualization: the demand that every single individual develops her human potential cannot be entirely harmonized with
the demand for standardized behavior and routine. What happens then
with those individuals of "supernormal ability and ambition" (Schumpeter
1943, p. 125)? They become entrepreneurs.

The entrepreneur is motivated by a constant, almost religious drive
for technical innovation (Schumpeter 1934). In this respect, he combines
Adam Smith's manufacturer with Max Weber's charisma.[18] Capitalism is

characterized by a "habit of mind": that of striving toward technical innovation for economic profit. Innovation is the motor of economic growth and capitalist expansion. The entrepreneur is not merely interested in science and technology for their own sake; he is interested in continuous innovation because he equates it with economic advantage. Innovations process major economic uncertainties and set the stage for imitators. Technical and economic processes are closely related to each other; technology is endogenous to the capitalist economic system (Rosenberg 2000, p. 12). The figure of the entrepreneur, then, assembles creative energies that do not find their place in the bureaucratic organization of economic life fostered by rationalization processes. This is an entrepreneurship different from Sombart's, one which is not driven by gambling fury but by the desire to challenge existing organizational forms.

Since rationalization processes are the dominant force of capitalism, they gradually narrow the "list of possibilities" from which individuals can choose. Even technology turns against the entrepreneur: mechanization promotes routines and, in time, leaves little place for entrepreneurial innovation. At the core of capitalism, then, lies a fundamental contradiction between routines and group conformity, on the one hand, and creativity and independent spirit, on the other. The entrepreneur belongs to this latter: "To act with confidence beyond the range of familiar beacons and to overcome that resistance requires aptitudes that are present in only a small fraction of the population and that define the entrepreneurial type as well as the entrepreneurial function. This function does not essentially consist in either inventing anything or otherwise creating the conditions which the enterprise exploits. It consists in getting things done" (Schumpeter 1943, p. 132).

Technological innovation is thus just one aspect of the broader entrepreneurial spirit. This allows Schumpeter to classify financiers as an "intermediate stage between entrepreneurial venture and mere current administration of an inherited domain" (1943, p. 134). In other writings, however, he stressed that the entrepreneur is different both from the manager and the "capitalist risk-taker" (i.e., the speculator) (Schumpeter 1991, pp. 407–8). The entrepreneur may put his talents in the service of joint-stock companies, but financial speculation is not his defining feature (Schumpeter 1991, p. 425n4, p. 425n9). At the same time, the logic of the capitalist enterprise, which strives toward automating progress, tends to be self-undermining. This logic is first and foremost promoted not by an abstract bureaucratic spirit but rather by the lively figures of entrepreneurs who speculate and create giant enterprises. In the very end, these figures turn upon themselves: "The true pacemakers of socialism were not the intellectuals or agitators who preached it but the Vanderbilts, Carnegies and Rockefellers" (Schumpeter 1943, p. 34).

The speculator thus occupies an ambiguous position: partly excluded from being an entrepreneur, because he is not associated with entrepreneurial organization, and partly counted among those possessing entrepreneurial spirit, because he channels energies which cannot find their place in bureaucratic organization.

More important, perhaps, is that in this account the rationalization processes which shape the capitalistic enterprise contain a mediating element which is temporarily resisted by some characters. It is this resistance (the "spirit of innovation") which moves capitalism forward, before succumbing to bureaucratization and routine. Since daring speculations belong here, it would follow that they, too, contribute to innovating capitalism. At the same time, and following this line of thought, financial markets themselves are subjected to automation and rationalization processes. "Heroic" figures of speculators would then counterbalance this process and act as examples of human creativity in the field of finance.

What we encounter is a stress on the role played by the charismatic, irrational features of market exchanges, combined with a reversal of Smith's notion of economic passions. Implicitly present here is the argument that mediating forces are needed in order to adapt to rationalization processes, as well as in order to resist them. While adaptation is ensured by routines, resistance is anchored in a special energy, or force, which only some individuals possess.

The Boundaries of Finance and the Capitalist Economy

Each of the figures examined here claims primacy in one or another explanatory account of capitalism. At a closer look, the picture is more complicated than we think. There are contradictions and tensions in these accounts, most visible perhaps in the cases of Marx and Weber. When it looks like the accumulating or the religious capitalist has taken center stage and that we have been offered a clear account of what makes capitalism tick, financial speculation pops up its head and the stage design is rearranged. Furnaces and conveyor belts go out, to be replaced by the trading floor.

TABLE 1. **Financial Speculation within the Context of Capitalism.**

	Main figure	What constitutes main figure	Site of constitution	How	Relationship between main figure and speculator	What constitutes the speculator	Site of constitution	How
Smith	Manufacturer	Skills Knowledge Pursuit of self-interest	Manufacture (increasing stock capital)	Talents and dispositions due to division of labor Self-interest	Opposition	Lack of knowledge Bad passions	The stock exchange	Lack of care
Marx	Accumulating capitalist (person)	Relations of ownership	Mainly industrial production Trade Also diffuse throughout society	Capital accumulation	Oppositions: Modernism/ atavism Accumulation/ expansion of abstract capital	Person: Willingness to transform savings into capital	The stock exchange	Metamorphosis of savers into investors
Weber	Religious capitalist (subject to externally imposed norms)	Set of religious norms and beliefs	Diffuse throughout society	Salvation-seeking Rationalization Calculation	Complementary: Double spirit of capitalism	Subject to behavioral prescriptions generated by the exchange Knowledge Willingness to enter tributary relationships	The stock exchange	Metamorphosis Power of attraction and transformation Charismatic authority
Sombart/ Schumpeter	Entrepreneur	Gambling fury/ Special energy	Present in some persons	Resistance to bureaucratization	Ambiguity: Subordination/ exclusion	Risk-taking Persuasion	The stock exchange	Powers of persuasion

For both Marx and Weber, as well as for Sombart, the boundary between the stock exchange and society is constituted by mediating processes (see table 1). The transformation of concrete savings into abstract and autonomous capital (Marx) cannot take place without a gigantic cultural, social, and political expansion of the stock market (Weber), an expansion which goes well beyond a limited set of economic functions (centralizing information, bringing together buyers and sellers, processing uncertainties about the future). In fact, these very functions, in Weber's account, depend on the ways in which the stock market expands culturally, a process which produces certain types of dominant attitudes and knowledge. Information cannot be centralized and uncertainties cannot be processed into risks without creating appropriate and legitimate tools for these tasks, tools which can be used in this very expansion. In *The Stock Exchange*, at least, Weber's insistence on the role played by knowledge in this process can hardly be overestimated. From Sombart's perspective, the interface between financial markets and society is a rhetorical one: markets work as promises and hopes, neither of which can take shape without a work of persuasion, without convincing the society at large.[19] Conceptually, project organization and planning depend on launching projects in the market, and a project-based economy depends on persuasion.

Cultural expansion implies a work of mediation, the creation of an expandable, stable boundary between the stock exchange and society. The social positions and the roles of financial actors are constituted along this boundary, allowing the public to participate in controlled ways to the activities of the stock exchange. It is this expandable, stable interface which mostly preoccupies Marx and Weber on several levels. On a conceptual level, they strive to account for the links between actors' positions in the capitalist order, on the one hand, and their actions, on the other. There is a sense in their writings that these positions, neither fixed nor exclusively given by external determinants, are subjected to transformations and shifts which cannot be explained without taking into account elements of social consciousness. Yet these authors (Marx included) sense the difficulty of reducing social consciousness to a collective or "class" consciousness, or to universal ethical norms. Such elements have to be binding, yet individual enough; individual, yet similar enough with each other. For Weber, financial knowledge and domain-specific norms (embodied in codes of honor and prestige) mediate between society and the stock exchange. Marx, by contrast, sees the separation between ethics and speculation as intrinsic to the mediation taking place in modern capitalism.

On another level, we encounter a contrast between the eighteenth and the nineteenth-century view (with Schumpeter belonging to this latter). For Smith, the mediation enabling economic action cannot be but ethical. Its normative and cognitive dimensions have a general character, valid in public as well as in economic life. This latter cannot be completely separated from the public sphere. Both need the same kind of heroic characters, which cannot be provided by the stock exchange.

More than one hundred years later, the notion of a general barrier between speculation and society is replaced by a different view. Weber's insistence on honor and prestige, his warnings that the stock exchange is too powerful and important to even think of dismantling it are in stark contrast with Smith's observations about bad passions and finance. The relentless transformation of persons into capitalists through financial investments (as seen by Marx) stands at odds with viewing the stock exchange as a social nuisance.

We can see this as a conceptual shift, of course, related to different theoretical frameworks. Yet it would be hard to dissociate here conceptualization from observation, theoretical reflection upon the state of things from the state of things itself. At stake here are not only different forms of theoretical reflection, which cannot be separated from observation, but also a shift in the conceptual take on finance, from the observation of speculation within the public and civic context (with the implied ethical norms) to the observation of a hard-to-penetrate, quasi-closed entity. Of course, this shift in theorizing is not unrelated to more general changes taking place in the nineteenth century in the social sciences. Yet in play here are different theoretical reflections on different forms of mediation. And since prestige and honor seem to have a significant role, both by being completely absent from Smith's observations and by being so insisted upon in Weber's analysis, I will start by investigating their place within the boundaries of finance.

CHAPTER TWO

Prestige, at Last: The Social Closure of the Stock Exchange

B oundaries mediate between the society at large and the stock exchange. They determine how the public (as well as social institutions) relates to the latter by determining what can be observed and what cannot. It remains unanswered, however, how possibilities for observation relate or don't relate to forms and processes of social closure which might affect stock exchanges. In other words, if observation is intrinsic to the boundaries set in place by specific groups, what other mechanisms of (social) closure might be put in place by these groups? Closure means drawing boundaries, setting distinctions and tracing ways of access which, in their turn, imply group positions and roles. Groups can take, change, or generate new positions for themselves within the larger context of society. By doing this, financial groups anchor the world of the stock exchange into society not just at the site of economic interests and profits, but in more stable, multi-sited ways. Nonetheless, the inner world of stock exchanges is not automatically made more transparent.

Structural Embeddedness and Legitimacy in Financial Markets

I shall start by examining the role of enclosure, as well as of the social and symbolic processes of group building, by relating (and contrasting) them with broader arguments made in economic sociology about the social structural underpinnings of financial exchanges. It has become almost commonplace to argue that the mooring of financial actors and transactions into social structures allows the processing of uncertainties into risks (Stinchcombe 1990, p. 5) and the reduction of information costs, together with the production and distribution of action-relevant information. Arrangements like networks and intermediary groups generate trust, routines, and standardized procedures (e.g., Baker 1984; Abolafia 1996; Carruthers and Stinchcombe 2001), which reduce the costs of procuring and processing information. Without this anchoring, financial action would collapse under the burden of uncertainties.

At least three aspects are relevant here: (a) trust, (b) routines, and (c) standardization. In order to engage in transactions, actors need to trust information providers and transaction partners. Personal trust is provided by social networks. Mark Granovetter argues that markets can work only when embedded into such networks (Granovetter 1985; also Polanyi [1944] 1957; Knight [1921] 1985). Since networks precede transactions, it would follow that markets evolve out of networks. Seen from this perspective, the latter are logically and empirically prior and external to market processes (Krippner 2001), intervening only when specific uncertainties arise. However, if price-, quality-, and partner-relevant uncertainties are processed by conceptually distinct networks, we cannot explain how and why markets emerge from networks. Indeed, there would be no reason for financial markets to emerge at all: apparently, networks can solve these problems much better than them. It becomes difficult, then, to maintain that networks are conceptually external with respect to market processes. Historically, networks may precede full-fledged markets; conceptually, the externality relationship between markets and networks has to be revised.

The solution would be to treat financial markets as networks *combined* with communication systems (White 2002, p. 27). Market actors continuously send observable signals to each other, around which relationships are built. This makes markets into self-validating signaling systems (White 2002, p. 31; also Podolny 2001), which can process uncertainties into information patterns. In this account, producer markets play the key role. They require monetization and networks of financial relations (White 2002, p. 246); therefore, financial markets are a second-order construction, based on the observation of producer markets (White 2002, p. 248).[1] Yet, since financial actors primarily observe each other (White 2002, p. 5), they monitor only internally generated (or second-order) representations of producer markets. Intermediary groups, like securities analysts, generate representations of the external world, which are then observed by financial actors.

Financial markets, then, are self-referential communication networks which do not need external forces or interventions in order to process the uncertainties they produce. Since actors are integrated into stable networks, they develop habits and routines, which in their turn contribute to processing uncertainties (e.g., Beckert 1996; Knorr Cetina and Bruegger 2002a). Habits and networks are mutually supporting: transacting with the same partners over relatively long periods of time produces routines, established deal-making procedures, and tacit knowledge. Routines enable financial actors to position themselves with respect to each other in a chiastic system of classifications (Bourdieu 1994, p. 80), which translates the logic of personal ties into that of impersonal transactions and vice versa.

Another important device is cognitive standardization (Carruthers and Stinchcombe 2001, p. 100). Market actors need tools with the help of which heterogeneous pieces of information are made comparable, interpreted, and used in financial decisions. Centralization of trading floors, for instance, allows participants to directly observe the same prices at the same time and to compare them. Tools like stock analytical techniques, pricing formulas, or theoretical models concomitantly disseminate and standardize information. Due to their complexity, however, formulas and models require a body of specialists in sense-making who provide market actors with interpretations. These tools have a performative quality (MacKenzie and Millo 2003): they are not mere representations, but market-shaping instruments. Cognitive standardization in financial markets leads to the emergence of a body of intermediaries (financial economists, stock analysts) who contribute to processing uncertainties.

Overall, then, networks and intermediaries are intrinsic to financial markets. Markets are not embedded in external formations, but *are* themselves networks and intermediary groups which produce self-sustaining communication patterns. In this way, financial markets become a reality sui generis, irreducible to rational calculation and efficiency criteria. This presupposes that transactions are integrated into (and compatible with) society. Integration and compatibility, in their turn, require legitimacy. This latter is irreducible to the possibility of making gains and consists in the instances of social control which are effective in given situations and for certain paths of action. Legitimacy is intrinsic to the actors' definition of their situation, to their trust and authority relationships (Lazega 1992, pp. 27, 37; Thévenot 2002, p. 190).

There is a further aspect to the legitimacy problem, though. Since such networks are also communication pipes circulating (internal and external) observations, their overall devices, processes, and results have to be legitimated. Economic espionage, for instance, may well include observational procedures, but is certainly not legitimate (nor legal). It cannot be practiced on a generalized scale and in the open. Observational instruments that allow a group to be observed from without have to be subjected to social scrutiny and appear as legitimate both within and outside the market. Social networks or intermediary groups alone, however, cannot act as adequate instances of social control. According to the logic of self-referentiality, these instances should come from within, not from without, markets. Legitimacy should be generated internally. Yet it is difficult to see how networks and intermediaries alone could be adequate instances of social control, acknowledged as such by and integrated into the larger society. The closed, inward-looking character of networks (actors who observe each other, but not their broader social environment) does not automatically generate a boundary allowing the observation of activities from the outside, nor does it automatically validate such activities as legitimate.[2] While network segments and clusters of firms may establish boundaries among them (White 2002, p. 285), such internal differentiations cannot in and by themselves solve the legitimacy problem.

Legitimacy and Status Groups

If markets are sui generis structures, then they cannot be conceived only as networks and intermediary groups. Markets need instances of social control compatible with the broader social fabric. Financial transactions are open activities and take place in the public sphere. Taken as a whole, financial markets are not secret, sectarian activities (this does not preclude the secret character of some transactions). This requires that participants (and at least a part of the nonparticipating public) acknowledge them as socially adequate. Without this acknowledgment, a public trading system would not be possible. Robust arrangements for symbolic sanctioning and control are needed, ensuring that market actors are integrated into the larger society as adequate public actors. Sanctioning takes place (a) among financial actors and (b) between these actors as a group and external observers. Robust control arrangements have to be different from networks and intermediary groups. Status groups are such a solution.

Since they involve symbolic sanctioning, and since this sanctioning partly emerges at the interface between status groups and the society at large, then we should look for the ways in which boundary work is implicated in these processes. A close caption discussion of status groups should clarify this point.

A status group is characterized through "a specific, positive or negative social appreciation of 'honor', related to common group characteristics" (Weber [1921] 1972, p. 534). Though often tied to a common profession, status groups are irreducible to professional groups. They are not exclusively defined through the same level of wealth or through a common social origin, although these may become selection criteria. Status groups are defined through common rituals, habits, tradition, prestige, and the "monopolistic appropriation of privileged professional chances" (Weber [1921] 1972, p. 179). Rituals regulate conduct of activities, access, time and space, and categorical identities, as well as personal reputations (Collins 2004, p. 274). Monopolistic appropriation can be achieved through a mix of economic and social criteria: for example, membership fees can be combined with apprenticeships or with social origin or both in order to restrict access. By combining monopolistic appropriation with specific rituals and traditions, status groups integrate two mutually reinforcing aspects: a charismatic, prestige-based one and a means-rational one (Weber [1921] 1972, p. 124).

Status groups imply but are irreducible to jurisdictional claims (Abbott 1988, p. 20), according to which the group sees itself as the only one entitled to adequately perform certain activities, on the basis of the special knowledge it possesses. Jurisdiction, however important, must be supplemented by features related to the group's social standing, to its respectability and honor (Barnes 1995, p. 139). These features are expressed in formal and informal rules of conduct, rituals, admission criteria, and public perception of honorability, which appear as guarantors of legitimacy. By displaying these features, the group represents itself as socially competent and as part of the broader order (Thévenot 2002, pp. 181, 191).[3]

The competence of group members does not allude only to skills, explicit knowledge, or professional abilities. It does not mean the trustworthiness of a particular person, or her track record in financial transactions. Social competence is irreducible to economic competence or to the competence of individual actors. It implies the ability to relate to the larger social order and integrate into it. Individual lack of respectability is represented as deviating from the group's standard and sanctioned as such. The social competence of the group also enables the trust relationship: we place trust in the group's activities because they appear as integrated into the larger order and therefore as legitimate.

Qualities like social behavior or manners may appear as peripheral in relation to a group's economic position (Bourdieu 1979, pp. 113–14). Yet the public display of such auxiliary qualities is constitutive of the group. Competence and entitlement are not exclusively expressed as economic acumen, financial knowledge, or jurisdiction, but also as social solidity, respectability and good social behavior. Groups of this kind would stress not only their mastery of transaction procedures, but also their social standing and honor which, whilst also processing uncertainties, act as legitimacy tools. Such groups would stress the trust they are entitled to by virtue of their standing and of their social competences.

Concomitantly, stabilization and reproduction of the group's actions require the capacity to self-repair and self-reconstitute when challenged (Barnes 1992, pp. 265–66). These efforts (not conscious all the time) require mutual symbolic sanctioning, which is produced among group members, as well as between the group and external observers. In its turn, symbolic sanctioning cannot do without social codes of respectability. It is exactly these features which allow "concerted efficacious action in the face of the unknown" (Barnes 2000, p. 147). This unknown can also include uncertain public reactions to the activities of the group. We can find many instances of groups who, when criticized, contested, or attacked from the outside, launch public offensives of charm and honorability, meant to persuade the public about their legitimacy. Such offensives can include rhetoric, as well as means of social control, such as the exclusion or public humiliation of "dishonored" individuals.[4] Displays of reputation to the outside world also help reinforce the control exerted by a specific group over its own social positions. Honor and reputation stabilize action and act as mechanisms of social control (Baxter and Margavio 2000, p. 399). Such displays legitimize the institution(s) associated with the group (Collins 1986, p. 146; Bourdieu 1980, p. 171; Barnes 2000, p. 147).

Thus, monopolistic appropriation of an activity requires prestige and codes of honor as instances of social controls and markers of the group's social adequacy. Such codes define the place of the group in the larger society and its adequacy to public life. Group action is stabilized by the mutually reinforcing relationship between monopolistic appropriation and honorability.

Status groups are exclusionary structures, reproducing through social selection, differentiation, ranking, and collective constraints. They show who can legitimately perform certain actions and who cannot, how actions are to be coordinated, and which "ideal or material goods" (Weber [1921] 1972, p. 537) are legitimate with respect to these actions. A status group which monopolizes a profession or access to certain goods or activities can entrain the emergence of subordinated groups. Together, they form a hierarchy which integrates into the larger social structure. Examples in this sense are profession-based groups and their apprentices (Abbott 1988, pp. 251–52).

Thus, when investigating the social structure of financial markets, we should look not only at social networks and established intermediary groups, but also at status groups in the process of their emergence (see also Podolny 1994, p. 461).[5] Through control of access, selection, ritual, and honor, status groups confer legitimacy upon financial exchanges. Rituals and procedures concerning location, access, and behavior, among others, confer the imprint of reputability and solidity, which plays a central role in the group's self-definition as well as in its perception by external observers.

Moreover, rituals of honor and prestige can tie subordinated groups to the main status group. Individuals working for brokers and traders can constitute themselves as a group of lesser status, with its own rituals, membership criteria, and admission procedures. They then monopolize activities tied to and required by the main group. For instance, back office clerks needed by brokers can be organized as a subordinated status group, with its own rules and admission criteria. Rules would specify, among other things, whether the barrier between groups is permeable or not: that is, whether clerks could ever become brokers and under what conditions. A status group can also select customers of comparable status: brokers may set a minimum order size which can be afforded only by wealthy customers, or may employ tacit selection criteria. Investors of lesser means will enter transactions with unofficial brokers, while the official ones will cater to a socially and economically exclusivist clientele.

If honor and prestige are required for the appropriation of activities on the stock exchange, for achieving monopolistic closure, and for setting in place exclusionary structures, then adequate discourses of honorability need to be set in place. They become even more important, since honorable behavior cannot be directly witnessed by external observers when access is closed. Monopolistic structures and exclusion prevent both direct external observation and the direct access of outsiders to rituals of honorability. Moreover, direct witnessing of behavior by outsiders can become counterproductive. Direct observation of trading behavior on the stock exchange by a larger public may undermine claims of honorability and, with that, the presentation of the group to the outside world. Yet such a presentation is essential to legitimacy claims.

One way to solve this problem is to replace direct, close-up witnessing of behavior on the stock exchange with virtual witnessing. This, in turn, requires setting in place an adequate observational apparatus, one which should be related to the group's closure and intrinsic to its boundaries. Veracity is not underwritten by virtue (Shapin 1994, p. 410), which may be shaky anyway. Verisimilitude is underwritten by observing representations of virtue, produced by group members both for each other and for the larger society. Social closure, therefore, compellingly includes an observational apparatus which substantially contributes to legitimating the group both with respect to its self-perception and to the society at large. Having argued this, I will turn to examining how financial honor and prestige are configured in relationship to the social closure of the stock exchanges, a configuration which structures external perceptions of the groups involved in financial transactions, as well as of the stock exchange as a social institution. While not being met without resistance, this contributes to defining the legitimacy of finance in modern society. In order to better understand its impact, I will first discuss the legal, spatiotemporal, and group boundaries of stock exchanges in the eighteenth century.

The Boundaries of Early Stock Exchanges

With respect to stock exchanges, at least the following legal boundaries can be distinguished:

(1) Boundaries concerning ownership of the exchange, of the entities being transacted, and of the by-products of these transactions. For instance, who owns the place/space/material arrangements which make transactions possible? What are the consequences of this ownership for the legitimacy and legality of ownership upon transacted entities? To what extent do transactions generate by-products which can be owned too, and who owns them? These are crucial distinctions with respect to how transactions can be reinforced and by whom, to

the possibility of extended intervention (regulation) in or of transactions, and for the circulation and control over essential entities such as price data.

(2) Boundaries concerning the relationship among categories of actors active on the stock exchange, as well as between those categories, on the one hand, and outside actors, on the other. These boundaries concern not only the relationship between brokers and customers, but also the relationship between inside and outside transactions: who is allowed to deal with whom, and under what circumstances?

(3) Boundaries concerning the status of transactions: are these defined as equivalent to commercial contracts, or do they have to be fixed down in writing, to be recorded in a specific manner? Could such a recording be seen not only as the memory of the market, but also used as evidence in litigation, as well as for regulatory interventions?

(4) Boundaries concerning the legal definition of specific classes of transactions, for instance as illegal or as void. An illegal transaction would be punishable, whereas a void one would be merely unenforceable in a court of law. At least the following classes of transactions are relevant here: (a) short sales, where the person selling the securities does not own them; (b) sales on margin, where the person buying the securities does not have the money to pay for them; (c) transactions in futures and options, where the date and price of the sale are ulterior to the moment when the transaction is done, or where only the right to buy or sell at a certain price and date is transacted; (d) bets that a certain security will attain a certain price at a future, set date.

Legal boundaries do not have to precede social and symbolic boundaries, and they do not mechanistically shape the latter. Arguments made within debates, representations set in place by specific groups, and established social boundaries can influence the ways in which legal distinctions are set. During the eighteenth and most of the nineteenth century, many of the above legal boundaries were not codified at all. What is more, their progressive codification, which actually takes shape around the dawn of the twentieth century, is directly related to established social boundaries, to representations and definitional efforts contained in brokers' writings, and to argumentative clashes between critics and apologists of the stock exchange.

In the eighteenth century, the absence of spatiotemporal and group boundaries made it impossible to establish legal boundaries on the ownership of the place where financial transactions unfolded. In seventeenth-century London and Paris, financial transactions took place in coffee houses and in the adjacent streets, with traders and customers being often chased by the police, and forced to move across various locations (Preda 2001a, pp. 282–85). The situation was similar in New York City and Philadelphia, where financial transactions took place in locations like the Tontine and Merchant's coffee houses, respectively, but also spread well out of them. The space of financial transactions encompassed whole neighborhoods (many of which already had a bad reputation) and overlapped entirely with other trades, as well as with noncommercial activities. The streets which came to epitomize eighteenth-century financial transactions, like the rue Quincampoix in Paris or the Exchange Alley in London, already had a very solid reputation for crime, due to various murders, some of which were famous at that time (like the murder of the Count Horn in rue Quincampoix).

Moreover, there were no clear-cut group boundaries in these places, which should correspond to the boundaries encountered in the society at large. Observers stressed with disapproval the mix of social classes and groups; the lack of social hierarchies, interpreted nowadays as an egalitarian utopia (Chancellor 1999, p. 29), was perceived by contemporaries as challenging the established order in an almost intolerable way. A pamphleteer of the South Sea Bubble of 1720 wrote that the Exchange Alley was inhabited by "Stars and Garters down to wooden Shoes . . . Turks, Jews, Atheists, and Infidels, mingle there as if they were a kin to one another" (Sherwood 1720, pp. 15–16).

The absence of legal boundaries concerning the ownership of exchange places was coupled with a lack of legal codification of the relationships between brokers and their customers. During the eighteenth century, there was no legal basis for holding a broker accountable to the customer, nor were the rights and responsibilities of this latter defined (France made an exception here). This resonated in the absence of a legal status of financial transactions and of their by-products. Marketplace transactions in financial securities were not legally acknowledged as commercial contracts during the eighteenth and nineteenth centuries. Short selling was prohibited, yet widely practiced in New York, London, and Paris (Duguid 1901, p. 188).[6] In the US, trading in financial securities was not considered a business and therefore not susceptible of public regulation (Wachtel 2003, p. 27). There was no legal fundament for negotiating debt issued before and during the War of Independence. Transactions were mostly oral and not automatically recognized in courts of law.[7] Many nineteenth-century legal cases concern the inviolability of brokerage orders (Fowler

1870, pp. 25, 70), the sole guarantee of which was the brokers' code of honor (Cornwallis 1879, p. 36; Chiswell 1902, p. 51). In the UK, brokerage orders were first acknowledged as commercial contracts in the Finance Act of 1909–10 (Poley 1926, p. 154). Only in 1909 did the New York State Property Law codify stock exchange transactions as commercial contracts.

Several aspects impeded on the legal recognition of stock exchange transactions as commercial contracts. First, it was not clear that financial securities were similar in nature with other goods.[8] Second, transactions on the stock exchange were oral; usually, such transactions were not followed by a written contract. The only proof of them having taken place was the slip of paper on which the broker had scribbled the order. During the nineteenth century, brokers did not always keep transaction ledgers;[9] they only wrote orders on slips of papers. These slips could be easily destroyed, lost, or forged. Without a written proof of the transaction having taken place, it was difficult to acknowledge it as a commercial contract. As a magazine writer formulated it at the turn of the twentieth century:

> When you buy a house even if both parties sign, the agreement is worthless unless you put up one American dollar and get the other fellow's receipt for it in writing. If you buy a horse or a cow, or anything else of value, the same precaution is necessary. So too if you sign a will. Your own word is not good enough. You must get two others to sign with you before the Surrogate is satisfied.
>
> None of this in the Stock Exchange. A wink, or two fingers held up, is enough. Often in the thick of the fight when the floor of the Exchange is a howling mob, when frenzied brokers shout themselves hoarse and stocks are going up and down by leaps and bounds, and ruin or fortune is measured by minutes, the lifting of a man's hand over the heads of the crowd is all that binds the bargain. (Quoted in Van Antwerp 1913, p. 293)

Mandatory account keeping for brokers was legally codified only in 1909 for the New York Stock Exchange (Goldman 1914, p. 243); the obligation of keeping account books open to the New York State comptroller was introduced in 1913 (Goldman 1914, p. 67). A certificate of stock, endorsed in blank, was not a negotiable instrument at common law (Campbell [1914] 1922, p. 83). Until 1922 at least, transactions on the New York Stock Exchange could be repudiated by brokers before clearing or comparison tickets were exchanged (Campbell [1914] 1922, p. 11), a process which could take several days. If a financial transaction was repudiated within this interval, it could not be reinforced in a court of law. The main (if not only) mechanism which enforced transactions was provided by the statutes and rules of stock exchanges (like the New York Stock Exchange), together with the code of honor backing them.[10] The relationship between brokers and customers, as well as the relationships among brokers, was not legally codified until the end of the nineteenth century (Schwalbe and Branson 1905, pp. 50, 102); reciprocal duties, rights, and responsibilities were not established by law, but in the best case understood as grounded in the customs of the stock exchange.

This lack of legal, spatiotemporal, and group boundaries was not without consequences for the legitimacy of financial actors and transactions. Above all, perhaps, it impacted upon the ability to integrate the social order and characters of the marketplace into the larger order of society. When they turned toward the stock exchange, eighteenth-century observers saw mostly darkness and dishonor.

Markets, Darkness, and Dishonor

On June 20, 1720, at the high tide of speculation in the Mississippi Company, Matthieu Marais, a prominent advocate with the parliament of Paris, reflected in his diary upon the nature of financial transactions:

> It is a trade where you do not understand anything, where all precautions are useless, where the most enlightened spirit doesn't see a flicker, and which turns according to the designs of the Movement of the Machine. Yet all the fate of the Kingdom depends upon it.

About six weeks later, on Saturday, August 3, 1720, Marais furtively goes to see the open air financial market in Place Vendôme; it is

> a vile place . . . which I went to see like everybody in my neighborhood. I saw the paper traders in their lodges, where everybody comes and goes at will, and where they get updated. [The traders] have beautiful women with them, and those who have [women] make more business than the others. (Diary of Marais, lawyer with the parliament of Paris, vol. 1, 1715–21, Paris, Bibliothèque Nationale)

Darkness, lack of knowledge, and powerlessness in face of the machine (to which I will come later) are not enough. Financial transactions, conducted in vile places (and which the whole neighborhood goes to see, but furtively or in disguise), are openly accessible, yet paired with an almost total lack of honorability. How shall society then conceive its relationship with market actors, how shall it open up stable and public paths of financial action, if these markets are below respectability? This is a question which constantly preoccupies eighteenth-century observers, one which does not emerge only in moments of financial crisis.

This question is not exclusively due to the (ethically doubtful) association of financial speculation with gambling. After all, gambling was an acceptable activity for noblemen (if kept under control), and eighteenth-century mathematicians were increasingly prepared to deal with it in a systematic fashion (Bernstein 1996). The question is rather due to the perceived incompatibility between society and financial markets, a central aspect of which is lack of honorability.

French stockbrokers are so skilled in stealing that they are worse than lawyers. They are all only "valets" and "Savoyards," writes an anonymous author who, having lost everything in financial speculations, is now forced to serve in the army (*L'Agio* 1789, pp. 5–6).[11] In Paris, it is the Savoyards and the Lyonnais who are seen as the prototype of the dishonest broker. In Geneva, it is French protestant refugees who takeover this role (*Le bon-homme* 1795). In London, it is the French and the Dutch, and everywhere it is the Jews, the absolute foreigners, who are seen as the paragon of the stockbroker. Society's incompatibility with the stock exchange is thought to be so great that the foreigner becomes a metaphor for the disreputable role of the broker.

And disreputable it is: "a change broker will out lie the devil for the advantage of stock" (*The Guardians* 1741, p. 126). The broker is "impertinent, noisy, and vain, without wit, a joke" who conspires with Jews and Tories against the American Revolution (Hopkinson 1780). He lacks moral education and "can write a variety of hands," forging documents (*A Genuine Narrative* 1763, pp. 7–8). Moral pamphlets tell the stories of Jonathan Wild, John Rice, Thomas Tyler, or Charles Price, brokers who in the eighteenth century are masters of impersonation and disguise, with "a natural propensity to dishonesty, servile, mean, effronteous, impudent, and given to palaver" (*A New Edition* 1786, p. 20; also *Some Seasonable Considerations* 1720; *A Complete Narrative* 1790). *Dr. Johnson's Dictionary* defines the stockjobber (a trader for his own account) as "a low wretch who gets money by buying and selling shares in the Funds" (cited in Wheeler 1913, p. 19).

Brokers should be below merchants in the social order, but in the order of the marketplace they are ahead of emperors (Colquhoun 1814, pp. 124–25). Yet the merchant is truthful, upright, courteous (*The Imperial Magazine* 1760, pp. 76, 78), while brokers are in fact con men (*The Life of Jonathan Wild* 1725, pp. 62–63). Thomas Mortimer, whose influential *Every Man His Own Broker* is continuously in print from the moment of its first publication in 1761 until the 1820s, pleads for abolishing stockjobbers and reducing the number of stockbrokers as a means of legitimating financial exchanges in the eyes of the public.[12] First, brokers are not intended for men, but for women, because men can conduct their own business. The "fair sex" must be "delivered from connections with the medley of barbers, bakers, butchers, shoemakers, plaisterers, and taylors, whom the *Mammon of unrighteousness* has transformed into Stockbrokers" (Mortimer [1761] 1782, p. xix). Moreover, stockjobbing is ruinous to merchants and tradesmen and, more generally, to any character, since it encourages deceit, falsehood, and dishonesty. Disorder and covetousness are encouraged by brokerage too; these lead to fraud, which in its turn leads to robbery (*The Fatal Consequences* 1720, pp. 9–10, 13, 24–25). Financial speculation is disorder and degeneration. There is no honesty and moderation, only exaltation and drunkenness, writes Mirabeau on the eve of the French Revolution (Mirabeau 1787, pp. 10, 19, 38, 50, 53).

Becoming Legitimate

Against this background of public mistrust toward stock exchanges and brokers (Bowen 1986), processes of monopolistic enclosure, including the virtual witnessing of honorability, shift the situation. Two aspects played a significant role in the emergence of status groups: monopoly granting by the state and self-constitution.[13] Among the most important mechanisms involved in the creation of status groups were controls of (a) space, (b) access to membership, (c) securities lists, and (d) honor. Groups of official brokers were accompanied by the emergence of subordinated and lesser groups (clerks and unofficial brokers, respectively), creating a hierarchy in which the transition from the lower to the higher groups was regulated by strict rules.

In England and France, the state granted brokers monopoly over financial transactions through the Act of the Parliament of 1697 (England) and the royal edicts of September 24 and October 14, 1724 (France), respectively. The Act of 1697 expired in 1707; the status group which had emerged was dissolved under the pressure of market forces. Starting in the 1770s, we witness the reemergence of this group by self-constitution. In France, sixty (non-nominated) brokers were granted monopoly in 1724. The group thus formed continued to exist, with some modifications, until well into the twentieth century. Initially, brokers were rich merchants and noblemen who could afford the licensing fees. In the US, a bill of the New York state assembly from April 10, 1792, banned public auctions of securities and made time bargains unenforceable (Sylla 2005, p. 307). This was followed by self-regulation only a month later (the Buttonwood Agreement of May 17, 1792): twenty-four partners agreed to fix brokerage commissions and to give preference to each other. In February 1817, twenty-four brokers constituted a board (Sylla 2005, p. 309), providing the basis for New York Stock Exchange as a status group during the next centuries. In all these cases, the granting of monopoly was officially justified as restoring order and security, and as eradicating improper practice (Jenkins 1973, p. 20; Duguid 1901, p. 12; Colling 1949, p. 72; Markham 2002, p. 118).

The Social Control of Space

From the beginning, control of space was an important mechanism: the place of financial transactions was the exclusive domain of official brokers. In some cases, this space was policed by the state as well. In Paris, for example, the royal edicts of 1724 stipulated that all financial transactions have to take place in the Jardin Royal, where stockbrokers (*agents de change*) had exclusive access. The presence of women was strictly prohibited. The business-conducting public was admitted only up to a rail fence. A company of archers, directly answerable to the general lieutenant of police, was posted to prevent all disorder (*Deux arrests* 1724). In 1801, Napoleon decided to build a new Bourse (Palais Brongniart), owned by the state and accessed only by official stockbrokers (Colling 1949, p. 155).

In 1761 in London, brokers attempted to form an exclusive club by controlling the coffeehouses. A group of 150 brokers rented Jonathan's for exclusive use during three hours each day and prohibited the access of nonmembers (Michie 1999, p. 31). A successful challenge in court led brokers to build their own premises and charge a fee for daily access in 1772 (Hennessy 2001, p. 16; Poitras 2000, p. 297). In 1801, the stock exchange building was reorganized as an exclusive subscription room, owned by a club of brokers, with a yearly membership fee of ten guineas (Francis 1849, p. 180). Being an official broker automatically meant being a member of this club, a co-owner of the building and of the company of the stock exchange (Michie 1999, p. 34; Jenkins 1973, p. 50).

In New York City, we witness a similar process. After the agreement of May 1792, the group rented the Tontine Coffee House and excluded nonmembers from access.[14] Organized as the Board of Brokers (later the Old or Regular Board), this group owned the stock exchange building. Outsiders were admitted to certain rooms (e.g., to the Long Room in the 1860s) upon paying a yearly fee (Fowler 1870, p. 50). The statutes of the New York Stock Exchange and the London Stock Exchange, respectively, explicitly defined the purpose of these private associations as furnishing rooms where members can meet like in a private club (Goldman 1914, pp. 1, 117; Cordingley 1901, p. 83; Giffen 1877, p. 37).[15] Control of space was essential for establishing jurisdiction and for the institutionalization of stock exchanges, centered upon a status group.

The spatial control of status groups over the stock exchange did not mean that the street ceased to be a place of financial transactions. Throughout the nineteenth century, for instance, the whole neighborhood of the Paris Bourse constituted the setting of the coulisse, the unofficial yet tolerated stock exchange.[16] In Lower Manhattan, brokers who resisted the authority and the monopoly claims of the Regular Board of the New York Stock Exchange formed the New (and later the Open) Board, dealing in the street. In the twentieth century, unofficial brokers resisted control by the New York Stock Exchange by refusing to move indoors until 1921 (*New York Curb* 1931, p. 31).

What spatial control achieves, in part, is to mark a boundary between legitimate groups, together with the institution they support, on the one hand, and a tolerated "rest," on the other. While not eradicating all suspicions of dishonor and dark tricks, this boundary usefully points to a realm (street trading) upon which blame can be easily transferred. This boundary, understood as formal exclusion, does not mean a complete and clear-cut division. Up to the dawn of the nineteenth century, some New York brokerage houses will practice multiple memberships—i.e., having one broker as an official member of the New York

Stock Exchange, another one as a member of the Consolidated and Petroleum Exchange, etc. (Wyckoff 1930, p. 102). Yet this formal distinction between the inside and the outside serves in its turn to legitimate
official brokers within society at large: once the disreputable elements
have been left outside, those inside (and their activities) are endowed with
honorability.

The Social Control of Membership

A second mechanism of boundary marking was control of membership.
Stock exchanges were organized as exclusive men's clubs. In 1772 in London, the explicit aim was the "desire of the proprietors to organize a small,
select, and exclusive membership from the great mass of irresponsible
dealers, many of them with poor repute, who gained all the privileges of
the market by payment of sixpence a day" (quoted in Duguid 1901, p. 71).
Two sets of formal criteria were relevant in this respect, albeit in different combinations: wealth and the status of applicants (defined through
nationality, religion, ethnicity). In addition to these, the club set informal
criteria of admission.

   In London, the Act of 1697 stipulated that brokers had to pay an admission fee of £2 and make a deposit of £500. In London and New York,
members had to buy a share in the association and were co-owners of
the building. The price of membership rose continuously throughout the
nineteenth century. In 1869, a seat on the New York Stock Exchange was
selling at $8,000 (Markham 2002, p. 288). Between 1858 and 1870, seat
prices increased fivefold; between 1871 and 1901, they increased thirtyfold
(Warshow 1929, p. 341). In Paris, the edicts of 1724 stipulated that brokers
had to be wealthy, according to a level set by a committee of ten prominent
citizens. Brokers received hereditary status in 1786. After a short suspension during Napoleon Bonaparte's reign, this status was regained in 1816
and maintained until the end of the century (Colling 1949, pp. 105, 188).
Membership lists of the Paris Bourse show largely the same family names
throughout the eighteenth century (Bouchary 1939, p. 97; 1940, p. 23).
In 1801, Napoleon set the deposit paid by stockbrokers at 60,000 francs
(Colling 1949, p. 156). Wealth as a condition of membership was meant to
make sure that brokers honored their contracts; combined with the other
admission criteria, it also had the effect of creating a status group which
was difficult to access.

In time, control over membership led to the legal definition of a seat on the New York Stock Exchange as private ownership, which could be sold (with the agreement of the exchange board), and which gave the owner a right to participate in the activities of a voluntary private organization (Goldman 1914, pp. 11, 14; Meeker 1922, p. 570; also *Hyde v. Woods*, 94 US 523, 1876; *Sparhawk v. Yerkes*, 142 US 1, 1891; *Page v. Edmunds*, 187 US 596, 1903). Corporations were not permitted to own seats on the New York Stock Exchange (Meeker 1922, p. 297); the presence of a corporation as a member would have opened the door to federal regulation.

In addition to wealth, applicants had to fulfill criteria of citizenship, religion, and nationality. In Paris, these were very strictly defined. Official stockbrokers had to be over twenty-five, French citizens, Catholics, and residents of Paris. Noblemen were permitted to be brokers. Foreigners were admitted to the Bourse as visitors or on business only if a French merchant resident in Paris vouched for them. In 1801, brokers were assimilated to civil servants, selected through a complicated procedure. A committee of eight bankers and eight merchants drew up a list of names, sent to the prefect of Paris, who added names up to twice that number. The list was then sent to the minister of the interior, who added further names up to twice the number of those selected by the committee and the prefect together. The list was then sent to the emperor, who named the official stockbrokers of the Bourse (Colling 1949, pp. 72, 156). Around 1900, the price of a seat on the Paris Bourse oscillated between $300,000 and $400,000, at that time's currency value (Van Antwerp 1913, p. 392).

In London, the number of seats on the Stock Exchange was fixed at five hundred. After 1772, only twelve of the seats could be occupied by Jews. In addition to the usual fees and deposits, "Hebrew applicants" had to purchase the privilege "by a liberal gratuity to the Lord Mayor" of the city of London (Francis 1849, p. 113). Normally, members of the London Stock Exchange had to be freemen of the city (Jenkins 1973, p. 43) and natural born British subjects. The selection process was at least as complex as in Paris, though less dependent on the state administration. From 1812, applicants and their wives had to renounce all other business activities, if admitted. The names of the applicants were posted on the exchange board and a vote was taken, with three black balls meaning rejection (Jenkins 1973, p. 55).

In New York, a rule adopted in 1817 forbade any business between a member of the official board and a nonmember broker (Markham 2002,

p. 123). The Regular Board of the New York Stock Exchange (and the Open Board too) prohibited members to attend the Evening Exchange, organized at the Fifth Avenue Hotel in Manhattan until 1865 (Cornwallis 1879, p. 13). Members of the London Stock Exchange were forbidden to attempt the legal enforcement of claims arising out of a transaction against the principal of a fellow member without the consent of the Committee for General Purposes; the Stock Exchange was its own tribunal (Brodhurst 1897, pp. 134, 137).

There was a very strong prejudice against Jewish brokers. The Regular Board was noted for exclusiveness: "one might as well attempt to visit the Kabla at Mecca without swearing by the Prophet, as to enter the sacred arena of the brokers, when lacking satisfactory introduction" (Medbery 1870, p. 26). In 1848, applicants had to show at least one year experience in Wall Street and pay an admission fee of $400 (*Stocks and Stock-Jobbing* 1848, p. 8). As in London, three black balls sufficed for rejection (Fowler 1870, p. 53).

The official status of stockbrokers had to be made visible at all times during business hours. On the Paris Bourse, the names were posted on the board and each broker carried a personal badge. Brokers had to be present at all time during business hours; the only excuse for absence was illness. In London, the Act of 1697 introduced personal silver badges for stockbrokers, which were to be produced upon each transaction.

The Social Control of Securities Lists

Besides control of space and membership, brokers had control over lists of traded securities. Paris brokers were hereditary civil servants and their transactions were exclusively acknowledged by the French law as commercial contracts. They were the only ones entitled to issue a quotation list and had discretionary power over which securities could be listed and traded (Colling 1949, p. 125). In spite of this monopoly, several unofficial quotation lists existed. The French state also licensed a second class of fee-paying brokers, the *coulissiers*, who were not civil servants and could not inherit the office. Their transactions were not acknowledged as commercial contracts and they were not formally allowed to issue lists of traded securities. New York and London official brokers had a similar monopoly over quotation lists (Brodhurst 1897, p. 281; Hamon 1865, p. 16); while their transactions were not acknowledged as commercial contracts, only they could decide which securities were traded and quoted on the list. Transactions in unlisted securities were subject to fines. Control over the official listing of securities, however, did not mean standardization of price data: parallel lists, official and unofficial, continued to exist well into the twentieth century. During the eighteenth century, London had at least two quotation lists, Freke's and Castaing's (Cope 1978, p. 18). The Paris Bourse, for instance, had in 1910 at least the official list, the *Cote Desfossés*, the *Cote Vidal*, and the *Cote du Syndicat* (Vidal 1910, p. 38).

Prestige, Honorability, and Codes of Behavior

Brokers elected a governing body: the Committee of General Purposes (London) and the Board of Brokers (New York), respectively. In Paris, official brokers were governed directly by the state. In nineteenth-century New York City, the Board of Brokers (i.e., the Regular Board) was seen as "a wheel within a wheel, an imperium in imperio, a government in itself" which dispensed with aid from courts of law (Fowler 1870, p. 58). These governing bodies set admission, transaction, and behavior rules (Jenkins 1973, p. 55). In New York, the board had the power to monitor telephone and telegraph lines (once these had been installed), and even to cut them off in order to protect the interests of the exchange (Van Antwerp 1913, p. 267; Goldman 1914, p. 28). The institutional regulation of financial transactions overlapped with the regulation of behavior meant to preserve the reputation and exclusiveness of a status group.

Status was made visible through rules and rituals appropriate for a select club. The necessity to distinguish between good and bad behavior was recognized very early. The Act of 1697 specified corporal punishments for defaulting on contracts: three days in the pillory for each default. In 1787, the black board was adopted by the full meeting of the members as the "moral pillory of the Stock Exchange" (Francis 1849, p. 147). At the opening of the Subscription Room in 1801, the *Times* declared that applicants must be scrutinized and balloted in order to "keep out improper persons and bad behaviour" (Hennessy 2001, p. 22). In Paris, the black board (introduced in 1724) listed the names of the brokers who had defaulted on contracts or had committed other grave misbehaviors. Even the manner in which brokers had to talk to each other was regulated: without raising their voice and without any gesticulation. Tailcoats and tall hats were mandatory at the sessions of the NYSE's Regular Board. Each member had his personal chair in the trading room. Buying a seat on the exchange literally meant buying a chair from a retiring broker.

Being a stockbroker also meant being privileged with respect to certain forms of behavior. London brokers, but not clerks, were allowed to smoke after 4 p.m., a restriction which applied in New York too. In 1865, NYSE's Constitution established fines for use of "indecorous language," for interrupting the president, for talking while the president speaks, for leaving the room, for standing on tables or chairs, and for smoking. Visiting other stock exchanges was completely forbidden: repeat offenders had their names published on a Black List (Hamon 1865, pp. 26, 30–31). Admissible practical jokes included bursting a sack of flour over the heads of a trading crowd, setting newspapers afire in the reading room, knocking off hats, and throwing paper darts at each other (Duguid 1901, pp. 170–73; Markham 2002, p. 288). However, these jokes were to be kept under control. Repeat offenders could be excluded from the club. The social propriety of stockbrokers was thus not exclusively defined through honesty in business or payment of debts, but also through good social behavior and gentlemanly conduct befitting an exclusive men's club.

Observers repeatedly stressed honor and respectability, which integrated stock exchanges into the broader society. In the absence of any adequate legal frame, honorability was the only means to ensure the inviolability of contracts (Hirst 1911, p. 50) and to present them to the public as similar to commercial contracts. This honorability, so essential, yet not directly observable, had to be at least virtually witnessed: "The standard of honor is high among stockbrokers in relation to their contracts with each other, as it necessarily must be when these are the work of a moment, and a single word, and involve large amounts of money. Contracts once made are never repudiated, even where ruin might be averted by doing so, and where it might be difficult to prove them to the satisfaction of a court of law" (Cornwallis 1879, p. 36).

The internal rules of the exchange, for instance, were regarded by courts of law as having binding power, even in situations where material proof of the transaction having been ordered (or conducted) was absent. In the case of *Louis Cohen v. Morris H. Rothschild and Bernard Hyman* (brokers on the New York Cotton Exchange), decided in 1918 by the Supreme Court of New York (1918 N.Y. App. Div. Lexis 7877), the plaintiff claimed that Rothschild and Hyman had never executed his orders, while pocketing the money. With telephone records destroyed and order slips not mentioning any names, it was very difficult to bring proof of the order having been put. The court ruled that the rules of the exchange included a "relation of the most delicate fiduciary character" between principal and agent, with the broker trading on discretionary accounts for fifty customers. The plaintiff knew that the brokers were allowed an opportunity to defraud, yet he entrusted them and acted on the presumption of honorability. Therefore, the plaintiff "should not without some proof of dishonesty or bad faith prevail in his contention that his trusted agents cannot recover unless they affirmatively show that they have not cheated him and could not have done so" (1918 N.Y. App. Div. Lexis 7877, p. 7). The presumption of honorability was held to compensate for lack of proof and destruction of records.

There was a sustained effort to convince the public that brokers are honorable: "The stockbrokers are almost without exception men of honor, without which virtue the Stock Exchange would be an impracticable chaos. [The broker] is genial in manner, liberal in his views, generous in his nature, a warm friend, a good liver and a keen observer. Like a lawyer, he must think on his feet; he must be quick in decision, for he cannot wait for public opinion to crystallize itself after an event; he must anticipate what the opinion will be" (Gibson 1891, pp. 30–31). There is "no place in the world where people are trusted so much on faith as they are in Wall Street; not even in the Church" (Clews 1888, p. 33). And, "New York stock-brokers are large-hearted, liberal-minded men; their generous impulses are known far and wide. Ever true to the interests of their customers, their mutual transactions form the daily varying barometer of the financial atmosphere" (*The New York Stock Exchange* 1887, p. 17). Another indicator of honorability was the compatibility between the church and brokerage: "a few years ago it was thought inconsistent for a member of the church to be a stockbroker, and now . . . stockbrokers are rather at a premium to be good members and vestrymen" ("Stocks" 1881).

Members of the Regular Board made "a highly respectable livelihood" (*History* 1887, p. 5), and were among the most influential citizens in New York City (Hamon 1865, p. 112). The brokers of the Paris Bourse gave a seal of authenticity to transactions by their mere presence (*La Bourse* 1854, p. 7). The broker's character justified the trust put in him: "If we entrust him with such important sums, it is because he guarantees it by his character, his morality and his experience" (De Mériclet 1854, p. 9). London brokers were "men of considerable standing and reputed wealth in the City; though their connexion in business lies entirely within the Stock Exchange, from which they are rarely absent during business hours, and they are mostly men of great experience . . . (they) must necessarily have a certain standing and character in the business world" (Playford 1855, pp. 17, 21).

The need to maintain honor required control over membership:

> And yet the Stock Exchange has rules for its own members, and it is exclusive, like the English society, the benefit of this exclusiveness being that a crowd of unknown little operators are kept out of the pale. . . . And no doubt the Stock Exchange escapes much inconvenience of the kind by closing its doors to the general public, and taking precautions that no unknown dealer shall be allowed to cover himself to excess with liabilities to pay or deliver stock, that in imitation of our rigid social rules a formal introduction shall be necessary in order to guarantee respectability. . . . The whole system could not be compared to anything more fitly than to a club. (*The Rationale* 1876, p. 110)

And, "That a stock-broker should be a man of good standing and character is evident, considering the magnitude and importance of the business which he has to transact. . . . So various and so numerous are the checks upon irregularity, and so jealous is the Stock Exchange of its honour, that in all intelligent circles the character of a stockbroker is looked upon with great and merited respect" (Fearn 1866, p. 96).

Such a group had the capacity to select its customers. Early on, stockbrokers imposed minimum order sizes. In London as in New York, the minimum size was one hundred securities, which could be increased only by sizes of ten. In 1865, the Regular Board did not accept any orders under $500 (Hamon 1865, p. 18). For comparison, in 1860 the per capita money value of all economic goods possessed by the people of the US was $513 (*Statistical Abstract* 1913, p. 628). Only the very rich could afford the services of the Regular Board. Less wealthy individuals had to conduct business with unofficial brokers. The correspondence of brokerage houses, as well as investor diaries, indicate that members of the Regular Board regularly socialized with the upper classes and had ties in "respectable" circles.[17] Directories of the respectable wealthy—regularly published in New York City since the 1840s—had stockbrokers as a permanent fixture (e.g., *Wealth* 1845).

Subordinated Status Groups

This exclusiveness was accompanied by the emergence of subordinated groups. In the range of rights and privileges, clerks were immediately below stockbrokers. Brokers had to vouch for the character and moral integrity of personally subordinated clerks, and apply for their admission. In London, the Committee for General Purposes approved clerks. They and their immediate relatives were forbidden to deal in securities. Under certain conditions, however, clerks could become brokers. They needed two guarantees and three recommendations from members of the exchange and had to be over twenty-one (Poley 1926, p. 37). Additionally, they had to pay all the required fees and deposits. In Paris, the state licensed unofficial brokers (*coulissiers*), but did not acknowledge their transactions or endorse their quotation lists (Tétreau 1994).

Throughout the nineteenth century, the consolidation of stockbrokers as a status group went hand in hand with the consolidation of the stock exchange as an institution. In some cases, official stockbrokers absorbed competing groups, or tried to limit their access to information and transactions. In New York City, street-trading broker groups like the New Board (aka the Outside, later the Open Board) emerged early. The Open Board was absorbed by the Regular Board in 1869 (Markham 2002, p. 288; Fowler 1870, pp. 55–56). Brokers operating on smaller exchanges in Manhattan were restricted to trading unlisted securities. Street brokers were clearly perceived as less honorable than the Regular Board (Hamon 1865, p. 129).

The stress on morality, character, respectability, solidity, strict admission criteria, exclusiveness, and good social behavior were meant to legitimize the stock exchange as a social institution. It propagated the idea that financial transactions are anchored not only in business acumen and economic savvy, but also in social respectability and solidity. This did not mean that all manipulation and dark dealing disappeared. It meant, nevertheless, that the lens through which society perceived this group had changed, and the emergence of a discourse of self-presentation which was not there before. The respectable, even conservative bourgeois replaced the adventurer and the villain as the character with which brokers could be most appropriately identified. Throughout the nineteenth century, we repeatedly encounter the view of official stockbrokers as an exclusive men's club which integrates into the broader social order and contributes to maintaining it, a view echoed by Max Weber ([1894] 2000a, p. 322; [1894]

2000b) in his perception of nineteenth-century stock exchanges as "closed clubs" and as a "monopoly of the rich" ([1894] 2000a, pp. 326–27).

Another effect of the social closure of stock exchanges (with the intrinsic emphasis on honorability) was the creation of a hierarchy of transaction places, out of the rumble and jumble of the streets where garters and wooden shoes had mingled earlier. These places were not completely isolated from each other, neither spatiotemporally nor communicatively. Official brokers could maintain informal connections with unofficial ones, while being able to further tout their honorability. It could then be argued here that such a hierarchy of groups is similar to the hierarchy of networks which, in Harrison White's argument (2002), constitutes a market. But then such a market—different from the tumult of a thousand adjacent, yet disconnected conversations—emerged as the consequence of setting in place boundaries to society at large, of putting a legitimate face to the world, and not only to adjacent networks.

Prestige and Authorship

During the eighteenth century, the social status of brokers was mirrored in a literary divide: while brokers provided the figures for a considerable number of moralizing pamphlets and comedies, they almost never embraced the authorial position. Low status meant, among other things, that they could not gain an authoritative voice in the time's public conversations. They were talked about, but could not talk themselves. Of course, the seventeenth and eighteenth centuries knew the occasional broker-turned-author, who wrote descriptions of speculation as a means of warning good citizens; nevertheless, theirs was not the authority to talk about the stock exchange in the public arena.

Yet as prestige and honorability became an intrinsic part of the brokers' self-presentation to society, things changed. On the one hand, the monopolistic closure of stock exchanges made necessary an observational apparatus, which in its turn required authoritative voices, voices claiming to directly witness market transactions and actors. On the other hand, once brokers were perceived as honorable, they could acquire public voices impossible to obtain under earlier conditions.[18] Their place was now in the almanacs of the rich and respectable, in books like *Famous American Fortunes* (Holloway 1884), which gave them an additional authority. Prestige and social recognition meant an authoritative public voice, among other things. Especially in the second half of the nineteenth century, brokers, financial speculators, and other actors associated with stock exchanges (like engineers and journalists) venture into the field of intellectual production, authoring investment manuals, theoretical treatises about financial markets, how-to books, memoirs, histories of stock exchanges, and even novels and poems celebrating financial investments.

This takes place against the background of a growing differentiation between economic writers and fiction writers, one in which economic and fiction writing become increasingly incommensurable (Poovey 2008, pp. 27–28). Within this process, economic writing is represented as factual and informative, while fiction writing claims for itself the domain of the imagination. The parallel emergence of financial journalism as a new genre in the 1820s (Poovey 2008, pp. 32–33), without any precise equivalent in the domain of fiction, reinforces this divide, while facilitating the engagement of brokers in literary production. What is more, claiming a new domain for themselves—that of factual financial description and information—does not prevent brokers from engaging in other literary activities as well, regardless of whether they pertain to the domain of the descriptive or to that of the imagination.

A telling example here is that of Edmund Clarence Stedman (1833–1908), an official broker of the New York Stock Exchange, who combines trading with writing histories of his institution (Stedman 1905), as well as poetry, achieving national recognition in this latter field. Another example is that of a book on sports published in 1898 by members of the London Stock Exchange, which stated in the preface:

> The "House" on sport is not meant to embody a series of great literary achievements but . . . the writers on and about the various sports thoroughly know their subject, and the greatest testimony that can be adduced to the value of each article . . . is that each contribution discusses *con amore*, and advises its own sport as the "hobbiest" of hobbies. . . . That the "House" should write on sport is perfectly natural, for ever since its inception, the old English sport of Bull and Bear baiting has been carried on right up to the present time, and even now it bids fair to last as long as any of the sports treated of in this volume" (Morgan 1898, p. vi).

It is in such examples that the difference to the eighteenth century becomes clear: while Defoe, Swift, Beaumarchais, and Mirabeau, among others, are writers who speculate, nineteenth-century speculators also write.

These interventions in cultural production,[19] intrinsic to redefining the tense boundaries between capitalist markets and the civil sphere (Alexander 2006, p. 35), occur against the background of more general social and intellectual changes which bring forth a bourgeois, or civil society in the nineteenth century (Beckert 2001; Kocka 1995, 2004; Morford 2001), a society in which the position of the writer and the intellectual is represented as autonomous (Bourdieu 1996), and defined with respect to "the public." Of course, the civil or public sphere does not embrace all classes and groups of society; in this sense, "the public" is rather a fiction, or "an essentially imaginary function" (Warner 2002, p. 144). It enables the impersonal circulation of publications, as well as authorial orientation toward a collective, abstract entity.

While making efforts to appear as honorable—an essential bourgeois virtue—brokers address this fictional entity (the public), situating their claims above class circumstances. Public, intellectual interventions of brokers qua authors include, among other things, claims that financial markets require a sort of knowledge and understanding which can only be provided by a systematic intellectual activity. The authority of brokers and financial speculators is grounded in a unique educational mission, in the quest for a systematic, scientific knowledge about financial investments, or in the depiction of heroic financial deeds. We encounter, for instance, the example of Henri Lefevre de Chateaudun, who in the 1870s devises a national education plan for French investors, and publishes several investment treatises aimed at a wide readership. Charles Castelli, a London broker who publishes *The Theory of "Options" in Stocks and Shares* in 1877, justifies his enterprise like this: "The interesting operations on the Stock Exchange, known as 'Options,' I have long felt to be deserving of a far greater share of public attention than they now secure. . . . It is hoped that the work may prove equally useful to the Broker and the Client, as not only are specimens of intricate combinations clearly worked out, but separate cases are given to show how each party is affected" (Castelli 1877, pp. 3–4).

Another example is that of Jules Regnault, a Parisian broker who in 1863 approached speculation on the Paris Bourse with the dispassionate eye of the physicist, searching to uncover regularities similar to those "of the Earth circling the Sun" (Regnault 1863, p. 7). Others, like Henry Clews (1888), recount their decades-long experiences both as a means of educating young men and of telling heroic narratives. Still others, like the speculator-cum-writer Edwin Lefevre, choose fiction as the means of recreating the stock exchange as a heroic and adventurous world (e.g., Lefevre 1901, 1907).

What these writers seek is the public acknowledgment of their social role. When A. G. de Mériclet, the eighth official stockbroker on the Paris Bourse (out of sixty) publishes *La Bourse de Paris* in 1854, he states the following: "A part of the public wealth, and numerous interests are engaged in stock exchange operations; I thought that it will be useful to make financial speculation known in its details, in its intimacy, unveil its secrets, avoid its dangers, and teach the best values which can be learned by speculation" (De Mériclet 1854, p. 5). In the preface to their *Business Methods and Customs of Wall Street*, the brokerage house of John Davis & Co. provides another eloquent justification: "In doing this, we address the readers of this book just as we would write or speak to any one who might apply directly to us for the information referred to. A few words here as to brokers and their functions: the business of the broker is as legitimate, of as much importance, and as honestly and honorably conducted as that of the merchant, manufacturer, or farmer" (*The Business Methods* 1888, p. 6).

Yet another stockbroker, writing in 1865 in Paris, resorts to seafaring metaphors in justifying his enterprise:

> The seas fullest of reefs, most fertile with tempests can be considered harmless when compared to the dangerous Ocean of the Bourse. How many hurricanes, how many shipwrecks, how many disasters happen every day in the vast quadrangle between rue Vivienne and rue Notre Dame des Victoires! How many desperations has this indifferent monument witnessed! The sea maps show seafarers the reefs to be avoided, but try and chart the countless reefs which make the Bourse so dangerous! Since I cannot draw them on a map, I want to show them at least in a book, and will have reached my goal if I can persuade my readers that the best way to stand firm when passing the threshold of the Bourse is to lean on the arm of a honest and experienced pilot. (*Les écueils* 1865, p. 5)

The broker is imagined as the necessary pilot who helps the public navigate the dangerous yet exciting waters of the stock exchange; this latter, in its turn, appears as an ocean which engulfs society. This seafaring imagery probably sums up best the role projected by the broker-writers (together with their associates) for themselves: to pilot society on an exciting financial adventure, to explore and discover, and, finally, in the manner of the true seafarers, to get rich. This adventure, however, requires an honest, honorable, trustworthy pilot, one who is fully integrated into the social order.

While the popular literature of the time has a more ambiguous position with respect to the pilot's honor, it develops and includes several genres which celebrate the stock exchange, brokers, and speculators. Biographies of the "kings of fortune," as well as popular novels celebrating speculative success, are integral to the wave of "success manuals" ubiquitous in the US between 1870 and 1920, and which were explicitly seen as a means of educating men (Hilkey 1997). Fiction, manuals, and biographies were part of a larger, sustained effort to convince the public that the stockbrokers belong to an honorable profession which has nothing to do with speculation or fraud (e.g., Emery 1896, p. 98; *The New York Stock Exchange* 1887, p. 17; Gibson 1891, pp. 30–31). This literature tries to counteract negative views and to represent the stock exchange and its figures as examples of a successful bourgeois life and career.

This new relationship with society would not have been possible in the eighteenth century, when the stock exchange was the place of dark powers and the stockbroker was seen as just another trickster and fraudster. Not so paradoxically, perhaps, the spatiotemporal and group boundaries set to stock exchanges in the nineteenth century make possible a reconfiguration of the observational boundaries between society and financial markets. The newly emerging status groups can now legitimately lay claim to new, public intellectual activities, and to leading social roles. The wave of stock exchange publications which rises during the second half of the century, their number and diversity, and the widespread implication of brokers (together with other associated figures) in writing and publishing activities play a significant role in redefining financial knowledge and transactions.

The transformation of brokers into a status group was accompanied by their entrance into the intellectual field as writers of various fiction and nonfiction genres (as well as honorable literary figures), an entrance which contributes to legitimizing financial markets, as well as the social position of their actors. From being (negative) characters in the discourse of others, brokers and other associated actors became an authoritative voice, creating a public, positive discourse on markets and speculation. With that, they actively participated in redefining the nature of financial knowledge, the character of financial actors, the relationship between speculation and morality, and the links among the state, the economy, and stock exchanges. While the New York and London Stock Exchanges remained privately owned throughout the nineteenth century and beyond, with private control over transactions and very little, if any, public regulation, their actors became public figures: not only characters to be talked about, but voices of authority speaking to the society at large. It is in this speech that the boundaries of finance continue their configuration, through the redefinition of an essential aspect: financial knowledge.

CHAPTER THREE

Financial Knowledge and the Science of the Market

W hen the actors of the stock exchange got a public voice of their own, a crucial task they were confronted with was to redefine the character of financial knowledge. Why a redefinition? On the one hand, they were confronted with the legacy of the eighteenth century which, as I will detail below, saw the nature of financial knowledge as incompatible with civilized society. Public visibility and honorability, however, required a kind of knowledge not only compatible with, but integral to, bourgeois society. On the other hand, having a public voice meant having definitional power over the nature and properties of the knowledge needed by financial actors, the characteristics of these actors, and the properties of financial transactions and information.

I have argued in the previous chapter that the view of markets as networks does not solve the legitimacy problem, since it cannot explain how the interface between markets and society is constituted. In an analogous way, we need to go beyond understanding financial knowledge as a series of signals about price and quality, signals which can be internally processed in these networks (White 2002, p. 16). In order to understand how internal signals are constituted and processed, we need to examine first the factors and forces which define what constitutes a signal, the modes of its processing, and the properties needed by market actors in order to be able to process signals appropriately. In other words, the internal organization of information processing cannot replace the broader epistemic constitution of stock exchanges. Financial knowledge requires more than signals; it requires a community of practice which defines itself as such (Foray 2004, pp. 4, 37), and which sets validity standards.

While we encounter price data in the eighteenth- and nineteenth-century financial markets, and while such data are taken as signals from the contemporary perspective, their meaning would not be independent from the time's broader understanding of financial knowledge, of the properties of financial actors, and of the observational tools needed for the valid interpretation of such signals. At the same time, the broader understanding of what constitutes valid financial knowledge cannot come from the outside, but must be constituted through the agreement of the community of practitioners. This agreement may be grounded only in the mutual recognition of tacit rule-following (Bloor 1992, p. 270), or it may be grounded in this mutual recognition *and* in a reflexive discourse on the properties of valid financial knowledge. When the nature of financial knowledge is determined mainly (if not exclusively) by market actors following tacit rules, when knowledge means little more than interpreting the shouts, the body signs, having the ability to elbow one's way through the crowd, or to gossip at corners, this knowledge may appear as problematic and illegitimate to the society at large. In the second case, when the community of practitioners is endowed with definitional power over what constitutes valid knowledge, its definitions constitute legitimate gates to the outside world. A reflexive discourse about the nature and properties of financial knowledge then becomes intrinsic to the boundaries of the market.

Having an authoritative, respected voice means being able to define what constitutes valid financial knowledge and to impose this definition as the legitimate one. The constitution of status groups on the stock exchange, accompanied by them acquiring a public voice, inevitably meant that a redefinition of financial knowledge was a crucial aspect of their discourse. In order to make clearer the centrality of this task, I will turn now to how eighteenth-century external observers saw financial knowledge in relationship to society.

The "Devil's Mechanick"

All too often, the eighteenth century has been characterized as the century of reason, enlightenment, and endeavor for knowledge. If there is something which fascinated the observers of that time, it is scientific knowledge:

the possibility to decipher nature in a systematic way, to learn from the laws governing nature and apply these laws to the not less systematic study of society. Factual study, accompanied by the art of reasoning upon data and followed by generalizations defines the "political arithmetick" of the eighteenth century (Schumpeter [1954] 1994, p. 211). Could then financial knowledge find its place, between celestial mechanics and political arithmetic, in the century's well-tempered order of knowledge?

The allegory, one of the century's preferred modes of visual representation, treats financial markets as Fortune in a chariot conducted by the two-headed Folly, and followed by "a great Throng of People of all conditions and sexes, running after Fortune to catch the Actions. In the Clouds is the Devil Making Bubbles of Soap which mingles with the Actions that Fortune distributes to the Fools, Caps which falls to the Lot of some and the little Serpent which denote the Besotted, the Envious & the Avaricious" (*A Monument* 1720).[1] Financial markets are the work of the Devil, founded upon delusion (*The History* 1797, p. 84); the exchange cannot find its place in the natural or social order. Brokers and financial speculators are "vampires thirsty for blood, shrouded in darkness" (*Liste Générale* n.d.), claims a poster published during the consulate period of the French Revolution, echoing other publications of the same period (Louchet 1793). Their speculations came straight out of hell (*Sur la proposition* 1789).

Something which is the work of the devil, something which lies in darkness and is practiced by vampires, cannot be characterized by positive knowledge. While a science of financial markets undoubtedly exists, this science is a deadly one and an illusion, proclaims Mirabeau (1785, pp. 8–9). As such, it remains opaque to any rational spirit; knowing about financial markets means becoming one of the vampires. Yet this opaqueness does not mean that there is no regularity at work in financial exchanges. Eighteenth-century observers liken the stock exchange to a machine which cannot be known, a description which makes them even more apprehensive. A tract published in Leipzig during the Mississippi bubble sees "the whole Machine" as chaos (*Kurze Remarques* 1720, p.7). One of this author's contemporaries, writing in London, considers that:

> To all Men whose Eyes are to be open'd with Reason and Argument it shou'd be enough to fill them with Abhorrence, to think that the scandalous Mechanick, Upstart Mistery of Job-brokering should thus grow upon the Nation; that ever the English Nation should suffer themselves to be impos'd upon by the New invented Ways of a few needy Mercenaries, who can turn all Trade

into a Lottery, and make the Exchange a Gaming Table: A Thing, which like the Imaginary Coins of Foreign Nations, have no reality in themselves, but are plac'd as things which stand to be calculated, and reduc'd into value, a Trade made up of Sharp and Trick, and Mang'd with Impudence and Banter. (*The Anatomy* 1719, p. 52)

It is not so much the analogy with gambling which makes the author rant against financial speculation, but its character, which deals with imaginary values (*Truth* 1733), replacing the calculating spirit and emptying transactions of their real substratum. This emptiness makes speculation radically different from trade,[2] and as such into an impossible object of systematic investigation. If anything, speculation is the antithesis of calculation. While the time's understandings of mechanics are those of "moving powers," applied mathematics, or the manual (i.e., vulgar, common) skill of building machines (Carroll 2006, pp. 30–31), the "mechanick" of speculation could be associated only with dark powers and dishonorable skills. Similarly, speculation is an "engine" in the sense of deception, a meaning specific to the time, along with that of material contraption.

During his stay in Paris at the end of the eighteenth century, Thomas Paine observes the "modern complicated machine" of financial speculation and concludes that its aim at perpetual accumulation works against both the laws of nature and those of society:

Do we not see that nature in all her operations, disowns the visionary basis upon which the funding system is built? She acts always by renewed successions, and never by accumulating additions perpetually progressing. Animals and vegetables, men and trees, have existed ever since the world began; but that existence has been carried on by successions of generations, and not by continuing the same men and the same trees in existence that existed first; and to make room for the new she removes the old. Every natural idiot can see this. It is the stock-jobbing idiot only that mistakes. He has conceived that art can do what nature cannot. He is teaching her a new system—that there is no occasion for men to die—That the scheme of creation can be carried upon the plan of the funding system—That it cannot proceed by continual additions of new beings, like new loans, and all live together in eternal youth. Go, count the graves, thou idiot, and learn the folly of thy arithmetic. (Paine 1796, p. 37)

Therefore, any calculation on which speculation might claim to be based on is but illusion and folly. It is impossible to bring this sort of knowledge in harmony with any known order of knowledge, impossible to give it the task of discovering lawlike regularities and integrate it thus into the hierarchy of science. No new Isaac Newton can do that. The fact that speculation is grounded in taking chances and might seem akin to gambling plays here a lesser role than the unnatural assumption of perpetual accumulation of wealth, or the substitution of imagination for calculation. All that is left is observing and describing the characters and conversations which unfold in places like the Exchange Alley or the rue Quincampoix. These characters, however, with their hard to penetrate order of bulls, bears, lame ducks, pigeons, projectors, and the like, seem to form a world entirely apart from that of society or of nature. Their conversations, short-lived and ever changing, apparently with no reference to the world of common-sense, provide little stable, valid knowledge to the outside observer. Being too shocking, observation of financial speculation cannot form the basis of financial knowledge, in the way observation of nature provides a basis for the natural sciences.

Inevitably, the consequence of an unknowable order, radically different from nature and from society, is moral decay. It is not gambling or taking chances per se which is morally condemnable. It is not because financial speculation interferes with divine design or with given ethical commandments that it is ascribed such a destructive force, as the work of vampires. It is because financial speculation is radically unknowable and does not fit any given order of inquiry that so many eighteenth-century observers condemn it so vehemently. The only way of knowing financial speculation is to practice it—to learn the ways and the manner of speech of bulls and bears, to look like them, to learn the glances, their bodily signs, their way of walking. But learning all this implicit knowledge means becoming one of them, and becoming one of them means being situated neither within the order of nature, nor within the moral order. This impossibility of knowing by means of systematic observation and reflection, of constituting the subject of speculation in accordance either with the laws of nature or with the moral imperatives of society, delegitimates financial markets.

Practicing something which is radically unknowable inevitably leads to social distress and moral corruption. To put it in more modern terms, the radical uncertainty of financial transactions cannot be processed by any sort of calculation. Something which cannot be calculated is outside human reason and should not be practiced. All those who practice financial speculation have lost their reason and are prone to moral perdition, with immense social consequences. This is why, among other reasons, Adam

Smith could not classify speculation along any activity enhancing the wealth of nations and the well-being of their citizens.

This lack of certain knowledge combines with the absence of a legal frame in which marketplace transactions could be acknowledged as commercial contracts; such transactions cannot support ownership. Financial transactions are legally situated in a twilight zone, neither banned nor acknowledged as contracts.[3] Conducted orally and without written proofs, continuously shifting sides, often reneged by the parties, or staged only for manipulative purposes, the transactions of the stock exchange cannot support stable relations of ownership. Many financial instruments are ephemeral; trading practices like short-selling, where one transacts instruments one does not own, heighten the public perception of a radical incompatibility between financial markets and stable, durable ownership. Same goes for practices like buying on margin (where one does not own the money one is supposed to pay), or for time bargains. This incompatibility, in its turn, generates a gap which cannot be filled by knowable chance. And, since a stable financial knowledge appears to be impossible, it follows that knowledge-based rules of action cannot be formulated but as rules of knavery, deception, and fraud. This makes the constitution of financial subjects impossible. How could such subjects be grounded in rules of action, when it is impossible to formulate these very rules?

This magnifies the initial problem, namely creating stable ownership via financial transactions. The instability of these latter, their ephemeral character, and their continued existence in a legal limbo combine with the impossibility of knowledge-based rules of action, in a mixture perceived by many observers as poisonous for the social order. Only against this background can we better understand the horror of large parts of the New World when financial speculation is introduced to New York City and Philadelphia.

Radical unknowability fitted well with the exclusion of financial transactions from the larger social order. However, as stock exchanges and their actors became legitimate parts of this order, as status groups of brokers achieved both social respectability and an authoritative public voice, the standpoint of unknowability became untenable. How could legitimate, respected members of society claim to conduct a business which cannot be known, one which can be integrated neither in the order of nature, nor in that of society? During the eighteenth century, unknowability was established by external observers, since brokers did not have a public voice. Now the situation changed: respected brokers could be respected authors and advice givers; respected authors could define themselves the nature of financial knowledge. This is what happens especially in the second half of the nineteenth century, when a visible shift occurs in the vocabulary, literary genres, and the cognitive tools used to represent financial markets, as well as in the definitions of its object and actors.

The Popular "Science of Financial Markets"

Acquiring definitional powers over the nature and meaning of financial knowledge does not mean changing or challenging the whole spectrum of tacit knowledge forms which support transactions in the marketplace. A bull could remain a bull and a bear a bear, with all the looks, talk, hand signs, glances, and elbowing needed there. Yet since outside observers did not have direct access to transactions anymore, and with the new authorial voices becoming louder, financial knowledge could be represented to the outside world as something higher than, and different from, glances, shouts, and elbowing other people. This something should realign markets with the social order and, why not, with the order of nature too. But which was the way to go, which model to turn to? Was financial knowledge to become a branch of moral knowledge, or maybe even a branch of political economy? While not neglecting these possible connections, most authors choose to follow the lead of the most impressive model of solid, valid knowledge: natural science.

From the mid-nineteenth century on, on both sides of the Atlantic, sustained efforts were mounted to represent financial investing as a science. Made possible, in part, by the brokers' newly acquired position of public authority and respectability, this science was closely connected to the drive to attract both individuals and institutions into the sphere of speculation (Preda 2000, 2001b). Attracting growing numbers of investors into market activities required not only that financial investments were economically rewarding, but also that they were socially legitimate and morally acceptable. After all, the stock exchange claimed now to be a respectable institution, fully integrated into the social fabric. Consequently, financial knowledge had to be integrated into the accepted order of knowledge too.

Starting in the 1840s, and initially related to the explosive growth in the number of railway companies, publications targeting the middle-class investor multiplied: manuals, journals, newsletters, and how-to books were published by brokerage firms, newspapers, speculators, or railway engineers. While not all periodicals survived over the decades, their number can give an idea of the effort put into representing finance to the outside world and into redefining its activities as legitimate. In 1881 in Paris alone, 238 financial periodicals were published (Hautcoeur 1997, p. 238). Britain had at least the *Money Market Examiner* and *Railway Review*, the *Corn Universal Reporter*, the *Financial and Commercial Record*, the *Commercial Daily List*, the *London Daily Stock and Share List*, and the *Brokers' Circular*, not to count provincial periodicals. Between 1800 and 1900, at least fifty-two periodicals related and dedicated to the London Stock Exchange were published in England (*Waterloo Directory* 1997). The United States was also well stocked with financial periodicals, headed by the *Commercial and Financial Chronicle* and by the *Wall Street Journal*. All this without counting the myriad of how-to manuals and books meant to educate the paying public about finance.

Integrating finance into the accepted order of knowledge required solving several problems; changing the public discourse about the nature of this knowledge was probably the most important one. Subordinated to it was the association with gambling (Fabian 1990), which, while not the main issue,[4] made investments socially unpalatable, and even more so to a respectable public.

A "science of financial investments" was meant, in part, to disentangle investment from gambling. It certainly helped that, at about the same time, gambling was dissociated from morals and transformed into a medical condition (Brenner and Brenner 1990, pp. 72–76; Reith 1999, p. 86). An effect of this double dissociation was that both gambling and investing became somewhat similar objects of scientific inquiry. While the former had already been made into an object of mathematical treatment in the eighteenth century, its medicalization during the nineteenth century meant that individual cases were treated as pathologies, as deviations from normal social behavior. At the same time, the general principles of gambling continued to be studied as before, by applying mathematical tools. Similarly, individual investors could be treated either as examples of normal behavior or as deviating from rules, while the market could be conceptualized and studied as an abstract entity, by applying general principles of inquiry borrowed from the natural sciences.

Presenting financial investments to the public as a science required at least two things, the consequences of which go far deeper than mere scientific pretense, mockery, or the use of a scientific vocabulary as a smokescreen. First, rules of action for financial actors had to be devised, rules based in a systematic body of knowledge, covering everything from skills and attitudes to the sustained, reflective inquiry into the character of financial markets. Second, the way financial markets were conceptualized had to change. If they were to be made into an object of systematic inquiry, an inquiry led by its own rules, then the eighteenth-century mode of seeing markets as an amalgam of people, cries, plots, plans, staged performances, and manipulations—in short, as an observable chaos—had to be replaced.

Chaos and manipulation were the old way of seeing things, from the time when markets lacked their own voice. Now that they had one, virtual witnessing of market events could get a new mold, that of systematic observation of regularities, not of chaos. At the same time, financial markets had to be rethought as being more than a mere amalgam of interactions among humans, a reconceptualization required by the very task of formulating rules of behavior for investors. Formulating rules meant talking about the regularities which made markets into something more than a rumble-jumble of cries, not to mention the fact that the new image of honorability forbade such a rumble-jumble.

Actors directly or indirectly associated with stock exchanges used their newly won authorial voices in order to change the modes of conceptualizing financial speculation and investing. Such changes required first a shift in the literary genres seen as adequate for embodying financial knowledge. While pamphlets and comedies dominated the eighteenth century, more honorable genres, befitting prestige-seeking groups, appeared on the stage. Self-styled "scientific" manuals explicitly promoted an active attitude of observation, inquiry, and intervention, as opposed to the passive contemplation of a theatrical spectator, an attitude common in the eighteenth century (Agnew 1986; Preda 2001a); they disseminated cognitive instruments with the help of which readers could examine the markets and intervene in them.

A new analytical language emerged, different from that of pamphlets and comedies. It was riddled with metaphors borrowed from physics, engineering, medicine, and meteorology, promoting the analogy between investing and the natural sciences. A language which stresses the similarities between financial and physical processes also suggests that both obey the same (or similar) laws, and can be studied with similar means. More precisely, it suggests that every investor can act as a scientific observer of the laws of financial markets. During the nineteenth century, neoclassical economists set out to model economics after the causal, deterministic program of nineteenth-century mechanics (Mirowski 1989; 1994; 2002, pp. 7, 9), a program echoed by efforts to comprehend financial markets as governed by the same laws which govern natural phenomena (Jovanovic and Le Gall 2001). In their turn, popular financial writers did what they could to promote the analogy between the stock exchange, on the one hand, and phenomena of nature, on the other.

This self-styled "science" promoted the notion that financial markets are governed by principles which are not controlled by any single individual or group. Even if some persons may occasionally manipulate markets, these principles will ultimately prevail. Investors can learn the principles, provided they adopt the right attitude. This dovetailed with a rationalization which did not appeal primarily to ethics, but relied on the idea that financial markets require a systematic investigation and a scientific attitude on the part of the investors. One of the most durable effects of this science was on how investment behavior was understood.

The Rational Behavior of Investors

In order to understand better the conceptual changes introduced by the efforts to make investment into a scientific activity, we have to take into account that how-to brochures were not just a new literary form. They wanted to convince their readers that investments were not only lucrative and relatively sure, but also legitimate sources of income, given that a few rules will be respected. These rules, incessantly repeated, concerned individual behavior, on which financial success was made dependent. This, to state again, was disconnected from the tacit rules of behavior underlying the brokers' transactions in the marketplace. They were meant to represent and prescribe norms for the use of a public who could not directly observe what was happening on the floor of the exchange, and who was incessantly told about the honorability of market actors.

Rules of behavior, in their turn, could not be directly modeled on a general template of economic behavior. First, the viewpoint that financial transactions were just another form of economic activity was not yet a universally accepted one, but an argument in the making, contingent upon many issues. Second, manuals and how-to brochures promoted virtual witnessing of ideal financial transactions, separated from any particular traits and peculiarities of concrete market actors. This sort of witnessing mainly stressed observational attitudes as a basis for any decision making. Third, if financial markets as a whole were to be made into an object of systematic inquiry, then the rules governing the individual behavior of investors had to be adapted to this higher goal. What better way, then, for formulating these rules than to model them on the rules of scientific observation? What authors set out to do, then, was to rationalize financial behavior as analogous to scientific behavior and as fitting the overall treatment of financial markets in a scientific fashion.

Lack of emotions, capacity of self-control, continuous study of the markets, and monitoring of the joint-stock companies were represented as fundamental conditions of successful investments. In the first place, the notion of market behavior was stripped of its emotional, unforeseeable side, of aspects like panic, or hysteria: principles and cold blood, not passions, govern the Stock Exchange (De Mériclet 1854, p. 31). This did not mean that financial panics did not happen or that they weren't anymore an object of reflection—quite the contrary. But panicky behavior could now be examined and explained in thoroughly rational terms as lack of self-control. Errors were made by the investors who did not respect basic rules, did not properly evaluate information, or were letting themselves be manipulated by others. In other words, financial panics were tied to cognitive deficiencies on the part of investors who did not fit the model of permanent monitoring and dispassionate analysis of market events. Behavior was also stripped of its moral aspects, because nobody asked anymore whether it was moral to invest in financial securities or not.[5] While a moralizing discourse on financial investments continued to exist in the nineteenth century, it was by no means dominant; it was articulated mostly in novels and journalism, and was pitted against the "scientific" character of investment manuals. Moreover, the morality (and necessity) of financial investments was amply legitimated with respect to the family, the state, and the individual's happiness. Financial behavior was made dependent on knowledge and presented as thoroughly rational: it was a matter of studying, observing, and analyzing. A successful investor has to rely on long studies and reasoning; one must always hear all the news (Crampon 1863, p. 48; *Notions génerales* 1877, pp. 54–55).

While attention to information was one of the main components of rational behavior, another one, at least as important, was acting according to rules. As a consequence, investor manuals sought to devise clear rules of investing, of assessing risks, of picking up stocks, and of computing the value of financial securities. Two kinds of rules were devised: on the one hand, there were rules according to which investors should examine and assess the value of securities, or calculate interest rates.[6] A railway engineering manual, for example, stated that assessing the value of railway stocks has to go through a series of steps like examining gradients and curves, analyzing balance sheets, and computing profits per share (Lardner 1850, p. 310). The investor's aim should be the maximization of financial value: that is, of the value of stocks and bonds in one's portfolio. This was not seen anymore as a matter of sheer luck, but as dependent on the efforts of each individual. Publications stressed cognitive abilities as intrinsic to the rationality of financial behavior: analysis of balance sheets, reading of stock price diagrams, examination and evaluation of news.

At the same time, there were rules according to which investors should make decisions about buying and selling. For example, an English manual from 1870 advised its readers to build classes of financial securities and to select the cheapest security in a class (*Beeton's Guide Book* 1870, pp. 6–7, 67). Problem-solving chapters—a must for every manual worth this name—showed the right decision for various trading situations, and how to act on the grounds of the information at hand. Here's such an example from a French manual published in 1877, a contemporary of Henri Lefevre and Jules Regnault:

> Q: We sell 6,000 francs of French 3% bonds at 71.50 at 1 franc premium and we buy the same quantity at 71.90 at 50 centimes premium. Which limits do we impose by that to our gains? Which limits do we impose to our losses?
>
> A: We limit gains to 1,000 francs and losses to 800 francs (*Notions génerales* 1877, p. 62).

This and similar problems show that decisions are represented as thoroughly rational and depending on rules for projecting profits and losses. Investor behavior was reduced to decisions according to certain, given situations; decisions were reduced to calculations. In order to decide, the investor needs to compute possible outcomes. Behavior was thus conceived as both embedded in calculations (of probable outcomes) and calculable—that is, foreseeable, since it took place according to standardized rules. Ethical problems related to investing were avoided by excluding them from the domain of scientific inquiry. Irrational mass psychology was superseded as an explanatory variable by the informed decisions of individuals. Actual interactions on the floor of the exchange were either bracketed out, or presented as the epitome of rationality. It is not per chance that, especially from the 1880s on, the organization of the stock exchange is celebrated as a model of efficiency, rationality, and speed (see chapter 4 for a detailed discussion).

Since decisions depended on information, and since information determined prices too, both could be represented and analyzed in a homogeneous, unitary frame. While a formal notion of information will enter the vocabulary of financial economics at a much later stage (Mirowski 2002, p. 21; Preda 2007), there is a constant preoccupation in the manuals of the time with identifying the communicational factors which should determine financial behavior.

Representations of market behavior as based on knowledge and observation could not bypass the brokers and jobbers of the stock exchange. Whereas the eighteenth century focused on moral storytelling and on the external markers by which bulls, bears, or jobbers could be identified at a glance (in order to be avoided), the new mode of understanding market actors had to define brokers as mere dealers in merchandise (Van Antwerp 1913, p. 105), and to classify them according to the functions they fulfill within the stock exchange. While this latter had specific economic and social functions within society at large (detailed in the following), brokers and traders had specific functions (and played distinct roles) on the floor of the exchange (Meeker 1922, pp. 91–112). They were nothing more than calculative agents preoccupied with ensuring fairness and profits to customers (Meeker 1922, pp. 121, 124). This redefinition of the actors present on the floor was accompanied toward the turn of the twentieth century by the legal reconceptualization of the relationship between clients and brokers as that between principals and agents in a fiduciary position (Schwalbe and Branson 1905, p. 102).

The effort of representing market behavior as grounded in knowledge played an important role in making the former apt for formal analysis. The realization (and maximization) of financial value was made dependent on rational, cognitively founded individual behavior. With this, another fundamental premise for their formalization in a coherent theoretical frame was fulfilled.

Information, Prices, and Behavior

Since investors were told to rely on study and research, it followed that information was key with respect to market-related decisions. At the same time, some authors shifted to the notion that the price of financial securities should be treated as information—namely, as the most important kind of financial information. More or less systematic attempts to gather and process information on financial securities had been initiated before 1850. Already in 1844, the Court of Directors of the Bank of England had appointed "John Beaton, of the 3 per cent Consols [. . .] to make such confidential investigations and inquiries in the various Funds as may be required, and to attend the Courts of Law and Equity, in relation thereto" (Minutes of the Court of Directors, Bank of England, October 10, 1844, London, Archives of the Bank of England). As one manual put it, the stock market is nothing more but the high organization of information:

> Taking the Stock Exchange as the pattern of high organization, it will be easy to point out the advantages and disadvantages which a market of the kind exhibits. It is too often forgotten that the eager speculation in securities makes it worth the while of the keenest business men in the world to obtain good information on the value of what they traffic in; and so a bad thing falls, a good one rises in market value, a paying speculation is immediately advertised to those who will imitate it, a worthless concern is publicly expressed by a mere figure on a list. (*The Rationale* 1876, pp. 25–26)

Investor manuals and brochures distinguished between several kinds of information: on the one hand, there was the information provided by newspapers and journals, gossip and rumors. On the other hand, there was the information an assiduous investor could gain from calculation, from examining the balance sheets and computing profits per share, or from examining the historical variations of securities' prices. With respect to the information disseminated by newspapers, one had to be careful, since a good portion of it was planted and not trustworthy; moreover, a successful operator always supplements public with private information (*Stock Speculation* 1875, pp. 4, 30). At the same time, calculating is key for successful investments; it is what makes investing a science. Accounts and balance sheets have to be examined in detail; the same goes for historical price variations. Therefore, investors' manuals published both, with the explicit aim of facilitating research and decisions (e.g., Train 1857, p. 213; Courtois 1862). Statistics of historical and seasonal price variations were relatively common in investor manuals since the late 1840s.

Since information was seen as key, and since manuals distinguished between narrative information and cognitive rules, they also tended to stress more the one or the other. Some authors argued that newspaper and private information matters more; others emphasized the importance of rules and formulas for determining the value of financial securities. Accordingly, the first were viewed as "speculators,"[7] while the latter formed the camp of "theorists" (e.g., Pinto 1877, p. 179). "Speculators" considered that the value of a stock is determined by investors' expectations, which in turn are shaped by the available information (Wayland 1837, p. 278).

The idea that the value of a stock is measured by the profit per share required formulae for evaluating income per share, as well as for extrapolating income—which served to estimate the future value of a railway company or any firm, for that matter (e.g., Blanchard 1861; Sourigues 1861, 1862; Lefevre 1870, pp. 114, 122). Other manuals, such as *Beeton's Guide Book to the Stock Exchange* (1870, p. 90) extrapolated the mode of computing rates of return on bonds: "to calculate what a security at a certain price pays the investor, multiply the rate per cent paid by the security by 100, and divide by the price."

A standard technique for evaluating stocks was calculating their relative value, which meant taking a (standard state) bond as a reference point and figuring out the variations in price differences (security to bond) over a chosen time interval. This method had been first introduced by Thomas Fortune's (1810) *An Epithome of the Stocks & Public Funds* at the beginning of the nineteenth century, replacing the old view according to which the value of a stock can be best estimated by comparing it with the value of land. Comparative tables of price variations were published (*Fenn's Compendium* 1854, pp. 52–53; Wright 1842, pp. 5–6), allowing readers to compare not only the variations in prices over a time interval, but also the variations in price differences, and to classify stocks according to these variations. An investors' guide from 1870 stated that this method has enriched all who have used it since 1800 (Medbery 1870, p. 209). Some publications went so far as to state that charts and tables of price variations were an indispensable instrument for any broker dealing in puts, calls, and straddles:

> To guard against these disasters, the new system of operating in stock privileges (known as puts and calls) has been devised, by which any person may increase their chances of operating a thousand fold, with a very limited amount of capital. [. . .] It is as much the duty of a broker to pilot his customers safely through the sea of speculation, as it is his business to obtain such a customer. [. . .] Now for a broker to be able to judge with any degree of certainty the course of a stock is likely to take, he must have had actual experience in the market under many

different conditions, and he must also base his opinion upon something more than the general indications at any moment, for appearances are often deceitful in a stock market. One of the oldest maxims of the street is, that "where a stock has once sold, you may reasonably look for it to sell there again." Therefore, it becomes almost a necessity that the broker or operator should consult a table of fluctuations of stocks before he can form an intelligent opinion of future prices. (*Secret of Success* 1875, p. 11)

Even more importantly, perhaps, prices and price variations began being acknowledged as intrinsic information, the most important an investor can get. The more detailed the price variations and the closer their recording was to the actual transactions, the more important was the information. Writers of popular manuals began to realize that real-time, minute price variations were important, and that investors should gather data on these. In order to better understand this shift of perception, one must keep in mind that the quotations published in financial newspapers and journals were not standardized until the late 1860s. Many authors of financial manuals complained about the difficulty of finding and accurately compiling securities' prices, advertising at the same time their own investigative and statistical skills (e.g., Martin 1886, p. iv). Price information depended on specific price-recording systems, which influenced the cognitive instruments available to investors.

Price, Information, and Market Models

Let us reexamine the background picture: investors' manuals promoted a behavior anchored in observation, analysis, and knowledge. They formulated rules according to which investors should conduct themselves in the marketplace. Rational investor behavior was dependent on knowledge, and this meant in the first place knowledge of price variations. Behavior was made into a discrete variable and tied to price movements. This implied that knowledge, behavior, and price movements could now be integrated and examined in a homogeneous frame. Hence, what counted was not so much an explanation of price movements based on causal external factors, but how behavior changed together with prices.

The shift to securities prices as the most important kind of information needed by investors required a separation between prices, on the one hand, and the particular authority and trustworthiness of those generating and providing them, on the other. This means separating two kinds of knowledge, which were fused together in the eighteenth century: knowledge about "objective" entities and knowledge about the idiosyncratic actors of the marketplace. In its turn, knowledge about prices as "objective" entities, independent of the peculiarities, track record, or personal ties of any market actors, meant either setting up a price recording system endowed with abstract authority, or studying price movements within abstract, theoretical models. In its turn, this latter kind of study implied the use of analogies with the natural world (mainly with physics), as well as a shift from representations of rational investor behavior to representations of price behavior.

Probabilistic modeling of gambling and its outcomes already had a long tradition (Bernstein 1996; Todhunter 1965; Hacking 1990; Desrosières 1998, p. 80). While the application of the probability calculus to the study of society was opposed as contradicting the principle of free will (Breton 1992), it was discussed as a possibility of grasping price variations. A manual from 1854, for instance, although skeptic, shows that probabilistic explanations of price variations were discussed at that time:

> I do not know about the power of probabilistic calculus applied to the operations of the Stock Exchange, but I know that Condorcet and the marquis of Laplace failed on all their calculations on the probability of moral events, on judgments on a plurality of votes, and on the results of parliamentary votes. A moral event depends on thousand unknown causes which cannot be submitted to any calculus. If we would want to try our fortune by some calculus, the method of the viscount Saint-André would be better. The marquis of Laplace has made a science out of the probability calculus. This science can be applied to life insurance, to ship insurance, it has a basis in the mortality tables and the number of ships which strand every year, but it is impossible to find it in the lows and highs of bonds. What produces the movements of these bonds is as variable as the golden arrow on the dome of the Stock Exchange. (De Mériclet 1854, pp. 88–89)

Other authors echoed the view that the causes of price variations were far too complex to be modeled probabilistically. In ranting against probabilistic calculus, they provided a clear view of how such methods were to be employed:

> I had a High Wrangler on my books (he is dead now), who thought that with his knowledge of mathematics he must succeed. He was not a gambler, but an

experimental philosopher. What he told me was this, and I tell you, dear "Out-side Fools"—"*Multiply each gain or loss by the probability on which it depends, compare the total results of gains and losses, and then you will have the required average, or, as it is termed, the mathematical expectation.*" In fact, he started with a *petitio principii*. In other words, he assumed that he knew the probability on which the gain or loss depended, which was a totally unwarrantable assumption. In Stock exchange speculation, and indeed, as I think, in all other things, it is impossible to gain such a complete knowledge of the "*sum of the conditions*" as to correctly predict the result of those conditions. The only people, my dear "Outside Fools," who have any approximate knowledge of this philosophical "*sum of the conditions*" are the powerful men who are behind the scenes, the directors, and wire-pullers, and financial magnates, who, possessing through their wealth enormous leverage on the markets, exercise it remorselessly; and I grant you this, that they, if any one, have this knowledge. And yet it would not be theoretically correct to say that they had this knowledge, for a war might suddenly break out, they might die, a money panic might suddenly occur, or a division in their own camp to frustrate their plans. (Pinto 1877, pp. 376–77)

This is a biting critique of the attempt to develop a causal explanation of price movements based on probabilistic calculus and the evaluation of (insider) knowledge. It shows, however, two entangled arguments: (1) the attempts to apply the probability calculus to price forecasts and (2) the im-possibility of causal explanations of price variations. Some may have been derided for their belief that the complex and changing causes of financial volatility could be grasped in probabilistic terms (Eggleston 1875, p. 79; De Mériclet 1854, p. 87), but the idea that probabilistic calculus could be used for analyzing price variations stuck at least with some brokers.

Against this background emerged the first formulation of the random walk hypothesis,[8] the cornerstone of the formal treatment of financial markets. In 1863, Jules Regnault, the employee of an official broker of the Paris Bourse,[9] published the *Chance Calculus and the Philosophy of the Stock Exchange*, in which he undertook to develop an abstract model of price movements. One of his declared aims was to supersede morals as a means of uncovering the dangers of financial gambling by "demonstrat-ing to the gambler how the natural course of events will inevitably lead to his ruin on a certain day, instead to make him feel that if he's getting rich, it cannot be but by robbing his fellows" (Regnault 1863, p. 3). Such a precise aim (predicting the day of one's financial ruin) rested on the belief that financial speculations are governed by objective laws, similar to those governing natural phenomena. These powers of prediction implied relegating chance to a superficial level, below which lies that of objective laws, which must be investigated by a "science of the Stock Exchange."[10] Moreover, it was perfectly legitimate to apply formal instruments (like the probability calculus) to issues which are only superficially moral (like financial investments): "many enlightened spirits are full of indignation that some dare introduce the calculus to questions considered to pertain to the moral order; but the moral world is governed by the same laws which govern the natural world" (Regnault 1863, p. 6). Therefore, "the variations of the Stock Exchange, like the Earth revolving around the Sun, are submitted to the laws of universal attraction; under certain conditions, the capitalist can be assured to realize proportional profits with the same certitude with which he expects the seasons to change" (Regnault 1863, p. 8).

Both the causes of price movements and their subjective evaluations by market actors are extremely diverse (p. 23); moreover, the stock exchange discounts the actors' expectations and incorporates them in prices (p. 24). The value of securities is determined only by the price; it is impossible to have a "true" value different from price (p. 30). Future movements of prices are independent of past ones (p. 39), and there is only one sure way of making profits on the stock exchange: "to operate only on certain information, unknown to the public, to have the secret of events important enough to influence prices" (p. 42). This may be a cause of social inequalities on the stock exchange, but does not influence the objective laws of speculation.

Writing at the beginning of the 1860s, when price recording was not yet standardized,[11] Regnault insisted on computing median prices as the absolute value toward which real prices tend. Under the influence of Quételet (Jovanovic and Le Gall 2001, pp. 333, 348), he insisted on the causal determination of prices. Regnault asserted that stock price variations have causes which remain constant over time and can be examined in a rational fashion. He classified these causes as general or particular, constant or variable (Regnault 1863, pp. 17–18, 110) and proceeded to study them. Information determines the investors' expectations, and with that price variations. Since these expectations are individual, and since they determine price movements, it follows that these movements do not depend on each other; future movements cannot be inferred from past ones. But this does not mean that we cannot find a method for analyzing them: this method, dubbed by Regnault "law of deviations" (loi des écarts) consisted in analyzing the relationship between time intervals and price variations: the aim was to find a regular, probabilistic relationship between time and price differences.

Regnault considered that the causal influence of events diminishes with time; what happened a month ago has less influence on prices than what happened yesterday. This led him to argue that shorter time spans cause smaller differences in prices, while longer time spans cause bigger differences in prices. His "law of deviations" concerns the relationship between price volatility and time intervals: if one studies price data over a long time period and calculates the deviations of prices over given time intervals, one can see that "price deviation is directly proportional with the square root of time intervals" (Regnault 1863, p. 50). With the help of this law, investors could compute how much they had to wait if they wanted to double or triple their profit.

Regnault's law of deviations is seen by historians of economics as the first validation of the random walk hypothesis (Jovanovic 2006b), in its turn crucial for modern financial theory. In contrast with other investment manuals of the time, Regnault shifts from the study of human behavior to that of price movements; he prescribes observation as the fundamental attitude of the market observer, irrespective of whether this observer is a speculator or a contemplating scientist. In fact, the two attitudes overlap.

Regnault (who, remember, was the employee of a brokerage firm and an investor in his own right) writes at the interface between investment advice and the analytical examination of financial markets as entities governed by objective laws. This enables him to distinguish between the appearance and the essence of markets (he talks about apparent and permanent causes of price variations), to locate this essence in the realm of natural phenomena, and to transfer mathematical principles and instruments to the study of price movements. From the "devil's mechanick," stock exchanges become both the realm and the object of positive knowledge, a transformation impossible to obtain without a redefinition of actor behavior and of information. This transformation, in its turn, reinforces the legitimacy of markets: financial transactions, now the object of positive knowledge and a quasi-scientific activity, become hereby socially acceptable, if not even desirable. Therefore, one can engage in debates whether physical or biological analogies are best suited to capture the essence of the market.

A decade later, Henri Lefevre, who was an investor and an actuary (Jovanovic 2002, 2006a),[12] considers that the analogy with physics has to be abandoned. Financial markets are to be conceived as a living organism and approached in a functionalist, not in a causal manner:

> The Stock Exchange is a circulation organ, its function is to make circulate, to appraise the quality of the materials submitted to its action. When you introduce poison, venom, in the veins of an animal, the heart makes it circulate through the entire organism. More or less grave disorders result, and the heart becomes a victim, but, again, its role is to produce movement and not to make chemical analyses. This is why most criticisms of the Bourse are off mark, like the legal dispositions they pretended to impose upon [the Bourse]. It will go on like that as long as we continue to believe that society is a mechanism whose movements and wheels can be controlled at will, when in fact it is a natural *organism* whose spontaneous functioning must be studied with the aim of supporting its development. (Lefevre 1874, p. 13)

The character of the stock exchange as a natural entity is not contested anymore: at stake here are the scientific disciplines which should guide its investigation. While organic and anatomic metaphors were not a novelty in the banking language of the time (Alborn 1994), Lefevre drew his consequences with respect to the explanation of prices. Accordingly, causal explanations of price movements, which rely on a mechanistic view of financial markets, are useless. What matters is to explain the functions fulfilled by markets in the society at large. A functionalist explanation, however, has to be supplemented by an adequate market model. Biological analogies and functionalist explanations did not exclude recourse to statistics. Quite the contrary: it was the analogy with biology which justified the application of statistics to economic and financial phenomena (Ménard 1980, pp. 533, 539; Breton 1992, p. 32).

This analogy is encountered not only in banking and financial advice manuals, but also in works of fiction, such as Émile Zola's *Money*, where Saccard, the speculator, encourages Ms. Caroline to insert a ban on futures and options in the statutes of her newly founded charity, saying that every firm has such a ban, and none respects it. But instead of bonds, which are "dead matter," she would do better to speculate:

> You should understand that speculation, gambling is the central cogwheel, the heart of a vast business like ours. Yes! It summons the blood, it takes the blood from everywhere stream by stream, it accumulates it, sends it in rivers in all directions, establishes an enormous circulation of money which is the very life of

business. Without gambling, the great movements of capital, the great civilizing works which result from it are radically impossible. (Zola 1897, pp. 119–20)

Such analogies between society and living organisms, representing speculation as a vital force, were not without consequences for the ways in which explanations of price movements were formulated. Lefevre, for instance, thoroughly rejected the deterministic approach. He considered that a causal explanation of price movements was totally superfluous. The (investing) public needed something completely different:

> The public does not need definitions and formulae, he needs images which are fixed on his mind (esprit), and with the help of which he can direct his actions. Images are the most powerful auxiliary of reason; thus, whatever properties of a geometric figure result from its definition and are implicitly contained within, it would be almost impossible to extract them without the help of the eyes, that is, of images, in order to help the mind. . . . Especially in the case of Stock Exchange operations, where the decisions must be prompt, it matters if one has in his mind clear images instead of more or less confused formulas, because the slightest hesitation or a false movement may cause considerable damages in some cases. (Lefevre 1870, pp. 184–85)

But, at the same time, there is a second reason: a science of the stock exchange should not be concerned with explaining the causes of price movements, but with "*differences*, one must look after the laws of *differences*, abstracting from the quotations in which they appear, which needlessly complicate the phenomenon, and abstracting from the concrete quantities with which one works, which confuse the reader. By eliminating from the problem any reference to quotations (cours) and quantities, in order to consider only the differences, we can easily determine their laws and make them visible to the eyes. [. . .] We shall consider first and foremost the unity of value which makes the object of the market" (Lefevre 1870, pp. 186–87). An abstract, formal model of the market is required because real quotations obscure "the unity of value."

If only the laws of differences should be taken into account, then one can focus the analysis on the differences between the price of an option and that of the underlying security. Starting from these arguments, Henri Lefevre proceeded to develop a graphic representation of decisions in the options trade, a representation which was employed thirty years later by Louis Bachelier in his doctoral thesis. When devising the payoff diagram and the *auto-compteur*,[13] Lefevre's strategy was to visualize individual decisions in a space of coordinates. His space of decisions is defined by two axes: the horizontal axis of the market, with downward (*baisse*) and upward (*hausse*) situations as its extremities; and the vertical axis of the investment's outcome, having gains and losses as its upper and lower extremities, respectively. These axes define four angles: two of them are angles of gains (in a bear and a bull market, respectively); correspondingly, two are angles of losses. The diagonal lines intersecting these angles represent the various situations of the spot seller and buyer, respectively, in various market situations (Lefevre 1870, p. 191).

Lefevre then proceeded to show that options contracts can be visualized in this graphical space; he also described the outcome and the right decision for each type of contract traded in the French 3% bond. The payoff diagram, published first in his *Traité* in 1870, was repeated in 1874 in the *Principes de la science de la Bourse*—a booklet which was officially endorsed by the union of the stockbrokers of the Paris Bourse. Starting from this diagram, he devised the "abacus of the speculator," an instrument to be used by investors on the floor of the stock exchange. This was a wooden board, divided into squares, with the axes of loss and gains drawn on it; it had mobile letters (similar to those of the auto-compteur), with the help of which traders could visualize the course of various options with respect to the corresponding security. By repositioning the letters, a trader could see the outcomes of his decisions on each type of option contract. Lefevre also devised a plan of national financial education based on his method, but the stockbrokers' union declined to invest any money in it. In 1873, the payoff diagram was taken over by Léon Pochet—an engineer from the École des Ponts et Chaussées—in an article published in the *Journal des Actuaires Français*, the stronghold of mathematical economy in France (Zylberberg 1990, pp. 92–93). Around 1900, this method was a fixture of investors' manuals, being known under the name of *polégraphie*; it was advertised as the one with the help of which the laws of bull and bear markets could be discovered (Roussel 1904).

While Henri Lefevre's perspective was that of individual decisions, thirty years later Louis Bachelier used the payoff diagram (a) for examining the behavior of prices, not that of individuals, and (b) as a starting point for an algebraic, not a geometrical model of price behavior.[14] His dissertation (Bachelier [1900] 1964, p. 18) gives only one page to the actions of individual actors. Similar to Lefevre, Bachelier ([1900] 1964, p. 17) considered a causal explanation of price levels only briefly; he declared it impossible to achieve in mathematical terms and that the study of quotations will never be an exact science. Instead, one should focus on price changes. Thus, the way for the formal treatment of price movements was opened, leading to the dominant role played by formal models in contemporary global markets.[15]

The Market and Its Functions

In the eighteenth century, options and futures (together with short selling) had been perceived as especially problematic: "imaginary chance," lack of ownership and means of payment was what they were all about (Anonymous 1721; Mirabeau 1787, p. 47). The fact that they posed particular conceptual problems to eighteenth-century market observers contributed to the bad reputation of stock exchanges. Options and short selling seemed not to be based on real chances, but on imagination; they did not imply a transfer of ownership, but the exchange of something transaction partners did not possess. Throughout the nineteenth century, the legal boundaries of transactions such as short selling, buying on margin, lending securities, and options and futures contracts were uncertain. In the US, state-specific legislation was sometimes contradictory. In the state of Illinois, for instance, options contracts were assimilated to gambling. In 1874, the Illinois legislature voted for an enlargement of the criminal code which would have defined options contracts as gambling contracts. While the initial formulation did not pass, the Illinois senate adopted a statute prohibiting options trading, false rumors, and market corners (Lurie 1979, pp. 55–56). The new law was ambiguous and spurned several legal cases in which courts upheld futures contracts. In the state of New York, short selling (as well as options and futures contracts) were declared void (but not illegal) in 1812, an act which was repealed in 1858 (Meeker 1922, pp. 547–48).

In Britain, during the eighteenth century, bills against transactions in futures and options were introduced in the Parliament (Anonymous 1736). In 1799, the Committee for General Purposes of the London Stock Exchange decided not to recognize transactions in puts and calls (Minutes of the Committee of the Stock Exchange, 1798–1802, manuscript 14600/1, Guildhall Library, London.). The Barnard's Act from 1733 declared short selling (together with time bargains) to be illegal, whereas the Gaming Act of 1845 declared them to be void, but not illegal (Brodhurst 1897,

p. 137). The applicability of Barnard's Act, however, was restricted by courts of law to English funds.

In Paris, the official brokers of the Paris Bourse were forbidden by the royal edict of 1724 to deal in futures and options. Options contracts were fully legalized in France only in 1885, while being widely tolerated by legislators and informally acknowledged since 1860. Of course, these legal definitions could also be (and were) exploited as loopholes by anyone wishing to default on a transaction. Nothing was easier than to pledge gambling and refuse to pay or deliver without any fear of legal consequences. Such cases were anything but rare during the nineteenth century.

The rationalization of market behavior and the increased attention paid to price data had to deal with the issue of the social status of such transactions, a status which had direct consequences for their legal definition. Against the more general background of the attempts to formulate rules and procedures concerning stock valuation, trading in options and futures was made into a standard feature of investment manuals, which explained trade operations, types of contracts, their consequences, and rules of behavior for each type of contract. Another no less important aspect was justifying options, futures, and short selling both with respect to trading behavior and to markets as sui generis entities. This meant finding specific roles, or functions, fulfilled by options and futures, functions which were both rational and vital to overall markets. Biological metaphors and analogies with the human body played a seminal role in the reconceptualization of stock exchanges as fulfilling specific functions within society (detailed in chapter 6). In this sense, attempts to conceptualize financial markets as function based echoed a broader preoccupation of the time's economic literature with biology and illustrate the efforts of building up a "science of the market."

Manuals argued that futures and options fulfill clear economic functions, like raising short-time money or ensuring that the laws of supply and demand are working. I will quote here the French socialist Pierre-Joseph Proudhon, who in 1854 wrote in his *Manual of Stock Exchange Speculation* that forbidding futures markets was an economic folly:

> Let the press be muzzled, a tariff be put on the library, let the post be spied, the telegraph exploited by the state, but speculation, by the anarchy which constitutes its essence, escapes all state's and police constitutions. To try putting a control on this last and infallible interpreter of opinions would mean to govern in the darkness of Egypt, which, according to the rabbis, was so thick

that even candles and lanterns went out. How, for example, to forbid *futures markets*?[16] In order to forbid futures markets, they should stop the oscillations of *demand* and *supply*, that is, to guarantee to the trade the production, the quality, the placement, and the invariability of commodities' prices, and at the same time to eliminate all the aleatory conditions of the production, circulation, and consumption of goods, which is impossible and even contradictory. (p. 31)

Proudhon was no exception in this respect. Many authors argued that futures and options allow smaller investors to become active in the market and distribute the chances of gain more widely. A put or a call contract benefits both parties and nobody loses, since the money is attracted anyway from other sectors of the economy (Proudhon 1854, p. 31; Noel-Fearn 1866, p. 103; *Stock Speculation* 1875, pp. 22, 25; Playford 1855, p. 58). Some manuals declared futures and options to be so well known that discussing them again was not worth the effort (*Stocks* 1848, p. 11). Glossaries of trading notions, together with problem-solving chapters, were a standard feature. Readers were required to compute the outcomes of trading puts and calls in a bull or a bear market (Rougemont 1857, pp. 11–12; *Les écueils* 1865, pp. 100–111).

Another strategy for endowing options with economic and social functions was to redefine notions like "speculation" and "gambling." Most (but not only) French manuals followed the strategy of differentiating between speculating (*spéculer*) and gambling (*jouer*) (Proudhon 1854, p. 81; *La Bourse* 1866, pp. 31–35; Playford 1855, pp. 57–58). While speculating designated the usual operations in stocks and bonds, gambling designated betting on price differences.[17] Speculation was a legitimate activity for the middle-class investor and a basic feature of human creativity. But if gambling was nothing more than a second-order speculation (Crampon 1863, pp. 158–59), a speculation on the speculation in stocks, it would follow that it is useful and creative too—and hence acceptable for a family father. The consequence was that these transactions should be studied with the same scientific methods employed in studying gambling or racing bets (Borel 1835, p. 9; *Les écueils* 1865, p. 12; Lefevre 1871, p. 7; see also Zylberberg 1990, p. 94, on Léon Pochet).

Options and futures were not represented anymore in terms of a "real" or "imagined" ownership, with consequences for the morality of financial transactions, but in terms of the functions they fulfilled within financial markets.[18] Once speculation was redefined as human creativity, or "divine unrest," as a stockbroker turned author put it (Van Antwerp,

1913, p. 35), it could be presented as a force of economic progress (Meeker 1922, pp. 170, 394). It could be endowed with economic functions such as foresight, insurance, and steadying price movements (Van Antwerp 1913, pp. 46, 81). Being universal (and hence on a par with what firms and merchants usually do), time bargains were of the same nature as the credit given to any other institution (Van Antwerp 1913, p. 83; Giffen 1877, p. 38).

Perhaps one of the most astute redefinitions of speculation in functional terms was undertaken by Edmond Guillard, a lawyer who, in his legal treatise on stock exchange operations, started by asking the question: is speculation merely identical with the "unloyal means condemned by morals and rejected by honesty or rather, by exploiting the financial market by underground means and insidious maneuvers," is it *agiotage*,[19] the horror of horrors of the eighteenth century (Guillard 1875, p. 512)? But, continued Guillard, why ask such irrelevant questions when it is clear that speculation fulfills economic functions and is beneficial to society: "[speculation] defends [the market] against the dangers of sudden deviations which sometimes menace the public fortune" (Guillard 1875, p. 540).

As for the relationship between gambling and speculation, the former could be either redefined as a special instance of the latter, or a distinction could be introduced which, while preserving the legitimacy of speculation, would have significant legal consequences. This distinction is anchored in the rational, calculative character of market actors, and is based on their assumed intention to deliver the securities they have contracted. Intention to deliver, then, whether fulfilled or not and however fleeting, became in the late nineteenth century the basis of a legal distinction between gambling and speculation. Besides reinforcing the legitimacy of transactions in options and futures, this intention-based distinction closed off possibilities for purposively defaulting on contracts by taking a plea of gambling.

The redefinition of speculation as functional, accompanied by (and inserted within) a broader shift toward thinking of financial markets as analogous with body organs performing specific functions, was finally echoed in legal definitions of options contracts. In France, options trading had become legal in 1885, when all financial transactions were placed under common law together with all other commercial transactions. This led an American observer to write, with a hint of envy, that France had first achieved financial democracy (Van Antwerp 1913, pp. 410, 412). In the US and in Britain, it was a series of high-profile cases which led to legal opinions about the character of options trading.

In Britain, the case of *Thacker v. Hardy* (1878) established that even if the intention to deliver is absent, a time bargain can be defined as the result of "two distinct and perfectly legal real bargains, namely, first, a bargain to buy and sell; and, secondly, a subsequent bargain that the first shall not be carried out" (Brodhurst 1897, p. 180). Further distinctions, such as between contracts of gaming and contracts by way of gaming, together with court cases which tied gambling to establishing the intention not to deliver (*Shaw v. Caledonian Railway Co.* 1890) culminated in *Forget v. Ostigny* (1895), which defined financial speculation as "a legitimate commercial transaction to buy a commodity in the expectation that it will rise in value and with the intention of realizing a profit by its resale. Such dealings are everyday occurrence in commerce" (Brodhurst 1897, p. 190).

In the US, legislative differences (as those between Illinois and New York) did not prevent options contracts from being legally enforceable in New York if intention to deliver was understood by the parties. New York courts, however, ruled that unlawful intention of one party did not make the transaction illegal (Goldman 1914, p. 54). In other words, it sufficed for one party to express or hint (however fleetingly) at the intention to deliver for the transaction not to be illegal. The borderline between legality and illegality was made dependent upon intent of delivery, a very ambiguous notion (Lurie 1979, p. 61).

In 1905, the case of the *Chicago Board of Trade v. Christie Grain & Stock Co.* was brought before the US Supreme Court (198 US 236). Christie, a Chicago bucket shop,[20] had tapped the telegraph wires of the Chicago Board of Trade in order to obtain price data and use them, in part, for transacting in options contracts. The Board of Trade introduced a lawsuit, which went through various courts of appeal up to the US Supreme Court, where the final legal opinion was delivered by Justice Oliver Wendell Holmes, Jr.

Christie & Co. made its case on several grounds; one of its central arguments was that, while Christie was a bucket shop specialized in options trading, this sort of trading was widely practiced by the official members of the Board of Trade themselves. Therefore, while Christie's activities may have been illegal, some activities of the Board of Trade were too.[21] Therefore, Christie's access to price data was legitimate. The defense's argument was that "if, under other circumstances, there could be property in the quotations, which hardly is admitted, the subject matter is so infected with the plaintiff's own illegal conduct that it is caput lupinum, and may be carried off by any one at will." (198 US 236).

In his opinion, Justice Holmes stated that members of the Board of Trade dealt in options only as a means of "self-protection in business." Moreover, "the contracts made in the pits are contracts between the members" and fall within the Charter of the Board of Trade. They differ from contracts made with the public. A third argument was that "in a modern market, contracts are not confined to sales for immediate delivery. People will endeavour to forecast the future, and to make agreements according to their prophecy. Speculation of this kind by competent men is the self-adjustment of society to the probable. [. . .] This court has upheld sales of stock for future delivery and the substitution of parties, provided for by the rules of the Chicago Stock Exchange" (198 U.S. 236). Consequently, transactions in options by (official) members of the exchange have a special character: they require special competencies and serve the greater society. Competence becomes the condition of legitimate speculation, which in its turn fulfills specific social functions. Acquiring competence means following the rules of behavior prescribed by those endowed with authority, and engaging in financial transactions. This reinforces the separation between financial knowledge and morals, while endowing the former with functionalist attributes; at the same time, the distinction between "competent," inside men, on the one hand, and outsiders, on the other, indicates that such knowledge is not evenly distributed or equally accessible.

Prestige, Authorial Voices, and Financial Knowledge

I will now return to my initial question about prestige, authorial voices, and the constitution of financial knowledge. Comparing the position of Marais (the Parisian advocate I introduced in the previous chapter) as an observer with that of the nineteenth-century authors discussed in this chapter, for the latter there is neither the need nor the possibility to furtively go on a Saturday afternoon to observe what the dealers are doing. The basic assumptions of what it means to observe financial transactions are radically changed. Observation, for the authors discussed here, means not looking after individual, peculiar features (aptly illustrated by Marais' tents). It does not mean looking for glances, gestures, fashion, bodily postures, or ways of walking. Observation means looking for regularities through a theoretical lens, searching for the deeper level of the principles governing price movements.

This lens is promoted with the authority conferred by claims of special knowledge, as well as by claims of being legitimate and respectable, an authority which the "devil's mechanick" could never gain. Gaining a public voice and speaking authoritatively about transactions implied that brokers and other financial actors had to become socially acceptable figures, a process which in its turn was promoted by the vast work of enclosure and monopoly building unfolding since the early nineteenth century. Once the actors of the stock exchange gained voices of their own, they began producing a literature radically different from that of the eighteenth century: it was different not only in genre or in vocabulary, but also in that it accomplished a redefinition of financial knowledge and, with it, of the position occupied by financial markets in society.

From radically unknowable and aleatory, financial markets are transformed into an object of systematic investigation, a process which includes redefinitions at several levels: that of individual behavior, as well as that of a sui generis entity called "the market." This latter now justifies its existence by the social and economic functions it fulfills, and is exonerated from whatever negative events it might entail. The market actor is defined through observation, analysis, and calculation, and reflected in the positions of those writing about successful speculation. Since special knowledge, akin to science, is a condition of success, the distinction between real market players and wannabes is now defined by knowledge. This, in turn, reinforces the authoritative position of those speaking about the market, while encouraging the idea (if not the illusion) that speculation can be done by many, provided they learn the "science of the market." However, there will always be a boundary between systematic, in-depth knowledge, on the one hand, and appearance of knowledge, on the other, a boundary which undermines widespread accessibility.[22]

The newly gained prestige of brokers and investors means a reorientation toward additional, palatable social roles: (more or less amateur) scientists, writers, and educators; these, at least in part, replace the con man, the swindler, and the reckless gambler, which dominate the eighteenth century. This is not to say that swindlers and con men disappear; quite the contrary. Nevertheless, they do not take the same place in the public perception of finance as they had before. As I will show in the chapters to come, the prestige which now defines the status of the stock exchange will allow for a reworking of darker aspects into a new, more ambivalent figure: that of the financial "hero" or "titan."

At least some of the brokers-cum-authors pay an increased attention to the natural sciences and have a scientific education. Their use of analogies and metaphors from physics and biology was meant, in part, to situate financial markets in the sphere of rigorous observation and investigation, to formulate a normative view of investor behavior, and to define price as the most important piece of financial information. The effort to model price variations provides the starting point for the formulation of the efficient market hypothesis, the random walk theory, and the capital asset pricing, among others (e.g., Mehrling 2005, pp. 61, 95) which, in the words of Michel Callon (2004, p. 123), define markets as calculated and calculable entities. Such instruments, or lenses, which restrict the viewer's field by pushing to the margins or blackening out idiosyncratic, unrepeatable elements, are put to work in the creation of new financial products and transactions (MacKenzie 2006). And much, much later, the rhetoric of finance as a branch of scientific knowledge, paired with mathematical tools, will become incorporated in academia, augmenting its legitimacy and prestige not only through the worldwide anchoring in academic departments, but also through public admission into the pantheon of science, an admission sealed with the Nobel Prize.

The notion that such markets are legitimated through their functions, however, raised several problems which had to be solved: first, conceptualizing "the market" as a larger and more abstract entity, to which exchanges are subordinated; second, redefining the links between financial markets, the larger economy, and the state in a fashion consistent with a functions-based view of society; third, reworking accordingly the very notion of speculation. If financial knowledge is something akin to scientific knowledge, then the activity flowing out of it, speculation, had to be endowed with a similar range of attributes, like universalism and progressiveness.[23]

Yet this remodeling of financial knowledge required not only a new range of attributes for speculation, but attention to price data as the object of observation. The new boundaries of finance needed devices which should generate price data and present these to public observation. All the exhortations to observe, to be attentive, to analyze, would be in vain without such devices. The boundaries of finance had to go beyond manuals and pedagogical admonitions, and incorporate concrete observational arrangements. In short, they had to include an objectified price-observational technology, to which I will now turn.

CHAPTER FOUR

Close Up: Price Data, Machines, and Organizational Boundaries

The redefinition of financial knowledge as grounded in observation, attention, and calculation represented price data as the most important kind of information available to market actors. This required an observational system for prices which, in its turn, raised a whole lot of problems. How can such small entities be observed? Moreover, are they material entities? What is authoritative price data? What does reliable data mean? How can price data be made observable to several people at once? How can they be transferred across various contexts without losing their properties? Who owns price data? The cherished rhetoric of observation, analysis, and calculation would have remained limp without an answer to these questions. This required a technology which should separate prestige and authority from the individual properties of market actors, a technology different from the bodily techniques through which bulls and bears signaled trustworthiness to their transaction partners (see Mauss [1950] 1999, p. 365).

Throughout the eighteenth century and during the first half of the nineteenth century, the trustworthiness of price data was inextricably tied to personal trust and authority. In their turn, these relied on bodily techniques like glances, hand movements, or attire, together with technologies of personal authority, such as letters. Price lists, while in existence during all these times, were infrequent, unreliable, and all too often subject to forgeries. Besides, no one could exactly tie prices published in the price lists to a particular time in the flow of transactions. Yet since the 1860s a preoccupation with technology is witnessed by observers of the stock exchange, a preoccupation which includes the development and durable implementation of the stock ticker as a custom tailored price-recording machine. Just a couple of years before its introduction, another (short-lived) attempt at using machines for recording transactions was undertaken on the Paris Bourse. From then on, we witness a continuous, uninterrupted preoccupation with implementing machines in the marketplace, machines which not only support or aid transactions but, more recently, also automate them.

This effort makes technology an intrinsic part of the modern boundaries of finance: we cannot conceive contemporary financial transactions without machines for recording prices and even for conducting transactions (Shiller 2003, p. 75; Preda 2007). Moreover, we cannot conceive price data as being irregular, dependent on the character and trustworthiness of particular persons, and accessible only locally. The whole discourse of market reliability and continuity and of rational actor behavior would be inoperable without a technology for observing price data, a machine which should endow these latter with objective authority and prestige. The fact that such machines are nowadays installed in public places, that they are almost omnipresent on television screens, offering broad accessibility to price data, speaks volumes about their place at the boundary between finance and society. Observation, modeled on science, is oriented to data. Yet in a fashion different from that of the lab scientist, observers of financial data do not manipulate or calibrate themselves the observational devices. These devices are presented to them; their way of working is in part at least obscured by the flow of data. Machines make observation possible, but how these machines work should not necessarily be observed.

A boundary which integrates price data machines, in its turn, raises the question of how these machines open up action paths which wouldn't be there without them; in other words, how machines become agents of institutional invention. It is this question which I examine here, while following the trajectory of the stock ticker, the first successful custom-tailored technology of the stock exchange. I will start, however, with a short presentation of the ticker and of its short-lived French competition, the pantelegraph.

The Stock Ticker and the Pantelegraph

In February 1865, a new machine—if not the first one—made its appearance at the Paris Bourse. The device was the invention of an Italian professor of physics, Giovanni Caselli, who had worked on it for more than a decade. The pantelegraph was a "chemical telegraph"—basically, a primitive fax machine which could transmit handwriting, signatures, or drawings on a 15 × 10 cm (ca. 6 × 4 in.) piece of paper, over a telegraph wire.[1] During 1867, over 5,555 "pantelegrams" were transmitted between Paris and Lyon—the only pantelegraphic line available. Of these 5,555 messages, only 7 were not related to financial securities' prices (Du Camp 1869, p. 191). In other words, for every single day of the year, 15 price-related messages were sent between Paris and Lyon. The pantelegraph attracted quite a lot of attention: it was widely lauded in the European press as a "genial invention" (Lardner 1880, p. 135). In 1870, Thomas Alva Edison received a contract from the Gold and Stock Reporting Telegraph Company for constructing a machine similar to the pantelegraph (Jenkins et al. 1989, p. 147)—which he never managed to do. Although a manufacturing company was formed for producing pantelegraph machines, neither the French state—which had a monopoly on telegraphic communications in France (Flichy 1995)—nor the Paris Bourse supported it. However, the Paris Bourse did not adopt another machine.[2] At least until well into the 1920s, it continued to work without any price-recording technology.

The stock ticker was invented in 1867 by Edward A. Calahan, an engineer associated with the American Telegraph Company. It was a printing telegraph with two independent type wheels, placed under a glass bell jar (to keep off dust) and powered by a battery (Jenkins et al. 1989, p. 153). The wheels were mounted face-to-face on two shafts and revolved under the action of an electromagnet. The first wheel had the letters of the alphabet on it; the second wheel had figures, fractions, and some letters. The inked wheels printed on a paper tape divided into two strips: the security's name was printed on the upper strip and the price quote on the lower one, beneath the name. In the 1870s, the ticker also began to record the traded volume, printing it on the tape immediately before the price. The machine could be manned with only one expensive Morse operator (at the recording end), instead of two (with one at each end). Ticker operators and machines were installed on the floor of the New York Stock Exchange and in the brokerage offices of David Groesbeck; Work, Davis & Barton; Greenleaf, Norris & Co.; and Lockwood & Co. in December 1867 (Calahan 1901, p. 237). The ticker has been in operation ever since, being continuously upgraded. The mechanical version was replaced in 1960 with the electronic ticker; this latter is now a ubiquitous presence.

While the failure of the pantelegraph deserves an attention of its own, I will not detail here its causes and context. Rather, I will follow the successful trajectory of the stock ticker, of its various mechanical off-spring, searching for its agential force, for the ways in which this machine, by allowing the observation of minute price data, opened up paths of action and of institutional invention. Grasping this force, however, first requires further theoretical reflection: how can such a force be attributed to machines? Until now, the argument has been that the boundaries of finance involve the agency of human actors, of the stock brokers and speculators who put in place rules of access, who wrote books and articles about the "science of financial markets," and who devised abstract models of price movements. This time, however, we have to do with a machine: how can electromagnets, wheels, ink, and paper have agential force?

Agency and Machines

We see agency as the capacity of (social) action to transform given structures and to reconfigure its own context (Emirbayer and Mische 1998, p. 970). The projective dimension is essential here: agency implies that the iteration of past actions is accompanied (or replaced) by the generation of new paths of action, leading to structural change and to contextual reconfiguration (Emirbayer and Mische 1998, p. 971; Giddens 1987, p. 204). If we ascribe this transformative capacity exclusively to human actors, then we have to define it as driven by desires or interests (Pickering 2001, p. 164), which sends us to the concept of intentional human action. A reduction of agency to intentional action is plagued by problems like conceptual regress and circularity (Schatzki 2002, p. 190; Lynch 1992, pp. 251–52). Part of the solution to these problems is to consider artifacts and technologies as "endowed with powers of determination that either render these entities as potent as social phenomena or make materiality and sociality codetermining" (Schatzki 2002, p. 108). A large body of research has examined how technology contributes to projecting new paths of action and to structural change (e.g., Pickering 1995; Woolgar 1991; MacKenzie and Wajcman 1985; Grint and Woolgar 1995; Bijker, Hughes, and Pinch 1987), while cautioning against treating all possible future courses of action as predetermined by technological structures.

Debates about machines and agency have focused on technology as a mediating agent (Pinch 2003, p. 248) in financial markets (Callon 2004, p. 121; Barry and Slater 2002a, p. 177). Mediating agents align the positions and interests of heterogeneous, dispersed actors (e.g., of traders and investors), by producing and distributing standardized information, which contributes to the rationalization of economic action. The aspects of mediation related to market standardization and rationalization are captured by the concept of calculative agency (Barry and Slater 2002a, pp. 181–82; Callon and Muniesa 2003; Callon 1998, p. 15). Technology standardizes financial data, allowing economic actors to rationalize their future courses of action and to project the outcomes of these actions, a process which establishes boundaries between efficient and nonefficient actions. This concept thus mediates between the sociology of technology's concern with sociotechnical agency, on the one hand, and the economic sociology's preoccupation with modes of economic rationalization (Weber [1920] 1988, p. 9), on the other.

Operating with a broad definition of technology, which includes theoretical and disciplinary aspects (Callon 2004, p. 123), calculative agency is defined by: (1) framing, (2) disentanglement, and (3) performativity. Framing designates the process through which technology creates calculable objects (Callon 1998, p. 15; Barry and Slater 2002a, p. 181) and separates them from noncalculable ones. Disentanglement is the marking of boundaries between what is relevant or nonrelevant with respect to calculability (Callon 1998, p. 16). Performativity designates the status of technology (including economic theories) as a set of intervention tools in market transactions.

At the core of this approach is the notion of technology as a standardizer.[3] Making objects calculable requires treating them as abstract, homogeneous entities characterized by a restricted set of properties, to which a set of context-independent operations is applied. Standardization implies boundary marking (e.g., between relevant/ irrelevant properties) as well as the projection of similar paths of action across various contexts. Economic theories together with material artifacts provide both the tools and the criteria for standardization.

Technology as a standardizer involves sets of rules, conventions, and tools which help transfer data across contexts. It plays a major part in the rationalization of decision making and in the constitution of financial transactions as separated from broader social ties and obligations (what Michel Callon calls disentanglement). With respect to financial data, trust and authority are dissociated from individuals and transferred to technology: trustworthy data are data produced or recorded by an authoritative technology, which can be transferred across heterogeneous contexts without losing their properties.

Standardizers can create new boundaries and/or shift existing ones with respect to at least (1) professional jurisdictions (e.g., Abbott 1988, pp. 219–20), (2) gender (e.g., Bertinotti 1985; Fischer 1992; Siegert 1998; Bakke 1996), and (3) time and space (Stein 2001, p. 115; Flichy 1995, pp. 10–11). The agential force of standardizers thus consists mainly in opening predictable and reliable paths of economic action across heterogeneous contexts. In doing this, they expand the sphere of economic transactions and make market actors adopt distinctions and operations incorporated in technology. By promoting order and efficiency, standardizers introduce routines which may preclude further reconfigurations of action contexts. Once a mode of calculation (i.e., a set of routines) has been established, unexpected paths of action are discouraged.

Against this background, it would be tempting to see a machine like the stock ticker as a standardizer which makes price data uniform and distributes them over a larger area. After all, such a view would reinforce the idea of a continuous process of rationalization underwent by the stock exchanges, a process including the preoccupation with formal models, the rational behavior of market actors, and the like. The boundaries of finance, however, require more than the invention of routines; they require a mode of seeing financial transactions which can incorporate the unexpected and accommodate surprises. Observing such a small thing as prices—thin lines on paper—does not mean that the machines used in this process only made observers more routine prone. There has to be room for discovery, surprise, and innovation. The "invention of invention" (Mumford 1967, p. 255) is intrinsic to the active character of observation, as opposed to the passivity implied by (at least) some routines.

Financial Machines as Generators

How can an observational instrument, a price microscope, generate paths of action? Let me first unfold the theoretical argument. The general starting point is the view of technology as a set of rules, conventions, and tools (MacKenzie and Wajcman 1985, p. 3), grounded in Karl Marx's notion of machines as "crystals of social substance" and "implements of labor" ([1867] 1996, pp. 48, 389), and in Émile Durkheim's insight that (practical) knowledge is incorporated in the artifacts with which we operate ([1915] 1965, p. 440). In this perspective, technology has an iterative dimension (skills and routines), as well as a projective one. To use Martin Heidegger's notion, technology is an "en-framing" (*Ge-stell*) of social action ([1962] 1977, p. 19).

Once we accept that technology is social action, we have to treat it as having its own temporal structures. Action that is directed toward other actors (users) and toward the future (the agency condition) is defined through an internal time structure (Schutz 1967, pp. 68–69). In the case of a price-recording technology, we cannot see it as reproducing a given, external time structure; technology as action generates time structures. For instance, a technology which produces data sporadically and at irregular intervals differs from one producing data continuously and at regular intervals. Data perceived as representing past transactions differ from data representing current transactions. Moreover, action which projects its own temporal structures toward other actors (users) elicits responses which also are temporally structured. The rhythm of price data requires temporally specific actions (as manifested in observation, attention, and interpretation, among others). Thus, at a first level, technology generates temporal structures visible in the rhythm of data and in the rhythm of the users' responses to them.

Furthermore, the temporal structure of action is visually articulated and presented *as* action to other actors. These articulations can manifest themselves as working action or as performed action (Schutz 1967, p. 214). Working action is generated in a continuous flow, in the present tense, while performed action refers to the past. Working action is visualized as a continuous flow of data; performed action is articulated in closed visual arrangements. Data presented as a continuous flow differ from arrangements like a table or a list which refers to the past. Thus, technology displays its own temporal structures, eliciting specific responses from its users. Technology provides an arrangement for the observation of its own time structures, a microscope containing the observed object, in a way similar to that in which in biology, for instance, a microscope holds the prepared cells enclosed between two glass plates.

Responses to price rhythms include, in part, adequate language tools for designating, describing, and interpreting both price data and the users' reactions to them. Taken together, visual arrangements, time structures, and language tools project avenues for interpreting and processing price data as transaction-relevant. This requires that users regard data not only as an object of contemplation, but also as a "manipulative area" (Schutz 1967, p. 223), acted upon with the help of interpretive tools.

Therefore, once we conceive technology as social action, we are compelled to take into account its temporal structures, visualizations of those structures, and the tools with which such visualizations are processed, as intrinsic agential features. If they are to be transferred across contexts, the temporal structures of technology have to be endowed with authority and tied to users' responses. This requires distinctions between users who are entitled and able to respond and those who are not; between users entitled to take up further tools and those who are not. Such distinctions, in their turn, are relevant to issues of access and control (intrinsic to the boundaries of finance): who is entitled to own the technology, to observe price data, to own them, to interpret them, to use them in transactions. A price-recording technology would thus be tied to status and access issues. It could reinforce existing status boundaries, but also create new, access-based ones.

Issues of status and access are related to distinctions like the one between public and private transactions. When the authority of price data combines reliability (iteration across contexts) with charismatic features (status and prestige), a double movement emerges: authoritative data are kept in the sphere of public transactions, but access to them is controlled. A means of control would be restricting access to data according to status; another would be restricting access to the tools which help interpret these data. This would imply both the emergence of a group which controls the tools (data analysts) and a reorganization of the activities related to their use.

To reiterate: when we conceive technology as social action, we are compelled to deal with its intrinsic temporal structures and with the modes for visualizing those structures. Temporal structures open up means of creative intervention in financial transactions, means that go beyond and embed data standardization. Technology appears thus as an observational instrument generating paths of action which are not predetermined or restricted to standardization and routines. What sort of observational instrument was the stock ticker then?[4] What ways of viewing the rhythms of the market did it produce?[5] The ticker was built for viewing very small entities: price data. Due to the machine's size, even the attitude of the observer was that of somebody bent over and peering through the lens at small, lively entities. (As I will show in the following sections, this machine was manned with a trained tape reader, who had to look down at prices all the time.) But, as it is sometimes the case, its impact can be better appreciated if we contrast it first with how securities prices were constituted as data before the introduction of the ticker.

The Constitution of Price Data before the Ticker

In spite of all its apparent benefits, the telegraph did not automatically induce investors to send price information by telegram. When we examine the correspondence of investors and stockbrokers, we can see that, even after the inauguration of the transatlantic cable in 1865 and the introduction of the first telephones to Wall Street in 1878 (Anonymous 1927, p. 753), brokers still used letters extensively. The business correspondence of Richard Irvine & Co. (a major New York brokerage house with an international clientele) with its British clients shows that in most cases orders were placed by letter. In other cases, Irvine & Co. included price quotations in letters to investors, and asked them to order back by cablegram. In 1868, Irvine was still providing quotations which were twelve days old to some of his clients. Of course, cablegrams were rather expensive (e.g., Winseck and Pike 2007, p. 147) and investors used them parsimoniously. At the same time, the fact that price quotations were circulated by letters between New York and Europe indicates two aspects. On the one hand, information was enmeshed with narrative structures generated in letters. When writing to clients about a successful shipment of fruit, Irvine & Co. offered some attractive stocks too, together with the latest New York quotations:

> We have shipped to you care of Messrs Lampart and Holt, by this steamer, the apples you ordered in your favor of the 20th September last. We are assured the peaches and oysters are of the best quality, and trust they will prove so. Below we give you memo of their cost to your debit. We think it well to mention that 1st Mortgage 6% gold Chesapeake and Ohio Railroad bonds can now be bought here to a limited amount at 86% and accrued interest. They are well thought of by investors, and were originally marketed by the company's agents as high as 14% and interest. We enclose today's stock quotations. (Letter of Richard Irvine, New York, to J. A. Wiggins, London, 1872, New York Historical Society)

This, among other documents, makes clear why brokers and investors cherished good old letters. They were a more efficient means of distributing information, networking, and deal making—in short, of producing knowledge and relationships at the same time. In this perspective, brokers were nodes in a network in which knowledge, deals, and private services overlapped. For all these practical purposes, letters worked very well. In this example, relevant information cannot be separated from a complex narrative structure evocative of deep social ties, of an economy of favors, and full of allusions impossible to render by means of a telegram.

On the other hand, financial actors needed *accurate, timely information about price variations*. It is more or less irrelevant to know that the price of, say, the Susquehanna Railroad Co. is at $53 ¹/₈. What is really relevant is whether it is higher or lower than thirty minutes ago, or an hour ago, or yesterday.

First and foremost, this kind of information required that prices be recorded in an adequate fashion. What the public got to see were price lists, published in the commercial and general press. But where did these prices come from? How were they processed in list form? In fact, it was impossible to determine what kinds of prices were being published in the lists and how they were recorded in the first place. The practice of publishing closing prices was not common everywhere. In New York City, publications like the *Wall Street Journal* began publishing closing quotations only in 1868. The New York Stock Exchange got an official quotation list on February 28, 1872. "Official" did not mean, however, that the NYSE guaranteed price data. In the 1860s in London, only the published quotations of consols (consolidated annuities) were closing prices. A closer inquiry into what "closing prices" meant provides us with the following specification: until 1868 "there were no official closing quotations. The newspapers would publish such late quotations as some broker, who remained late, saw fit to furnish" (Eames 1894, p. 51). Besides, some prices were compiled from the floor of the exchange, while others were compiled from private auctions, which ran parallel to those on the exchange floor (Martin 1886, p. iv).

There was also a long history of forging price lists. Typographic errors were all but infrequent. Stock quotations published in newspapers were accordingly not always perceived as reliable; in fact, stock price lists had a singularly bad reputation in the US (and not only there) for being unreliable and prone to manipulation (e.g., Anonymous 1854, p. 10).

Thus, price data,[6] not price variations data, were regarded as relevant information. Technologies of private communication (letters) were used in order to confer credibility upon price data. These communicative technologies emphasized personal authority and trust over accuracy and timeliness. The boundary between private and public price data was tilted in favor of the private domain.

Temporal Structures, Price Data Boundaries, and Status Groups

This brings us to the question of the organization of knowledge production underlying financial transactions. In the 1860s, just what did the words "Wall Street" designate? Trade in securities was in fact carried out by two wholly distinct classes of brokers.[7] One comprised members of the Regular Board, who inherited or paid hefty sums for their privately owned seats (they actually traded in tailcoats and tall hats, sitting on their personal chairs, from a fixed place in the room). The other class comprised brokers of the Open Board, who did not inherit any seats, paid much lower membership fees (under a tenth of what Regular Board members paid), and traded *in the street* (standing, of course). The Open Board had evolved out of the Outside (aka the New) Board, which included the curbstone brokers active at the Coal House in William Street. Until 1865, there was also the Evening Exchange, held at the Fifth Avenue Hotel in Manhattan (Cornwallis 1879, pp. 3, 26–28). The public could not join the sessions of the Regular Board, but constantly mixed with the Open Board (Anonymous 1848, pp. 8–9). The trading volume of the Open Board was estimated by some contemporaries to be ten times that of the Regular Board (Medbery 1870, p. 39).

The Regular Board traded by calls: securities were called out loudly, one by one. For each call, stockbrokers bought and sold according to orders received in advance; afterward, trading was interrupted. The Vice President of the board repeated the price to his assistant secretary, who repeated it to a clerk, who wrote it down on a blackboard. Then the next call was traded, its price was ceremoniously repeated, and so forth. The Open Board took the ground floor, the entrance to the building (the doors stayed open), and the street. The public was in and out all the time. The Open Board traded uninterruptedly and moved in the evening to the Fifth Avenue Hotel, so that its market was open for about twelve to fourteen hours a day. By contrast, the Regular Board traded between about 10 a.m. and 2 p.m., and its members made sure they did not miss their lunch breaks (Eames 1894, pp. 51–57; Smith 1871, pp. 76–77; Meeker 1922, p. 33).

What do we have, then? We have a closed status group operating a discontinuous market (the Regular Board) and a relatively open group operating a continuous market (the Open Board). There were multiple prices for one and the same security. The prices of the Regular Board were recorded after each call, but were discontinuous. The prices of the Open Board were—according to contemporaries—more or less continuous, but not all of them were necessarily (and certainly not accurately) recorded.

Brokerage offices employed messenger boys to record prices from Broad Street. In an article published in 1901, Edward A. Calahan (the ticker's inventor) reminisced that each office employed twelve to fifteen boys (rarely over seventeen), who had to ascertain prices from the street and from the building (see also Downey 2000, pp. 132–33). Each boy focused on certain stocks and yelled prices to other boys, who wrote them down on paper slips, which were lost, misread, misdirected, or forged on a daily basis (Stedman 1905, p. 433). Sometimes, messengers were robbed in the street (Cornwallis 1879, p. 13). About thirty to forty brokerage houses sent their armies to 10–12 Broad Street (Calahan 1901, p. 236):

> intermittent messenger-boys twist in and out, carrying hurried whispers back to offices, or dashing forward with emergent orders for brokers whose names are shouted by the page boys in shrillest treble. The roar from the cock-pit rolls up denser and denser. The President plies his gavel, the Assistant Secretaries scratch across the paper, registering bids and offers as for dear life. The black tablet slides up second by second with ever-fresh figures evolved from the chaos below. Every tongue in every head of this multiform concourse of excited or expectant humanity billowing hither and thither between the walls, is adding its contribution to the general bedlam. (Medbery 1870, p. 30)

On the first floor of 10–12 Broad Street, agents listened for the prices of the Regular Board, wrote them down, and sold the information in the street. This privilege was sold for $100 a week (Clews 1888, p. 8).[8] Seen up close, this was "perfect bedlam" (Smith 1871, p. 76). Seen from afar, this technology was well adapted to multiple prices. Messenger boys were highly mobile, and the tools they employed (paper slips, pencils), while neither accurate nor forgery proof, could be easily carried in their pockets. Nevertheless, they were essential for the execution networks which underlined the workings of the market: while transaction networks would have implied direct dealings (technologically mediated or not) among actors, execution networks were required by the closure of the New York Stock Exchange (Knorr Cetina and Preda 2007, p. 126).

Under these circumstances, it was understandable that even big brokerage houses did not bother much with telegrams: the telegraph did not solve a basic problem of the marketplace, namely that of tying price data directly to floor transactions. In between there was a myriad of paper slips littering the floor, crowds of courier boys running in all directions, shouts and yells, and also, not infrequently, forgers and robbers. In the Open Board market, contracts were written down by back office clerks at the end of the working day. In the Regular Board market, stockbrokers stopped the market to record transactions. In this arrangement, the time at which prices were recorded could be estimated with some accuracy, but this did not help much, since on the ground floor, where the Open Board reigned, prices changed continuously. The existence of two markets in the same building—one continuous, the other discontinuous—contributed to multiple prices and to parallel, heterogeneous time structures. The technology obscured any direct relationship between the published price data and the interaction side of financial transactions. These transactions were, in the eighteenth century (Preda 2001a) as today (Knorr Cetina and Bruegger 2002a) conversational exchanges: securities prices were set by conversational turns.

All this meant that the interactional price-setting mechanism of the marketplace was the speech act. Speech acts had to fulfill specific felicity conditions in order to be valid, of course: participants had to know each other, had to have legitimate access to the floor, and had to have a transactional record, among other things. But this does not obscure the fact that it was the perlocutionary force of a speech act (Austin [1962] 1976) which set the price. Paper slips fixed and visualized this conversational outcome post hoc and only for momentary needs. They were an ephemeral trace left by conversations which, if observed from the visitors' gallery, appeared as a cacophonous jumble of shouts and wild gestures. This spectacle was intriguing enough for tour operators to routinely include a visit to Wall Street in their "visit New York" packages, marketed to the middle classes from provincial cities. A special gallery was built on the first floor of 10–12 Broad Street, so that tourists could contemplate the "mad house" (Hickling 1875, p. 12). Conversations could not be directly and individually witnessed; the paper slips, sole proof of their ever having taken place, were less long-lived than a fruit fly.

In the same way in which the speech act's felicity conditions required that the broker was honorable and known to the other participants on the floor, the paper slip had to be handwritten, signed, and certified as original and emanating from its author. This, of course, made the price dependent on the individual, context-bound features of conversational exchanges.

The higher status group of brokers had a monopoly on trust and credibility. The Regular Board, through its elaborate rituals of recording price

data, invested it with authority. The lesser group of brokers, working continuously in the street, did not invest its data with similar features. The
boundaries between authoritative and less authoritative price data, between higher and lesser social statuses, were not affected by paper slips
and messenger boys.

Paper slips and pencils were a technology with a ragged temporal structure (irregular intervals, parallel times, and holes), which neither presented actual transactions to observers, nor represented (accurately) every
transaction. The assemblage of price data in lists was separated from the
generation of data. Market interactions were not made visible to the public. Existing boundaries between public and private transactions and between status groups were kept in place.

The Ticker and Price Data Monopolies

With the advent of the ticker, the brokerage office was directly connected
to the floor of the exchange and had access to real-time prices. However,
technical problems were soon to arise: the stiletto blurred and mixed up
letters and numbers instead of keeping them in two distinct lines, and tickers required batteries, which consisted of four large glass jars with zinc and
copper plates in them, filled with sulfuric acid; this, together with noninsu-
lated wires, made accidents frequent in the tumult of a brokerage office.

These problems were solved in the 1870s by Henry van Hoveberg's invention of the automatic unison adjustment and by the construction of
special buildings for batteries, respectively; brokerage offices were now
connected to a central power source (the battery building) and to the floor
of the stock exchange. The gold exchange received a similar instrument,
the gold indicator; a clocklike indicator was placed on the facade of the exchange, so that the crowds could follow price variations directly (Stedman
1905, p. 436).

After technical problems had been dealt with, several companies competed for the favors of brokerage houses and investors alike. Samuel Law's
company, the Gold and Stock Reporting Telegraph Company (which reported gold prices) competed with Calahan's Gold and Stock Telegraph
Company until 1869, when they merged. The outcome, the Gold and Stock
Telegraph Company, merged in its turn with Western Union in 1871. In
the early 1870s, Western Union's competition was the Gallaher Gold and
Stock Telegraph Co. (Jenkins et al. 1989, p. 357). Technical improvements

were accompanied by conflicts about patents: Thomas Alva Edison set out to circumvent Calahan's patent by developing his own "cotton ticker" with the type wheels mounted on the same shaft. In 1869, he developed a one-wire transmission technology, which competed with the three-wire technology of the Gold and Stock Telegraph Co.

According to Calahan, Samuel Law's company had secured an exclusive contract with the New York Stock Exchange even before the technology was developed. When Calahan appeared with his ticker, he replaced Law as the exclusive supplier of the stock exchange. Official brokers competed for being first on Calahan's delivery list (Calahan 1901, p. 237).

In the 1870s, for instance, the New York firm of Ward & Co. paid a monthly rent of $25 for their "instrument." Other firms rented tickers at a rate of $1 per day. While the figures for the number of tickers in use at the turn of the twentieth century are contradictory, it is clear that the ticker was present in provincial towns, at least between the Midwest and the East Coast. Around 1900, there were 1,750 tickers in Manhattan, Brooklyn, and New Jersey (Pratt 1903, p. 139). Edmund Stedman (1905, p. 441) claimed that twenty-three thousand US offices subscribed to ticker services. The *Magazine of Wall Street* (Anonymous 1927, p. 753) stated that in 1890 there were about four hundred tickers installed in the US; in 1900, there were over nine hundred and in 1902 the number had reached twelve hundred. Other publications (Gibson 1889, p. 82) claimed that by 1882 there were one thousand tickers in New York City alone, rented to offices at a rate of $10 per month. Peter Wyckoff (1972, pp. 40, 46) estimates the number of tickers in use at 837 in 1900 and 1,278 in 1906. Bond tickers were introduced in 1919. Contemporary observers thought that price recording over the ticker was less prone to errors than it was over the phone (Pratt 1903, p. 142); the ticker thus expanded even after the introduction of telephone services.[9]

Edward A. Calahan (1901, p. 236), who had worked as a messenger boy in his youth, wrote of the necessity of quelling the noise and the confusion emanating from the stock exchange. It appears that his motivation for developing the stock ticker was not tied to issues of increased efficiency or speed in disseminating the price data. The main issue was eliminating the disorder that affected the working of the Regular Board. Another issue was paying only one skilled, expensive Morse operator. As I will detail below, the users, on their part, were not motivated by ideas of efficiency or of increased access to price data. They were driven by their desire to consolidate their status. They wanted a monopoly over authoritative data and sought to have exclusive deals with telegraph companies. The technology brought together engineers, who developed competing machines, the telegraph companies, which sought to secure exclusive contracts, and the official stock brokers, who wanted exclusivity of use. The ticker was not wanted for efficient, accurate, and broad diffusion of price data. It was wanted because it helped reinforce social status and a monopoly over authoritative price data.

The Observation of Time

The ticker endowed price data with a new temporal structure, visualized in a new way. It made visible price variations, which now flowed uninterruptedly. Irregular, large time gaps were eliminated, or made imperceptible. Shrunken time intervals required more attention and coordination on the part of market actors. In the morning, actors set their watches before the tickers began to work (Selden 1917, p. 160), so that individual schedules were coordinated with the schedule of the machine. The time for the delivery of stocks, for example, was marked on the tape by "time" printed twice, after which the ticker gave fifteen distinct beats (Pratt 1903, p. 139). The ticker worked as a device for reciprocal temporal coordination. From the perspective of the brokerage house, it helped orient the participants' time and rhythm to that of Wall Street. In this sense, the ticker is an example of what Bruno Latour (1999, pp. 28–29, 306) calls an "immutable mobile": a networking technology which allows the transfer of temporal patterns across various contexts and the coordination of future paths of action.

Many commentators became aware of time differences, complaining about the fact that during peak hours the ticker fell behind, or that it could not record the entire volume of traded securities (Pratt 1903, p. 136; Selden 1917, p. 160; Wyckoff 1933, p. 24).

The flow of price variations visualized the results of ongoing conversational exchanges, and disassociated their results from the individual authority of the participants in those conversations. At the same time, the flow linked the results to each other, made the ties that bound them visible as the tape unfolded, and made the market in its turn visible as an abstract, faceless, yet very lively whole. All the felicity conditions which made the speech act valid (intonation, attitude, look, wording, pitch of voice, and so on) were blanked out. Authority and credibility was transferred from the broker's person to the machine. The flow of figures and letters on the ticker tape became an appresentation of market transactions (Husserl [1912] 1977, pp.112, 124–25). In other words, perception (of price rhythms) and representation (of floor transactions) fused together. The ticker made transactions present in several brokerage offices at once, as the unseen, yet necessary, side of the names and numbers on the tape.[10]

Since market transactions themselves were understood as representing events in the world at large, the flow of the ticker tape could be taken as appresenting the world. The observer related to this world not in a contemplative fashion; the observer rather directed his will upon the world, as the following fictionalization makes clear: Sampson Rock, Lefevre's main character

approached the ticker and gazed intently on the printed letters and numbers of the tape—so intently that they ceased to be numerals and became living figures. Williams was ten million leagues away, and Rock's vision leaped form New York to Richmond, from Richmond to Biddleboro, from Biddleboro back to the glittering marble and gold Board Room of the Stock Exchange. The tape characters were like little soldier-ants, bringing precious loads to this New York office, tiny gold nuggets from a thousand stock holders, men and women and children, rich and poor, to the feet of Sampson Rock. It may be there would be shrieks and sobs, pain-squeals and imprecations; but they would not reach the ears of a man whose soul had soared so high that the entire State of Virginia was spread before him in miniature like an outrolled map, glowing and glittering polychromatically in a flood of sunshine. And through this map ran a line, not a ticker tape, with towns instead of abbreviations or bridges instead of dashes, but a vein; and it was not a vein of human blood or of human tears, but of human sweat, a living thing, born of work, stretching tentacle-like arms every wither, reaching to every corner of the State of Virginia, to the great Atlantic; and more faintly, the same net-work of life-giving and life-creating veins extending to the Great river and the Great lakes, and perhaps—if Sampson Rock lived long enough to realize the dream of every railroad emperor—even unto the golden remote Far West and the blue Pacific—from ocean to ocean. (Lefevre 1907, pp. 16–17)

The new technology also meant that printed stock lists lost some of their importance as decision instruments—a fact already noticed by observers of the period. While stock list compilations separated the process of composition from the process of inscription (putting together the prices

of various securities came after each price was recorded), the ticker integrated them (Collins and Kusch 1998, p. 109). At the same time, lists
became more sophisticated and began to show not only opening and closing prices, but also prices at different times of the day—a fact mirrored
by more detailed market reports in the New York and provincial newspapers. In 1884, with the ticker now a solid market fixture, Dow Jones &
Co. began publishing average closing prices of active representative stocks
(Wyckoff 1972, p. 31), thus initiating the first stock market index.

The ways in which brokers and investors worded their decisions had
to be adapted to continuous data about price variations. This made brokerage houses adopt and distribute telegraphic codes to their clients, fitting the language of financial transactions to the new temporal structure.
For example, the house of Haight & Freese (known in Street parlance as
"Hate & Freeze") could telegraph a client "army event bandit calmly" instead of "cannot sell Canada Southern at your limit. Please reduce limit to
23" (Anonymous 1898, pp. 385, 396). Here, "army" stood for "cannot sell
at your limit," "event" for "Canada Southern," "bandit" for "reduce limit
to," and "calmly" for "23." Had the investor wanted to sell, say, 150 shares
Pacific Mail, he would have telegraphed back "alpine [sell 150 shares] expulsion [Pacific Mail]." This language was exclusively centered on representing the world of finance: one could build sentences using the word
bandit, but it was impossible to formulate sentences about bandits.

Some code books reached mammoth dimensions: in 1905, the Hartfield
Telegraphic Code Publishing Co. published *Hartfield's Wall Street Code*,
containing about four hundred and sixty-seven thousand cipher words, all
related to securities and financial transactions in Wall Street (*Hartfield's*
1905). Others, like the *Ticker Book and Manual of the Tape*, published in
the same year, included not only codes, but also maintenance instructions
for the machine and tips for tape reading.

An effect of the new transactional language was that investors were
bound to their brokers even more closely than before: as an investor,
one had to learn a special telegraphic code from the broker's manual and
spend as much time as possible in his office. Brokerage houses advertised
their codes as a sign of seriousness and reliability. Some distributed them
to their clients for free, while others charged a fee. This was a means of asserting the prestige of the brokerage house, but also an attempt to keep a
record of the investors using the code and thus limit forged orders. On the
other hand, free telegraph codes were a means of attracting more clients
and increasing business, as well as of saving money on relatively expensive

telegrams. A contemporary noticed that Haight & Freese was particularly skilled at attracting new clients by means of free statistics, diagrams, and code books (Wyckoff 1930, p. 21).

The ticker abbreviations of the quoted companies became nicknames, widely used by market actors:

> because MP stands on the tape for Missouri Pacific, that stock is generally called "Mop." NP stands for Northern Pacific, which goes by the name "Nipper," the common being called "little" and the preferred "big." PO standing for People's Gas Light and Coke Company, that stock is often called "Post-office." The same law of economy in the use of words applies to all the active stocks. (Pratt 1903, p. 136)

Not only was the new language standardized and adapted to the rapidity of transactions; it was tied to the visibility of price variations. The observer of financial markets could no longer be equated with the confused tourist standing in the visitors' gallery. The observer of the market was the observer of the tape. In this sense, the ticker contributed to a radical abstraction and reconfiguration of the visual experience of the market. Moreover, it certainly contributed to creating a visual culture of financial markets as a "way of seeing that *simultaneously* both *reflects* and *shapes* how members read the world" (Henderson 1999, p. 25).

This is perhaps best illustrated by subsequent developments. Due to its physical size, the ticker tape could be observed directly by only a few people at once. An operator, or tape reader, sat by the ticker and read the data. In 1923, a device called the Trans-Lux Movie Ticker was developed and tested on the floor of the NYSE. It projected the image of the ticker tape onto a translucent screen in real time, so that the flow of quotations was visible at once to all those present. Built according to NYSE's specifications, the Trans-Lux machine had a projection bandwidth of at least twenty quotations. Its success was so great that the parent company also developed the Trans-Lux Movie Flash Ticker and the Movie News Ticker. They were installed in banks, brokerage offices, and at different locations in the NYSE building. The Movie Flash Ticker projected a single, flowing line of business and political news onto the screen, while the Movie News Ticker could project a block of eight lines of text. The Trans-Lux company claimed that in 1929 there were one thousand, five hundred Movie Tickers in operation in 211 trading centers (Burton 1929, p. 14). After the introduction of the Trans-Lux machine, a new time lag appeared, because the speed of the ticker tape was greater than the movie ticker's projection speed. By increasing spacing between quotations, this time lag was eliminated (Wyckoff 1934e, p. 20).

While the use of the ticker provided the same data everywhere, these were contingent upon temporal structures and the related mode of visualizing the market. The ragged time structure of paper slips was replaced by the smooth, uninterrupted, unique time of the ticker tape. The visualization of this structure replaced the rhythm of conversational transactions, but at the same time was equivalent to it. Price variations became the most important kind of data *and* a representation of market transactions. The ticker unveiled patterns of repeatability in both conversations and price variations. This mode of visualization promoted observational and sociolinguistic principles superimposed on and equivalent to economic transactions. This should not imply that it was built according to abstract economic principles. Quite the contrary: its way of working generated temporal structures directing investors and brokers along specific paths of action, orienting them toward price variations, re-entangling authority with human actors, coordinating individual schedules, changing the language, and so on. Following distinctions developed by Harry Collins and Martin Kusch (1998, p. 119), the ticker was neither a tool, nor a proxy for human action: it did things that market actors could never have done without it.

Technological Attention and Market Attachment

Perhaps not entirely by accident, the ticker was invented at a time when US psychologists (but not only these) were engaged in heated debates about constant attention as a fundamental condition of knowledge (Crary 1990, pp. 21–23). The ticker firmly bound investors and brokers to its ticks. Constant presence, attention, and observation were explicitly required by manuals of the time. The duty of the stockbroker was simply to be always by his "instrument," which "is never dumb" and ensures that the US is "a nation of speculators" ("Stocks" 1881). Investors too felt motivated to spend more time in their brokers' offices, watching the quotations and socializing: "July 26, 1893. Erie going into the hands of a receiver, was the cause of the great decline in stocks in Wall Street to day & I passed the entire day in the office of Mssrs. Webb & Prall watching the ticker" (Edward Neufville Tailer, Diary 1890–1893, New York Historical Society).

In his reminiscences, Richard D. Wyckoff (1934b, p. 37), a stock operator and pioneer of chart analysis,[11] wrote that in 1905 friends of his could
sit and watch the tape for an hour and a half without any interruption.
Wyckoff himself had trained hard so that he could watch the ticker tape
for up to an hour. He remembered how in 1907 James R. Keene, the financial speculator, fell into a "ticker trance":

> I used to stand facing him, my left elbow on his ticker while talking to him. He
> would hold the tape in his left hand and his eye-glasses in his right as he listened to
> me, then on went the glasses astride his nose as he bent close to the tape in
> a scrutiny of the length that had passed meanwhile. I might be talking at the
> moment his eye began to pick up the tape again, but until he finished he was
> a person in a trance. If, reading the tape, he observed something that stimu-
> lated his mental machinery, I might go on talking indefinitely; he wouldn't get a
> word of it. . . . He appeared to absorb a certain length of tape, and to devote to
> its analysis a specified interval, measured by paces. Sometimes he returned to
> the ribbon for another examination, followed by more pacing. (Wyckoff 1930,
> p. 148)

The ability to watch and be in touch all the time was a key condition
of playing the game (Wyckoff 1934b, p. 38; 1933, p. 26). Some brokerage
offices tried to restrict access to the customers' rooms, where the tickers
were placed, on account of the great number of "chair warmers, just sitting there and watching the ticker and talking, who repel the better class
of business men" (Selden 1917, p. 106). Not only was one's presence in
the stockbroker's office a must, if one was to be au courant with the latest
price variations; it was also a must for the investor eager to hear "scientific" interpretations and analyses of price variations.

The importance of continuous attention and observation resonates in
the private diaries of some investors of the time. Edward Neufville Tailer,
a rich (although not among the richest) woolen goods wholesale merchant, kept a detailed diary between 1848 and 1907. When he undertook
a business trip through the Midwest and South in 1880, Tailer regularly
went to brokerage offices in cities like Nashville and Cincinnati, in order
to watch the ticker. First of all, his participation in financial transactions
seems to have increased after the introduction of the ticker; second, this
participation became a reflexive one. Up to 1870, Tailer (who traded in
woolen goods) bought stock only occasionally, and gold only for the pur
pose of covering his import-export activities. Whenever he bought gold

on margin and gold futures between 1866 and 1870, he admonished
himself for risking too much. In mid-1867, he began recording stock prices
regularly. Moreover, he started monitoring his actions with respect to the
evolution of stock prices and commented upon his past decisions. Edward
Neufville Tailer minutely recorded in his diary not only the actual dates
he went to his brokers' offices—during the years 1880–82, at least once a
week—but also the times when he should have gone, expressing regret
for not doing so:

> Dec 2 1880: I telegraphed today to L. T. Hoyt from Nashville to buy me one
> hundred shares of Western Union at nincty. It was quoted in Nashville @ 90 ½
> at noon. Dec 4 1880: The special to the Cincinnati Commercial reports money
> tight in NY, plus a commission of $1/32$ @ ¼ of 1% per day. Mr. L. T. Hoyt bought
> me 100 Western Union @ 90, a good purchase. [. . .] Feb 24 1882: Stocks are
> better today. I sold Louisville and Nashville @ 72 ½, Erie @ 36 ¼, and they
> have since advanced 1 ½ to 2%. I bought Union Pacific @ 111 ½ in the mar-
> gin and sold it @ peak @ 114. It was a lovely afternoon for riding . . . I missed
> it by not being at Louis T. Hoyt's office this afternoon, as stocks fell off 1 @
> 2 points. Feb 27 1882: Stocks are all better this morning, I missed it by not
> being at the opening of the market, as I later in the day paid an advance of
> 1 @ 2 % on the closing prices of Saturday, upon which I visited Mr. Hoyt in
> the morning. (The Diaries of Edward Tailer 1880–1882, New York Historical
> Society)

He admonished himself whenever he felt he should have been at his
broker's office instead of riding in Central Park. He pasted newspaper
clippings in his diary and commented upon his own transactions as corresponding or not to what newspapers said was the right thing to do.[12] When
on trips to Europe or in the US, he took care to go to stockbrokers' offices
and record prices.

Permanent attention to market events also meant permanent attention
to one's own doings, systematic reflection upon the satisfactions derived
from one's own behavior. Is riding in Central Park giving me a greater
satisfaction than a visit to my broker? What is the right thing to do? At
the same time, investors like Tailer seemed very reluctant to sell certain
stocks, even when they were losing money. He held Lake Shore and Michigan Railroad Co. stock for years (in spite of its continuously decreasing
price) and expressed joy over a small dividend, although the gain was written off by the price decline:

Sept 28 1874. Stocks have been excited in Wall Street today and Lake Shore has advanced to 82 ¾ at this price I could get out without a loss having purchased in the panic at 91 & last April @ 74 ½ for an average. [. . .] Jan 7 1876. I am pleased to see that the Lake Shore and Michigan Southern railway, in which I am interested, has earned a dividend of 2%, payable on the 1st of February next out of the earnings, for the six months ending with Dec 31 1875. [. . .] May 5 1876. I bought today 200 shares of Lake Shore, through Broke & Smith @ 52 ½. (The Diaries of Edward Tailer 1874–1876, New York Historical Society)

This "stickiness" or "frame dependence" (e.g., Shefrin 1999, p. 23; Andreassen 1990; Scharfstein and Stein 1990)—that is, the apparently irrational unwillingness to sell bad stocks—is not to be confounded with apathy or indifference. Someone like Tailer was anything but indifferent with respect to his portfolio, but he still couldn't bring himself to sell a stock the value of which had decreased by more than a third. It is to be speculated here that permanent (price) observation (induced, at least in part, by the ticker) had effects on personal attachment. The increased frequency and technological ease with which investors could monitor the performance of their stocks in the late nineteenth century encouraged emotional attachment. A continuous monitoring could also encourage investors to "give stocks another chance" and "wait a little longer," since under the new conditions they could in principle be sold any time. Increased cognitive preoccupation with financial securities necessarily leads to the development of emotional ties. This phenomenon has been noticed and described at least as the emotional attachment of scientists to the object of their research activities (Knorr Cetina 1997), and as the emotional attachment of professional traders to market processes (Knorr Cetina and Bruegger 2000).

The ticker—by requiring permanent presence and attention to the marketplace—encouraged (if not generated) a continuous monitoring of one's own behavior, together with emotional ties to securities one could associate with private and public events. Permanent observation, reflexivity, and attentiveness—the very same qualities preached by investor manuals—were now not only prescribed in an abstract and normative fashion, but also enacted in the concrete setting of the brokerage house. The observation of prices, encapsulated in machine-generated rhythms, bound actors to the marketplace in a way which no manual could have achieved.

The Ticker as a Device for the Organization of Knowledge

The rhythm of price variations required temporally structured responses from users, which led to a rearrangement of (1) the relationship between the brokerage office and the trading floor, and (2) trading floor activities.

The ticker transformed the stockbroker's office into a kind of community-cum-communications center, where investors could spend the whole day watching quotations, talking to each other, and placing orders. In the customers' room, rows of tickers (attended by clerks) worked uninterruptedly, while clients seated on several rows of seats watched other clerks updating the quotations board. The modern brokerage office had a separate telegraph room, an order desk, a ticker room, and a back office. It is not evident from the available evidence that brokerage offices had been organized in this way before the introduction of the ticker. At the center of this spatial arrangement was the ticker room. In the more important brokerage houses, this room was often elegant, but noisy; in it, the "ever-changing position of the great markets is like a kaleidoscope" (Pratt 1903, p. 162). Advertising articles praised the stockbroker's office as a model of efficient communication, accuracy, and machine-inspired modernity:

> A passenger standing on the observation platform in the engine-room of a modern ocean-liner will observe great masses of steel, some stationary, some whirling at terrific speed; he may go down into the boiler-room where is generated the power with which the great ship is driven, but all this will give him only a crude idea of the actual workings of the machinery of propulsion. [. . .] So it is with the machinery of a large banking and brokerage house. A client may spend many days in the customers' room, from which vantage point he will observe much, but his knowledge of the inner workings of the machine, built to handle orders in the various markets, must still be superficial. [. . .] Everything is run with clock-like precision. No matter how large a business is being done, there is no confusion, the plant being designed to handle the maximum volume of orders. (Anonymous 1908, p. 7)[13]

Cognitive organization was one of the central features of the "modern brokerage house," where knowledge-producing activities were centralized and bundled. Customers had to show up regularly in order to access this knowledge.[14]

Moreover, the broker's office could influence the market by bringing the ticker into action. Richard D. Wyckoff recalled that in 1905 some friends of his were sitting in the New York office of Eddie Wasserman, a known speculator of that time. Noticing that

> the tape was barely moving, he (Wasserman) said to the clients in the office: "Let's make up a little pool in Southern Railway and start a move in it. I'll buy thousand if you will." Eddie went over on the floor and bought a few thousand shares all at one price. "It came easily," he said. Then he called up friends and told them there was going to be a move in Southern Railway. When all these trades appeared on the tape and in such an absolutely dead market, it did look as though something had started. Here was a chance for some of the thousands of people sitting around hundreds of tickers all over the country to get a little action. Outside buying orders began to come into the crowd; in a few minutes Southern Railway was up a point and a half. Eddie and his friends quickly took their profits. The evening papers said Morgan had been buying Southern Railway. (Wyckoff 1934b, p. 37)

In this account, "moving the tape" and "moving the market" are treated as synonymous; the idleness of the tape requires action and intervention. At the same time, this episode is indicative of the possibilities for manipulating a market that is perceived as the flow of letters and figures on a tape. On yet another level, this manipulation could now be performed anonymously: one did not have to show up in the marketplace in order to corner the market. It became more difficult to know who was actually "moving the tape." The ticker appears not only as an instrument of passive observation, but also as one of active intervention: observation triggers action. This mode, which combines contemplation and action, reconfiguring the observed world, and relationships with other observers, sends us to analogies with the scientific laboratory, where nature is reconstituted within and through observation instruments (Knorr Cetina 1992, p. 122). In a similar way, the interactions of actors on the trading floor, the buying and selling orders coming from outside, the cries, glances, and hand movements are reconstituted as "the market" in the rhythms of the ticker.

The floor of the exchange was reshaped too. Before the advent of the ticker, the Regular and the Open Board were spatially separated; one was a discontinuous and rigidly organized market, the other was a continuous and formally disorganized one. Multiple prices were the rule. In 1868, members of the Open Board began adopting a particular place for each security traded. Later, the Regular Board moved downstairs and began trading in the same room with the Open Board, mixing up with its members. The two were officially merged on May 8, 1869 (Cornwallis 1879, p. 26). After the merger, seat prices rose to $10,000. The practice of trading by calls was abandoned. The redrawing of the boundaries—which happened shortly after the introduction of the ticker—allowed the market to become a continuous, single-price entity (Eames 1894, p. 69; Smith 1871, p. 71; Selden 1917, p. 90). The merger created a larger status group, but excluded from access to data all those who were not members of the former Open and Regular Boards. The boundary between authoritative and less authoritative price data was redrawn by absorbing old competitors and by keeping out any new ones.

The stock exchange floor was organized in specialized "crowds"—brokers and market makers trading a single security, or a group of similar securities around a ticker, under a streetlamp-like signpost (Nelson 1900, p. 19; Anonymous 1875, p. 9; Anonymous 1893). Each trading post had an indicator showing the latest quotations. Trading posts were connected by pneumatic tubes, so that orders would be sent over without sending a messenger across the floor (Meeker 1922, p. 57). In the northeast corner of the floor was the loan crowd, specialized in lending securities to short-sellers (Van Antwerp 1913, p. 290). The crowds around trading posts were taken to represent "the world's demand and supply" (Meeker 1922, p. 56). Four telegraph stations were installed on the floor between trading posts; transactions were reported from these stations to the headquarters of the ticker company, situated on the upper floors of the same building (Meeker 1922, p. 41). Speculators were relegated to a special, enclosed area on the floor, the access to which cost $100 a year (Cornwallis 1879, p. 27). Tourists had access only to the gallery. The public could no longer mingle freely with brokers. Stockbrokers were issued personal identification numbers; an electric panel was installed, and every time a stockbroker was called, his number was flashed in a color corresponding to the category of the caller—client, back office, and the like (Selden 1917, p. 90).

Redrawing the Boundaries: The Fights around Ticker Use

Official stockbrokers adopted the ticker in order to maintain their monopoly over credible, authoritative price data. Yet, since the technology brought together social groups with heterogeneous interests (developers, operators, users), the boundary between credible and less credible data soon became fragile. These groups engaged in both competition and cooperation: ticker operators, for instance, cooperated with stockbrokers, but competed with each other. Official stockbrokers wanted to keep unofficial brokers away from the ticker, while the brokers sought access to ticker operators. Because operators wanted to expand their business (after all, there was only a limited number of official brokers), they started selling the technology to unofficial brokers. Struggles arose for control of ticker machines and tapes. Engineers fought about patents, founded ticker companies, and got involved in mergers. By the early 1870s, Western Union emerged as the dominant (though not the sole) provider of price quotations. Patents on existing machines were circumvented by patenting new models, with minor modifications; the result was that in the early 1870s there were gold, stock, and cotton tickers which differed only slightly from each other.

Bucket shops sought access to the ticker and wanted to compete with official brokerage houses (Hochfelder 2006, p. 345). The price of a seat on the New York Stock Exchange fell dramatically in the late 1880s, compared with the early 1870s.[15] The willingness of operators to sell their services to unofficial brokers threatened the monopoly of the official brokerage houses. Power struggles raged over who should have access to price data; in 1889, in a short-lived attempt to drive bucket shops out and restore the value of the stockbrokers' seats, the NYSE banned all stock tickers (Wyckoff 1972, p. 33). By then, however, nobody wanted to go back to the preticker system of price recording:

> Wall Street was infested with bucket shops in 1889 and for many years afterward. The New York Stock Exchange had always fought these outfits bitterly. One day, driven to the last extremity in its endeavor to shake off the bucket shop, the Stock Exchange suspended the ticker service, even to its own members. We boys replaced the tickers. We had to run back and forth between the offices and the Exchange to get quotations and prices and report what was going on. No one in any of the offices knew prices until his boy arrived. This could not last. Nobody wanted to trade when the ticker wasn't ticking. (Wyckoff 1930, p. 19)

In 1887, in another short-lived attempt, the president of the Chicago Board of Trade destroyed the tickers on the floor of the exchange and cut all the electric wires (Hochfelder 2006, p. 335). In 1909, the report of the Hughes Committee (set to investigate stock market practices) suggested licensing all the tickers operating in the state of New York and, one year later, the New York Stock Exchange reached an agreement with Western Union to control the stream of ticker quotations (Cowing 1965, pp. 40–41). The reasons for these actions were manifold: on the one hand, some bucket shops dealt primarily in derivatives, taking thus a chunk of the business from the more established brokerage houses.[16] On the other hand, the big houses argued that the combination of shaky bucket shops and derivatives was ruining the reputation of financial investments.

Together with the NYSE, official brokerage houses tried hard to control the flow of price information. In 1890, the New York Stock Exchange bought a controlling interest in the New York Quotation Co., which received the exclusive right to furnish quotations to the members of the exchange (Pratt 1903, p. 134). The public was serviced by other quotation companies, under certain restrictions. Tickers could be installed only in brokerage offices approved by the NYSE (Selden 1917, p. 158). This triggered bitter litigation between the NYSE and brokerage houses, which ended in 1892 in favor of the NYSE. In the late 1880s, and again in 1909, the New York Stock Exchange tried unsuccessfully to deprive the Consolidated Stock and Petroleum Exchange (a much smaller exchange located in Lower Manhattan) of its ticker service,[17] so as to restrict the Consolidated to unlisted securities (Goldman 1914, pp. 27–28; Wyckoff 1930, p. 23). The latter fought back, and was able to retain its tickers for a time. (The 1909 prohibition was rescinded in 1913.)

On yet another level, the ticker greatly stimulated arbitrage activities (and competition) between the New York and the London stock exchanges. In the 1890s, it took only minutes for New York prices to reach London and vice versa. The NYSE saw arbitrage as damaging to its interests and to its control over price information, and in 1894, in another short-lived attempt, it withdrew all tickers (Eames 1894, pp. 65, 91). Some ticker operators had to learn the codes of the arbitrageurs speculating on price differences between New York and London (Nelson 1904, p. 59). At that time, the London Stock Exchange was actively trying to win business away from the New York Stock Exchange and build up an "American Market" in London (Michie 1999, p. 79). Banning the ticker was seen as a means of discouraging arbitrage, maintaining a tight hold on price information, and keeping business in New York. For its part, the London Stock Exchange protected its business by furnishing incomplete price information over the ticker, much to the distress of American brokers. The tickers of the London Stock Exchange did not print the price and the volume of each trade (Gibson 1889, p. 83); this made "an American stock trader in London feel as though he had no information about the market worth mentioning with only these meager figures to go upon" (Selden 1917, p. 162). At the same time, in London, prices were recorded by the ticker not from "crowds," but from inscriptions made by brokers on a blackboard on the exchange floor (Gibson 1889, p. 35). Incomplete inscriptions, made in haste, led to incomplete price data.

The enlarged Regular Board continued to have a monopoly over authoritative, continuous price data. By redrawing the boundary between authoritative and less authoritative data, the ticker rather reinforced the social position of the Regular Board. It wiped out whatever informational advantages (i.e., continuity) unofficial brokers may have had before. Deprived of them, many unofficial brokers reoriented themselves toward unlisted securities, which were outside the NYSE's monopoly. At the beginning of the 1920s, unofficial brokers dealing in unlisted stocks founded the American Stock Exchange.

Differences in the organization of knowledge and in price data were thus perceived as critical for access to financial transactions.[18] The organization of the stock exchange was synonymous with the "high organization of knowledge" (Anonymous 1876, p. 25). How to monitor and collect quotations efficiently and how to transmit them further without missing anything were topics regularly repeated by brokerage houses in their advertising brochures and manuals. In this sense, the ticker triggered a process of self-monitoring at the institutional level and generated principles of organization superimposed on the sociolinguistic view it disseminated. Both the organization and the individual had to pay more attention to what they did and weigh courses of action.

Technology and the Boundaries of Finance

Technology created patterns of perception, observation, and attention, patterns anchored in the rhythms of price data and in the visualization of these rhythms. The stock ticker replaced a ragged temporal structure with a smooth one, with the consequence that price variations became visualizations of market transactions and objects of symbolic interpretation. Market exchanges were made visible as they happened, were disentangled from local conversations, and transformed into something which is both abstract and visible in several forms to everybody at once. They were visible in the flow of names and prices on the paper strip, but also in the financial charts, which are nowadays also produced in real time. The quality of price data changed: instead of multiple, discontinuous, heterogeneous, and unsystematically recorded prices, we now have single, continuous, homogeneous, nearly real-time price variations. This does not mean, of course, that financial fraud and manipulation were eradicated forever: the evidence points to the contrary. When moving the market means moving the tape, the possibilities for anonymous manipulation all but disappear.

The new visual experience of the market was an abstract one, radically different from that of the eighteenth-century marketplace. Not only did one not need to be present anymore in places like the Exchange Alley or the Tontine Coffee House in order to "see" the market, but this latter became something very different from the noise and the conglomerate of colorful figures associated with these places. This new observational experience was one of virtual witnessing, only that the phenomena being witnessed—uninterrupted, near real-time price variations—were new too. Before the ticker, minute, continuous price variations could not constitute any real information for actors who were not permanently present in the marketplace; traders did not have the memory of a whole herd of elephants and the computational capabilities of an army of accountants. Moreover, this technology opened up the gate for the constitution of a market memory as abstract and distinct from the limited memories of individual actors.

It is relevant in this context that some of the most important subsequent developments were directed toward the construction of an automated market memory, which could record and store all transactions. Usually, memorization and classification required clerks who processed data and archived them in a table format, an activity which was time consuming and prone to errors. In 1934, the Teleregister Service was introduced in New York brokerage houses; it tabulated and displayed price data, replacing conventional quotations boards (*New York Curb Exchange* 1946, p. 29). The electromechanical price data tabulation opened the possibility of memorizing and archiving data while these latter were generated. The data were recorded on paper sheets; retrieving them was still a manual operation. It was performed by armies of operators, who worked in the quotations department, in groups differentiated according to classes of securities. Each group was assigned a telephone number. The broker wanting the price history of a certain security dialed the respective number and got the data from the operator (*New York Curb Exchange* 1946, p. 31).

The company providing the Teleregister Service was acquired by Martin Marietta (an air defense contractor) in the early 1960s, but continued to provide financial data services to members of the New York Stock Exchange. In 1964, the then chairman of Martin Marietta, together with a computer engineer, formed the Bunker Ramo Co., which provided computerized data systems to brokerage houses (Anonymous 1983, p. 60).

Not only did the creation of an objectified market memory allow the introduction of new kinds of evidence in the courts of law; it also got a public character, which was made available in the street:

> It is only a few years ago that opening, high, and low quotations were considered sufficient to satisfy those interested in the stock market and for forty years there had been no improvement. This primitive method was superseded by a careful compilation of the day's trading, printed in tabulated form and including every sale made or transacted from the ticker, reproduced in an afternoon paper and sold on the street for a penny twenty minutes after the closing of the Stock Exchange. [. . .] And so accurate has that service been that it has been accepted in courts of law as official in lieu of any better or as good service from the Stock Exchange itself. (Nelson 1902, p. 90)

The observer of the market was now the observer of abstract variations, not of picturesque and more or less morally dubious characters, a shift which dislocated transactions from their local embedding even more.[19] The abstract visual reconfiguration of the market required tools of symbolic interpretation and groups monopolizing these tools; a new market figure, the analyst, was just around the corner.

The forms of attention required by the observation of price data could be perfectly echoed by manuals, but also practiced by real actors. This was not, however, reducible to the transformation of market actors into calculating machines. Boundaries were set in place or redrawn, in the very process of generating perception patterns and attachment. Issues of monopoly, prestige, and authority were at least as important as before, if not even more important. The transfer of authority upon machines did not mean that market actors lost their powers of control. It meant rather the emergence of new forms of control over the capacity to interpret the abstract visual experience of the market. This capacity required cognitive tools and an adequate vocabulary, but also groups exercising a hold on them. And indeed, such groups were rather quick to emerge; market analysts became a new fixture of the financial world. It is to them that I turn now.

CHAPTER FIVE

From Afar: Charts and Their Analysts

The stock ticker purred out visual representations of transaction rhythms, requiring tools with the help of which the ink traces on the paper ribbon could be further processed into meaningful data framing and orienting at the same time the actions of market actors. These tools, as well as the interpretation of price and volume data, required boundaries between groups entitled to generating interpretations and groups entitled to using these interpretations. A monopoly over interpretation implies the constitution of this latter as a body of expert knowledge, raising problems at least with respect to its legitimacy, diffusion, use, and persistence. At the same time, this monopoly implies the emergence of a specialized group controlling this knowledge, an emergence which takes place in the absence of any preestablished professional structures. In this perspective, we are confronted with a series of questions about how such groups emerge and position themselves in relationship to users; how they gain legitimacy and authority both in relationship to the stock exchange and to the public at large; and how the monopolized knowledge is used. In the same way in which specific groups can establish a monopolistic closure over the space, time, and access to financial transactions, closure which is intrinsic to the boundaries of finance, other groups can establish monopolistic closure over the interpretation of financial data. Such interpretations mediate the actors' understanding of the significance of this data, their access to financial transactions, and their own actions within the market. Consequently, control over interpretation belongs to the boundaries of finance as much as control over space, time, and data observation.

Before the introduction of the stock ticker, the gathering and processing of financial information for the use of market actors (brokers, investors) was neither systematically practiced by third parties on behalf of an agent, nor specialized or professionalized. True, some banks (including the Bank of England) employed clerks to gather data about companies. Such inquiries, however, were not systematic, nor were they conducted by a specialist or made available to the public. While their tasks required skills and might have been complex, the clerks mandated to investigate did not claim a monopoly over special knowledge or expertise; their job was solely to investigate, not to interpret. Moreover, no set of specific methods of analysis were codified.

It is also true that, before the introduction of the stock ticker, tools like financial charts were produced and disseminated in financial circles, as well as to a larger public. Yet the price and volume data used in these charts were not endowed with any authority besides that of the chart compiler, many of whom complained about the difficulty of finding reliable, accurate, and gap-free data. Charts would show at best monthly prices and volumes, but not daily or even weekly ones. The discontinuous character of the data, together with their close attachment to the authority of individual compilers, made pre-ticker charts a relatively unreliable base for the formation of a body of expert knowledge. Chart compilers and drawers could be skilled economists: William Stanley Jevons, for instance, earned his living by drawing charts and selling them to London offices (Jevons 1886, p. 156). At the same time, he saw chart drawing as a means of earning money in dire times rather than as directly connected to a specific body of expert economic knowledge. In spite of them being produced and sold, in the pre-ticker era price charts failed to provide the basis for the development of expert financial knowledge, together with expert interpreters.

After the introduction of the stock ticker, we witness a situation in which a group creates a knowledge monopoly, while its members position themselves as specialized providers of financial interpretations. This group grounds its claims in using a special method and in a special relationship with a particular kind of financial charts, produced using ticker-generated data. In the decades between about 1900 and 1930, this group evolves into a semiprofessional cluster of analysts, employing a particular method.

They call themselves technical analysts and their method chartism.[1] They claim to be able to forecast price movements based on the interpretation of charts, and develop a specific vocabulary, together with the corresponding interpretive procedures. We witness therefore a situation in which a new form of expertise and a group of experts arise in relationship to a particular price-recording technology, gather a following, and manage to constitute themselves as a semiprofessional (and later a fully professional) group with growing success.

This form of forecasting differs from the one based on computing theoretical prices, grounded in abstract models, or from examining the fundamental data of listed corporations. It relies on assembling observations of price data and arranging them in a particular visual formation (the chart), which is then looked at, decomposed into its constituent parts, and "analyzed." Future price movements are "seen" or predicted based on these operations. The close-up observation made possible by the ticker is complemented with observation from afar. In order to be able to "see" the future in price movements, one has to step back from the flow of prices and look at larger formations. As a second observational mode intrinsic to the boundaries of finance, seeing and analyzing charts complements microscopic observations of price flows. What is far away in the future can only be seen if one steps back and looks through the chart.

Financial Chartism as a Form of Expert Knowledge

Financial chartism (aka technical analysis) is defined as a "method of forecasting the prices of stocks, futures contracts, indexes, or any kind of financial instrument" (New York Institute of Finance 1989, p. xiii). It is one of the major methods for analyzing financial securities, the other one being fundamental analysis. While fundamental analysts attempt "to discern cause-and-effect relationships between a security and its price [. . .] technical analysts do not attempt to explain why prices move as they do. [. . .] They attempt to detect patterns in market action that they can identify as having happened often enough in the past to be reliable as an indicator of future price levels" (New York Institute of Finance 1989, p. 2). Financial chartists thus claim that they are able to forecast the prices of financial securities without postulating a causal relationship between prices and fundamental economic data, such as profits and losses, balance of payments, or interest rates. This claim is grounded in the thesis that observing price movements and detecting their regularities do not need any additional data: future movements can be inferred by studying past regularities. Therefore, their main analytical instruments are financial charts, or minute diagrams of variations in price and volume, diagrams which are nowadays produced in real time. In addition to charts of individual prices and volumes, analysts also use diagrams of price indexes, which aggregate securities by economic sectors and industries, among others.

Chartism uses a special vocabulary in order to designate patterns of price movements: for example, analysts talk of breaking gaps, flat bottoms, sauce bottoms, falling flags, head and shoulders, or symmetrical coils, among others.[2] They geometrically process charts in order to highlight patterns of price movements. For instance, chartists draw channel lines in order to identify deviations in these movements, or trend lines in order to identify general market trends (New York Institute of Finance 1989; DeMark 1994).

The tenets of financial chartism run counter to the commonsensical tenet that there must be a relationship between the prices of financial securities, on the one hand, and fundamental economic data, on the other. They also run counter to academic financial economics, which maintains that price movements are random. Therefore, future movements cannot be inferred from past ones. The US economics literature of the 1910s and the 1920s did not treat financial markets as an object of systematic theoretical inquiry. In some cases, academic economists stressed the importance of the stock ticker as a means of getting fresh data (e.g., Huebner [1922] 1934, pp. 217–21), thus confirming the importance attributed to this machine by financial chartists. The situation, however, changed in the 1930s, when economists and statisticians started questioning the predictive claims of technical analysis. In 1933, Alfred Cowles 3rd published a paper based on his talk given at the American Statistical Association meeting a year before (Cowles 1933), in which he examined the forecasts of financial services, publications, and insurance companies, concluding that there was no true predictive power in these forecasts. Criticisms continued in the 1950s and the 1960s; papers published in major economics journals claimed that chartist patterns were nothing more than statistical artifacts (Roberts 1959) and that chart reading is "perhaps an interesting pastime" (Fama 1965, p. 34).

In spite of these contestations, technical analysis managed to maintain its authority within financial markets, to continue its professionalization, and to expand its circle of practitioners. Chartism has made a very good career in financial markets.[3] There are professional associations at the local and national level in North and South America, Europe, Asia, Africa, and Australia. More than thirty national associations are members of the International Federation of Technical Analysts. The US Market Technicians Association, for instance, has a membership of 430 full members and 1,841 affiliates.[4] In the US, the first professional association of technical analysts was founded in 1970 in San Francisco.[5] Technical analysts, however, were active as a group several decades before formal organization occurred. Banks and other financial institutions employ technical analysts. Professional bodies at the national and international level are responsible for certifying technical analysts; they organize schooling, conduct examinations, publish books and periodicals, have annual meetings and seminars, and aggregate job market information.

Expert Knowledge as Legitimate Mediation

How did this expertise emerge as a legitimate mediation of access to financial activities, mediation different from that of investor manuals? While such manuals claimed that access is conditioned by acquiring specific, quasi-scientific forms of knowledge and attitudes, this form of expertise is characterized by enclosure, by denying the possibility of direct access to seeing the future. The impersonal authority of manuals is forced to coexist with the group-specific authority of expert knowledge, which cannot be acquired from manuals (except for situations where the manual becomes a vehicle for a specific, acknowledged authorial voice). This tension characterizes financial knowledge up to our days: the promise of accessibility by learning, expressed in the tenet that everybody can learn to play the market, is paired with the claim that financial knowledge is enclosed within the expert domain.

A possible answer should be sought in the emergence of this expert domain and the group associated with it. Before examining this, however, a brief theoretical reflection appears useful. Several arguments have been made with respect to the emergence of financial analysts. A first argument is functionalist; according to it, analysts are necessary for "digesting the large corpus of information" required by regulators (e.g., in the Securities Exchange Act of 1933/1934) and generated by modern stock exchanges (Fogarty and Rogers 2005, p. 337; Bruce 2002). Financial analysts constitute themselves as a quasi-professional group, marked by internal differentiation, and sharing with academic economic theory a set of core assumptions about economic value (Fogarty and Rogers 2005, pp. 333–34). They classify, order, and process information with the aim of reducing uncertainties about value. Furthermore, it is directly assumed that fundamental value constitutes the most important piece of information with respect to market decisions; it is exactly because of this that it must be rendered calculable. Once this has been done, market actors can compare fundamental value with the price, and decide whether securities are over- or undervalued. In addition to developing a set of calculation procedures, analysts develop ceremonial structures which display their legitimate hold upon expert knowledge: professional associations, certifications, and meetings, among others. Thus, they confer legitimacy upon financial securities on the symbolic as well as on the operational level (e.g., Zuckerman 1999).

This account does not entirely fit the case of technical analysts or chartists, who emerge well before the Securities Exchange Act, are not concerned with value as the most fundamental piece of information, do not develop a quasi-professional structure from the outset, and do not share with academic economics a set of common theoretical assumptions about value (quite the contrary). In fact, technical analysts seem to be the exact opposite on each of these counts. Even if we admit that the stock ticker generated an increased volume of data, this does not answer the question why this particular form of expert knowledge emerged; there is no immediate relationship between more price data and chartists.

A second account can be produced starting from more general analyses of experts and professions. Since a profession is characterized first and foremost by integration in a system of jurisdictions over domains of expert knowledge—that is, in a system of legitimate claims over exclusive rights (Abbott 1988, p. 59), it would follow that analysts emerge as a profession by establishing and successfully defending their claim to a body of knowledge, both with respect to competing professions, like financial economists, and to users. They would then develop institutional arrangements different from those of competing professionals (e.g., their own organizations, accreditation procedures, conferences, and the like), and would monopolize a specific set of occupations (e.g., in investment banks and brokerage houses). While the existence of a professional group does not necessarily imply its formal professional organization from the start, the social organization of a profession has three major aspects: groups, controls, and worksites (Abbott 1988, p. 79). Before formal professional organization takes place, a group can establish jurisdiction over the expert knowledge it produces.

In this account, the emergence and establishment of a body of expert knowledge is tied to that of quasi-closed groups and their worksites, whereas professional organization can occur later. Chartism as a particular set of theoretical statements and methods for analyzing financial markets could thus be asynchronous with the evolution of institutional arrangements like professional associations, courses and seminars, or examinations. The emergence and evolution of technical analysis shows that the two aspects are asynchronous indeed: the theoretical tenets and methods of chartism emerge around 1900, whereas the first professional associations, institutionalized teaching, and professional degrees appear around 1970. We encounter then a long period during which this body of expertise successfully works in the absence of professional or quasi-professional structures. What remains to be explained, however, is how this form of expert financial knowledge emerges, how workplaces and tools are constituted, and how expert groups establish themselves. In other words, an account of the constitutions of jurisdiction should include and start from the content of this expert knowledge and its generation.

A third account aiming to include this content comes from the sociology of science. It examines not only how jurisdiction is established, but also how specific contents are used in particular settings by actors with specific aims and agendas. The general argument is that economic theories are not mere representations, but tools of active intervention (e.g., Barry and Slater 2002b; Callon 1998, 2004; MacKenzie and Millo 2003). This emphasizes the agential force of economic technologies (including theories and classifications), which allow market actors to calculate paths of future action and to process thus transaction-relevant uncertainties. Financial analysts coordinate classifications, analogies, and metrics which, taken together, make value calculable (Beunza and Garud 2007, p. 34). By being made calculable, financial securities are also invested with legitimacy.

In this perspective, technical analysts create an instrument (i.e., a theory) which is used by market actors to process uncertainties irrespective of the theory's capacity to withstand empirical tests. In the process of using the theory as an uncertainty-processing instrument, new entities are created, corresponding to the theory's representations. In other words, the theory represents things or states which have been created in the process of its use. This is ante hoc, not post hoc, representation. What counts most then is not the theory's representational force, but its power to create these entities. If we accept this argument, it follows that performance (i.e., the instrumental character of the theory) is logically prior to representation. Applied to the case of chartists, it would follow that technical analysis is a calculation instrument, with the help of which transaction partners process data-related uncertainties, by producing more entities (price data) which fit the prediction. If we reduce technical analysis to calculation, we would have then to explain how this mode of calculation remains stable while at odds with other modes of calculation like financial economics. Besides, we would have to investigate first whether technical analysis is indeed a mode of calculation. It should be noted here that technical analysis does not calculate future prices in a way analogous with that of the Black-Merton-Scholes formula. It is rather a tool of prediction than one of computation.

These accounts of how expert financial knowledge and experts emerge alternatively focus on the emergence of expert groups or of knowledge, without entirely managing to bring the two together. An attempt to solve this problem will have, at least in the present situation, to start from the role of expert knowledge in the constitution of the boundaries of finance.

Expertise and the Boundaries of Finance

My overall argument has been that these boundaries are generated in the process of legitimating stock exchanges as socially closed yet valid and accessible institutions. This process requires producing witnessable forms of financial knowledge, which can lay a claim to general validity. This means not only that the entity called the market must be made visible to observers, but also that this has to occur in a form invested with authority. Authority, in its turn, requires that market processes and trends are witnessed and revealed as true or "authentic" to participants. This necessitates a technology generating appropriate data and integrated in the social enclosure of stock exchanges.

This technology, which visualizes the temporal structures of market exchanges, makes price data transferable across various contexts. At the same time, being integrated in the social enclosure of the exchange, with access and user restrictions, price data requires proper witnessing, irreducible to the mere observation of ink dots on the paper strip. Data witnessing here means bringing testimony of them as reliable, durable representations of stock exchange transactions. Since ticker-generated price data represent transactions on the stock exchange, witnessing data means witnessing transactions, without having been on the floor of the exchange at the moment when these took place. This requires a body of specialized knowledge which can reconstitute social interactions, groups, and movements on the exchange from the flow of price data on the ticker tape. Capacity to witness means capacity to reconstruct in a reliable fashion the movement of actors from the movement of prices, and represent this movement of actors to the public. This enterprise is irreducible to a simple narrative of what has happened on the floor of the exchange. Such an analytical capacity is grounded in methods, tools, principles, and experience—that is, in a corpus of expert knowledge which becomes repeatable itself.

The validity of analytical methods and principles is inextricably tied to the validity of the field of expertise (Gross and Mnookin 2003, pp. 146–47), but where does the validity of interpreting price movements as a field of expertise come from? In the first place, from the fact that such movements are taken to be representations of transactions which cannot be directly accessed by external observers. The social closure of the stock exchange makes transactions nonobservable, except via price data, a sort of witnessing which further reinforces enclosure. Expertise at witnessing the market needs to be enclosed and invested with charismatic features, like prestige, its own invented tradition, and special abilities. In a way analogous to that in which the social closure of the stock exchange required representing brokers as endowed with charismatic features (good citizens, honourable, charitable, etc.), the enclosure of expertise implies representing experts as possessing attributes others do not have: special powers of concentration, attention, inquisitiveness, and the like. As a general principle, the social closure of stock exchanges includes privileged witnessing. A new status group would thus crystallize: some brokers and clerks would turn to fashioning expertise. This differentiation in status means that expert witnessing can be made into a commodity and sold to brokers and investors, leading to the emergence of firms specialized in selling this expertise.

This authority of expert knowledge is tied to persuasion devices and to the ability of enclosing a specific domain (Turner 2003, pp. 49–50). What counts, then, is the group's successful, legitimate monopolization of a domain of knowledge rather than it responding to a functional need of that domain. This monopolization requires control over access to knowledge production, but also the successful persuasion of users that they need a special form of knowledge in their activities. It requires a reciprocal tuning of the interests of user and producer groups, but also a tuning of users' interests to the expert knowledge which they acquire.

Bought and sold expert knowledge coexists then in tension with the argument (propagated in investment manuals) that financial activities can be accessed only through special forms of knowledge. Everybody can acquire financial knowledge (together with the necessary scientific attitudes), but not everybody can witness market transactions. Hence, this knowledge is incomplete without authoritative market testimonials, which remain the privilege of a closed group. The closure induced by the charismatic features of expertise (the access to which is no way equal) undermines claims about equal participatory opportunities.

In the account I suggest here, financial expertise emerges neither as a response to functional needs, nor as a pure instrument used to achieve group interests or as the establishment of a jurisdiction disconnected from knowledge contents. Expertise emerges as intrinsic to the boundaries of finance, which require that visualizations of time structures (price data generated by a specific technology), to which market actors react, be witnessed by and revealed to participants as representations of market transactions. The work of witnessing is constituted around a closed set of tools and methods; it implies the constitution of a specialized group (analysts) who reconstruct, explain, and forecast the market starting from price data. The validity of this field of expertise is ensured by (a) transactions on the exchange floor being closed to outside observers and (b) the analysts' claim of being able to access these transactions using specific tools and methods of observation and processing. (The claim about future price movements depending on past movements, made by technical analysts, is rather a corollary of witnessability.) Based on the claim that "the market" can be observed/witnessed with the help of the chart, technical analysis emerges as one of the first specific bodies of financial market expertise able to develop a quasi-professional structure. With this argument, I will turn to showing how a particular group established chartism as expert knowledge, persuading brokers and investors alike that it was indispensable.

The Constitution of an Expert Group

In the pre-ticker era, as well as in the first two decades after its introduction, information-processing employees had a marginal position in banks and brokerage houses. Tape readers were employed on the floor of the

exchange and in brokerage houses; their tasks, however, were not to interpret price data, but to extract specific data from the flow of the ticker
tape and to assemble price charts and tables for a specific security or group
of securities. Their expertise, therefore, consisted mostly in haptic, ocular,
and mnemonic skills rather than in a body of methods enabling data interpretation. While some brokerages employed statistically trained clerks,
gathering and processing data was mixed with menial clerk jobs. Some
banks did not employ professional statisticians at all, but required clerks
to gather statistical data in addition to other tasks. Overall, gathering and
processing financial data was not ranked high in the hierarchy of brokerage houses:

> Every city bank, investment house, and Stock Exchange firm had a "statisti-
> cian," who ranged all the way from office boy to one of the partners. Some of
> these statisticians had been salesmen on the side, as was my case. None of them
> was especially interested in his work. There was much duplication of effort.
> (Babson 1935, p. 134)

And,

> Little or no attention was paid to the statistical side—unearthing opportunities
> or trading in a scientific way. In fact, this seemed to be the rule throughout the
> Street. For every one who considered the statistical side of securities, there
> were twenty trading on tips. (Wyckoff 1930, pp. 52–53)

Reacting against the low status of information-processing employees
in brokerage houses, against attempts by brokers to control evaluations,
as well as against restrictions and controls (e.g., the ban on advertising), a
group of actors created an autonomous body of expert knowledge which
could be fenced off and marketed to investors and speculators. Around
1900, a group of stock brokers active on the East Coast reoriented themselves toward producing and distributing expert knowledge about price
movements. Initially, some of these brokers saw a business opportunity in
compiling statistics and information about bonds, selling this information
to banks.[6] They noticed the errors and unreliable character of the statistics
supplied by brokerage houses and began to produce their own statistics.
An example in this sense is Richard Demille Wyckoff, who started studying statistics in the 1880s (Wyckoff 1930, p. 27).[7] Another example is Roger
Ward Babson, who studied engineering and business at MIT in the 1890s,

graduated, worked for a brokerage house in Boston, and in 1904 founded the Babson Statistical Organization (Babson 1935, pp. 53, 76).

In his memoirs, Wyckoff wrote that he decided to abandon brokerage and switch to analysis because as a broker he could not find time for the study of the market (1930, p. 117). In Roger Babson's account, what inspired him to switch to data compiling and analysis was a lecture given by Booker T. Washington about his social experiments at Tuskegee.[8] Babson adopted Washington's emphasis on the division of labor and combined it with the insight that data compilers had a shaky status in banks and brokerage houses. He decided then to get out of brokerage and specialize in data compiling and analysis as a separate line of business (Babson 1935, pp. 133–34). In both accounts, there is a stress put on the special status of financial knowledge: theory requires contemplation, not action (Wyckoff) and is not given due respect by brokers (Babson). Therefore, the production of theory has to be separated from its use, yet remain related to it.

While initially working in brokerage offices, Wyckoff and Babson soon turned to the analysis of securities prices and ceased to conduct financial transactions. They did this at first independently of each other, but got in contact and, together with others, established themselves as experts in the analysis and interpretation of price data. Around 1900, Wyckoff worked as a stock broker for the firm of Price, McCormick & Co., where he was also in charge of gathering information on stocks and writing a newsletter for customers (1930, p. 95). He tried to develop brokerage by mail, but was prevented both by the firm's owners and by the restrictions put in place by the New York Stock Exchange on advertising done by brokers.[9] He left and founded his own brokerage firm in 1903; four years later, he shifted entirely to publishing investment advice literature. In October 1907, he started the *Ticker* magazine, where the first technical analyses appeared. The first issues of the *Ticker* were a mixture of gossip about famous investors, investment advice, and technical analyses (primitive compared with the ones we encounter today) (Wyckoff 1930, p. 159). In the beginning, the *Ticker* was a one-man show, with Wyckoff writing all the gossip articles (a task for which he was well-positioned) and compiling all the statistics. In 1910, Richard Wyckoff (under the pseudonym Rollo Tape) published *Studies in Tape Reading*, which used some of the core concepts of technical analysis (Tape 1910). By 1917, however, Wyckoff had managed to enrol as contributors both other chartists and known speculators, who could confirm chartism as the best method available (Wyckoff 1930, p. 219).

One of the chartists who published articles in the *Ticker* was Roger Ward Babson. In the beginning, Babson's firm indexed the circulars of bond offerings and sold this monthly information to brokerage houses. He won Boston's brokerage houses, as well as houses from New York, Chicago, Cleveland, Detroit, and Saint Louis, as his customers. (Babson had met Wyckoff on an advertising trip to New York.) He then sold this information service to Arthur B. Elliott, the founder of the National Quotation Bureau (Babson 1935, p. 138). The National Quotation Bureau (NQB), founded in 1911, compiled price and volume data from various brokerage offices active in the over-the-counter market (the Pink Sheets). In other words, the NQB service circumvented the monopoly of the Western Telegraph and of NYSE on price data and bundled together price data coming from smaller exchanges and offices which were not members of the NYSE.

After selling the bond information newsletter, Babson started another information service, collecting and compiling data on stock earnings. This information was sold to banks and brokerage offices alike. Shortly thereafter, Babson added evaluations to this newsletter, but met with resistance from banks and brokers whenever he issued critical evaluations of stock (Babson 1935, p. 139). Since the income on this service fluctuated according to how stocks were evaluated, Babson abandoned it. In 1907, he bought the Moody Manual Company from his friend John Moody. The Moody Manual Company compiled information on the earnings and stock prices of listed stock companies. In 1907, Babson started the *Babson Reports*, which introduced the Babsonchart. He also sold the Babson Desk Chart, and the Babson Desk Sheet, which provided customers with handy visualizations of price data variations.

Relevant here is the fact that these former brokers and information providers knew each other and acted as a group: Babson published articles in a magazine edited by Wyckoff. John Moody was a friend of Babson and sold him the Moody Manual Company. In the 1920s, Wyckoff's associate editor at the *Ticker*, George Selden, published books promoting technical analysis as the true method of forecasting the market (Selden 1922). Another acquaintance of Wyckoff, Samuel Armstrong Nelson, republished in 1902 Charles Dow's articles from the *Wall Street Journal* (Nelson 1902, chaps. 7–20).[10] Wyckoff republished the articles in 1920 in the *Magazine of Wall Street* (heir to the *Ticker*), with a preface by Selden, under the title *Scientific Stock Speculation*. In his articles and memoirs, Wyckoff systematically promoted Charles Dow as the man on whose ideas technical analysis is based.

This group compiled, published, analyzed, and sold financial data through specialized companies. Babson did this with his Babson Statistical Company, co-owned with his wife. Wyckoff followed him in 1920 with the Richard D. Wyckoff Analytical Staff, Inc. Subscription to its services cost $1,000 per year. The company provided a Trend Trading Service, an Analytical Staff Service, and an Investors' Advisory Board (Wyckoff 1930, p. 249). While Wyckoff sold both to brokerage houses and the investing public, Babson sold exclusively to brokerage houses and banks. Wyckoff, for example, had in 1911 an exclusive contract for technical analysis with Thompson, Towle &Co, but he also sold the *Ticker* to the general public (Wyckoff 1930, p. 188). The group also actively sought contact with brokerage houses. Wyckoff was frustrated that, as a broker, he was not allowed to advertise on a large scale (e.g., by sending circulars). Initially, Babson sold his newsletter door-to-door to brokerage houses. At least some of the group members had brokerage experience: Wyckoff and Babson were former brokers, and John Moody worked for a brokerage house in New York. Wyckoff systematically enrolled known speculators (with whom he was friends) as contributors to his magazine, for confirming, from the viewpoint of practice, the adequacy of technical analysis.

In the 1930s, technical analysis became firmly established, with several organizations selling it as a product to brokerage houses, and several publications (books, magazines) promoting it to investors. The use of the typewriter and of the mimeograph made it easier to publish and distribute chartist books on a larger scale. Thus, at least the following books were published in the 1930s as mimeographs: Orline Norman Foster's *Ticker Technique* (New York, 1935); D. W. McGeorge's *Tacking in the Stock Market* (Oakmont, PA, 1934); Meyer H. Weinstein's *The Real Boom in the Stock Market Is Here* (New York, 1936). In addition to them, there were at least the printed books of Wyckoff (*Studies in Tape Reading*, 1910), Babson (*The Future Method of Investing Money. Economic Facts for Corporations and Investors,* Boston, 1914), and William D. Gann (*Truth of the Stock Tape,* New York, 1923; *Wall Street Stock Selector,* New York, 1930). Authors like Weinstein and Gann worked for firms like the Financial Information Company (Weinstein) and the Financial Guardian (Gann). By the 1930s, there was already a body of chartist literature available to investors and brokerage firms, and this literature was at least in part published by firms specialized in the collection and interpretation of financial price data.

The Invention of a Chartist Tradition

The constitution of financial expertise implied not only relationships among practitioners and the founding of specialized firms and publications, but also the emergence of charismatic features which should mark the group's closure. Prominent among these features was the invention of its own tradition and the search for intellectual forerunners, who were enlisted from at least three directions: prominent figures from the world of finance; figures from the world of science; and "rediscovered theorists." As mentioned above, financial chartists created their own figure of a founding father in the person of Charles Dow. Dow, who had died in 1902, was the editor of the *Wall Street Journal*. His only publications consisted in editorial pieces giving general investment advice and outlining general principles of prudent financial investments. He did not produce a systematic theory; rather, his aim was to outline the general lines of reasoning which should be followed when observing the market. Richard Wyckoff, George Selden, and Samuel Armstrong Nelson republished these articles and represented financial chartism as following the general lines of reasoning formulated by Charles Dow. Accordingly, there are three general lines of reasoning in the market: (1) surface appearances are deceptive, (2) cut losses short and let profits run, and (3) correctly discounting the future is the road to wealth. The market has three kinds of overlapping movements: (a) day-to-day; (b) the short swing, running from two weeks to a month; (c) and long time movements of four years or more (Nelson 1902, pp. 36, 39). Applying the general lines of reasoning to these three movements (which should be studied with specific methods) will ensure financial success. Moreover, according to the way in which the general principles are applied to market movements, several methods of trading and types of traders can be distinguished, with different consequences (Nelson 1902, pp. 58, 65).

Academic support was mobilized too. Roger Babson mentions in his memoirs that he discovered the "Babson line" (a.k.a. the trend line) together with Professor George E. Swain from the MIT. This discovery was presented as grounded in Newton's "Law of Action and Reaction," which "may apply to economics as it does to physics, chemistry, astronomy, and other fields" (Babson 1935, p. 147). In Babson's interpretation, this law stated that "after a depression area, equal in area to the preceding area of prosperity, had developed, another period of prosperity would be due" (Babson 1935, pp. 147–48). The "law of action and reaction" was discussed in Dow's articles too, which defined it as "a primary movement in the market will generally have a secondary movement in the opposite direction of at least three eighths of the primary movement" (Nelson 1902, p. 43).

Concomitantly, chartists sought to "rediscover" publications as a support for their principles and methods. Babson (1935, p. 146) was influenced in his thinking by *Benner's Prophecies of Futures Ups and Downs in Prices* (Benner 1876) and *How Money Is Made in Security Investments* (Hall 1908).[11] Benner, who signed as "an Ohio farmer," considered that future prices of commodities could be predicted, although not on the grounds of agricultural statistics, which were unreliable (Benner 1876, p. 23). Instead of statistics, price prophecies should be founded on the following ideas: (1) prices are exponents of "accumulated wisdom"; (2) ups and downs of prices are repeated in cycles; and (3) extreme ups and downs alternate: "An up and down or down and up in average prices, is in this book denominated a cycle. . . . And inside this rule, like a wheel within a wheel, is to be found our 'Cast iron rule,' which is that *one extreme invariably follows another*, as can be witnessed in all the operations of nature, in all the business affairs of man, and in all the ramifications of trade and industry; and in every cycle of average prices it is shown to what extent these extremes run" (Benner 1876, p. 27).[12] Benner, who did not purport to provide the reader with any explanation of why cycles happen, stated that "we will risk our reputation as a prophet, and our chances for success in business upon our 11 year cycle in corn and hogs; in 27 year cycle in pig iron, and in our 54 year cycle in general trade, upon which we have operated with success in the past" (Benner 1876, p. 122).

Benner's notion of cycles,[13] similar to those of "the law of action and reaction" and of "market swings," expressed what intuition and experience had shown most traders and investors: prices go up and down. Yet, this seemingly trivial notion of ups and downs was formulated as a lawlike repeatability, one which cannot be revealed from the study of unreliable statistics about production. The distrust toward what could be called "fundamental" data was corroborated with the chartists' own observations about the low prestige of statistical work in brokerage firms. This rhetoric of tradition combined three distinct kinds of voices, with different authorities: that of practical experience and commonsense (the "Ohio farmer"), that of natural science (the MIT professor), and that of prestigious finance itself (Charles Dow). With all the potential public appeal of this combination, such an invented tradition could not have led by itself to the constitution of a body of expert financial knowledge. In this respect, a major task was persuading the public and, above all, the potential users in brokerage offices that this sort of knowledge required special abilities.

The Configuration of Users

Through its relationship with brokerage houses and known speculators, this group strived to generate an interest in using the tools and the interpretive methods they promoted. Chartists managed to enlist the support of well-known speculators for their theories. Known speculators like J. W. Harriman, Frank A. Vanderlip, and Theodore E. Burton published articles in the *Ticker*, supporting the theories promoted by Wyckoff as an editor (Wyckoff 1930, p. 219). Successful speculation was represented as depending upon the cognitive tools promoted by this group, tools which could not be directly accessed by nonexperts. Some of the persuasion strategies employed in this respect were described by Richard Wyckoff in his memoirs:

> I had a friend who had been a member of the Exchange and who was well up on the technique of the market from the standpoint of the floor trader. We often discussed the difference between reading the tape simply to follow price changes (as most clients did) and reading the tape to judge the probable action of stocks in the immediate future. [. . .] This ideal tape operator should have no hopes or fears. He must play the game without a sign of nerves or mental strain; look upon profits or losses with equal equanimity. He must develop the kind of intuition that becomes a sixth sense in trading. Such an operator, we agreed, was generally evolved from a series of failures over many months or years; his education could be completed only through a long series of transactions, spread over long periods, which would perfect his operating personality into one that could play the game cold. He must have persistence to carry him through adverse times without discouragement, until his expertness and self-confidence match that of the surgeon who performs many operations, losing some patients but never losing his nerve. Such a man, with such a character and with that experience, should be a success at reading the tape. (Wyckoff 1930, pp. 168, 170)

True forecasting requires character; concomitantly, only experienced men, "operating personalities," can become successful tape readers. The analysis of price data was presented as appealing not only to the intellect, but to the entire personality of the trader. This analysis required the use of specialized machines (the ticker) and cognitive tools (the chart), which in their turn requested permanent attention and devotion, making thus necessary an early division of labor. The mass of recorded data was substantially higher compared to the pre-ticker period, when the price recording system was diffuse, unstable, and unreliable. Clerks employed as tape readers,[14] different from statistics compilers, had the task to extract data from the flow of the ticker tape and tabulate it. Theirs, however, was an activity grounded in tacit skills. Compiling price data in near real time required attention, concentration, and exclusive dedication, which stock brokers and speculators could simply not afford to invest in this task. The division of labor between compiling and using price data was tied to the need of interpreting data in a way adequate to its continuous and massive character, and by specialized actors. Market judgment was reconceptualized as distinct from yet tied to market action. Those involved in decision making and market action had neither the time nor the attention and concentration necessary for judging the market:

> A broker's time is so occupied with the routine of the business that he is rarely able to devote sufficient time to the study and analysis of the stock market. Few people—stock brokers or others—are mentally equipped for the difficult work of forecasting price movements on the Stock Exchange and selecting the stocks that will yield more profits than losses to those who make commitments. Almost anyone with some years of experience in Wall Street can be correct in his judgment from time to time; but the problem is to be correct *most* of the time. (Wyckoff 1930, p. 116, italics in original)

A complementary line of argument was that expert knowledge provided protection to users, a protection which cannot be offered by brokers. Selling securities is grounded in a set of specific interests, which do not always overlap with the users' own perspective. Lack of knowledge makes these latter vulnerable; their interests have to be therefore championed by experts. Conversely, this championing of user interests requires the withdrawal of the expert from speculative activities and the transformation of expertise into a commodity:

> Mrs. Babson and I then burned all bridges behind us and determined to devote the rest of our lives to selling pure protection, first the protection of capital and income. At this point my father took me once more on a buggy ride. Said he: "If you are to be free to give unbiased advice, you must not borrow, indorse, or go

on bond." I am proud to say that thus far we have followed my father's advice
to the letter. Since *Babson's Reports* were started, neither one of us has ever
borrowed a dollar, and I have never lent a dollar to an individual. Those giving
advice should never become involved with the borrowing or lending money or
in speculation of any kind. (Babson 1935, p. 143)

At about the same time, in the *Ticker* magazine, Richard Wyckoff
loudly requested the establishment of the stock analyst as a distinct profession, one whose purpose was to ensure the impartial distribution of
meaningful information to investors and help them make their decisions.
A stock analyst would be on the same plane as a physician who recom-
mends a medicine solely on its curative merits; he "would have to stand
on a plane with George Washington and Caesar's wife. He must have no
connection with any bond house or brokerage establishment, and must
permit nothing whatever to, in any way, warp his judgment. He must know
all securities and keep actual records of earnings and statistics which show
not only whether a security is safe, but whether it is advancing or declining
in point of safety" (Wyckoff [signed anonymous] 1908, p. 35).

With an intellectual tradition to support it, a group of converted brokers as active supporters, and the users persuaded that they were buying
protection, chart analysts became an established presence in brokerage
offices, as well as in investor magazines:

> There was a chart-fiend in our office—a wise-looking party, who traveled about
> with a chart book under his arm, jotting down fluctuations, and disposing in an
> authoritative way, of all questions relating to "new tops," "double bottoms,"
> etc. Now, whatever may be claimed for or brought against stock market charts,
> I'll say this in their favor, they do unquestionably show when accumulation and
> distribution of stocks is in progress. So I asked my expert friend to let me see his
> "fluctuation pictures," my thought being that no bull market could take place
> till the big insiders had taken on their lines of stock. Sure enough, the charts
> showed, unmistakably, that accumulation had been going on at the very bottom.
> (Wyckoff 1907, pp. 2, 4)

Building up a following also meant controlling the distribution of this
expert knowledge and making it more difficult to access. The social closure of expertise implied, among other things a careful control of the charismatic features associated with the personality of the analyst: a system of
"star analysts" implied that not everyone could get access to their advice:

I had been often told that I had a personal following larger than that of any individual in Wall Street since the days of Governor Flower in the 'nineties. But I was not proud, or boastful of this. I was more cautious in every move, more concerned as to the final result. I did not seek or desire such a following; I dreaded it. [. . .] Rather than have my name on everyone's lips, I preferred not to be recognized. It better suited my plans to restrict those who acted on my advice to subscribers only, and not too many of these. I wished my advisory business to proceed in a sane, orderly and healthy manner, with no excitement and no effect on the stock market. (Wyckoff 1930, p. 217)

Wyckoff's account highlights two apparently contradictory themes, which complement and amplify each other in the culture of star analysts prominent in the late 1990s: cult status and inaccessibility, public presence and distance from the public (as exposed, for instance, in the contradictory public and private pronouncements about the value of stocks).

Users were configured as depending upon a body of specialized knowledge which they cannot obtain by themselves, and as needing experts in the interpretation of price movements, the mere existence of whom appears as a moral guarantee of unbiased judgment. At the same time, the technological apparatuses on which this knowledge depends (stock ticker, charts) are represented as requiring special skills and powers of interpretation, which brokers, being too busy, have not fully developed. In other words, this expert discourse claimed an epistemic monopoly over the observational apparatus, and declared the validity of user judgment to be contingent upon their services. Purchasing expert knowledge from producers was seen as conferring legitimacy upon brokers and speculators alike.

Forecasting the Market

Surely, experienced brokers and speculators would not have adopted technical analysis just on the basis of skilful exhortations. Chartists claimed that ticker-generated price data, together with price charts, helped explain and forecast price movements. One reason for the attractiveness of technical analysis as an explanatory tool lay in the changed conditions under which such movements could be explained. During most of the nineteenth century, the changes in price data were explained with reference to political and economic events, which were considered to be the causal factors of price movements. This explanatory frame worked well with discontinuous data: one could explain the price data from, say, April 14, 1865, as being caused by the assassination of Abraham Lincoln. The frame, however, didn't work well with continuous variations in price data, which showed price movements in the absence of any grand political and economic events. A solution then was not to look anymore for exogenous explicative factors, but to make the market itself into an explanation: price movements should become explainable on the grounds of market events themselves. The processing of market events into explanatory factors, however, required at least a twofold operation: representing events in terms of the concrete actions of market actors, while not reducing these actions to individual psychologies and particular interests; and making these events observable on the grounds of price data.

After the introduction of the stock ticker, the exchange floor was closed to observers, who could only sit in the visitors' gallery, a position which did not allow them to closely monitor transactions. Even without this spatial enclosure, the limited capacity of direct human observation would have allowed witnessing some transactions, but not all transactions at the same time. Therefore, an instrument of observation was needed, one which could allow observers see at once and from afar all transactions in a security or group of securities. These transactions, however, were represented by price data; therefore, seeing price data variations at once meant seeing the respective transactions at once. This inference made daily, weekly, and monthly price charts into a nearly ideal instrument of market observation.

Initially, tape reading and chart analysis were distinct procedures: tape readers had to sit by the ticker and watch the flow of prices together with others, whereas chart analysts could work alone. Tape readers were seen as listeners to the authoritative voice of the tape; however, understanding them as passive obscured the proactive character of expertise, and diminished their authority:

> The most expert type of tape-reader carries no memorandums, and seldom refers to fluctuation records. The tape whispers to him, talks to him, and, as Mr. Lawson puts it, "screams" at him. Every one is not fitted to become an expert tape-reader, any more than in the musical world can every one be a Paderewski. The greatest difficulty of the tape-reader is that he becomes so sensitive from working close to the tape, that his judgment is rendered narrow. (Wyckoff [as Rollo Tape] 1908, p. 34)

The chart, by contrast, allows a more active attitude: one can make his own charts from tables of sales, and the detection of manipulation is made easier (Wyckoff [as Rollo Tape]1908, p. 35). While tape reading allowed social interactions and incorporated opinions and gossip into the end re-sult, chart analysis relied exclusively on the observation of price varia-tions. Soon enough, it was argued that social interactions and gossip are rather damaging both to the analysis and to the traders' decisions, because reasoning is tainted by subjective opinions. Instead of sitting by the ticker, the tape can be read from afar:

> Then it is *necessary* to *know how* to *read* the *tape without seeing it*, or without watching it all the time. Market movements of importance, i.e., the long swings, require weeks and sometimes months to get ready, or for accumulation and dis-tribution to be completed. [. . .] Therefore it is not necessary to watch the tape every day, or every hour, in order to determine what stocks are going to do. [. . .] While this process is going on, you can keep up a chart of the stock you are interested in and judge much better when the big move starts, than you can by *watching* the *ticker every day*. (Gann 1923, pp. 6–7; emphasis in original)

Reading without seeing, witnessing without being there, required spe-cialization and dedication. The tape, however, could become too close to the observer; consequently, other tools were needed as well, tools with the help of which things could be seen from a distance: "The man who tests everything by the tape is one who examines phenomena through a micro-scope; while one who investigates international economic and political conditions is like one who looks through a telescope" (Pratt [1903] 1912, p. 237).

Commentators saw the price chart as "the bird's eye view of the stock market" (Pratt 1903, p. 138). "Reading charts is like reading music, in which you endeavor to interpret correctly the composer's ideas and the expression of his art. Just so a chart of the averages, or of a single stock, reflects the ideas, hopes, ambitions and purposes of the mass mind oper-ating in the market, or of a manipulator handling a single stock" (Wyck-off 1934a, p. 10). The ticker tape is "the recorded history of the market" (Wyckoff 1934f, p. 16). It is the resultant force of fundamental statistics, economic changes, and political developments (Wyckoff 1934d, p. 12) and requires a type of analysis fundamentally different from statistics (1934c, p. 23). The chart was the market, as well as the means of understanding the market as one collective being with a mind of its own: "Another way was to look at the market as if all of the transactions were made by one person. I called this person the *composite operator*. The successful trader must endeavor to ascertain what is in the back of the head of that fellow and to anticipate his moves" (Wyckoff 1930, p. 177; emphasis in original).

While the chart contributes to understanding the market as an entity of its own, observing price variations also means witnessing interactions, being on the trading floor without physical presence, as if a clairvoyant:

> The *Studies* represented a person studying the tape under the suggested plan as one looking upon a large room where a social gathering is being held. At first glance one would be merely seeing a lot of people; closer observation would disclose some individual traits. But by going in and mingling with them, the student would be able to detect many of their personal qualities—their hopes, wishes, desires; their habits, their weak and strong points; their probable actions under certain conditions. (Wyckoff 1930, p. 176; emphasis in original)

And,

> Stocks are no different than human beings—they have their peculiar habits and moves. It's just as easy to tell what a stock will do by getting acquainted with it and watching its moves over a long period of time, as it is to tell what a human being will do under certain conditions after you have known him for many years. (Gann 1923, p. 59)

Such a disembodied witnessing required a new language, which should summarize the actions observed in price movements in a few words. The new financial charts—unlike the older ones—came with their own metaphorical luggage and discursive modes: there were now "double bottoms," "tops," and "shoulders" to enrich the analyst's arsenal. As Wyckoff wrote, "I found myself obliged to invent terms that more clearly described the various phases. One of these was 'point of resistance'—a term which has since been widely used as indicating the level where, at the end of a decline, the buying power at length begins to overcome the selling, or the level where, after a rise, the selling begins to balance the buying" (1930, p. 178). In a manner appropriate for observation from afar, this analytical language is full of visual metaphors: we do not need any references to the bricks, furnaces, tracks, and machinery of stock companies any more. Price variations suffice. Discursive modes supported the chart as a cognitive instrument, which in its turn conferred authority upon the stock analyst as the only one skilled enough to discover the truth of the market in the dotted lines.

Analysts began refining the charts and adapting them more and more to the witnessing process. Roger Babson, for instance, introduced the "Normal Line" (known today as the "trend line"), which he concocted in discussions with Professor George E. Swain, the head of the civil engineering program at MIT. His technique consisted in plotting price variations on a chart, and then drawing a line through the sinusoidal curve in such a way that each area above the line approximately equalled the immediately following area below the line. Babson called this the "area theory," according to which cycles of prosperity and depression are represented by similar surfaces on the chart (1935, pp. 147–48). According to Babson himself, the Normal Line could be located only after the cycle had come to a close, while the sizes of prosperity and depression areas could only be calculated after the Normal Line had been drawn (1935, p. 148). This sort of circularity, however, did not prevent Babson from claiming that his area method could forecast business cycles and therefore when to buy and when to sell:

> The Law of Action and Reaction is assumed in making the areas equal in order to fix the Normal Line; but the Normal Line is always carried along in the same general direction. This enables business men and investors very closely to forecast how long a period of depression will last. By this trial-and-error method one continually approaches a closer and closer forecast, until the dotted line can finally be changed to a permanent line. (Babson 1935, p. 150; emphasis in original)

There are three kinds of stock market movements, each corresponding to a class of investors. Daily fluctuations cannot be foretold in any way and have no relations to the intrinsic value of the securities traded. The class of gamblers corresponds to this movement. The second kind is given by "broad breaks and rallies of from five to ten points, extending over a few weeks." These are due to the "impatience and avariciousness" of professional traders. Finally, there are the "long swings extending over one or more years." To these corresponds the class of "those with money and the courage of their convictions" (Babson 1914, pp. 13–18).

Babson's area theory was echoed later by William Gann's distinction among seven zones of market activity, equally situated above or below the "Normal Zone" (which was in fact a line) (Gann 1923, pp. 55–57). The "normal zone" corresponds to "something near actual intrinsic value, as far as human judgment can be depended upon and as far as the ticker tape can analyze it from supply and demand." Then there is the "First Zone above Normal," corresponding to periods of rapidly advancing prices. The "Second Zone above Normal" means active pools of speculators who try to get the public interested in the market. The "Third Zone or highest above Normal" corresponds to the public buying madly and will end in rapid and violent fluctuations, followed by a fall to the zones below normal. The "First Zone below Normal" is the one when people who have missed the third stage above normal sell out. The "Second Zone below Normal" is the one where conservative investors become active. Finally, the "Third Zone below Normal" is marked by panic, "great excitement throughout the country and reports of poor business." While the "normal zone" is something rather abstract, all the others are dominated by a certain class of market actors.

The notion of cyclical price movements, together with that of zones of activity, supported the argument that (1) patterns of price variations are repeatable and (2) these patterns repeat themselves in repeatable situations, grounding thus the claim that chart analysis can forecast price movements:

> A lot of people say that charts are of no value in determining the future; that they simply represent past history. That is correct; they are records of the past, but the future is nothing but a repetition of the past. Every business man goes on the past record of business in determining how to buy goods for the future. He can only judge by comparison with past records. We look up the record of a man, and if his past record has been good, we judge that his future will be good. (Gann 1923, p. 51)

Claims of forecasting price movements had been made before in the popular investment literature. These claims, however, were mostly tied to idiosyncratic knowledge of the "market conditions"—that is, of the specific coalitions of speculators at work in the market at a given time, of their ties with politics, of their interests, and the like. By contrast, technical analysis did not rely on knowledge of specific, historically contingent coalitions of interests. It claimed that there are repeatable patterns of such forces, and repeatable reactions to them.[15] These reactions are psychosocial in nature and follow general rules. Regular patterns are fully reflected in patterns of price movements. As Wyckoff put it, "the market is mental":

The market is made by the minds of many men. The state of these minds is reflected in the prices of securities in which their owners operate. Let us examine some of the individuals, as well as the influences behind certain stocks and groups of stocks in their various relationships. This will, in a sense, enable us to measure their respective power to affect the whole list or the specific issue in which we decide to operate. (Tape 1910, p. 38)

The classification of the "market" in specific zones of action arranged around an ideal of normality produced a vernacular sociology of economic actions, grounded in knowledge about classes of market actors: it included a typology, knowledge about what these classes do in certain situations, how they react to events, and the like. At the same time, the knowledge crystallized in this theory is also the knowledge used by market actors in their actions. Knowledge about panic in the "Third Zone below Normal" is also knowledge used in panics happening in this zone. Seen from this perspective, forecasting market movements, as technical analysis claims to do, is grounded in witnessing the actions of the market actors starting from the observation of price movements. In achieving this, technical analysis appears not only as a gloss on market actions (i.e., an interpretation of this latter), but also as a formulation of the social order of the market (Garfinkel 2002). As a formulation of what is going on,[16] technical analysis is different from particular transactions, yet intrinsic to market action. In truly Durkheimian fashion, it contributes to the creation (by witnessing) of a collective entity called "the market," irreducible to individual transactions. In this sense, at the very bottom, its forecasting capacity consists in its account of the market as an orderly (i.e., repeatable) social phenomenon. By using technical charts, this account is integrated in the market action itself. What appears as dizzying price movements can be translated at any time into the language of classes of actors, of strategy patterns, and of emotions—that is, it can be made intelligible as an orderly social phenomenon. It is this intelligibility which is captured by the expert language of technical analysis.

This kind of forecasting implies prophesizing the past, a mode based on the assumption that events belong to knowable types and categories. It is the mode of Teiresias, the blind prophet of ancient Athens who could see in the future in spite of not being able to see the present. It relies on categories-based "anticipations of everyday life [which] will be [all] realized *modo potentiali*, as chances" (Schutz [1945] 2003, p. 260). Such anticipations are grounded in the assumption of the orderliness of social phenomena, subsumable to known types and categories. Teiresias saw the future which had already happened, a future contained in the same categories with which we judge the past. Similarly, chart analysis "sees" future price movements because they will comply with the categories, "zones," "phases," and "lines" which contribute to making the market a collective phenomenon, observable from afar.

This form of prophesy contributes to creating orderly phenomena, by legitimating and reproducing operational categories of order. In this perspective, technical analysis did something other forms of financial expertise could not do: it provided market actors with an account of "the market" as an orderly, totalizing phenomenon, which could not be derived from isolated, individual experiences (Durkheim [1915] 1965, p. 489). This account, based on observing and processing mechanically generated price data, did not come from outside the market, from ethnographers observing transactions (which could not even be observed in their totality), but from within, from market practitioners turned observers. It became intrinsic to the phenomenon of "the market," indispensable for traders and investors acting from the observation of abstract numbers.[17] Technical analysis created social categories (both actor and action types) which could be identified on price charts.

In this sense, it is perhaps more interesting to ask why technical analysis became so stable in spite of not creating the prices it attempted to forecast. Here, my answer is that as intrinsic to the financial boundaries of modern markets, technical analysis represented these latter to users as orderly, intelligible entities, without the users being able to (or in need of) directly access the totality of financial transactions supposed to constitute the market. Technical analysis endowed a group (the analysts) with powers of representation, contributing to the social closure of stock exchanges, yet reproducing the notion (if not illusion) of wider accessibility. Seen in a broader perspective, it is part of the process through which the power of representation, the authorial, authoritative voice about finance, is concentrated within specific groups tied to financial institutions.

This also helps elucidate how technical analysis survived and even flourished in spite of being at odds with financial economics. We should not forget here that, historically speaking, chartism was constituted as a body of expert knowledge before fundamental analysis emerged as a form of financial expertise in the 1930s, and before the main principles of financial economics were systematically elaborated in the 1950s and the 1960s. Once this power of representation became concentrated, it allowed for internal differentiations according to principles, methods, schools, and styles of analysis for a variety of groups gathering around different forms of expertise, competing with yet mutually supporting each other in this competition.

As intrinsic to the constitution of the boundaries of finance, expert voices of authority and the machine-supported generation of price data are irreducible to a relentless process of rationalization and depersonalization of financial transactions, of a strive towards cold, pure calculability. In fact, such calculability could not have worked without controlling the access to data, inventing a new vocabulary, redefining legal concepts, reorganizing the exchange floor, inventing new machines for collective witnessing, and building up a faithful customer base ready to buy market forecasts. And, while these processes unfolded, creating, in the terms of nineteenth century commentators, a microscope, as well as a telescope through which to observe the market, something else was needed too: an account of how financial transactions and speculation should be observed (from a distance) in their relationship with the state and the national economy. Such an account had to be assembled from words, showing the principles according to which the broader world works, and speculation's place in it.

CHAPTER SIX

The Kaleidoscope of Finance: Speculation, Economic Life, and Society

Witnessing the market from a distance meant not only seeing transactions without being there, but also creating an observational system which should place financial transactions in the social world in an accountable way. Such a system of the market-in-the-world is based on words. But not only words: witness, for instance, the placement and appearance of traditional stock exchange buildings, situated, at least in London and Paris, in the middle of the city and designed to convey splendor and grandeur. Actors accessing speculation have to be provided with a view of the world as a judicious arrangement of little pieces.

Seen from a different angle, this amounts to the following: understanding the boundaries of finance as including self-validating observational systems grounded in social closure almost automatically raises the problem of the worldview generated at these boundaries, and of the ways in which such a worldview is intrinsic to the mechanisms of self-validation. The social closure of authorial voices, meaning that only certain classes of actors can authoritatively speak in public about the domain they control, is related to the reformulation of domain-specific knowledge as systematic and going beyond mere tacit skill or knowledge of other people. It is exactly this "knowing better because one is on the inside" which, in a chiastic turn, decisively contributes to social closure, while obscuring at the same time wealth-based control: not money and social origin, but special knowledge provides true access. Knowledge is special not only because it provides access to a specific domain, but also because it can account for how this domain fits into the broader world. Explaining the fit also means explaining misfits, deviations, "exceptional" cases which only confirm the rule, irrational elements which cannot be avoided by or excluded from systematic knowledge. The boundaries of finance thus include representations of the social and natural world, not limited to rational, regular occurrences, but justifying irrational, exceptional ones too. In other words, the little pieces forming the worldview are combinable in different ways, so as to provide an explanation of "good" and "bad" speculations. The capacity to generate such a worldview, one claiming general validity and anchoring in universal principles, confirms the special status of authorial voices: only a truly special knowledge can explain how financial markets integrate into the larger world.

Such a worldview includes, among other things, classifications which enable the orderly positioning of speculation in the world. It is not so much fixed categories which are central here, but classificatory operations which recombine and redefine categories. Being operations-based, a worldview opens up avenues of possible action and endows actors with agential capacities. Being able to situate their action in the world in a meaningful way, and acting within a flexible classificatory system, actors can project paths of future action which are not the mere reproduction of routines. Actors can project the resources of their domain beyond its confines and formulate significant programs for the larger world. Once their domain of action (i.e., financial speculation) is seen as meaningful within the world, it can be accepted or contested within a given categorical system. In the same way in which a kaleidoscope produces various images combined from the same little pieces of colored glass, the boundaries of finance provide different programs of action based on categorical combinations.

This means that voices of authority writing about the stock exchange and financial speculation not only claim that true access to financial transactions (and success) is ensured by special knowledge; they also elaborate representations of the social and natural order in which to integrate financial speculation with its successful occurrences, as well as with its failures, representations supported by and emanating from this special financial knowledge. Such representations, based in classificatory operations about financial speculation and the stock exchange, can support different programs of action with a broader relevance. For instance, they can support reformist (changing the world starting from speculation) or conservative programs (keeping the world as it is). They can compete or clash with programs generated by exogenous social groups. Seen from this angle, the boundaries of finance go beyond the walls of stock exchanges and offer a blueprint for the whole of society.

The Bad Speculation

Yet, in the nineteenth century, assembling such a blueprint was confronted with a problematic heritage. During the previous century, the answer to any question concerning the relationship between financial speculation, stock exchanges, economic life, and society would have been a short and clear one: bad influence. An incomprehensible form of knowledge cannot serve as the ground of any moral order, and therefore cannot be seen as in harmony with the public interest, with the state, and with economic life. Consequently, the places where this knowledge is accumulated and put into action, as well as the actors making use of it, are inimical to the state and to public interest.

At least four arguments about the incompatibility between speculation and public interest dominate the writings of pamphleteers, politicians, and philosophers, arguments which become even more heated during the French and American revolutions:

(1) Speculation weakens government and social order. The state has created public debt, which in its turn fuels marketplaces and financial speculation (Webster 1785, pp. 7–8; Pole 1987, p. 48; Hamilton, Madison, and Jay [1788] 1961, p. 192). As a state creation, public credit must be subordinated to the political system but, by allowing its debt to be negotiated, the state has created something with its own dynamic, something which cannot be controlled. Speculation is "an evil of the first magnitude" (Mortimer 1801, p. 414), which undermines the mutual trust between the government and the people, and with it the very fundament of public credit (Defoe 1701, p. 14). Lack of political control over financial transactions weakens the central power, and undermines social order. A weakened order, together with a growing debt mass, mean that the citizens' ability to pay taxes is diminished, which in its turn increases the disorder and decay (e.g., Paine 1796, p. 5; Webster 1791, p. 8; Laporte 1789, pp. 55–56). Thus, financial speculation, which springs from civil liberty (Mortimer 1782, p. 39), turns against liberty itself, which cannot exist without order.

(2) Financial speculation diverts both capital and human resources from manufacture, commerce, and agriculture, and thus weakens the economic system.

A weakened economy means a weakened state and an eroded public confidence (e.g., Laporte 1790, p. 75; Mortimer 1801, p. 422). Moreover, the true and sure source of wealth is industry, which should be alimented by money. Diverting money from industry to financial speculation means that money circulates now without producing anything, and without supporting labor, being reduced to gambling (*An Essay* 1721, p. 5).

(3) Financial speculation creates a monopoly, and monopolies are always detrimental to the public interest and to freedom. Once the state allows public debt to be traded, cliques of speculators will monopolize this trade and subvert thus the very freedom in the name of which they pretend to act; monopoly is the "worthy acolyte of speculation," writes Mirabeau (1787, p. 20). While speculators act in the name of the freedom to "dispose of property" and of natural rights, when selling what they do not possess and when buying without having any money they hollow out the very notion of property (Anonymous 1748, p. 7). Undermining property means subversion of freedom, which in its turn means destruction of the social order; speculators have thus declared civil war on the nation, and the government must intervene to reign in their influence (Anonymous 1750, p. 22). Speculation is nothing but a slow poison eroding all parts of the state (Laporte 1789, p. 50).

(4) Financial speculation encourages conspicuous consumption,[1] unsupported by labor or by investments, a consumption which in its turn weakens the moral order. Frugality and industry are good for the nation, insists Benjamin Franklin in *Poor Richard* (Franklin [1774] 1777, p.8), but speculation creates inflation and luxury, which lead to debauchery, and to the sacrifice of prudence and decency, as Peletiah Webster, Franklin's cocitizen and fellow politician, adds a few years later (Webster 1791, pp. 9–10). The desire to get rich quick and the monstrous luxury displayed by speculators deepen social inequalities and contribute thus to destabilizing social order. In the vision of the French Revolution, out of these inequalities emerges a society "where vanity and inhumanity dominate,/ where vile egoism has dried out the souls/ where esteem is submitted to infamous calculations/ where only the rich get attention,/ where, once poor, one lives in dishonor" (Charlemagne 1796, pp. 25–26).

In this context, financial speculation and speculators are not seen so much through the lens of an association with morally reprehensible gambling, as through that of an inability to integrate in and contribute to the given social order, paralleling the impossibility to find a place for financial knowledge in the order of knowledge. It is thus a matter of order, as seen by an external observer, a rational order which leaves no place for financial

speculation. What happens, though, when the position of the external observer is replaced with that of the internal observer, when this observer
acquires the authority to speak from within speculation? What happens
when that who speaks claims a privileged position, grounded in the possession of a special form of knowledge, akin to science, and in social status
and honorability as well?

When actors associated with stock exchanges gained an authorial voice,
one which reflected their respectability and privileged access to a form of
special knowledge, they sought to reposition financial speculation in harmony with the broader order of things. The representations of finance
related to the social closure of stock exchanges had to include not only
a redefinition of the relationship between speculation and gambling. A
more challenging task, one on which such a redefinition depended, was
to generate a worldview reconciling speculation and the social order, and
articulating a positive link among transactions on the stock exchange, the
economy, and the state. The arguments about weakening government,
diverting capital, creating a monopoly, and perversion by luxury had to
be countered, if not replaced, by such a worldview, in relationship to reworking the distinction between speculation and gambling. While such
a distinction was in principle relevant with respect to the constitution of
financial subjects, the redefinition of financial knowledge as akin to science and as a form of expertise already introduced a separation between
financial transactions and morals. Now financial knowledge had to be integrated into a broader view about the natural and social order, one in which
the place of financial speculation should correspond to the respectability
of brokers and speculators themselves.

Speculation as a Universal Force

The solution to the bad speculation problem was to redefine it, not according to whether it contributes or not to society, but as a universal force,
as intrinsic to human nature and as present in all societal domains. The
definition of speculation as vital force and energy occurs against the background of a general presence in the economic discourses of the nineteenth
century of organicist metaphors, which assimilate the circulation of money
to that of the blood flowing throughout the organism and thus legitimate
banking institutions in a functionalist manner, without however generating any price theory on this basis. At the same time, the preoccupation of

nineteenth-century engineers with notions of energy and efficiency combines, on a more general philosophical level, with a reconsideration of the
notion of life as formulated by Leibniz, namely as a force capable of resist-
ing stasis (Caygill 2007, p. 22). Vitalism emerges as a philosophical current
influencing not only Henri Bergson, among others, but also the scientific
works of Helmholtz (thermodynamics) and Rudolf Virchow (cell physiol-
ogy), for instance (Caygill 2007, p. 24). The general preoccupation with
the links between energy and forms of life, a preoccupation present in
philosophical discourses and in concrete scientific research programs, as
well as in economic discourses, provides the intellectual background for
the redefinition of speculation.

In its turn, this allows distinguishing various forms of financial speculation, with their various effects on the state, the economy, and the individual. Moreover, the distinction between speculation and gambling
can be reworked according to these categories of speculative activity,
with the effect of either removing gambling from the sphere of ethical
concerns, or of distinguishing various forms of gambling, only some of
which can be seen as unethical. At the same time, postulating speculation as universal and as pertaining to human nature removes it from the
confinement to financial transactions. Financial speculation now becomes
comparable with speculation in various other domains and, consequently,
its preeminent locale, the stock exchange, is made comparable with other
social institutions. With one strike, speculation is integrated into the social
order.

At the core of this rhetorical strategy is the image of progress as characteristic for human nature, paired with that of speculation as a force of
progress. While this strategy is always set in a local context, responding to
specific political arguments and becoming embroiled with specific political forces, it is flexible enough to be applied on both sides of the Atlantic.
Whether it is New York stock brokers trying to counter agricultural interests from the Midwest or French socialists arguing against the coalition
of official brokers and state officials, the voices being heard say the same
thing: speculation is progress, patriotism, and education (Meeker 1922,
pp. 394, 426, 436).

On November 12, 1891, George Rutledge Gibson (a speculator and
banker who played a seminal role in the establishment of technical analysis in financial circles) expressed this viewpoint at the convention of US
bankers in New Orleans, endowing it with an authority above that of a
mere pamphlet or prospect:

Now, that I am at once met with the possible criticism that Wall Street is merely the seat of an unproductive, useless and injurious speculation. I want for an instant to debate this point, to see whether the common judgment of unthinking people may not do an injustice to this portion of the financial mechanism. Large undertakings require large capital, and to accomplish great industrial results it is necessary to amass capital. The fortune of no individual would be ample to set in motion the forces which have produced the prodigious results of modern material civilization. The subdivision of the title of ownership of such great engines of progress as manufacturing, shipping, mining, banking, trading, telephone, telegraph, cable, water and gas companies is indispensable to their organization and operation. [. . .] The principle of speculation is inherent in all business; it is, indeed, but another name for foresight and progress. It expresses itself perhaps more quickly and palpably in a stock exchange than in purely commercial circles, just as a wave of heat registers itself more quickly on a bulb of mercury than upon a bar of iron; but the heat is there the same in both instances. (Gibson 1891, pp. 10–12)

While being the motor of progress and civilization, speculation is also the rare, wild spirit of adventure, completely different from the drudgery of the merchant making one small gain after another. It is a force of nature which nobody can tame and, as such, indispensable to the community:

The speculator is a very different person. Like the last new comet, he acknowledges a law of his own. He does concern himself in the rise and fall of prices, for they deeply concern him. The trader depends on customers; the speculator has none. The trader depends upon small, but regular gains; the speculator looks to sudden and eccentric enrichment. The world is his market. No doubt speculation is a lottery, but so is going to California. Since the suppression of lotteries in Massachusetts, mercantile speculation, daring, dashing, hazardous, break-neck adventures, have greatly increased, not only in actual amount, but proportionally in comparison with regular trade. The fact is, there is a certain quantum of the spirit of wild, and eager, and hazardous adventure ever in the community, and it *will* seek exercise and gratification in some form or other. (Freedley 1852, p. 153)

The universal nature of speculation was put forth, for instance, in investment manuals, which suggested to readers that they could escape their walk in life by speculating. Speculation becomes hope for upward mobility:

Everyone, from the highest to the lowest, has a speculative nature, and large
fortunes are being amassed by persons who, without this venturesome spirit,
would probably be wearing out their lives as struggling salesmen or poorly-
paid clerks. The great fortunes of this country were not made by investing in
Government bonds but by speculation of the boldest kind, and in the case of
European fortunes it is well known that their foundations were laid by dealing
in stocks and bonds in the most instances. It may be not possible for us all to
become immensely rich but anyone may, by going to work carefully and wisely,
place himself in an independent financial position, even from a small beginning.
(Anonymous 1898, p. 44)

Civilizing factor and untamed natural force at the same time: by operating with this oxymoron, repeated by countless authors,[2] this discourse
manages to simultaneously integrate speculation into the natural and social order, to bring together the rational and the irrational into one over-
arching view, and to rank speculation with respect to other domains of
human activity. While the civilizing side is characterized by hard work,
attention, observation—all qualities intrinsic to speculation as a privileged form of knowledge—the wild, adventurous side means taking risks,
developing emotions, being caught in the ardor of the game as a means of
escaping the boredom and dullness of ordinary life.[3] This drive may lead to
excesses, and even to financial failure, yet it contributes to rank financial
speculation as above other economic activities, and speculators as above
ordinary humans. From the pariah of society, speculation is made into an
activity both comparable with other economic pursuits and situated above
them.
    While speculation is life spent lowly, it is life itself, and includes an ex-
cess of passion without which economic progress is impossible. In Zola's
novel *L'argent* (Money), Ms. Caroline reflects upon the project of building
a railway in Lebanon (set up as an object of speculation in Paris), when it
suddenly dawns upon her that

> money was the manure out of which tomorrow's humankind grew. [. . .] without
> speculation, there would be no grand enterprises, lively and fertile, in the same
> way in which there would be no children without bawdiness. One needs this
> excess of passion, all this life lowly spent and lost, in order to reproduce life
> itself. [. . .] In the fury of gambling, it rained money in Paris, money rot every-
> thing. Money, poisonous and destructive, became the ferment of all social veg-
> etation, was the humus necessary for grand works, the execution of which will
> bring people together and peace to the world. (Zola [1891] 1897, pp. 245–46)

Perhaps no one treated the oxymoron of civilization and wildness in a more systematic (and poetic!) fashion that Pierre-Joseph Proudhon (1809–65),[4] who sought to integrate financial speculation into his social theory as well as into his political program. Proudhon saw private ownership as grounded in power relationships, based on force and theft (Proudhon [1848] 1938, p. 290; [1840] 1926, pp. 131, 295). Yet ownership is at the same time a formal relationship among social actors; it is expressed in exchange, conceived as a "fusion of all values produced by private industries into a single body of social wealth" (Proudhon [1847] 1923, p. 107). As a formal social relationship cemented into social exchange, ownership cannot be replaced; yet its basis must be work and not "a fictive occupation or an idle will" (Proudhon [1841] 1938, p. 128). Exchange, which fuses together all values into social wealth, creates more than has been brought in, because social wealth is not the simple sum of individual values; therefore, exchange is similar with work, a "mode of creating wealth with nothing" and a rival of capital (Proudhon [1848] 1938, p. 313). Yet, exchange is not reducible to buying and selling commodities; there is another force at work in exchange, one which is intrinsic to human nature.

In the anonymously published *Manuel du spéculateur à la Bourse* (Manual of the stock exchange speculator, 1854), Proudhon made speculation into a fundamental principle for the production of wealth. Speculation is eminently productive and designates the genius of discovery; it constitutes the fourth power of the social economy, the first three being the capitalist, the working, and the mercantile "faculties" (Proudhon 1854, pp. 6, 9, 23–24). At the same time:

> By the very nature of things, speculation is most spontaneous, incoercible, most refractory to appropriation and privilege, untamable by power, in a word, most free. Infinite in its means, like space and time, offering everybody treasures and mirages, a transcendent world, offered by the sovereign God (Ordonnateur) to the investigations of mortals, *tradidit disputationibus eorum*; more than once has the political power tried to stretch its regulating hand under the pretext of public morality, and [speculation] has always convinced it of its own ineptitude and powerlessness. (Proudhon 1854, p. 31; emphasis in original)

Offered by the ordering, sovereign God to the investigation of mortals; free and irrepressible; untamable by political power, able to resist the latter and to convince it of its own stupidity! As a social power in its own right, financial speculation was at last on a par with work and capital. This view on the existence of a vital creative force was echoed later both by

Jules Regnault (who played a seminal role in formulation of the random walk hypothesis; see Regnault 1863, p. 102) and by Henri Lefevre, another key figure in the prehistory of financial economics (see Jovanovic 2006b). This latter saw speculation as intrinsic to any commercial operation, necessarily tied to the merchant's obligation of making provisions for unforeseen events. Thus, speculation is nothing else than "human providence," a necessary element of any activity (Lefevre 1870, p. 168; see also Van Antwerp 1913, p. 46).

The integration of financial speculation into the social and natural order makes it possible to redefine it as a sort of commercial activity, and to distinguish between "good" and "bad" speculation, between its productive and its destructive forms. Once more, this distinction allows repositioning speculation with respect to gambling; bad or destructive forms may have some associations with gambling, but productive or good forms are something entirely different. While acknowledging that in practice "serious speculation and parasite speculation are inseparable" (Lefevre 1870, p. 171; also Van Antwerp 1913, p. 257), Henri Lefevre saw the latter as being the necessary price to be paid for enjoying the benefits of productive speculation, which "corresponds to real needs." It is only the abuse or excess of speculation which is immoral (Lefevre 1870, p. 167); yet, not only is it hard to distinguish abuse from moderate speculation in practice, but the excess itself is intrinsic to this vitalistic view on speculation, as expressed both in the unbounded, heroic figure of the grand speculator and in equating speculation with a natural, almost uncontrollable force.

Regnault, in his turn, considered that good speculation is:

> the only one which deserves this name, has the talent to create, build, transform, having as goal the common utility; it corrects the exaggerated movements that blind trust or an insane panic would bring onto the quotations, and serves credit by maintaining a constant equilibrium among the various securities according to their utility and their products, keeping an always open market at the Bourse, where sellers and buyers are certain to find a counterpart, a profitable investment and a sure opportunity; it is this speculation which operates by means of capital, and this [fact] could not be praised or encouraged enough by all governments, because [speculation] is the true source of public credit. (Regnault 1863, pp. 102–3)

While "abusive speculation asks for the emotions of gambling" and the chance to deliver a "blindly earned fortune, without pain and without work" (Regnault 1863, p. 103), good, honest speculation goes slowly, but surely.

It is the means by which "the entrepreneur, the merchant, the worker are assured to arrive at fortune or at least at the comfort which is enough for happiness" (Regnault 1863, p. 103). But how to distinguish the two in practice? Where does evil speculation end and where does the good one begin? Well aware of the difficulty of this task, Regnault stated that "the true gambler, the influence of whom is most pernicious for the credit of a country is the uncovered speculator,"[5] that who does not possess either the security or the means of delivery (Regnault 1863, p. 107). Yet, since they are indistinguishable in practice, the only means of capturing them is to "imagine what would happen if they were entirely abandoned to themselves, if there was no relation, no possible alloy between them" (Regnault 1863, p. 107).

Whether "uncovered speculation" is the truly bad form or not is a matter of discussion, and others will argue that while the "principle of the margin is the mainspring of speculation," "mankind, since the beginning of things, has been doing a vast amount of business on a very thin margin indeed" (Medbery 1870, pp. 58, 64). While options contracts may approach bets, "an absolute equivalent to gambling is not to be found in any phase of speculation" (Medbery 1870, p. 101). Arguments concerning the economic functions, as well as, more generally, the legitimacy of speculation, were anything but rare (Kahn 1917, p. 10; Meeker 1922, pp. 96–97, 170, 198).

Perhaps more important than the discussions about how to distinguish bad from good speculation, though, are several other aspects enunciated by Regnault, with significant consequences. First, the true means of distinguishing between the two is not observing them directly, since they are indistinguishable in practice. Second, good speculation has a common utility and brings together the merchant, the capitalist, and the worker, contributing to social harmony. This argument, which echoes Proudhon (and which I shall discuss below into more detail) repositions the stock exchange as a potential source of social harmony, instead of class conflict. The true means is imagining what would happen if they were completely separated and analyzing them as if they were apart—that is, conceiving them through the lens of a theoretical apparatus which will enable the true observation of speculation. This position, which completely removes any ethical element from the study of speculation, entirely resonates with the notion that at the root of this former lays expert knowledge:

> Speculation is a business that must be studied as a specialty, and though it is
> popularly believed that any man who has money can speculate, yet the ordinary

man, without special training in the business, is liable to make as great a mistake in this attempt, as the man who thinks he can act as his own lawyer. . . . The common delusion, that expert knowledge is not required in speculation, has wrecked many fortunes and reputations in Wall Street, and is still very influential in its pernicious and illusory achievements. (Clews 1888, p. 23)

It is expert knowledge, in its different forms, which gives access to speculation both as an activity and as an object of intellectual contemplation. At the same time, intellectual access to speculation as a universal force meant access to the functions performed by speculation, functions which in the first place are economic. This rethinking of financial speculation in terms of its economic functions contributed further to integrating it into the realm of economic phenomena, which are studied by economists, a view which gained hold in the academia. In a PhD thesis submitted at Columbia University, published in 1896, Henry Crosby Emery noticed that financial speculation has been wrongly neglected by economists, and that its criticisms are unfounded. Moreover, the resemblance between gambling and financial speculation obscures some essential differences: in gambling, one party must necessarily lose what the other wins, but in speculation this is not the case (Emery 1896, pp. 98, 100). The growth in knowledge itself makes speculation necessary, since merchants do not have the time anymore to monitor the world:

With the advance in knowledge, the trading element and the speculative element in their business [the merchants'] had come to be more sharply distinguished, and the more important the speculative element became, the greater was the burden on those who pursued their business for its trading profit. As merchants they were primarily concerned with buying, storing, and moving their actual commodities, and had little time to watch the ever shifting conditions of the world market. What was now needed by the trader was a distinct body of men prepared to relieve him of the speculative element of his business, that is, of the risks of distant and future changes, just as he had formerly relieved the producer of his distinctly trading risks. A new body was wanted to cope with the *Konjunktur*. (Emery 1896, p. 108; emphasis in original)

In this argument, financial speculation is integrated into the division of labor; it constitutes an observational and actionable system dealing with risk and anticipating the future. As an observational system, it should be itself observed and analyzed by economists. This, again, radically departs from the eighteenth-century position that direct observation of financial speculators, as they act in the marketplace, can tell something about the character of speculation. When social closure intervenes and direct access to the trading floor becomes impossible, the boundaries of finance include an observational system providing the intellectual categories according to which speculation can be judged. Function, differentiation, and knowledge are among these and, since we cannot have functional speculation without an appropriate institution, these categories require a social repositioning and redefinition of the stock exchange itself. A reconceptualization of the social order along functionalist and vitalistic lines thus becomes necessary; speculation as a universal force and as fulfilling specific social functions means that society has to be represented in terms of forces and functions too, with the stock exchange at its core.

The Heart of Society

This general reconceptualization of society takes place against the broader philosophical background of vitalism and biologism characteristic of the second half of the nineteenth century, which conceived society as analogous to a living organism, and social institutions as performing different functions, similar to those performed by specialized organs in a body. Tied not only to the rise of biology as a natural science, but also to social changes brought about by industrialization, which made different sectors of society interdependent and raised new problems like public health (Alborn 1994, p. 173), the imagery of society as analogous to a living organism equated money with the blood flowing throughout this latter. While this view (in contrast with physics) never provided the conceptual grounds for price theory (e.g., Limoges and Ménard 1994, p. 338; Schabas 1994, p. 322; Mirowski 1989, p. 271), it became quite influential in social philosophy and in sociology, particularly due to the impact of Herbert Spencer, Auguste Comte, and (later) Émile Durkheim (e.g., Mayr 1982, p. 386; Schumpeter [1954] 1994, p. 789; Radcliffe-Brown [1910] 1984, p. 113), as the basis on which these disciplines tried to establish their social scientific status. Biological analogies, which failed to unfold their epistemic potential in economic theory (dominated by physical metaphors), also became essential with respect to repositioning the stock exchange within the social order, from a marginal and dubious gathering to a key institution.

Conceiving (financial) speculation as a vital force meant that that the overall social significance of its locus—the stock exchange—had to be reevaluated, a reevaluation which required a comprehensive view on how society is organized. What better analogy, then, than that between society and a living organism, with the stock exchange taking the place of the heart which pumps the lifeblood of public credit through the veins of society? Good speculation, then, ensures that this heart beats regularly, and that society progresses; it is the very motor of civilization. This view was repeated time and again, by Pierre-Joseph Proudhon and Henri Lefevre, among others: the stock exchange is at the center of the social order. The former started by asserting that, for the true economist, society is "a living being, endowed with its own intelligence and activity, governed by special laws which only observation can discover, and the existence of which manifests itself not in a physical form, but by the concerted and intimate solidarity of all its members" (Proudhon [1847] 1923, p. 123). This organism, driven in part by speculative power, needs a specialized organ or temple, which is none other than the Bourse (Proudhon 1854, p. 25).[6] This organ transforms capital into a merchandise like any other commodity, so that the stock exchange is nothing but a "market of capitals" bringing together "the man of millions and the man of ideas," forming thus a complete reflection of society (Proudhon 1854, pp. 76, 113).

Not only is the stock exchange the heart of this complex organism; it's also a heart which entirely reflects society, and where the four basic social powers (capitalist, working, mercantilist, and speculative) unite. In his turn, Regnault chose to close his book on the *Calcul des chances* exactly with these considerations:

> The Bourse is the expression of public Credit. The public Credit is the expression of the state of advancement of a society. In our era, so material and progressive, everything must converge towards the Bourse. Like in a great body, the *heart* receives life and diffuses it throughout all the limbs. When the heart has unequal and convulsive movements, the man and the society are ill. The morality of individuals consists in knowing how to keep a right middle of the road in all circumstances; virtues are nothing else but the equilibrium of our faculties, and even our qualities, when they vary too much, produce only vices. Peoples advance in civilization, morality and welfare only if the variable social elements oscillate within the narrowest limits; let the political calm consolidate, let the great commotions disappear; then trust grows, and with it the power of Association and Credit. (Regnault 1863, p. 210; italics and capitals in original)

Only a couple of years later, Henri Lefevre repeated the same premises: human societies are not simple collections of individuals, but true living organisms, characterized by internal differentiation and by specialized organs (Lefevre 1870, p. 242). At the center of a superior organism is the stock exchange:

> At last, in superior beings and societies all these scattered centers group themselves in a common center, which is the *heart* or the *Bourse* which we see functioning in the individual as well as in society according to absolutely similar processes. Like the heart in the individual, the Bourse aspires *veinous* money scattered throughout all the parts of the social body and sends it to the industry, where it revives itself, similar to the dark blood which is sent to the lungs where it refreshes itself and is redistributed anew throughout the individual or collective organism, in various forms, but with fertile and nutritious qualities which it didn't have before. These qualities are exhausted in their circulation: money, like blood becomes dark again and recommences a new evolution. (Lefevre 1870, p. 243; italics in original)

In this "functional world, which the social organism resembles more and more," there are two circulatory systems, both governed by the Bourse: the pulmonary or industrial circulation, on the one hand, and general circulation, on the other (Lefevre 1870, p. 245). If the Bourse will cease to work, these circulatory processes will disappear and a superior society will cease to exist (Lefevre 1870, p. 246). In this picture, the stock exchange is more than just the center of a monetary circulatory system; it is the organ coordinating general social circulation, the one ensuring social cohesion, progress, and the continued existence of society as a superior organism. All these qualities are predicated on the "organ and temple" of speculation (as Proudhon formulated it), a syntagm which summarizes its overall position: speculation performs necessary social functions (e.g., processes uncertainties about the future, channels funds into industry), but is also an uncontrollable vital force. As a functional component of social and economic life, speculation can be analyzed and known; as a vital, creative force, it is worshipped in its own temple, without which the organ cannot exist. This makes the stock exchange into a natural force, which can be put to use, but never fully controlled: it is on a par with natural phenomena, it is like a living being, and disturbances or illnesses are unavoidable.[7] In the same way in which the illness of a living organism is a symptom of broader biological disturbances, financial turbulences are symptoms of broader economic disturbances:

As steam is explosive, electricity deadly; as tuberculosis lurks in milk, typhoid fever in water, and trichinae in meat, so the stock market is full of manholes and pitfalls. [. . .] Financial storms may manifest themselves with a greater cyclonic fury within the precincts of the Stock Exchange, but they are equally destructive in commercial and industrial circles. Bonds and shares are the most mercurial and sensitive forms which capital assumes, but as a sudden wave of heat registers its arrival more quickly on a bulb of mercury than on a bar of iron, so the former more quickly recovers its normal temperature. It is so with Stock-Exchange markets, which are first to feel a financial barometric depression, but likewise the first to record a better atmosphere, while real estate, for instance, is the last to detect, as well as the last to recover. (Gibson 1889, pp. 9–10)

The vital force of speculation, which is not possessed in equal measure by everybody, justifies in its turn both the social closure of the exchange and the social inequalities generated in the process of speculation itself. The enclosure started in the name of honor (the actors of the exchange being honorable citizens, men of their word, and so on) and metamorphoses into a natural system, grounded in the possession of a mysterious quality. Different degrees of financial success due to hard work, observation, and learning may turn out to be due just to the different degrees in which one possesses the gift of speculation. Max Weber's lament at the speculative involvement of nonprofessionals, which he saw as unfortunate, his insistence that financial speculation should be left to the grand players, are perhaps not entirely due to a difference in knowledge and information opportunities, but also to one in giftedness: the small, nonprofessional investors do not possess this force to the same degree as grand speculators.[8]

The Mystique of the Stock Exchange as a National Symbol

The overall view on functional differentiation as a consequence of a vital force at work in society is important not only because it is formulated in the writings of two pioneers of financial economics, and of a major figure of nineteenth-century European socialism; it is echoed in countless investor manuals and descriptions of the stock exchange which, in the same breath, stress the social and economic functions of speculation and the special character of the stock exchange, irreducible to these functions, considering that "there cannot be a great people without a great stock exchange" (Medbery 1870, p. 7), that the "colossal achievements" of capitalists (and, implicitly, of capitalism itself) could not have been possible without the stock exchange (*The New York Stock Exchange* 1887, p. 17). A US investor manual written as a collection of letters from Europe saw finance as a force more powerful than politics itself: "So from *politics* let us turn to *finance*—simply remarking that just now they are most intimately associated—like England and America—a Siamese twins connection; cut the band and thrones will tumble! The stock exchange is more powerful than the monarch—and the treasury has always had a wonderful influence on the cabinet. At present the peace and happiness of Europe depend somewhat upon the amount of bullion in the national banks!" (Train 1857, p. 18). With that, the stock exchange enters the sphere of the political in a way which is not reducible to it fulfilling specific economic functions. While it can be argued that, in the eighteenth century, stock exchanges have been ultimately political creations, engendered by the debt-raising activities of the state (Neal 1990; Carruthers 1996), in this discourse, on entirely different grounds, the stock exchange becomes an expression of the political force of the state, and of the nation's standing (see also Kahn 1917, p. 18; Meeker 1922, p. 329).

By concentrating vital, creative forces in one place, by controlling not only the circulation of capital, but also the general circulation of society (understood in an abstract fashion as a system of exchanges which ensures social cohesion), the stock exchange becomes a national symbol, an institution integral to an advanced society. Such an institution can then be minutely compared with the stock exchanges of other nations, highlighting its modus operandi, its advantages, and the myriad of ways in which it works better than in other nations. And, as a symbol of the nation's strength, the stock exchange should be defended from any attempts to denigrate it or deny its importance, a view which is echoed nowadays in the public outcries triggered by attempts to takeover or merge established stock exchanges (the various attempts of the late twentieth century and early twenty-first century to buy the London Stock Exchange are a case in point here). In France, already in the early nineteenth century the construction of a new building for the Bourse (the Palais Brongniart, started by Napoleon in 1807 and finished in 1826, in the form of a Greek temple) was projected in a fashion "worthy of the capital of the French empire, . . . [a building] with more splendor" (*Avis rélatif* 1807), but then it was a state institution anyway. However, investor manuals published in the US and the UK praised the stateliness of their respective stock exchange

buildings too and—what's more important—their role as national symbols and assets.[9] A description of the New York Stock Exchange published
in 1887, for instance, provided detailed data about the size of the building,
its most important rooms, and all the amenities, stating that "there is in
fact no feature of modern convenience and improvement which has not
been introduced into this superb building" (*The New York Stock Exchange*
1887, p. 33).

More important, perhaps, than the praise of stately buildings is the understanding of the stock exchange as a national symbol, grounded in the
notion of a vital force, creating the mystique of a quasi-inaccessible center
of power on which the whole nation depends. This mystique is conjoined
(in a not so paradoxical fashion) with the idea that systematic knowledge,
study, and observation are the keys to access. In his address before the convention of American bankers in 1891 in New Orleans, George Rutledge
Gibson asked the rhetorical question, what is Wall Street to America? To
some, he said, Wall Street is the red, cruel dragon of capital; to others, it
is just another Monte Carlo, or a mad and cruel racecourse; to the knowl-
edgeable, it is a great reservoir of fluid capital which irrigates wheat and
tobacco plantations, and sets the wheels of factories in motion. Ultimately,
however, Wall Street is "a sundial into which the rays from all sections of
the country are converged, an epithome of American finance, and yet an
integral part of the country in close touch and in fact identical with all its
interests. Let us seek briefly to discover not only its characteristic face
but its true inwardness, to note its utilitarian value and its ethical quality"
(Gibson 1891, p. 4). The stock exchange may thus fulfill specific economic
functions (i.e., "irrigating" the economy with capital), but, beyond that, it
is a spiritual force in itself and, as such, it brings the nation together: this
is its true ethical quality. The separation between speculation and ethics,
supported by the rigorous knowledge inherent to the former (and emphasized by Gibson), is superseded here by the spirituality of this very
speculation; the two are reunited on a superior level.

At about the time of Gibson's address, political movements like progressivism were taking off, arguing that speculation and the stock exchange
were weakening the nation, wasting its assets, creating monopolies, and
serving narrow group interests. The country's assets were found not in
Wall Street, but on the wheat fields and cornfields of the Midwest (e.g.,
Wiebe 1962, p. 11). Influential books such as Henry George's *Progress and
Poverty* ([1880] 1971, p. 194) argued that speculation means not only one's
gains but also somebody else's loss. Yet George was mainly concerned

with land speculation as the source of all evil and less with financial speculation, acknowledged in passing.

   While George's ideas had an impact on clergymen (Caine 1974, p. 13),
some of whom spoke out against financial speculation, others were less
decidedly against it. Thomas De Witt Talmage, one of the most prominent preachers of the second half of nineteenth-century America, whose
sermons were attended by up to five thousand people in Philadelphia and
Brooklyn, had an ambiguous attitude toward financial investing and was
castigated for it in some manuals.[10] However, in his sermons directed to
clerks he urged them to keep in mind that "the seat of national power
is not in an English palace, or Paris, or Washington, but in the Bank of
England, in the Bourse, in Wall and Third Streets" (Talmage 1866, p. 12).
In his sermons on speculation, he offered his audience a simple solution
in order to avoid sinful financial investments. Investors may escape hell's
fire and ruin if they make proper Christian investments, which means two
things: first, donating a part of the profits to a Christian charity; second,
praying, because praying brings financial healing and financial prosperity. If these simple precepts are followed, wrote Talmage, then "Christian
generosity [will] pay now, pay in hard cash, pay in government securities"
(Talmage 1888, p. 418). With redemption in reach of every investor, there
were little moral obstacles, if any, in the way of a broader participation in
financial markets. The sentiment that there was no contradiction anymore
between religious feelings and financial investments was expressed by one
of Talmage's contemporaries as follows: "The gentleman remarked that a
few years ago it was thought inconsistent for a member of a church to be
a stock broker, and now, he said, stock brokers are rather at a premium to
be good members and vestrymen, merely showing that the religious community has lost its aversion to speculation" ("Stocks" 1881).

   The transformation of the stock exchange into a national symbol meant
that, under certain circumstances, speculation became a patriotic duty.[11]
This was more than an often-repeated mantra during the Civil War, when
East Coast brokerage houses mounted a massive effort to make Union
bonds attractive to the population, by publishing brochures and prospects,
organizing road shows, and developing networks of sales agents (Berk
1994, pp. 28–29). In Europe too, and in times of peace, pamphlets asserted
that "the centralization of French capital in French hands is an absolute
necessity," and that good citizens do not pay attention to the anomalies
of the Bourse, but do "loyal speculations . . . trusting our commerce, our
industry, which are the force and glory of our country" (*La Bourse* 1868,

pp. 5, 13); others considered that the national interest is menaced by trading foreign securities (Blanc 1861, p. 23).[12]

After the Franco-Prussian war of 1870–71 and the Paris Commune, the Paris Bourse and its unofficial counterpart, the coulisse, were publicly praised for raising the money necessary to pay the war reparations:

> When more than one political skeptic and discouraged thinker allowed themselves to write down upon the crumbling walls of our burned-down palaces "*Finis Galliae*," the Bourse kept its faith in France and her fortune, and that faith in France was spread by it all around, at home and abroad. Speculation was patriotic in its way; it has exhibited a confidence in our resources which the discretion of many a wise man rated as foolhardy. (Vidal 1910, p. 221 note *a*)

Needless to say, a couple of decades later, in the wake of the Dreyfuss affair, a nationalistic campaign was mounted against the coulisse, which had Jewish and foreign members. The members of the Paris Bourse (who, since 1724, were all Catholic and French citizens) were said not to be strangers to this campaign; they were defending their monopoly by any means necessary (Vidal 1910, p. 241).

The notion that the stock exchange is the true seat of national power, radiating a spiritual force which can be harmonized with religious precepts, is not only a far cry from the eighteenth-century view of the exchange's destructive influence, but it also begs the question of the ways in which financial speculation could support alternative political projects. In other words, if such a powerful force justifies the present order and cannot be renounced or dismantled without putting the whole order in peril, could it serve as the basis of alternative projects too? If it supports an order grounded in closure, hierarchy, competition among speculators, and social differences, could it also support the project of a cooperation-based order? With that, the improbable realm of political utopia opens, one in which financial speculation becomes a tool for achieving a better society.

Speculating on a Better World

The idea of a general system of exchange which holds society together (the "general circulatory system"),[13] irreducible to the particular interests of individuals involved in concrete exchanges, coupled with that of speculation as a universal creative force (both found in the writings of

Pierre-Joseph Proudhon) lead to the notion that financial transactions mean not only competition, but also cooperation. Proudhon saw the Bourse as bringing together men with money and men with ideas, as reproducing society in a concentrated form, and as forcing various categories of actors to interact and cooperate. This position resonated with his notion that private ownership (which is theft and an expression of power relationships) can be superseded not by means of abolition, but by bringing owners and nonowners together in a system of cooperation. Put together, all these ideas provided the outlines of a cooperation-based social arrangement with the stock exchange at its core, an arrangement in which social classes will live in harmony. Proudhon distinguished between three social classes: the superior, the middle, and the lower class. The superior class corresponded to the ancient French aristocracy, and its privileges have been acquired by force; the lower class is the working class, and the middle one is the bourgeoisie. There should be an alliance between the lower and the middle class, and this can be achieved by providing them with the possibilities of financial speculation, by creating joint-stock associations and companies which are then traded on the stock exchange. Only such an alliance, grounded in speculation, can emancipate the working class from its eternally inferior position:

> Is it possible to admit that this association movement, resulting not from utopian theories but from economic necessities, and which invades all branches of production, will stay eternally closed to the worker? That securities will be accessible only to money, and that labor, by its essence and destination, will forever turn down partnership? Shall we believe that the commercial society, which spreads with such an irresistible force, has the resuscitation of castes and the deepening of the rift between the proletariat and the bourgeoisie as its providential aims, instead of bringing these two classes to the necessary and definitive fusion, to their emancipation and triumph? Fifty years from now, all national capital will be mobilized; all securities, engaged as instruments of production, will be subordinated to a social justification, the field of individual ownership will be reduced to objects of consumption, or, as the [Civil] Code says, to fungible objects. Will then the salaried man, this ancient slave excluded since the origins of the world from ownership, be excluded from society until the end of days? Fifty years from now, work will have the exact weight of capital, does anyone think that the former will not think of absorbing the latter, and, should this idea surface, that anything will prevent its execution? (Proudhon 1854, p. 337)

Far from being reactionary, financial speculation appears thus as the way to class reconciliation and harmony, leading finally to the disappearance of all class differences and to reaching the ultimate stage of societal development, that of a free association of producers (Proudhon 1854, pp. 343–44). This resonates with rather than antagonizes the notion that any criticism of the stock exchange, "this grand and useful institution," is just a plot to introduce "a split between finance, bourgeoisie, and the proletariat" (*La Bourse* 1854, p. 3). While Proudhon the socialist probably did not dare publish such a blueprint under his own name, having already attracted enough criticism and scorn (from Marx, among others), this utopia did not remain without echo in financial circles. Reenter here Henri Lefevre, who (while calling Proudhon "one of the most powerful revolutionary critics") considered land ownership as being one of the main sources of social evils. The "industrial movement" produces a vast mass of financial securities, and speculation has the potential of remedying social inequalities by bringing together social classes which otherwise would antagonize each other. In order to reach this social harmony, however, knowledge was necessary. The public of potential investors always needs guidance, and study is the prerequisite of speculation. What was needed then was a plan of national financial education, which Lefevre devised based on the graphic methods and devices he had invented. The official stockbrokers' union of the Bourse, however, declined to invest any money in it, and his plan was never put into practice.

In 1900, during the International Congress of Securities organized at the Paris World Fair, the congress's president Alfred Neymarck declared:

> There is no longer a plutocracy, but a veritable financial democracy; when these thousands of millions of certificates are minutely segregated, these are only found atoms of certificates of stocks and bonds, and atoms of income—so great is the number of capitalists and independent individuals who divide these securities and these incomes among themselves. (Quoted in Vidal 1910, p. 167)

There was another aspect besides financial education, however: the social closure of the stock exchange. A utopian plan for broader social participation and harmony could easily be translated into a protest against this closure and a call for free access to financial transactions, something which did not fail to appear. If financial securities are like any other commodity, they should be traded like any other commodity, and not be controlled by a closed group. Moreover, if speculation is such a universal force, then everybody possesses it in some degree or other. Therefore, everybody should be able to transact securities without the interference of a stock broker:

> Let free the operations of the Bourse, give to everybody the right *to bet himself*, at the hours set for auctions, on the commodities called *stocks, debentures, bonds*, etc., as if they were bets on a *piece of furniture*, a *painting* . . . which an auctioneer is charged to sell in a public place or on a site designated by law (Paoli 1864, p. 17; emphasis in original).[14]

The protest against the social closure of the Bourse, against the discrimination between official and unofficial markets (present not only in Paris, but in New York and London too), positions itself on grounds other than the social melee characteristic of eighteenth-century financial marketplaces. Neither these grounds nor the eighteenth-century melee are identical to the idea of universal economic rights, of financial access and participation justified by the equality of all human beings. The often-heard arguments that financial markets embody egalitarian yearnings, that they represent in themselves a utopian egalitarian project which tears down the barrier between social classes (Chancellor 1999, p. 81), that modern financial markets are grounded in (more or less symbolic) social inclusion instead of social exclusion (e.g., Staeheli 2002), needs correction. While in the eighteenth century lack of social control (and not any idea of economic rights) is perceived as destabilizing order, the boundaries of finance set in place in the nineteenth century do not include a notion of universal economic rights either. They include a kaleidoscope of rational and irrational elements, and out of this mixture emerges the utopia of a social community, of a broad association centered on the stock exchange. In this kaleidoscope, notions that speculation is not different from a commercial transaction, that the stock exchange fulfills specific economic functions, are mixed with those of the social organism powered by the vital force of speculation, participating in the community not by virtue of equal rights but by virtue of sharing in this force.

The flexibility of this kaleidoscope is such that it can support both the status quo and reform, both exclusion and yearnings for accessibility. In a way similar to that of recombining little pieces of stained glass in order to achieve different patterns, knowledge and vitalistic force and economic function and political symbol are combined in patterns which shape observation from afar. Consequently, calls for exclusion (allow only national securities or capital, keep outsiders away) can comfortably coexist with calls for inclusion, and rational calculation does not banish but begs for the charismatic features of those individuals endowed with the "special powers" of speculation. As such, this kaleidoscope does not dismantle social closure and unequal access to financial transactions, but rather contributes to perpetuating them, by anchoring marketplace-related distinctions not only in social indicators of honorability (which, in time, may become questionable), but also in such special powers, irreducible to knowledge and hard work, powers which we see celebrated even now in so many accounts of daring "predators," cunning financiers, "bond kings," and the like.

There is a vast amount of popular literature on the figure of the charismatic speculator, a genre started in the latter nineteenth century and periodically bursting out into the public awareness. Examples of such waves of public attention are the 1920s and the 1980s–1990s, the latter two decades bringing to the center of interest junk bond kings, takeover virtuosi, dotcom operators, and many more. While individual publications are often critical toward the particular figures they discuss, this popular literature as a whole perpetuates the idea that special powers of cunning, invention, energy, or, in a word, a particular force residing in these individuals helps explain their financial success, in spite of often questionable morality and even plain illegality. Sometimes, this force is represented as "criminal energy," an expression which should not obscure the heavy emphasis on "energy." At other times, this energy is clothed in the rhetoric of outright heroism, with the financial speculator taking on (and defeating) bad governments, ossified bureaucracies, and the like. The media celebration of George Soros bringing down the Bank of England in 1992 is a case in point here.

Yet, concomitantly with this celebration of special energies, the notion of broad, popular participation in financial speculation is publicly promoted as a chance given to ordinary people to overcome their social situation, to "make it," provided they take the study of markets seriously. In an unintentional echo of Lefevre's national plans, widespread financial education (undertaken by brokerage houses, for instance) is seen nowadays as a means of enhancing popular participation in investments, a participation which in fact remains highly dependent on income, status, and ethnicity (De Bondt 2005; Swedberg 2005). What is even more, the stock exchange is put at the core of social reform projects (like the pensions reform in Western Europe, or the Social Security reform in the US) and (irrespective of whether these projects are concretized or not) invested with the capability to promote and support broader social changes, something which would not be possible without implicitly accepting markets as political institutions. The utopian strain launched in the nineteenth century thus continues to exist, in various forms and on different sides of the political spectrum, up to our days.

Does this mean then that this kaleidoscope is nothing else but false consciousness, an ideological smokescreen set in place to mask the real operations of finance? Not at all. My overall argument has been that the constitution of observational and discursive boundaries is intrinsic to the process of social closure which lies at the heart of modern financial markets. They provide the means for coordinating various paths of action for dispersed, unrelated actors. Among these means are observational frames and standpoints which help integrate financial markets into society at large. A socially closed institution based on the coordination of dispersed actions precludes direct and widespread observation of its activities, yet needs observational arrangements. Without these, it would neither be able to sustain its claim to legitimacy nor to reproduce its transactions, which by definition require both attracting new actors *and* staying in control. New actors must be persuaded that investing or speculating are economically profitable *and* socially acceptable; at the same time, a closed institution must maintain control over all features of its transactions, including symbolic ones. This cannot be achieved without providing an observational system which does both, one which gives actors a standpoint from which to rationalize their financial activities in the overall context of society, while maintaining control over the symbolic features of financial transactions. This is why authorial voices of nineteenth-century financial markets are so preoccupied not only with understanding the economic functions of speculation, but also with overall views of society and with social projects. This is why some brokers and speculators invest their time in writing about society and devising plans for its betterment. With that, I should stress here again that such discourses do not come from nowhere, but are generated from within the market, by actors who feel compelled to write, to expose a broader view of things—a kind of compulsion which we do not encounter during the eighteenth century.

The solution embraced by these writers—biologism and vitalism— necessarily requires paying some attention to the darker features of financial transactions. Yes, financial markets mean not only knowledge, but also a vital force; they mean not only study, but also charismatic figures.

THE KALEIDOSCOPE OF FINANCE: SPECULATION, ECONOMIC LIFE, AND SOCIETY

Yet what happens in darker moments, when calculation does not seem to help much, when charisma doesn't seem to work? What happens in financial panics and in moments of distress? Putting in place the boundaries of finance meant confronting these issues and integrating them in the whole picture, and it is to them that I turn now.

CHAPTER SEVEN

On the Dark Side of the Market

In his novel *The Gambler*, published in the same year as *Crime and Punishment* (1866), Fyodor Dostoevsky presents us with the rather curious (for the uninitiated) case of Antonida Vasilevna Tarasevicheva, a wheelchair-bound Russian who arrives in the German spa town of Roulettenburg (a thin disguise for Baden Baden), where her relatives have spent months playing at the casino and awaiting her death (together with the corresponding inheritance, which should save them from the incurred debts). As a rich merchant's widow, Antonida Vasilevna is cynical, haughty, and calculating. She manages her money well and is a wealthy landowner herself. She knows very well that her relatives look forward to her death, for the news of which they have regularly telegraphed to Moscow. She wants to surprise them by her arrival and send a signal that they should not count on her soon demise.

Once she arrives in Roulettenburg, her demeanor is taken for that of an aristocrat and she is addressed as a countess and a general's widow (titles which she could never have laid claim to, being of bourgeois extraction and not associated with the military, but which she tacitly accepts). After having scolded her nephew for squandering his money at the roulette, she asks to see the casino, where she observes the players and loudly urges some to leave the table, otherwise they'll be ruined (Dostoevsky [1866] 1991, p. 199). She is shown how roulette is played and, after having learned it by heart and observed the players, she starts playing herself. From now on, she can hardly quit the roulette table, to which she is compelled to return day after day. Resolutions of leaving the town and returning to Moscow are broken; in the end, Antonida Vasilevna loses her fortune (which, interestingly enough, partly consists of financial securities she has brought along from Moscow). With that, she is brought down from the status of a countess and general's widow to that of a semisenile grandmother, and her trajectory is seen by her entourage as a journey backward into infantilism.

Dostoevsky's fictionalized account of gambling and financial loss, based on his own experiences as a gambler between 1863 and 1871 (Jones 1991, p. xv), presents us with the tension between two intertwined yet radically opposed modes of profit, one provided by longtime accumulation, the other by winning at the roulette table. The relatives of Antonida Vasilevna are waiting for her death in order to squander their inheritance at the casino. She is a merchant's widow, the beneficiary of a fortune accumulated over a long time, and she has herself skillfully managed this fortune before coming to Roulettenburg. Her relatives live with the hope of winning a fortune over a couple of evenings; spend it, win again, and so on. Accumulation is not part of their plans.

At the same time, the narrator (who tutors the great-nephews of Antonida Vasilevna and is himself a gambler) makes this tension explicit when he states in a conversation that "roulette is simply made for Russians" and then explains:

> The ability to acquire capital has, historically, emerged as practically the most important item in the catechism of the merits and values of the civilized man in the West. On the other hand, a Russian is not only incapable of acquiring capital, but he even squanders it disgracefully, and to no purpose. "Nevertheless, we Russians also need money," I added, "consequently we are very glad to have, and very susceptible to, methods like roulette, for example, where one can make money on the spot, in a couple of hours, with no effort. It is very attractive to us; and since we gamble to no purpose, with no effort, we lose!" (Dostoevsky [1866] 1991, p. 149)

The narrator, who would rather spend his life in a Kirghiz tent than "bow down to the German idol," presents this latter as follows:

> Here every family is in a state of complete servitude and submission to the Vater. They all work their asses and they all save money like Jews. Let us suppose the Vater has already put away a certain sum of gulden and is counting

on handing over his trade or plot of land to his eldest son; to this purpose his daughter is not given a dowry, and she remains a spinster. To this purpose the younger son is sold into bondage, or the army, and the money is added to the household capital. [. . .] Finally, about twenty years later the fortune has increased; the gulden have piled up honestly and virtuously. The Vater blesses his forty-year-old elder son and the thirty-five-year-old Almachen, with her withered breasts and her red nose . . . as he does so he weeps, reads a moral, and then dies. The elder son himself turns into a virtuous Vater, and the same story starts again. And thus after fifty years, or after seventy years, the grandson of the first Vater has indeed realized a significant capital and he hands it on to his son, as he does to his, and he to his, and after five or six generations we get Baron Rothschild himself, or Hoppe & Co., or the devil knows whom. Well, sir, what a majestic spectacle: a hundred, or two hundred years of continuous work, patience, intelligence, honesty, strength of character, endurance, reckoning, the stork on the roof. [. . .] Well, sir, this is the point: I would far rather create an uproar, Russian-style, or get rich at the roulette. I don't want to be Hoppe & Co. after five generations. I need money for myself, and I don't consider myself in any way as something necessary and subordinate to making capital. (Dostoevsky [1866] 1991, pp. 150–51)

This discourse, which seems to prefigure some of Karl Marx's and Max Weber's insights, respectively, is less a contrast between two "national spirits" (German vs. Russian) than a tension between two different modes of profit: one based on longtime accumulation and personal submission to a supraordinate, abstract principle (capital), the other with much shorter temporal horizon (a couple of hours) and grounded in an individualistic perspective (I need money for myself). While prima facie this is a revolt against the principle of capitalism, it emerges in fact as its very own product: the individualization inseparable from the process of accumulation creates a time horizon which undermines the notion of multigenerational accumulation.[1] This spurious revolt drives the narrator toward a different machine of the system, which sets the individual "against the Gods," without any other apparent purpose than to beat the unknown. Here, the promise of absolute individual freedom (the chance of winning) is coupled with apparent effortlessness. This promise, if and when fulfilled, will reveal the whole power of the individual, his victory over the gods. One does not need to toil for this, to make sacrifices, or to wait years for a small gratification.

Yet the notion of effortlessness is subverted by the narrator's further description of his own gambling at the roulette table, based on hours of observation, on learning by heart, on counting and calculating, or trying to detect outcome patterns in the roll of the ball. The game is less irrational and impulse based than one might think, but requires learning and toiling. Nevertheless, these cognitive elements seem to be paired in a specific way with emotions, with sudden bursts of joy and fear, with hope and excitement. These bursts, in their turn, seem to be contagious. They expand uncontrollably among those gathered at the roulette table, players and observers alike. They seem to be compulsive: the narrator can neither leave the table (true gamblers, he explains, never leave) nor control his joy or fear. He is bound, attached to the table by invisible chains, and this inescapable position makes him much less free than he might think. The contradiction between the promise of individual freedom and spiritual enslavement (not much different from the enslavement to "capital") is a fundamental one.

The Kaleidoscope of Speculators

There is a similarity here between the narrator's reflections on gambling as an alternative to capital accumulation, on the one hand, and financial speculation, on the other, perceived as grounded in individual confrontation with chance and as having an analogous time horizon. Speculation, too, appears as detached from (and even contradicting) the toils of long-term accumulation, of restraint, and of self-imposed savings. With respect to the boundaries of finance, however, the above reflections outline two sets of questions. The first concerns the ways in which these boundaries include the figures of speculation not only as examples (see Fraser 2008), but also as lenses through which financial activities can be observed. Since speculation, like gambling, is an individualized activity, antagonistic to the idea of common toil, its justification cannot be limited to a rationalization of the links among speculation, the state, and the national economy; it has to generate figures or templates through which the concrete activities of concrete speculators can be made sense of.

Second, and at least as important, is the question of the relationship between calculation and emotions, as illustrated by Dostoevsky's narrator. Financial speculation is not devoid of calculation; quite the contrary. Yet it is interspersed with emotions like euphoria, fear, or panic, which cannot be straightforwardly deduced from calculation. The biggest problem of the speculator is not errors of calculation; the biggest problem is given by these seemingly uncontrollable emotions which take hold of you, spread like wildfire, and, in an eye's blink, seem to annihilate all calculative efforts. Noticed since the early eighteenth century at least, emotions like overexcitement and, above all, panic have appeared as one of the greatest challenges for understanding financial markets. How is it possible that stretches of apparently wild panic emerge in the midst of calculative efforts and bring ruin, how is it possible that the dark shape of panic lurks behind calculation? Apparently, this is a paradoxical situation: financial speculation is an individualized activity, one which, while requiring interactions, is oriented toward individual, not collective goals (as Dostoevsky's narrator puts it, "I want money"). Such an activity should not be so susceptible to collective phenomena like panic, which undermine its own very essence.

With this, I go back to the finance-centered worldview I discussed in the previous chapter. My argument was that this works, in part, as a definitional and classificatory system allowing the representation of the social world as orderly; this classificatory system provides the lens through which financial operations can be observed in relationship to larger entities like the state or the national economy. Of course, this kind of observation is the antithesis of unmediated, direct perception. It requires that the institution to be observed is socially closed and hardly accessible to outside direct perception. The lens coconstitutes the entities offered to observation: the stock exchange in its relationship to the national economy cannot be entirely separated from the process of justification which makes it observable as such, placing it in a socially legitimate relationship with other social institutions.

A lens for observing the inaccessible must correlate the level of large social institutions with that of individual actions and actors. It must generate mutually consistent categories for observing both the stock exchange in toto *and* its individual actors. Consequently, we should expect that the same generative principle which produces supraindividual categories will produce individual ones too. This principle is that of a tension between financial activities as grounded in knowledge and observation, on the one hand, and the very same activities as being driven by a vital force, irreducible to knowledge, on the other. Financial speculation requires diligence, skill, knowledge, and calculation; at the same time, it embodies a force one is born with or not.

This tension, which automatically implies a hierarchy (given by the degrees to which one possesses such a vital force), legitimates the stock exchange as the crucial organ of the modern social body, an analogy which, in its turn, introduces the notion of specific economic and social functions performed by the exchange. Specific functions, then, require a detailed knowledge, on the side of participants, as well as on that of observers. Both the speculator and the social scientist observing him must use knowledge in order to perform that specific function or to identify it, respectively; this brings us back to the notion that speculation (and the stock exchange with it) is anchored in cognitive operations and explainable in rational terms. The technology of price data recording (the market's microscope) and analysis (the market's telescope) work toward reinforcing this tension: they require knowledge and skills, and explicitly disseminate the idea that financial success is ensured by study and observation; yet, as they come under social closure, as the privilege of specially endowed persons (witness the special "powers of the analyst"), they perpetuate the notion of a vitalistic force one must possess. Thus, the tension which lies at the core of this worldview reproduces itself in its constituent elements, making knowledge inseparable from quasi-religious belief, and entwining calculation with charisma.

This lens through which both the stock exchange as a whole and its individual figures are observed can absorb and engulf apologetic as well as critical stances with respect to financial speculators. In the same way in which it supports reformist and conservative projects (according to how these tilt on the side of accessible knowledge or on that of privileged charisma), the kaleidoscope of speculation encompasses laudatory stances toward speculators, as well as critical ones. During the nineteenth century much of the criticism nests itself within fiction writing, due to protesting voices being partially displaced by the authority of brokers and investors writing "factual" accounts of speculation, "histories" and "documentaries." Nevertheless, criticism, as well as an apology of speculators, operates to a large extent with the same categories and figures. This is due in part to the fact that the apology of finance expands into the area of fiction writing as well; for instance, in the genre of educational fiction directed at preparing young boys for successful business careers (e.g., Hilkey 1997). This expansion imports the classification system used to "document" the stock exchange into the realm of fiction, thus engulfing many of the possibilities for conceptual criticism and protest.

Heroes, Conformists, and Fraud

A classificatory system enabling the observation of speculators at a distance is not a new product of the nineteenth century; one had already been in place in the eighteenth century, required by society's need to make sense of financial transactions. The eighteenth century generated an array of figures which have become entrenched in the financial vocabulary: the bull, the bear, the lame duck, as well as (perhaps less popular today) the monkey, the pigeon, the sharper, and the projector. The classification works as one anchored in habits and embedded in certain literary genres. Its aim is to provide observational tools so that readers can recognize a bull or a bear should they encounter one. Therefore, authors aim at providing a description of the looks, the clothes, the walk, the ways of talking, and the places of congregation of bulls, bears, and other figures; they provide a field guide for the observation of transaction-related behavior (Preda 2001a), with the aim of instructing the reader about the moral pitfalls of speculation. This guide is included in publications like pamphlets, comedies, satires, and visual allegories, which, by definition, require radical doubt toward the observed characters.

While neither pamphlets nor caricatures vanish in the nineteenth century, a parallel classificatory system emerges, one which is grounded in authorial voices coming from within, not from without, the stock exchange. Claiming to possess better knowledge about speculation, and asserting that this latter is nothing else but systematic (if not scientific) knowledge, these voices produce an alternative classification with distinct properties. While some of the old figures continue to exist as general appellations for trading positions (the bulls and the bears), the new classification does not work anymore as a sort of field guide for the observation of speculators in their natural habitat. First, the sites of speculation are not accessible to direct observation anymore; sitting on the visitors' balcony of the New York Stock Exchange, among the tourist crowds, rather discourages close observation.

Second, at least some of the classifications set in place operate along functional distinctions which emphasize the economic roles and functions performed by specific classes of actors on the floor of the exchange. Such classes (like brokers, traders, odd lot traders, or specialists) are represented according to the rational purpose of their activities. They are presented less as oriented toward profit making than as subordinated to a greater scheme: specialist traders are calculative agents, dealers ensure a continuous market, odd lot traders make sure lesser investors have access to the market too and smoothen the trading process, bears correct the excesses of the market, and so on (Van Antwerp 1913, p. 75; Meeker 1922, pp. 91, 98, 112, 149; Schwalbe and Branson 1905, pp. 14–15; Cordingley 1901, pp. 10–11).

Third, observation means having a lens through which one can make sense of actors in a broader frame, as legitimate social actors. What are needed here are figures identifiable with larger social roles, and not a zoo of monkeys, pigeons, ducks, or bears.

This stands in stark contrast to eighteenth-century observations, which did not attribute speculators any superhuman powers (bar devilish ones) and did not take the hierarchy (or the assembly) of speculators as normal, natural, or superposed on other social roles. When, on October 29, 1720, the Paris police clean out the neighborhood where financial transactions take place, Marais, the lawyer with the parliament of Paris, writes in his diary:

> Since this morning the foot guards and the companies have swept the Hôtel De Soissons, the Bourse Place, the streets de Grenouille and d'Orléans, and the street de Bouillon, where I live. The Place has been fumigated, all speculators have been chased, all protesters thrown in prison, and during the whole day the mass has been exalted. At last the evening is free and all this robbery has disappeared. The servants are back at their homes, the craftsmen at their workplace, the peasants [. . .] are back at their labor [. . .] and everybody has regained his natural place." (Diary of Marais, lawyer with the parliament of Paris, vol. 1, 1715–21, Paris, Bibliothèque Nationale)

Legitimate speculation requires that its figures be anchored in knowledge, discipline, hard work, observational skills, and specific cognitive tools. All this, however, should not impede upon the idea that speculation is driven by a vital force, one strong enough to make the stock exchange into the core of social life. This vital force required by the excitement of speculation may make this activity unhealthy, but at the same it licenses speculators to be different, yet socially acceptable:

> light-heartedness and joviality undoubtedly lessen the strain of a wearing and exciting occupation upon the nervous system very materially, and what is sacrificed in the way of dignity is gained in health; for it may be safely assumed that if the Stock Exchange were a serious body its members would die under their anxieties far sooner that they actually do. At best they lead for the most part lives of feverish excitement, and the death rate among them is abnormally high, while nervous prostration, heart disease, Bright's disease, and apoplexy, are the maladies that most frequently assail them. (Cornwallis 1879, pp. 34–35)

The notion that speculation triggered intense mental excitement, which in its turn required a vital force to bear it, might not have been just media hype, but also a sincere belief in at least some actors involved in financial transactions. During the gold mania of 1864, Edward Neufville Tailer, the New York dry goods merchant, wrote in his diary about "the Fifth Avenue Hotel & its halls one night crowded with stock brokers, who keep up the excitement of gambling in stocks until a late hour— One can notice upon their features the marks of care & anxiety, caused by a life of such intense mental excitement" (Diary of Edward Neufville Tailer, February 23, 1864, New York Historical Society). Since not everybody possesses such a force to the same degree, a hierarchy of speculators ensues. This hierarchy, in its turn, can adopt and adapt larger social roles, reworking speculators into easily recognizable figures. This generates a heterogeneous hierarchy comprising military strategists, barons, scientists, educators, and gentlemen, among others.[2]

At the top of this hierarchy is the grand speculator, akin to a military strategist. This figure, celebrated in countless accounts about the exploits of Vanderbilt, Jay Gould, Jay Cooke, James Fisk, or Daniel Drew, among others, is portrayed as relentless in his pursuits, ruthless, single-minded, and disciplined, "with a splendid and daring ability in the art of cornering" (Burnley 1901, p. 226), and driven by an almost superhuman force. Such figures become live examples for smaller investors, who should emulate them, without ever attaining their feats.

The power of this example is not exclusively directed at smaller investors, unknown to institutional contexts, or antiquated. In January 2008, for instance, the French Bank Société Générale discovered that one of its traders had lost over seven billion dollars in trades gone awry, setting up an elaborate deception system in order to hide trades which were not approved by his supervisors. The deception had unfolded over several years, and required going to great lengths in manipulating electronic accounts, performing fictitious trades, and the like. The ensuing investigations (as echoed in media reports) revealed that a major motivation was the desire of the trader to be acknowledged as equal to the stars of the trading floor, to overcome his status as a lesser trader, and to be shown the respect and consideration he thought he had deserved. The same investigation revealed that setting up systems of deception with the help of which riskier trades could be undertaken was not uncommon at all. It belonged in fact to the practice of showing off large trading profits, in which traders currently competed with each other in order to achieve a better place in the prestige hierarchy of the trading floor. What the culprit did was to imitate what the star traders were doing.[3]

The grand speculator possesses almost superhuman powers, duly eulogized by writers like Edwin Lefevre in his novel, *Sampson Rock of Wall Street*:

> Rock's friends often spoke of his habit of thinking in lightning flashes, of the marvelous quickness with which he abandoned old and settled on new policies, and, at the same time, of the systematic, von Moltke-like manner in which he planned some of his market campaigns. In their heart of hearts they sometimes doubted that any human mind could think so much and so quickly, or see so far and so clearly. Their minds did not. Therefore they half thought that Rock often closed his eyes, jumped, and landed safely on a golden feather-bed, compelling fortune's smiles by sheer audacity. [. . .] But it was not difficult for Rock to know, in the twinkling of an eye, what to think or what to vision to himself and why. His untiring patience in the conduct of the subsequent campaign, and his final success so deliberately led up to, alone shook his friends' confidence in the "blind plunge" theory. (Lefevre 1907, pp. 3, 4)

The myth of superhuman powers of the speculator became entrenched in the repertoire of popular culture, being recycled time and again throughout the 1980s and the 1990s, up to the present days (see also Fraser 2008, p. 110; Khurana 2002, p. 69). More prominent contemporary features of this myth are the unsurprising predilection of various financial speculators to identify with characters from the Star Wars film series (e.g., Tillman and Indergaard 2005, p. 87), as well as the speculators' depiction as David-like heroes who bring down Goliath-like "anachronistic" social institutions. The media styling of George Soros as the man who single-handedly fought and defeated the Bank of England in the early 1990s also is a case in point here. This myth helps perpetuate the social closure of financial institutions and the accompanying symbolic hierarchy of investors and speculators: not everyone possesses the special powers of a grand speculator and, therefore, not everyone can achieve comparable success. At the same time, the myth of the speculator as superhero helps obscure the complex processes and networks of relationships which enable financial speculation; in the public imagination, as fed by this myth, speculative success means not whom you know and what influence you yield, but what superpowers you have. Some speculators themselves may come to believe in their own special powers, as indicated by projecting fictional characters (like Star Wars heroes) upon themselves.

As a variation on the theme of the vital force characteristic for financial speculation, superpowers can also be used to justify acts of transgression or, in other words, fraud. Fraud as an ethical and legal term implying intentional breach of law and trust is replaced with loss or blurring of powers as an explanation for behavior which, for other actors, would be simply called stealing. In May 1890, for instance, Washington Quinlan, a member of the New York Stock Exchange, simply disappears with his money and a number of securities left in trust to him, after having sold short about forty thousand securities. Edward Neufville Tailer, the investor whom I discussed in chapter 5, clipped in his diary a newspaper article explaining Quinlan's disappearance in terms of temporary loss of power and control, and confidently declaring that Quinlan (who had actually left for Europe for good with the money) will be back shortly: "It is feared that his brain has been affected. His fellow-brokers say that he has probably become 'rattled.' This is, in fact, the only explanation that can be given. He was not a drinking man, and the idea that he has committed suicide is indignantly repudiated by those who know him well. They declare that he will return and make good his losses dollar for dollar" (Diary of Edward Neufville Tailer, May 7, 1890, New York Historical Society).

In the similar case of Frederick Ward, a broker who had forged contracts, stolen more than half a million dollars from his clients, and then disappeared, the *Chicago Daily News* presented his capture as that of a romantic hero who lost his powers of control but who, in essence, cannot be evaluated in the ethical terms of fraud:

"Mr. Ward, will you be kind enough to explain the causes leading to this arrest?" asked the DAILY NEWS correspondent, as he entered the room in which Ward was to-night. Ward made a faint effort to smile. His hitherto pallid countenance assumed a deep flush for a moment, but this quickly died away, leaving an ashen paleness. "I care to say nothing," he finally replied, with an effort to stifle his emotion: "the matter is in the hands of my attorney. I have been persecuted and blackmailed." . . . Ward finally said that he had concluded to make a clean breast of the entire transaction of his firm, as he did not propose to stand all the blame himself. He will tell a story more remarkable than romantic novels, and will show that for eighteen months he has been persecuted and blackmailed by parties who guessed his secret and compelled him to pay for their silence with millions of dollars actually stolen from trusting customers. . . . Mrs. Ward is said to be dying of nervous prostration at her mother's home in Brooklyn. It is confidently expected that Ward will make a startling confession and then blow out his brains with a revolver. He told a friend that he would never face a criminal trial. ("Ward Made Prisoner. The Ex-Stock Dealer Arrested," *Chicago Daily News*, May 23, 1884; from the diary of Edward Neufville Tailer, New York Historical Society)

The resistance, if not unwillingness, to present to the public fraudulent acts in ethical and legal terms has been noticed in many contemporary situations too, where, for instance, financial machinations like Enron's and WorldCom's have been reshaped as pioneering enterprises, as fulfilling valuable economic functions, or as due to a degree of sophistication not matched by ordinary mortals (Tillman and Indergaard 2005, pp. 256–57, 272). Considerably different from the perception of the eighteenth century, the ambiguity of the public imagination toward grand speculators (even when seen as villains, there is a nod to their superhuman feats) indicates the degree to which representations set in place in the nineteenth century have been successful in legitimating financial speculation as a non-ordinary activity to which everyone should take part.

Superpowers, however, do not prevent the grand speculator from combining courage and business sense with social conformity. In his memoir about Jay Gould, written in 1893, the former general auditor of the Erie Railroad Co., G. P. Morisini, stressed that one of Gould's strengths was his single-mindedness with respect to financial markets and his indifference to any kind of entertainment. Jay Fisk (Gould's partner), by contrast, was

> a man of undoubted talent and full of generous impulses but he lacked the cold business tact and farseeing abilities of Jay Gould. For while Mr. Gould proceeded to work quietly and smoothly, Mr Fisk by his liaisons with notorious women, his theatrical ventures and the crowd of unscrupulous heelers by which he surrounded himself, attracted to the Erie management great many enemies in America and abroad and lead the way to the disasters that followed. (*Jay Gould and the Erie Railway*, manuscript, New York Historical Society)

It is this conformity, the unwillingness to challenge established norms and codes of behavior outside the stock exchange, the outright yearning to be accepted at the top of the social hierarchy, which characterizes the speculator as part and parcel of the "society," of the small circle of very rich people spending their time at balls, dinner parties, horse races, the opera, and spas. While not susceptible to generalization, we can see this obsession in the diaries kept for almost seventy years (1848–1917) by Edward Neufville Tailer, the New York City dry goods merchant already invoked in this story. From the early 1880s on, when he achieves wealth through speculation and retires from the dry goods business, Tailer became obsessed with society events, minutely recording every single ball and every single dinner party to which he and his family were invited, pasting invitations, dinner menus, and society columns in his diary. The Astor ball; the Vanderbilt wedding; the Newport, RI crowd; and the tennis tournaments became intrinsic to a self-contained universe, regularly punctuated only by Tailer's visits to his broker. This universe was hierarchically organized, solely dedicated to conspicuous leisure and consumption, to the cultivation of manners, and apparently completely separated from any form of industrious employment (Veblen [1899] 1949, pp. 54, 76). In a manner similar to that of Antonida Vasilevna's, speculators admitted into this universe are treated as "counts" and "generals" as long as they do not experience financial failure, which would entail exclusion and regress to the status of "old men."

An episode of "loss of vital force" leading to rapid senescence is fictionalized in Frank Norris's *The Pit*, when Curtis Jadwin, the Chicago grain speculator, appears before his wife, Laura, after having lost everything. Laura was ready to leave him for another man (an artist), when Jadwin appears in the room: "Then an uncertain hand drew the heavy curtains aside. Jadwin, her husband, stood before her, his eyes sunken deep in his head, his face dead white, his hand shaking. He stood for a long instant in the middle of the room, looking at her. Then at last his lips moved: 'Old girl . . . Honey' (Norris [1903] 1956, p. 411).

The obsession with becoming part of "society" implied not only a transformation from "savage" to "civilized and cultivated," but also "the claim made constantly for the baron that he might rightfully take command of popular institutions" (Josephson [1934] 1962, p. 316). In the words of one almanac of the rich published at the turn of the twentieth century, "to write about American millionaires and not refer to the Astors, Vanderbilts, Goulds, and other money kings of the country, who by operations apart from trade and industry have achieved great fortunes, would be like writing about the Civil War and leaving out the name of General Grant" (Burnley 1901, p. 490). Belonging to "society" also meant laying a legitimate claim to leadership, thus reinforcing the notion that financial speculation and the stock exchange are the heart of economic and social life.

The fascination with the grand speculator and with Wall Street as the center of life spilled out into the realm of fiction,[4] triggering both high-brow and popular novels celebrating the warrior cult and the "financier as übermensch" (Fraser 2005, pp. 243, 279). Popular novels like

Frank Norris's *The Pit* were processed into silent movies and board games still available in the 1990s (Fraser 2005, p. 220). While a cultural counterreaction did not fail to emerge (e.g., in Thorstein Veblen's criticism of financiers as predators and as disconnected from industry), it should be said here that the utopian or critical imagination embodied in works of fiction and social criticism, respectively, operated according to the lens set in advance by the authorial voices of the stock exchange. The notions of financial speculation as relying on a vital force, of the speculator as endowed with superhuman powers, do not appear as the invention of "culture," of autonomous works of fiction. They are rather part and parcel of the observation lens set in place by writers of investment manuals and stock exchange histories, a lens through which the individual actors of the exchange can be seen in their relationship with entities like the state, the economy, and the society at large. While such a lens can and does include elements like educational fiction (addressing teenage boys, for instance), it does not primarily claim esthetic autonomy. Its aim is not contemplation and reflection as such, but observation as a path to action.

In this sense, it could be argued that the boundaries of finance set topics to which the utopian imagination (as embodied by the arts) reacts, either by adopting or by questioning them. One can either become fascinated with the "superhero" or reject him, but both stances are reactions to this topic and, as such, help reproduce it. This is so because the voices speaking about finance are not perceived as having the same authority and the same degree of expertise. Claims to authority and expertise are largely based on the enclosure of the domain being talked about. Those who claim to speak from the inside have greater authority than outsiders, an authority which includes control over themes and means of access. In other words, debates and controversies around the status of financial speculation and of speculators evolve around topics set within the boundaries of finance, not by a neutral or adversarial instance, and certainly not by a contemplative, reflexive one. Consequently, rather than undermine or dismantle this lens, continuing controversies reproduce it. In contemporary popular culture we notice the same controversies around the heroism of finance present at least since the 1880s, only that now heroic images are grafted on newer cultural products like Star Wars characters. It is therefore plausible that both the topic and the controversies around it will persist in the future, only adapted to newer cultural products.

Two related aspects, which have not been given much attention in the critical discussions around the financial übermensch, are that (1) the notion of vital force supports not only a particular figure, but a system of classifications forming a hierarchy and (2) this notion does not work on its own, but in conjunction with that of financial knowledge, which is supposed to provide access to financial activities. Often, criticism of the speculator's superhuman powers has been conjoined with statements about the esoteric character of financial knowledge and about its inaccessibility to ordinary mortals (e.g., Tillman and Indergaard 2005, pp. 87, 177, 212). This undermines the criticism itself: assuming that financial knowledge used, for instance, in the construction of derivative products is too sophisticated to be understood by common people (and even by regulators) indirectly reinforces the notion of special powers. At the same time, this latter notion works to support a whole classification system, not just an isolated figure: it provides orientation and hope for those on the lower rungs (maybe one day a smaller speculator will discover this force in her), legitimates inequality, and allows financial knowledge to be the gate through which speculation can be accessed. Yet what happens when this force is called into doubt, not by external critics, but by those who believe in it and claim or yearn to embody it? Apparently, this is hard to imagine, but there is at least an instance when radical doubt arises: the panic. In this instance, the charisma holding the classificatory system in place seems to unravel, while calculation appears to be helpless.

CHAPTER EIGHT

Panic!

Witnessing one of the first Wall Street turmoils in 1792, Harriet Golden, a member of the New York middle classes (and an investor herself), wrote to Colonel John Laurence, member of the US Congress (who also happened to be a business partner of hers), that

> the whole fabric of speculation has been so connected that a General Failure is supposed to be the inevitable issue amongst the dealers in stocks. Happy are you not to witness the Shocking Scenes that daily take place here. The depravity of the human Mind has been exhibited in its worst stage. The Speculators are daily boxing in the Streets, Cursing and Abusing each other like Pick Pockets and trying every fraud to prey on each other's distresses. This is the *real* state of Things at this moment. (Letter of Harriet M. Golden to Col. John Laurence, Esq., and member of the Congress of the US. New York, April 11, 1792, New York Historical Society; emphasis in original)

This scene belongs to what later historians of finance will later call the first Wall Street panic (e.g., Sobel [1972] 1999, p. 8), caused by the default of William Duer. Among others, it is instructive that the street turmoil, characterized as shocking, is conceptualized in terms of depravity and fraud, not in terms of disrupting economic functions. More generally, it appears that many, if not the majority, of eighteenth-century observers did not use a notion of panic similar to that we encounter in the nineteenth century.[1] Moments of collective agitation and grief seemed all too normal to observers who saw financial transactions as grounded in an incomprehensible, devilish "mechanick."

Relevant in the present context is not only to see how characterizations of financial panics change over time, but, perhaps more important, to investigate the role played by the boundaries of finance in these changes. For somebody like Harriet Golden, observing a panic meant describing what she saw on the street and framing these descriptions with moral judgments. Yet, once spatial and social boundaries are set in place, it isn't that simple anymore. First, scenes of turmoil on the stock exchange cannot be directly observed. Second, observation of a panic requires something more than seeing agitated people shouting at and elbowing each other. Observation has to relate to a scheme or definitional frame in which that which is being looked at is seen as an instance of a more encompassing class of phenomena or actions, the relevance of which can go beyond the confines of a local situation. Such schemes are often incorporated in the lenses helping us see events or phenomena which are either too large or too dispersed to be contained in a well-bounded situation like a street fight. The observation of individual activities on the stock exchange cannot be effected directly, due to institutional closure. Restricted access allows only observation from afar. This kind of observation requires an instrument, a lens which formats the activities in question as recognizable in specific ways to the observer.

When do figures on the ticker tape show a panic? How can we evaluate its consequences for the national economy and the state? What are its implications with respect to the fundamental justifications of the market? Answers to such questions have to take into account how market participants use the observational instruments at their disposal in order to make sense of the situation and to define their own positions within that situation. In other words, the question is to see whether and how such observational instruments, which are intrinsic to the boundaries of finance, play a role in the definition of what is going on, thus contributing to shaping the phenomena being observed.

Earlier in this book, the argument has been made that the boundaries of finance are flexible and adaptable enough to account for extreme as well as for "normal" situations. Normality and extremes, however, are not disconnected. If "normal" market situations are legitimated based on a combination of knowledge and vital force, what happens to them during extreme situations such as panics? What happens to the hierarchy of speculative figures which should serve as behavioral examples for smaller speculators and investors? Before turning to these questions, it is worth examining how financial panics have been dealt with by three disciplines: psychology, sociology, and economics.

Panic as Pathology

The notion of panic as a pathological belief, in which sociological conceptions are actually rooted, was configured in the second half of the nineteenth century in relationship to Platzschwindel,[2] a new diagnostic entity put forth by German doctors around 1870 (Hinton et al. 2002, p. 137). Initially, psychologists considered that panic was caused by a strain put on the eye muscles by a complex visual environment and suggested agoraphobia as a suitable alternative name. The increased attention given to hysteria by clinical psychologists at the turn of the twentieth century included an awareness of financial panics as appropriate examples of hysterical behavior. For instance, the psychologist Boris Sidis included a chapter on financial panics in his book *The Psychology of Suggestion*, published in 1897 (Zimmerman 2003, p. 70).

Laboratory experiments conducted in Germany shortly before the outbreak of World War I sought to generate empirical evidence for the "basal collective impulses" which can lead members of a group to react to (and follow) their fellow members' body movements (Moede 1920, p. 79). While these experiments aimed explicitly at improving the efficiency of group work, the author also underlined the necessity of group leadership as a means of avoiding negative collective phenomena such as panics (Moede 1920, pp. 97, 147).

In the 1960s, panic became a clinical term and was recognized as a separate psychiatric entity in 1980[3] (Hinton et al. 2002, p. 145). It is seen nowadays as belonging to the class of anxiety and mood disorders and defined as the development of anxious apprehension, a clinical manifestation of fear (Barlow 1991, pp. 61–62). It is widely agreed that panic as an emotional disorder includes physiological changes (but not necessarily a biological dysfunction), and that these changes are cognitively processed in an adaptive fashion. Psychiatrists disagree about whether panic symptoms are culturally determined. It is argued that there are actually distinct diagnostic entities encountered with different frequencies in various cultural settings. An example in this respect is the distinction made between panic attacks and "nervous attacks" (Lewis-Fernandez et al. 2002).

Sociology's Panic

More than two decades after the transformation of panic into a diagnostic entity, Gustave Le Bon made the crowd into an analytical entity of social psychology (Le Bon [1895] 1917). He saw the phenomenon of crowds as being triggered by the growing individualization of modern societies, a process which conferred "agglomerations of men" properties different from those of individuals. Yet the crowd was not identical with masses of people assembled in the same place; rather, Le Bon's definition of the crowd is that of dispersed individuals acting in step and sharing the same beliefs, in spite of their spatial dispersion. Social classes and electorates are instances of such crowds (Le Bon [1895] 1917, pp. 181, 201). Crowds are "only capable of thinking in images and are only to be impressed by images" (Le Bon [1895] 1917, p. 76); it is not rational explanation which moves them, but "startling and very clear image(s)" (p. 78). These images must not necessarily be only visual in nature; images can be formed by words too. Repetition of images and personal prestige is what moves the crowds, ensuring contagion of beliefs (Le Bon [1895] 1917, pp. 143, 148–49). Le Bon's account is an organicist one: peoples, or societies, are "an organism created by the past, and, like every other organism, it can only be modified by slow hereditary accumulations" ([1895] 1917, p. 93). Within this organism, the crowd reacts to images and to prestige.

Relevant here is the parallel introduction of two notions in two different disciplines. One is panic as a clinical entity; the other is the crowd as a dispersed mass of individuals coordinated by the means of images and by a common orientation to prestige, developing the same sentiments at once. Initially thought as caused by visual strains in public places (one sees too much; the eye muscles are strained), panic is fear of the crowd (hence the idea that it overlaps with agoraphobia). The crowd, in its turn, can neither be directly observed, nor can it directly observe, since it is mostly dispersed. Both notions require observational systems: the crowd is constituted by coordinated observation of the same images, while panic is a specific reaction triggered by perceptions. One sees or observes something which triggers fear and then flight. Observation does not necessarily mean here direct observation; only in a few cases could the crowd, according to Le Bon, observe something directly.

Perhaps the best-known case of panic triggered by observation of images (and one which almost certainly influenced sociological research) is that of *War of the Worlds*, performed in 1938 by Orson Welles and the

Mercury Theatre on the Air and broadcast on the Columbia Broadcasting System. Welles reworked H. G. Wells's novel about an alien invasion from Mars (set by Welles in New Jersey) into a radio play which was broadcast on Sunday, October 30, 1938, from 8:00 to 9:00 p.m., triggering a real panic. In spite of the introductory caveat about the play being only fiction, many listeners believed an alien invasion was actually taking place; some fled the area or reported later seeing flashes of the fighting in the distance. Examining Welles's script can provide some valuable clues about how this panic was triggered without any direct, actual observation of invading aliens. The characters of the play are observers who report to each other and to the reporter what they have witnessed. The audience witnesses several, superimposed accounts of observations made by persons enjoying either professional authority or eyewitness status. For instance, in the opening of the broadcast tango music is played and then interrupted by the announcer, who reports unusual astronomical events and then talks to astronomers from Princeton University supposed to have made the observations (Wells 1938). The public listens to reported observations which are then corroborated by other reported observations. These reports appear to be spontaneous and interrupt the supposedly usual broadcast. Moreover, the public witnesses the reactions of the imagined public—the "crowd"—to these observations and develops reactions similar to those reported to be observed on the radio. In this case, panic was triggered not by any direct observation of events, but by reported observations of both the invasion and the public's reactions to it.

Welles's episode highlights the significance of panic, understood not simply as a disruption of usual functions (economic, political, or otherwise), but as the dissolution of a given order, a notion which reverberated in subsequent sociological research. Panic, as well as order, require the coordination of dispersed actors (the crowd) by means of an observational system to which they simultaneously orient themselves. In Welles's case, the observational system was the radio broadcast reporting the multivoiced witnessing of events supposed to take place in real time. In contrast to, say, a stampede at a theatre exit during a fire, when visitors panic because they observe other visitors rushing to the door, in the broadcast of *War of the Worlds* the panic ensued because radio listeners imitated the imagined behavior of a public in the play.

Small wonder, then, that sociological research discovered panic as an object of empirical investigation in the late 1930s, in relationship to new media such as the radio (Orr 2006, pp. 37–38). Paul Lazarsfeld, who worked on the Radio Project, initially based at Princeton and later at the Columbia University, was interested in the study of radio-induced panics too (Orr 2006, p. 57). After World War II, sociological investigations of panic intensified, in relationship to the threat of a nuclear attack (Tiryakian 1959; Foreman 1953; Forman 1963, p. 285). Initially, panic was conceptualized as nonsocial behavior and as disintegration of social norms (Quarantelli 1954, p. 270), but since the 1960s the view on panic as a specific form of collective behavior has prevailed (e.g., Smelser 1962; Forman 1963; Coleman 1990, pp. 215–18). While this view endorsed the notion that panic was a form of rational behavior, distinct from psychoses and neuroses, it retained an irrational component at its core.

During the 1980s and the 1990s, the topic of moral panic rose to attention. Against the background of infectious diseases such as AIDS and later BSE, the notion of moral panic sought to highlight in the first place the media mechanisms through which social resources are mobilized to the exclusion and isolation of specific groups. In this case too, hysterical beliefs diffused by the media were regarded as playing a key role in setting in place exclusionary mechanisms. At the same time, moral panics include a blame-placing component and operate with a distinction between pure and impure groups or persons. After a period of eclipse, panic seems to have been rediscovered by sociologists in relationship to the threats posed by global terrorism and the recent series of natural disasters (floods, tsunami waves, heat waves).

The sociological view of panic as a form of collective behavior, which stresses the conditions for panic as intrinsic to the group, are (1) structural conduciveness (given by opportunities for communication and escape), (2) strain (the threat as perceived by actors), (3) hysterical belief (anxiety and fear), and (4) mobilization for flight (Smelser 1962, p. 133). While the first two conditions are necessary but not sufficient for triggering a panic, hysterical belief and collective mobilization play a crucial role (Mann, Nagel, and Dowling 1976, p. 232). As emotional collective phenomena, panics then raise the question of how this "mob hysteria" emerges and takes hold of dispersed actors; how everybody feels the same in spite of a lack of direct contact. In other words, how is a "herd" produced when there is none there to be seen?

This question is related to the sociological treatment of emotions as changes in bodily states accompanied by cognitive reactions (Berezin 2005, p. 110), or as (dis)trust relationships "constituted within and between powerful organizations for rationally coping with the unknown in decision processes" (Pixley 2004, p. 20). These two views seem to be mutually exclusive: according to the first, cognitive reactions succeed and attempt to process changes in physical states. Therefore, emotions arise as a cognitive response to changes in one's body. Consequently, we would need to explain how collective emotions arise: how do dispersed actors develop the same cognitive reactions to bodily states which they cannot share? Seen in this perspective, this is a variety of the solipsism problem discussed in the sociology of scientific knowledge during at least the past two decades (e.g., Lynch 1992, p. 222). According to the second view, emotions are not individual, but collective reactions to uncertainty problems. This echoes a vision of emotions as Durkheimian "facts," irreducible to their individual components. If this is so, then it becomes difficult to explain how emotions arise in the first place as a collective phenomenon.

If hysterical emotions are actually cognitively processed changes in bodily states,[4] then we could perhaps explain contagion within one locale: panics arise when actors observe such changes and send signals about them to other actors, who then imitate these signals, spreading them further. In this case, imitation is the key explanation; this would work well for the case of traders acting on the same floor, but less so for dispersed actors, who cannot reciprocally observe changes in their respective bodily states.[5] As for the alternative concept of emotion (as interorganizational trust relationships), this would have to account for how emotions emerge in the first place as a collective phenomenon.

These crucial questions—how "hysterical beliefs" emerge and how they spread—are grounded in at least two assumptions: the first is that of a pathological character of belief (anxiety/fear), which pertains to the medical domain. The change in bodily states does not fall within the boundaries of medical normality; therefore, the cognitive processing of these changes is disorderly and may have pathological traits. The second assumption is that of a "crowd," mass," or "mob" through which these beliefs spread. Thus, the sociological treatment of panics as a paradigmatic form of extreme behavior does not actually renounce the irrational element (the hysteria, irreducible to rational behavioral elements), combined with the social element of "mass" or "crowd." The conceptual difficulties arise not only when this "crowd" is not actually present in one place, but also in trying to account, on purely sociological terms, for how fear emerges and why it spreads so quickly. Arguing that fear is spread by imitation actually undermines any attempt to treat collective behavior as rational, since it amounts o saying that, in the manner of the experiments conducted by

Walter Moede before World War I (Moede 1920), group members follow and imitate the physical manifestations of their fellows.

In an attempt to avoid recourse to fear while preserving the definition of panic as a form of collective behavior, James Coleman (1990, pp. 202, 205) emphasized the role played by transfer of control in the emergence of panic phenomena. Transfer of control means that members of a group, crowd, or audience react to events unfolding in the situation according to norms and conventions, as well as to the expectations of their peers. In a theater fire, for instance, those taking initial action "on their own without transferring control" (Coleman 1990, p. 202) may ensure an orderly exit instead of panic. In this case, those taking the initiative choose not to comply with the expectation of panic shared by at least some in the audience. Transfer of control would thus mean conformity, while keeping control over one's own actions would mean nonconformism. Thus, the problem of panic behavior is seen as one of agency.

While Coleman sought to avoid emotions in this explanation, others have acknowledged their role. Charles Smith, for instance, considers that crowd behavior emerges when market participants lose faith in their own view of events, succumbing to accounts and opinions which they had earlier dismissed (Smith 1999, p. 125). This abandonment points toward tensions and conflicts involving not only opinions and arguments, but also emotional energies, or what Smith (1999, p. 129) calls "the emotional pull of the market." Therefore, emotions cannot be completely avoided when accounting for agency during panics.

A better understanding of the link between agency, emotions, and panic behavior would require a closer look at the face-to-face situations where panic unfolds. In such situations, individuals confront each other not only intellectually, but emotionally as well, through bodily actions and verbal exchanges. Confrontations are part of the participants' attempts to control the situation, and can lead to tensional buildup (Collins 2008, p. 90). Buildup can be accompanied by fear that control will be lost, which in turn can increase aggressivity and violence, thus leading to what Randall Collins calls forward panic (2008, p. 94). Thus, notions similar with Coleman's transfer of control are applied to situations (instead of isolated individual actions) and seen as part of an ongoing interaction with uncertain outcomes. Paying close attention to the interaction order helps explain how localized panic behavior emerges. The issue here is to understand its dispersed emergence and diffusion as well. Moreover, fight or loss of situational control often implies that the definition of a situation changes.

In dispersed panics, the mechanisms through which such definitions are produced and diffused cannot be reduced to direct observations of an event (like a theater curtain catching fire). Therefore, the question is how arrangements for indirect observation contribute to producing situational definitions adopted by dispersed actors. Before examining this further, it is worth taking a short look at how economists have dealt with the same phenomenon.

The Economics of Panic

While already present in financial publications in the 1820s, panics became an object of systematic description in the 1860s. They were classified according to the area in which they were manifest (e.g., mercantile, banking, stock exchange panics) and described in terms of monetary mass and price variations (e.g., Gassiot 1867), while psychological aspects were mentioned in passing. A central preoccupation was identifying past events as panics and reformulating them in appropriate terms. Economists like John Stuart Mill and Stanley Jevons also developed an interest in the study of panics and crises; while Mill saw them as essentially psychological phenomena, Jevons connected them to the periodicity of natural phenomena like sunspots (Selwyn-Brown 1910, p. 158). Toward the end of the nineteenth century, financiers acknowledged the psychological element in panic as central, turning to and citing psychologists like Boris Sidis and Cesare Lombroso (Zimmerman 2003, p. 79). In a paper written for the American Academy of Political and Social Science, Myron T. Herrick, the chairman of the Board Savings Society from Cleveland, Ohio, wrote: "The immediate circumstances that produce a financial or industrial panic are never the same, and it is these circumstances that determine the direction that the disturbance is to take as well as the duration and the severity of the depression that usually follows. The periodicity of crises is undoubtedly a psychological phenomenon and is an expression of the erythmic movement between hope and despair, optimism and pessimism, that has ever characterized society" (Herrick 1907, pp. 10–11).

Among the psychological factors responsible for financial panics, passions were prominent: "The fundamental cause of all these misfortunes was excessive passion for speculation, which inflated credit to the bursting point. And as speculation will always exist where surplus wealth exists, recurring panics will always hold a place in the normal order of things this side of the social millenium" (Stedman 1905, p. 261).

Economic historians have defined financial panics as part of a crisis and as tied to a crash or collapse in asset prices: "a panic, 'a sudden fright without cause' [. . .] may occur in asset markets or involve a rush from less liquid securities to money or government securities" (Kindleberger and Aliber 2005, p. 94). Panics are induced by asset shocks and asymmetric information, compounded with uncertainties and the market actors' preference for liquidity (Calomiris and Masson 1997, p. 863). Uncertainties and asymmetric information contribute to generate a collective irrational phenomenon involving "mob psychology" and person-to-person contagion (Chen 1999, pp. 947–48; Kelly and O Grada 2000, p. 1110):[6] the fright spreads through "group thinking" throughout the mass of market participants, who begin to "move as a herd" (Kindleberger and Aliber 2005, p. 36). They are similar in this respect to financial manias, which also involve herd behavior and hysterical beliefs (Smelser 1962, p. 131); panics, however, may be more intense and take place within a short time span, which increases the damage. Panics are also tied to manias, being usually understood as accelerating the decline of asset prices after a period of economic expansion and boom. From this point of view, financial panics are an essentially irrational phenomenon, of an emotional nature, which disrupts market functionality. They are triggered by sudden changes in the mind sets of market actors, by mood swings from confidence to pessimism (Kindleberger and Aliber 2005, p. 77).

We encounter here the same treatment of extreme behavior within a psychological framework of irrationality, coupled, this time, with an emphasis on the role played by the circulation of information. While this latter helps account for the simultaneous occurence of panic in different places, the key role continues to be played by the fear element. Perhaps with the exception of psychology itself, which has nowadays embraced a neurological model, disciplines like sociology and economics largely continue to treat panic on the grounds of a nineteenth-century view of irrationality and imitatory impulsiveness, a view which the psychology of that time had developed based mostly on financial panics. When this impulsiveness, equated with disorder, spreads, social order (and indeed sociality) unravels.

Yet one cannot but notice here that this presumed impulsiveness leaves aside the symbolic elements present in panics, elements which play a considerable role in the coordination of dispersed actions. For instance, when social and personal hierarchies perceived to support the order of the marketplace crumble, this latter can unravel. When personal symbols of power and authority suddenly disappear or lose their charismatic force, disorder can spread. Social arrangements relying on combinations of rational and irrational elements (of knowledge and personal charisma) can be particularly susceptible to the unravelling of symbolic elements. Such unravelling does not necessarily have to be observed directly: symbols work on the basis of their representational force.

Financial panics include and rely on tools for the dispersed observation of something which cannot be directly accessed (market transactions). This is not to say that financial turmoils emerge first with such tools. The argument here is that the very concepts of panic and crowds emerge in the later nineteenth century; both imply dispersed imitative behavior, of a kind irreducible to direct observation of the marketplace. Consequently, we should distinguish here between a restricted, economic definition of financial panics as sudden price slumps and depreciation of assets and a broader sociological definition, which needs to take into account the specific social mechanisms related to panic behavior.

In this sense, panics can be seen as coordinated indirect observations of disruptions,[7] observations that increase behavioral uncertainties. Indirect observations provide actors with situational definitions, helping them make sense of their own behavior in a broader frame. Sharing the same observational instruments means sharing the same situational definitions, even if market actors are spatially dispersed.

An instrument like the stock ticker, for instance, allows observations of price data variations at a distance. Since these variations represent financial transactions,[8] they provide patterns of real-time order. Making sense of these patterns (as slow, rapid, frenzied, and so on) requires additional observational instruments, like the financial charts I have discussed in chapter 5. They allow observers to see price movements as orderly or disorderly, as normal or not. Observers, however, should be able to account for why price movements are seen in a specific way. Such an account presupposes not only the ability to identify visual patterns, but also to relate them to a narrative of real-time events, one which should also include the observer. Narratives of market events operate with figures provided by the kaleidoscope of finance. Speculators need to relate to this figural hierarchy as a mode of observing the market. A questioning of the force underlying this hierarchy can generate disorder and uncertainties, and imitations of represented behavior can amplify the perceived disruptions.

Panic and Imagined Behavior

I will return here to Edward Neufville Tailer who, during his half-century
career, witnessed several financial panics in New York city, and was directly implicated in some of them. What is noticeable from the perspective of the individual involved in a panic is the apparent lack of erratic or
hysterical behavior.[9] Of course, the behavior displayed by one investor in
his diary entries cannot be taken as representative for all investor behav-
iors. Nevertheless, such entries reveal behavioral patterns which cannot
be considered solipsistic; if they were so, then the actor in question would
have noticed that his peers manifest incomprehension and give signs that
his behavior is inappropriate. Over decades, this would result either in
the actor's isolation or in behavioral changes. None of this is observed in
the diaries of Edward Neufville Tailer. Therefore, while I do not take his
reactions to panic to be representative for all financial actors, I take them
as having the significance of a pattern shared by several actors. These reactions become even more significant if we contrast them with descriptions
of panic published in the newspapers of the time, which Tailer clipped
and pasted next to his own observations. We thus get two parallel, clearly
different perspectives: one is that of the individual directly observing the
failure of his investments, or his increased incapacity to honor debts; the
other is that of indirect observations of panic. These observations act as
a sort of lens for seeing a broader and different phenomenon, and as a
tool for making sense of the personal situation in a broader context. This
sense-making tool rather increases than reduces the behavioral uncertainties of its user.

   As a speculator, during panics, Tailer was under the pressure of financial obligations which he could not easily meet. However, from the
perspective of the individual the main issue during a panic is that of maintaining a degree of control over his own situation, and working toward a
solution. In many cases, finding a solution simply meant calling on various business partners and obtaining extensions and additional loans from
them. Thus, the panic of September 1873, caused by the failure of Jay
Cooke (a prominent speculator), caught Tailer with his guard down. He
had to find money to meet his obligations, and started calling on his old
acquaintances, cultivated during years of socializing:

   Sept 17 1873: There has been a great panic in Wall Street today owing to the
   failure of Jay Cooke and Co—at noon I bought for my own acct 100 shares of

Chicago & Rock Island @100 and at 2 pm I bought for Mr. J. A. Hamilton on a telegram from Newport 100 shares @ 98 ½. This stock ten days ago was selling @ 108. My brokers are Messrs Leonard Sheldon & Foster. Western Union Telegraph stock fell 10% in a short time.

Sept 18 1873: I found it exceedingly difficult to raise money today to pay for the 100 shares of Rock Island, which I had purchased the day before through Messrs Leonard Sheldon & Foster. I finally succeeded at 2 pm in getting my note for $6,000 ten days to run discounted at the German American Bank, the President Mr. Emil Sauer conferred this favor upon me. . . . The financial panic is the main topic of conversation at the Newport Club, and Mr. J. A. Hamilton came to see me in relation to it. (Diary of Edward Neufville Tailer, February 12, 1872 to May 28, 1874, New York Historical Society)[10]

A decade later, during the panic of May 1884, Tailer showed the same kind of attitude; while permanent observation of events, watching the ticker, and calling upon acquaintances are essential activities, erratic or hysterical behavior is not part of the picture he provides. Neither he nor the persons he spends time with seem to behave in a panicky fashion, although they are under considerable financial stress. This does not mean, of course, that hysterical behavior was completely inexistent. Tailer gives us a hint of the stress he was submitted to when he mentions the struggles to get cash, that he will long remember this panic, or that he and L. T. Hoyt, his broker, remain together until midnight:

May 14, 1884: The panic to day in Wall St. will long be remembered by me, at 10 ¼ am I sold at the opening, 300 shares through LT Hoyt of N.P. Pref. @48, it after wards sold down to 43 ½. I. H. Prall &Co. sold [afterwards?] for me, 200 L.N. @ 41 ¾—200 Central Pacific @ 40 ¼—the former sold to day for 32 ½ and the latter 35. I am a stock holder in the Metropolitan Bank and was [found?] to notice the suspension of my old time friends O. M. Bogart & Co.

May 15, 1884: The Metropolitan Bank resumed business today at noon— but towards 3 PM confidence was again shaken by the failure of Fisk & Hatch and A. W. Dimock & Co. At the Union Club the evening I met Messrs. Cottin, Wm.L. Strong and Mr. Kendell discussing the situation later I called upon Mr. L. T. Hoyt and remained with him until 12 o'clock.

May 16, 1884: The great struggle back yesterday and to day has been to get the ready cash to perform the usual function of settling the differences in financial transactions. The Union Trust has called in a call loan which I have with them for $50,000, but I hope to convince Mr. Edward L. Strong to let it

remain on Monday should the market let off. (Diary of Edward Neufville Tailer,
1884–85, New York Historical Society)

Ten years later, in the panic of 1893 caused by Erie Railroad Co. going
into receivership, Tailer mentions the first signs of physical strain put on
him by panics. He is sixty-three now and needs to take electric baths and
consult doctors in times of financial distress. Nevertheless, the same old
pattern of behavior is there—watching the ticker, calling upon business
partners, regretting not having sold earlier:

> Sep. 26, 1893: I have not been feeling very well. [Sunday?] I dined with Mr.
> Berger at the Swedish Restaurant something that I eat on that day must have
> hastened me—my bowels have pained me ever since, and I consulted a Dr.
> about them at the Hyde Park Hotel. The stock market is upset today and all
> stocks have fallen from 2 to 8%, Erie which touched 16 last week has been to 12
> $^5/_8$ Atchinson from 22 to 18 ½ N.P. Pref. from 23 ½ to 18 ¾, what a sell they all
> would have been last week if one had had the courage to sell. (Diary of Edward
> Neufville Tailer, 1893–94, New York Historical Society)

However, when one turns to the newspaper clippings which Tailer
pasted regularly next to his own entries, the situation changes radically.
That these clippings mattered to Tailer is indicated, in part, by his habit
of repeating article headlines in his own handwriting, as if "Panic in Wall
Street" would indeed define a panic in Wall Street. They appear to work
as a material instrument, a lens through which Tailer reconsiders his own
observations of events and redefines them accordingly. This lens allows
him to connect what was going on in the offices of C. T. Hoyt or of the German American Bank with the larger social world. On June 22, 1884, for instance, Tailer pasted a newspaper clipping (half a column) bearing the title
"Wall Street To-Day. The Stock Market Very Weak and Panicky." Next
to it, he wrote: "The stock market to-day is weak and panicky," between
notes about leaving Annandale for NY and about dinner that evening. On
the left-hand margin he wrote "Panic." This is indicative of how imagined
observations of panic, such as those included in a newspaper report, can
become definitional resources for speculators. A panic is that which is observed by others as a "panic."

These clippings provide, among other things, an all-encompassing definition; panics are seen as biological phenomena (and hence uncontrollable) marking the evolution of humanity:

History is made in these times with great rapidity; the old story of wars and re-
bellions, of financial crashes, of plagues and pestilence, which in earlier generations it was the task of a quarter of a lifetime to catalogue within the memory,
is now the story of everyday experience. Human sensations are swift in their
successions as the varied chatter of the telegraph wire. (Newspaper clipping,
"Panics and Their Power," June 23, 1866, Diary of Edward Neufville Tailer,
1862–66, New York Historical Society).[11]

Such clippings provide an observational system of something which
cannot be directly witnessed by speculators: behavior different from that
of a group discussing panic over the dinner table, or of a broker sitting
together with his clients. These are crowd scenes as observed for a dispersed public, one that doesn't have any means of directly observing what
is going on. One such scene is from September 1873, during the panic
caused by the failure of Jay Cooke, when Tailer was busy securing money
from the German American Bank, and it was published by the *New York
Times* under the telling title "The Panic. Excitement in Wall Street." Before reproducing it here almost in its entirety, and as paradigmatic for
this imagined observation of crowds, I will stress again that more general
conceptualizations of panic echo the general theme of a loss of vital force.
Panic, wrote a commentator, is "the evil genius of industry, commerce,
trade, and finance" which human ingenuity cannot prevent (Eadie 1873,
p. 2). Panics are "correlative of great activity of mind in business affairs"
and raise the mortality among businessmen (Eadie 1873, pp. 38–39). They
destroy "the vital energy," arrest development, and ruin whole generations (Phillips 1826, pp. 35–36).

Crowds can be astute and insane at the same time; they can be mobilized by speculators in their fights with each other, acting as an instrument
of destruction. But they can also act on their own: therefore, it is crucial
to realize whether they are the instrument of somebody's will, of an individual force which can be fought off, or whether they are express pure
disorder. In the following excerpt, a fictional speculator is terrified by the
crowd until he realizes that the apparently senseless actions are orches-
trated by his main opponent:

They did not know how much more was coming until Dunlap, his face convulsed as with mingled anger and terror, shrilly implored the crowd to buy five
thousand from him at thirty-seven. . . . That clearly, unmistakably, meant that
a bad break was coming—it was coming whether Rock was selling to be rid of

stock he had and didn't want or whether he was selling stock he did not have but wished to buy cheaper. Then the astute mob went mad, visibly and audibly insane, and offered a car-load of Virginia Central stock at thirty-six, at thirty-five and one half, and the commission houses that had "stop loss" orders at thirty-six also sold—real stock, theirs, not merely contracts—and the specialists sold and everybody sold—excepting Dunlap, his face no longer panic-stricken, but watchful. (Lefevre 1907, p. 132)

While another individual can be successfully opposed, once his manipulations have been seen through, pure disorder means loss of force. How can this loss occur? I will turn now to the New York Times article clipped by Tailer and look for an answer in its description of the 1873 panic. The first signs are rumors about an apparently unexpected event, followed by excitement, stunned silence, and excitement again:

> The first intimation which came into the Stock Exchange of any change in the programme was contained in a brief notice, which said authoritatively that Jay Cooke & Co had suspended payment. To say that the street beamed excited would only give a feeble view of the expressions of feeling. The brokers stood perfectly thunderstruck for a moment, and then there was a general run to notify the different houses in Wall Street of the failure.

This sets in motion the observation of human mass movement in the marketplace, followed by an immediate mobilization of forces. Time becomes compressed, and deliberation is replaced by action:

> The brokers surged out of the Exchange, tumbling pell mell over each other in the general confusion, and reached their respective offices in race horse time. The members of the firms who were surprised by this announcement had no time to deliberate.

This mobilization is followed by the first round of a fierce battle; the enemy was already at work on the trading floor, in a move which seems to contradict the initial element of surprise. Now the reader can observe the battle taking place on the floor, one which brings about defeat and demoralization:

> The bear clique was already selling the market down in the Exchange, and prices were declining frightfully. Of course every one gave orders to sell holdings as

quick as possible, in order to obtain the best prices, and in this way when the brokers returned to the Long Room a fresh impetus was given to the decline, which brought about a fearful panic. There was no one on hand with nerve and money to arrest it either, and so the bear clique, taking advantage of the general demoralization, made confusion worse confounded.

With the spread of the news, a new wave of soldiers is mobilized and a second round of violent fighting ensues, one which is decisively won by the enemy:

> The news of the panic spread in every direction down town, and hundreds of people who had been carrying stocks in expectation of a rise, rushed into the offices of their brokers and left orders that their holdings should be immediately sold out. In this way prices fell off so rapidly that even Vanderbilt could not have stemmed the tide. The Stock Exchange had been the arena of many desperate conflicts between bulls and bears, and it is hard to discriminate as to the violence of the respective melees, but it was said by old frequenters of Wall Street that no panic so frightful had ensued since the failure of the Ohio Trust Company in 1857 as that witnessed yesterday.

This time, the lost battle leads to loss of reason and to actions which cannot be accounted for in rational terms anymore. As if on a battlefield, the survivors lose the capacity of thinking clearly:

> The sellers and purchasers in the Exchange seemed to have lost their reason in many instances, and shouted out one offer in one minute, and then, either completely demoralized or oversanguine, put the price up or down one or two per cent. At one time there seemed to be no bottom to the market, and if the bears had pressed their advantage, it is likely that stocks would have declined much lower than was the case.

All that is left now is the bare instinct for individual survival; scavengers appear on the battlefield:

> Men went about the street with blanched faces, and requested piteously of their brokers that their stocks should not be sold out as more margin would be obtained in the morning; but self-preservation seemed to be the first law of nature with every one, so the accounts of the customers were closed out, and the losses became a fixed fact. [. . .] At the corner of Broad Street and Exchange Place a

wild crowd of money lenders and borrowers collected and tried to fix a rate for loans. It seemed almost impossible to do so for a time, as everyone was afraid to take stocks as security for fear of a terrible fall and consequent loss. The matter hung in the balance for some time after the extent of the panic became positively known until borrowers were afraid they would not be able to strengthen up their bank accounts unless action was taken at once. Then they bid until the price of money touched one half of one per cent per day and legal interest. (Pasted in the September 19, 1873, entry of the Diary of Edward Neufville Tailer, from Feb 12, 1872, to May 28, 1874, New York Historical Society)

This account forms an abstract narrative, with a self-contained temporal structure, one which is disconnected from external reference points. We do not know, for instance, the time of the day when the news comes, or when the battle begins. We do not have here the perspective of the individual actor. It is as if the observer sees everything that happens in the marketplace from above and at once, never descending and mixing with the actors. The focus is on the crowds, of which at least two types are present here. First, there is the crowd listening to the news, stunned yet eager to mobilize and take action. Second, there is the fighting crowd, one which battles "the bears" in the market, mobilizing twice and losing. (Interestingly enough, these "bears" appear more like a faceless enemy who has been long awaiting this moment. They are not surprised or stunned by the news, and they rush nowhere. They are already in the market waiting for the others to come and fight.) While the first crowd observes, the second crowd acts. The reader is incorporated within the narrative from at least two vantage points: that of the stunned observer, and that of the acting speculator.

In another narrative, pasted again in a diary along with personal observations of events, the collapse of a whole social order requires the intervention of armed forces:

Representatives of almost every class were there. The great merchant stood side by side with the *sans culotte*—the gutter stripe of society; the man of law compared notes with the Wall Street "goat," an individual known only to brokers; and, in fine, everybody, not forgetting the bootblacks and a few City politicians, found standing room opposite the Gold Room, and looked in gaping astonishment at the kaleidoscopic indicator. . . . Inside the room the scene almost beggars description. While the "bull" party were frantically bidding above the market rates, in one part of the room, the "bears" were offering gold in another at much below them. Around the fountain, which occupies the centre of the room, some 200 persons were collected, and he who can imagine the din created by 200 human voices, all hoarse and discordant from over-use, and all exerted to the outmost at the same moment, may perhaps form a slight conception of the Bedlam here presented. Nor did the doughty bulls and bears confine themselves to bellowing and roaring. Their gesticulations, their jostling and crowding, their restless change of position, all indicated the excitement under which they labored. A stranger, viewing them for the first time, would have supposed that their excitement would lead to unpleasant results physically, but further inspection would have convinced him that they were not actuated by anger, but by a passion much more to be deplored—avarice. [. . .] It is said that the Adjutant-General of the State ordered that two Brooklyn regiments be kept in readiness to move on Wall-Street in case of a riot. (Newspaper clipping, "The Gold Excitement," *New York Times*, September 25, 1869; pasted in the September 23, 1869, entry of the Diary of Edward Neufville Tailer 1866–70, New York Historical Society)

The plot of the above narratives is surprise/mobilization/fight/mobilization/fight and final defeat/loss of reason/hopelessness and flight for self-preservation. The dramatic character of this loss of reason comes from the absence of vital force it implies, and from the shattering of the existing hierarchy, which is rendered powerless. The traders cannot withstand the "bears" that inflict damage after damage; no grand speculator (not even Vanderbilt) can stop this destructive force. Incidentally, this structure is identical to that of Orson Welles's *War of the Worlds*, which triggered a real panic. The broadcast starts with surprising observations of unexplained astronomic events, followed by direct, on-site observations of the landed spaceships. The first alien attacks are followed by mobilization, fight, defeat, an even larger mobilization, fight, and total defeat. Finally, the two survivors, the Stranger (who seems to have has lost reason) and Professor Pierson are disoriented and clinging to their lives. Toward the end of the play, Professor Pierson asks, "What is there left?" The Stranger retorts, "Life! That's what! I want to live. Yeah, and so do you" (Wells 1938). Clinging onto one's bare life as the last horizon left appears to be an essential component of panic.

Both in Welles's radio broadcast and in Wall Street's panics, we encounter a dispersed crowd observing (through a lens) a crowd which observes a surprising event, then engages in a battle and is radically defeated. The dispersed crowd looking through the lens assumes to share the situation of the imagined crowd, and takes this imagined crowd to be its own mirror. Based on this assumption of sharing the same disruptive situation, on the identification of the dispersed crowd with the imagined one, actors orient their behavior to the situational definition provided by indirect observations.[12] They identify themselves as part of a situation shared with others, who are not immediately present, yet with whom they coordinate by means of the same observational instruments. The shared situation is not reducible to downward price movements; while quite stressful, these latter are not automatically perceived as life threatening. The shared situation (which involves engagement in a life-significant battle) is one produced in the observational lens. One of its key elements is the possibility of a life-threatening outcome, which the existing social hierarchies cannot prevent.

Returning to Edward Neufville Tailer, our New York merchant and speculator, I want to reexamine his habit of pasting newspaper clippings along with his handwritten daily entries. True, his entries during panics do not show any signs of erratic or hysterical behavior; they are the notes of somebody confronted with practical problems. During the panic of 1873, he finds it "exceedingly difficult" to raise money and spends days with his broker. Yet his activities are paralleled and complemented by an observational system which helps him make sense of his actions. It is exceedingly difficult to find money because there is a panic, not because he personally has fallen out of favor. He sells at lower prices during a panic, not because of something else. He has to incur losses on stock because of the panic.[13] This is an observational system which helps him define larger situations and account for his own behavior; it's not only that he repeats in his own handwriting the titles of newspaper clippings (like "Panic!"), but he also relates what he sees and what he does in this shared situation of panic. After the panic he notes that "the travel to Newport is now becoming very light" (September 26, 1873), that the "financial situation is still dark and [. . .] owing to the unsettled state of the stock market, there was a small crowd at Jerome Park today" (October 16, 1873, entry in the Diary of Edward Neufville Tailer, from Feb 12, 1872 to May 28, 1874, New York Historical Society).

A similar observational system is employed by Tailer with respect to his other main preoccupation, namely social life. The newspaper clippings describing society events to which he was invited, and which mention his name, appear as both a confirmation of his status (acknowledged member of society) and as an observational system through which he makes sense of his own actions. Even if he was at the Astor ball and observed what was going on there, he could not have observed "the Astor ball" as a whole. It is this perspective from above which he apparently needs, and which is provided by the imagined "Astor ball." Needless to say, such an observational system does not have to be exhaustive or reveal the whole backstage in order to be effective. It rather reassembles various elements (e.g., descriptions of the dresses of Mrs. Vanderbilt and Mrs. Astor, of the menu, of the flower decoration, etc.) as "the ball" to be seen by everybody from a distance.

In a similar way, the observation of "panic" from above, made with the help of newspaper clippings, of narratives incorporating the reader as an observer and providing him with a specific vantage point (not identical to that of his own personal experiences) works as an instrument for making sense of situations and for positioning one's activities in a broader frame. Yes, Tailer was at the Astor ball, as constituted not only by the dancing, the menus, and the ball gowns, but also by descriptions of the whole. And yes, Tailer was in several panics, as constituted not only by his efforts to get credit, but also by descriptions of larger processes, implying battles and loss of charisma.

With this, I return to the example of Dostoevsky's narrator, who contrasts gambling as individual freedom with subordination to the abstract principle of accumulation. A similar kind of freedom is supported by the notions of speculation as a vital force and by the grand speculators as its ultimate embodiments. It is the freedom to defeat chance and to win "battles" against "the market." This individualistic view resonates well with the idea of speculators as calculating individuals, steeped in observation and knowledge. This freedom, together with the force which supports it, are central features of the speculator's charisma, of which Max Weber was aware when he argued that trading should be left to the grand speculators. Yet this individual freedom is never on its own, but grows in the dark shadow of the crowd. As such, it is a rather fragile plant, since it can be easily destroyed by the compelling force of masses, real or imagined. When these begin to move, the social hierarchies which legitimate speculation begin to crumble; the charisma of individuals is trampled upon, the order of the market is undermined. The celebration of individual freedom and force, cultivated even in our days, is replaced by the crushing movement of the crowd. The dark side of rationality, the nemesis of the calculating individual, is not so much uncontrollable hysterical behavior as the imagined mass. This, of course, does not mean that concrete individuals cannot make profits in a time of panic. It means rather that a discourse which justifies and encourages broad participation in financial transactions by appealing to freedom and vitality reveals itself in such situations as illusory.

With this, I want to reexamine the ways in which the notion of observational boundaries can help advance our understanding of panic phenomena. Two interrelated aspects should be stressed here: first, dispersed panic behavior (encountered in but not restricted to financial crises) sends us back to the uncertain coordination of action, discussed in the introduction to this book. Systems of indirect observation contribute to coordinating uncertain actions by providing actors with situational definitions. These can increase behavioral uncertainties and thus encourage extreme forms of behavior, without automatically triggering the latter. This helps us to understand better issues like struggles for control over the situation (emphasized by James Coleman and Randall Collins, among others), a control implying situational definitions.

Second, we have to notice that, at least in financial panics, such definitions imply at least a suspension of the assumptions that justify finance, and which are significant for trust relationships. If the boundaries of finance include representations of financial "heroes" (be they individuals or institutions) having exemplary force, panics delegitimize these representations. A more recent example in this sense is the rapid unraveling of the investment bank Bear Stearns, which happened over the course of a weekend in March 2008. Sudden loss of trust, leading to the unwillingness to extend lines of credit, occurred in spite of public assurances by executives about the bank's solidity. It can be argued that this loss was tied to a broader situational definition that delegitimated specific claims of trustworthiness. Such claims rested not only on financial figures, but also (and perhaps more importantly) on the bank's prestige, long history, and ranking at the top of the league. Yet the crumbling of hierarchies (as seen, for instance, in the repeated questioning of big bank's portfolios) rendered such claims ineffectual.

Back to the Future

Culture and the Boundaries of Finance

The problems I have dealt with in this book are intrinsic to what has been called at least since Max Weber "the spirit of capitalism," understood as the system of beliefs, attitudes, and routines underlying the West's modern economic order. This order has financial markets at its core; it relies more and more upon them as an answer not only to economic but also to social issues (the reform of pension systems being a case in point here), a reliance which presupposes the widespread if not universal acceptance of markets as socially legitimate, even desirable. The legitimacy question is in its turn closely related to that of the boundaries of financial markets. These boundaries concern the system of distinctions representing markets as integrated in society, their public presence, as well as the mechanisms through which market transactions can be accessed.[1] Setting robust boundaries (which implies putting in place definitional mechanisms for market activities too) is not possible without a socially entrenched system of beliefs. Therefore, the argument is that the "spirit of finance" is central to that of capitalism, an argument which can be traced back to the writings of Karl Marx and Max Weber, among others.

Yet what does this "spirit" consist of, concretely speaking? How can we pin down "beliefs" in a productive, methodologically robust fashion?

Things become here a bit muddled. Oftentimes, this "spirit" has been understood as "discourse"—that is, as a prescriptive account of modern financial transactions and institutions which frames and constrains individual actions.[2] Such an account, however, cannot entirely explain either the role played by key features of modern financial institutions (technology, for instance), nor the boundaries of financial markets. (Discourse, for instance, cannot entirely explain the arrangements allowing social actors to access financial transactions.)

I have suggested in this book that there are more adequate ways of understanding how financial markets gain legitimacy and how they set their boundaries. They include a set of observational arrangements proving financial knowledge as legitimate and enabling actors to project specific courses of financial action. At the more general theoretical level, the observational arrangements intrinsic to the boundaries of finance stress the mediated character of social action, as well as its cognitive constituents. The concept of boundary, as it is used here, aims at providing a solution to the coordination problem, namely to show how dispersed, unrelated actors coordinate their actions in an uncertain fashion. The general notion of discourse cannot capture the whole complexity of coordination devices, or their observational character.

All too often, debates among economic sociologists have been set in terms of networks versus culture, asserting either the primacy of relationships for price setting and for the stabilization of exchange processes, or the importance of interpretive frames. Seen in this perspective, the arguments about financial knowledge and observational systems could be understood as culturalist. I have attempted, however, to go beyond the network/culture dichotomy, by arguing that the very structures set in place in the early nineteenth century (the emergence of closed status groups on stock exchanges) bring about observational systems which in their turn became intrinsic to modern finance.

I have argued that the consequences of the boundary work taking place in the nineteenth century go deep: if we are to understand markets not as a simple agglomeration of parallel, more or less unrelated, and fragmented transactions, but rather as a stable hierarchy of groups and networks with internal boundaries, transacting on a systematic and continued basis (White 2002, p. 284), then financial markets as we know them today are shaped by this boundary work. Yet this latter is never exclusively structural or institutional: it is never exclusively the work of excluding outsiders, or of setting in place and defending institutional rules. It is also necessarily the work of putting a face to the world, of reaching out and adopting authoritative cultural roles, and of grafting them onto technological systems. Without such work, neither institutional distinctions nor integration could be accomplished: neither the distinctive place of markets as the functional "heart" of the economy, nor their social integration, could be possible.

The significance of this cultural work is perhaps better brought to the fore if we keep in mind that, until very recently, major stock exchanges such as the New York and London Stock Exchanges, respectively, have been organized as private associations (and in many ways closed to public scrutiny), while holding enormous economic and social influence. This brings us back to Max Weber's observation, discussed in chapter 1, that stock exchanges are necessarily institutions of power. This can be the starting point for a reflection on the relationship between culture and power, this time centered on economic (and not, as in many other cases, on political) institutions. In a Weberian vein, it could be argued that the power of stock exchanges (understood as their capacity to influence decisions and organizational forms of other economic and political agents) relies at least on their capacity to create reciprocal obligations across society (what Weber called "tributary relationships"). Such obligations contribute to increasing societal complexity, while encouraging individualization processes. Yet this capacity cannot be put to fruition without the ability to lay claim to honorability and force as the grounds of enclosure and hierarchy building. And these claims are formulated with a public voice and from established cultural positions. Power, in this sense, rests ultimately on the insertion into civil or bourgeois cultural production, an insertion which, as mentioned above, is grafted onto the authority provided by control of technological transaction systems.

Nevertheless, if cultural boundary work can be seen as a source of power, it also provides opportunities for public intervention. It has often been argued that, during some periods (e.g., between the Great Depression and the early 1960s), the rhetoric of speculation diminishes and stricter regulatory measures are set in place. The fall of 2008 seemed to be such a period. Indeed, several market actors I have interviewed, as well as some readers of this draft manuscript, have made this observation. For instance, a trader active on the New York Stock Exchange since 1959 has told me that when he started trading, public opinion was not in favor of financial markets and that many viewed such activities with reticence, if not outright suspicion. The boundaries of finance do not expand automatically and relentlessly. Rather, what makes them durable, among other things, is the capacity to withstand periods of public reticence. Moreover, the fact that the rhetoric of speculation may be scaled back during some periods does not mean that other components of these boundaries do not expand. Technicalization of market transactions, centered upon the creation of an encompassing observational system, together with a market memory, was pursued during the late 1950s and 1960s, for instance, in a period when exhortations to speculate were rather rare. The emergence of regulatory bodies like the Securities Exchange Commission (SEC) has rather contributed to the process of market automation.

In April 1963 (at a time when public rhetoric was rather reticent about financial markets), the SEC sent to the Committee on Interstate and Foreign Commerce of the US Congress the *Report of Special Study of Securities Markets*, a document of over seven thousand pages. This document contained a factual description of the operations on the NYSE's exchange floor and of OTC (over-the-counter) brokers, statistical analyses of trading volumes and price movements, and a series of recommendations to the US Congress. Several sections were dedicated to the "possibilities of automation" in financial markets. The *Special Study* acknowledged that computer systems for the recording of price and transaction data were implemented in NYSE brokerages, and that OTC trading had also been "slightly touched" by automation. It stated that

> if securities markets are to be truly public institutions, as they have been under the law for 30 years, the public interest in questions of automation must have a voice. The Commission should equip itself to keep abreast of electronic and computer developments in the securities industry. Otherwise, these may be neglected or suppressed for want of any consideration of the public interest. (SEC 1963, part 5, chap. 6, part E, p. 93)

The SEC made to Congress the recommendations that the potential impact of automation is affected with public interest (SEC 1963, part 5, chap. 6, part E, p. 108) and that automation should be used by regulatory bodies as a surveillance technique, in the same way it was used by the NYSE (SEC 1963, part 5, chap. 6, part E, p. 122; chap. 12, part B, p. 180). Automation was also recommended as a means of regulating OTC trading. Discussing the need to identify the "primary market makers," the *Special Study* recommended that

> beyond this data-supplying function, a system of continuous classification and identification would serve as a basis for whatever degree of further regulariza-

tion and regulation of over-the-counter markets may seem warranted, now or in the future, in what should be a continuing effort to improve and strengthen such markets generally." (SEC 1963, chap. 7, section F, p. 670)

Automation (implying the construction of a comprehensive observational system and of a market memory) is taken as a defining feature of markets as institutions; it appears thus not only as intrinsic to market definitions, but also as constituting the interface between regulators and markets. This marks the beginning of an accelerated market technicalization which will flourish in the late 1970s and early 1980s with the adoption of the first automated trading platforms and the large scale expansion of computer terminals in brokerage services. Thus, at a time when relatively few apologists of finance were heard in public, long-term programs for market technicalization were set in place, with the effect that, among other things, financial transactions became easily accessible decades later to anyone with a personal computer and a broadband connection.

Theories of Markets

With the empirical data used here covering mostly the second half of the nineteenth century and the early twentieth century, some readers might want to question the arguments' relevance for contemporary financial markets. Are these boundaries something pertaining to the past or are they relevant to how financial markets work now? Have they been displaced or are they still in place? More importantly, perhaps, how do they matter?

I argue that these boundaries are very much with us and that they have influenced developments in some decisive ways. Let me start with the way in which we perceive the nature of financial knowledge today. Very few, if any, would argue against financial economics as a rigorous science anchored in the stochastic analysis of price movements. Historians of economics may discuss whether the random walk hypothesis was formulated first in the 1860s or around 1900; financial economists may debate whether markets are efficient or not. Nevertheless, all these debates are firmly grounded in the belief that price movements can be recorded and analyzed, and that inferences about the behavior of market actors can be made on this basis. In fact, most discussions about whether financial markets are efficient or inefficient center on the notion of the available information being fully reflected in prices or not (e.g., Mehrling 2005,

p. 66). The idea that price movements are a source of information about the actors' behavior and that these movements should be studied as a fundamental condition of market participation is a cornerstone of conceptual transformations initiated in the nineteenth century, transformations related to the closure of financial markets and to the effort of creating observational systems which confer legitimacy upon transactions.

These transactions have also created a way of thinking about financial markets as having a specific ontology, characterized, in part, by the absence of extraordinary events which could escape an observational system geared toward a certain spectrum. It is difficult to capture the rare, the extraordinary, the unique event with microscopes and telescopes calibrated for a certain range. It is also difficult to capture unique events when such observational modes are not calibrated toward human behavior, but toward prices conceived as signals. This, however, does not mean that unique events do not occur, or that they do not have concrete consequences. An illustration of this is provided by the recurring discussions after each crisis and collapse, discussions about "who could have foreseen," "the data did not show anything," and the like. Among those rising against this ontology is Benoit Mandelbrot, who, in his criticism of the received view on price variations, discusses the reception of Cauchy's distribution at the French Academy of Sciences in 1853, a distribution different from the Gaussian one on which most market models are based. Cauchy was criticized because "you would have frighteningly discordant observations. And there is no doubt that they would be rejected and that the instruments, or the observation process, would be submitted to profound correction. [. . .] An instrument governed by such a law of probability would never be put on sale by an ordinary craftsman" (quoted in Mandelbrot and Hudson 2004, p. 39). In this perspective, the observation instrument is not so much meant to capture all market events, but to reassure participants about the reliability of observations conducted within a given range.

Moreover, as recent research has made clear, financial economics does not simply describe markets; it can intervene and contribute to their transformation. This is the key aspect of the performativity argument in economic sociology: financial theories are not a mirror of actual transactions, but a tool for active intervention and for market creation (e.g., MacKenzie 2006; Callon 1998, 2007). An example in this sense is the options market created in Chicago in the 1970s by traders using the Black-Scholes-Merton formula, a process studied by Donald MacKenzie. The transformation of financial knowledge into a highly specialized expert field raises a series of issues related to accessing it, as well as to its incorporation into technologies of observation. I will discuss these issues in more detail below, but not before examining another contemporary facet of the boundaries of finance, namely price data observation.

Technology's Lens

During the last two decades or so, stock exchanges and brokerage houses have invested billions of dollars in trading technologies, a large part of which was devoted to computerized price recording and price display. Trading automation has been implemented on stock exchanges like the Paris Bourse (now part of Euronext) since the 1990s, and even earlier on some other exchanges (e.g., Muniesa 2003; Levecq and Weber 2002). This process has been accompanied by increasingly blurred distinctions between traditional, trading floor–based exchanges, on the one hand, and electronic communication networks, on the other. Electronic communication networks (ECNs), which emerged in the late 1960s, allow market participants to interact with each other within a dispersed computer network. Nowadays, over 30% of NASDAQ's overall volume, for instance, is traded within ECNs. Stock exchanges like the New York Stock Exchange (NYSE) have recently merged with ECNs like Archipelago, while over-the-counter exchanges like NASDAQ had previously merged with networks like Instinet and Brut. Financial institutions are nowadays dependent on computer networks to such an extent that their demand for electrical power (and demand growth) far outstrips supply capabilities. For instance, the power demand of the City of London—that is, London's financial district—alone is 1,000 MW, expected to rise by 80% over the next few years (Warren 2008).

Brokerage houses have been intensely involved in the development of trading software, a process that has accelerated since the early 1980s.[3] Price recording and trading, two activities which until the 1990s had been largely separated, have become increasingly integrated.[4] The computerization of financial trading and the rise of electronic brokerages have been accompanied by an increased nonprofessional participation in electronic trading activities. Day trading,[5] a phenomenon which emerged in the 1990s and which, contrary to some expectations, was not vanished during the dot-com burst, is a consequence of this process. Day trading has been made possible, in part, by the widespread availability of secure, real-time financial data over broadband; this has been accompanied by an increased visibility of financial data in the electronic media, as well as in public spaces. Witness here the giant electronic tickers in places like Times Square, or the financial screens in the Science, Industry, and Business section of the New York Public Library, to give but two examples.

While it could be argued that the technicalization of financial exchanges has increased trading efficiency and market functionality, let us not forget here that the very notions of efficiency and functionality have been generated within the same boundaries which include the stock ticker, the updated successor of which is now installed in Times Square. Neither should we think here that market technicalization started with the computer. The evidence shows that, from the introduction of the ticker onward, stock exchanges have gone through a series of technological innovations, many centered upon price data recording and display. My argument is that what I have called the observational mode of the microscope, allowing the continuous observation of price flows in real time, is the dominant mode of global financial markets, and that it has real consequences with respect at least to market access, market memory, and market definition.

First, access is increasingly centered on computerized, real-time, continuous price observation. Without this sort of observation, participation in financial transactions would be very difficult nowadays, if not impossible. In fact, ethnographic observations of electronic traders suggest that they spend most of their time with the observation of price movements, while normal transactions take a small amount of time.[6] Increased observational efforts seem to be required both by the amount of financial data available, as well as by the electronic integration of various trading networks and places.[7] Second, price observation has been integrated with price recording since the stock ticker, allowing thus for an objectified market memory to replace the fractal memory (Bowker 2005, p. 9) of paper slips, individual records, and minds. This memory has triggered organizational changes on the stock exchange (e.g., the centralization of price records in the 1930s) and has been instrumental with respect to regulatory measures. The SEC's *Special Report* of 1963, for instance, which played a seminal role in the creation of a national market system, as well as the 1950's investigations preceding it, would have not been possible without an objectified, technology-supported market memory. Third, this price recording contributed to shift the definition of financial markets toward them being invested with public interest, in circumstances when such a shift could not have been supported by ownership-based legal interventions (the NYSE, as well as the London Stock Exchange, for instance, being private associations until very recently).

Nowadays, we can see how this definition of markets invested with public interest is invoked in debates about the regulation of hedge funds, which act as private and (to outside observers) inscrutable entities. Since their ownership structure as private associations does not offer a legal basis for public intervention and regulation (in the form of disclosure standards, for instance), regulatory calls ground their appeal in the notion of public interest. It should not be forgotten here that this notion arose in relationship to a price recording technology, and that it continues to rely on technologies of market observation and memorization.

The expansion of electronic trading has brought about the vision of one integrated, global market for the allocations of all resources. In 2005, for instance, the chairman of a major US electronic brokerage house drew the following picture:

> We, the electronic exchanges, electronic market makers and brokers together constitute the platform on which global economic planning and resource allocation will take place. This process is both centralized and fully distributed, in the sense that any participant from anywhere, based in any currency, has direct access to any and all nodes in the network. The number of participants is unlimited. Their size and impact is variable, but their access is equal. Just as in the Universe at large, wherever you may be, you effectively are at the center of the network. [. . .] Technology has given us the opportunity and the means of spreading the benefits of a market driven, entrepreneurial economy to every corner of the world. (Peterffy 2005, pp. 2, 6)

This is the vision of one observational system for all mankind, on which all resource allocation will take place. True, lasting equality created by observational access! This vision does not rely only upon the notion of efficiently performing allocation functions, a notion which, as I have shown, takes shape in the nineteenth century. No, it also relies upon the idea that the observational system at the core of financial transactions has the special force required to spread the gospel all over the world. Such a global system raises a whole series of ethical questions about fairness and justice, questions which cannot be answered within the system itself.[8] Moreover, because such a system narrows down the range of the phenomena defined as observable, it also raises questions related to an increased potential for volatility and instability,[9] questions which, again, cannot be answered exclusively by the internal system.

The Lens of Financial Expertise

Not only has technical analysis not died, in spite of all the contestations concerning its predictive power, but it has continued to flourish and has acquired a firm institutional structure. Not only that, but various forms of financial expertise have come to play prominent public roles, as highlighted by the media during both the boom and the burst of dot-coms, telecoms, and other coms. While this structure is doubtlessly supported by the longstanding ties between analysts and brokers, I would venture here that there is an additional element which has contributed to chartism's contemporary success. The expansion of electronic trading has greatly increased the amount of price data available, as well as the observational effort required from market actors. Spending hours every day on the observation of numbers flickering on the computer screen requires more than ever an instrument, a telescope with the help of which all the columns of multicolored figures can be brought together in a coherent view. This telescope, the chart, has been now integrated into the financial software and made available in real time. Traders watching real-time price data have the possibility of interpreting them by instantly calling up real-time charts. Up to a certain extent, this observational mode has contributed to diminishing the perceived importance of other types of financial data.[10] Electronic trading appears to lock in a certain type of data in conjunction with a certain type of interpretive tool. It is to be expected, therefore, that the expansion of this kind of trading will amplify the use of technical analysis.

At least two other issues are at stake here. One is related to the longevity and vitality of technical analysis, to its ability to withstand criticism. The other is related to its status as a body of expert knowledge. With respect to the first issue, the following can be said: criticisms of technical analysis very often focus on its lack of predictive power with respect to price movements. Strictly speaking, technical analysis cannot predict future prices; it does not provide a formula for computing them. Nevertheless, if we look at the ways in which financial charts are used by traders, we can see that this analysis provides them with a tool for seeing "the market," as well as for inferring other actors' actions from price movements.[11] Returning to the performativity argument discussed earlier, it cannot be said that technical analysis creates prices in the same sense in which the use of the Black-Scholes-Merton formula creates them, for instance. Nevertheless, charts appear as indispensable observational instruments, ones which become even more so in electronic trading. While recent news has highlighted the elimination of entire teams of technical analysts, as in the case of Citibank (e.g. Goldstein 2005), chartism has become widely available in electronic form and is now embedded within trading programs. There are numerous electronic subscription services providing real-time charts to nonprofessional traders and investors alike.

This brings us to the next issue, that of chartism as a body of expert knowledge. This expertise is what Stephen P. Turner (2003, p. 28) and Harry Collins and Robert Evans (Collins and Evans 2002, p. 252) call the third kind, namely groups and individuals who create their own following. While technical analysis is professionally organized, with associations at national and international levels, training programs, and certification procedures, the body of knowledge as such is not seen as being on a par with academic economic theories and is frowned upon in established business schools. Nevertheless, it is quite popular with professional and nonprofessional traders alike, and is practiced by many people who have not gone through any institutional training program. What is more, electronic trading programs now embed technical analysis; traders have, among other things, the possibility of programming alerts or trading instructions within the chart itself.[12] We encounter here both a popularization and an automation of financial expert knowledge. Technical analysis is partly transferred from the closed domain of experts to that of popular practice;[13] everybody can learn to do technical analysis. Learning how to do analysis, however, does not replace instructions for action. Consequently the analyst as a charismatic figure who instructs traders does not disappear. Personal authority is combined now with the authority of technical systems, a process which leads to the proliferation of online experts and "gurus." Their authority is given by academic credentials (e.g., a PhD in applied mathematics), aura of prestige (past predictive successes, ratings in the financial media), as well as the techniques they use in their analyses.[14] In some cases, the charismatic figure of the electronic analyst speaks to the trader via a podcast, lending more weight to his recommendations and contributing to creating an imagined sociality as the frame for financial transactions.

We witness then the emergence of a hybrid form of expertise which (1) combines personal and technological authority; (2) is situated below academic financial expertise, but above common knowledge; (3) combines populist and charismatic features; (4) is made permanently available; and (5) is integrated in the trading system. I would venture here that these developments strengthen rather than weaken the position of financial experts and expertise. What is more, these developments run counter to what is perceived as the separation of analysis and trading installed by regulatory measures like the Sarbanes-Oxley Act of 2002. While this separation may be implemented now within investment banks, electronic trading is characterized by an increased merger of these aspects.

The Force of the Market

It follows from the above that observational technologies and expertise—intrinsic to the boundaries of finance—have evolved, interlocked, and expanded in such a way that it is almost inconceivable now to conduct transactions without them. What about the social and political aspects of the legitimacy of financial markets? To recall the argument, the boundaries of finance are characterized by a tension between knowledge as an access gate to financial transactions and the idea of a vital force which (a) places stock exchanges at the core of economic and social life, and (b) creates a hierarchy of financial figures. Knowledge as a gateway implies that financial success depends on diligence and observation. Vital force implies that charisma is the main factor of success. This force endows stock exchanges with specific economic and social functions and makes them into national assets.[15]

Surely, in the era of economic globalization this must have changed. This notion must have been displaced by the view of markets as entities which know no nations and no borders. Well, think again. The almost religious trust in the market as ecumenical, omniscient, and omnipresent, which has been noticed by commentators (e.g., Cox 1999; Frank 2000), appears as worship of a superior force,[16] and goes hand in hand with the notion that nations too benefit from this force, which should not be controlled by foreigners.

Witness here the never ending debates about the "national" or "European" champions which must stay European, US, French, German, or British. For instance, when the merger between the New York Stock Exchange and the Euronext was recently announced,[17] political opposition was mounted up without much delay, with the aim of keeping Euronext

"European."[18] On this occasion, the German media declared openly that "stock exchange is politics too. A big stock exchange reinforces the prestige of a country" (Rhee-Piening 2005). At the end of 2004, when a merger between the London Stock Exchange (LSE) and the Deutsche Börse was attempted, similar patriotic concerns were raised on both sides.[19] When Anglo-Saxon investment funds (with the tacit acceptance of German stockholders) torpedoed the merger and imposed firing both the CEO and the chairman of the Deutsche Börse, the now famous expression "locusts" was born: speculators who are set on destroying the nation's assets (e.g., Weidenfeld 2005).[20]

The vision of the nation as benefiting from this force was expressed in a particularly telling way by James P. Gorman, the 2006 Chairman of the Securities Industry Association (SIA),[21] in a speech delivered on several occasions in the spring of 2004:

> As I started my remarks, I talked about how the securities markets are driven by two powerful emotions: greed on the one hand, fear on the other. These emotions have routinely driven the market to the euphoric highs we've seen and then the desperate lows. And yet, every cycle has resulted in reform, improved regulation, a market system that's stronger and fairer, more transparent and ultimately and, most importantly, increased public participation. This amazing process of wealth creation has been a progression, continuously moving through the history of this country. We've learned from the successes and failures. We're unafraid to change. And we at Merrill Lynch are fundamentally optimistic, because we believe in the ability of the markets to bring great value to individuals. We remain "Bullish on America." (Gorman 2004, p. 10)

Since Gorman was talking about the financial scandals of the late 1990s (Enron, WorldCom, and the like), it follows that emotional forces, not calculation, not economic efficiency, not better resource allocation (and *definitely not* ethics) are at the core of this "cycle of life" which makes the country stronger. "Fraud and regulation" is translated here as "death and renewal," and the "increased public participation" has to actually rely on the prospect of continuing this cycle, including future frauds. In a speech delivered in 2005, Gorman designated the "free flow of financial capital" as the "third fundamental freedom" of American leadership in the world (Gorman 2005). Financial markets are "all about creating opportunity" and are playing "a critical role . . . in advancing the general prosperity." Celebrating investor education as one of the most important SIA activities,

Gorman stated that "in the end, strong markets depend upon engaged and informed investors. People who understand the opportunities that market creates, but who are also fully aware of the risks" (Gorman 2005). Freedom appears as guaranteed by the flow of financial capital which creates a world of opportunity and general prosperity, a world of education and engagement. Yet, if greed and fear are the fundamental forces underlying markets (and hence the flow of capital), it follows that freedom is actually guaranteed by greed and fear. Does not this reverse the enlightened ideal of opportunity and access into a vital struggle, where the only freedom is actually achieved by the greediest at the cost of the others?

Very little is made here of the fact that, until now, there is no public, widespread, and sustained education in finance of the kind made necessary by global financial markets. Educational efforts are mostly seen as an added-on feature of financial services providers, but not as a public necessity or as a right.[22] Yet both the logic of transactions as grounded in knowledge and that of access to financial knowledge as a fundamental prerequisite for access to transactions require this kind of education. If physics and biology are part of the public education system, why isn't finance (whose theories are modeled on physics and, increasingly, on biology—see Mirowski 2007, p. 211) part of it too? In the absence of a public educational system in finance,[23] capable to reach the widest possible public, the tension between the necessity to promise participation and access, on the one hand, and the view of markets as a struggle won by force, on the other, is continued and replicated as something we have to live with.

Small wonder, then, that the cult of the financial übermensch continues to thrive today. Throughout the 1980s and 1990s, a heterogeneous array of figures like Michael Milken, Andrew Fastow, Nick Leeson, and many more have given wings to the public imagination, which celebrated them as innovators, geniuses, bureaucracy-fighters, industry liberators, entrepreneurs, and so on. Small wonder, too, that at least some of these figures identify with the superheroes of popular culture or with larger-than-life predators. What has been sometimes seen as a juvenile enthusiasm (e.g., Eichenwald 2005, p. 379) for *Star Wars* and *Jurassic Park* on the part of some traders makes perfect sense within this cult. True, some of these figures have in the meantime graduated from the federal prison system or are in the process of doing so. Nevertheless, since greed is acknowledged as the driving force of markets, exceedingly greedy people cannot be entirely shunned, even when sent to prison. There is always admiration for and fascination with hubris, with excess of force.

Among the more recent public debates which reverberate the tension between knowledge and vital force as sources of empowerment and legitimacy for speculation, the discussions about the salaries and bonuses of traders, hedge fund managers, and finance executives are perhaps the most relevant. Seven- and even eight-figure bonuses for institutional traders are a relatively recent phenomenon, evolved from the marginally more modest bonuses paid in the 1980s. In part, the recent emergence of such bonuses has to do with the fact that until the 1960s, financial trading was dominated by individuals, not by institutions. It was only after institutional players became dominant in international finance that ever increasing bonuses were brought into public consciousness. Bonuses are reported to have topped £14 billion (over $28 billion) in 2007 in the City of London alone.[24] How can they be justified both within the respective institutional contexts and in society at large?

The justification of eight-figure bonuses as remuneration for paid work is not entirely convincing, to say the least. It is not convincing in relationship to society at large: what socially significant value do trading activities produce that it is equivalent to the sum of hundreds of teachers', engineers', or bus drivers' work? The justification is not convincing within institutional contexts either: how is the generated organizational value equivalent with the sum of hundreds of back office workers' value, while being at the same time impossible without these latter? Remuneration for salaried employees is usually justified with respect to the skills and the knowledge these bring to the institution, skills and knowledge which have to relate somehow to the existing ones—that is, to be comparable and commensurable with them. Pay scales are one of the tools used by organizations for this purpose. Skills and knowledge, however, can hardly justify an extra $28 billion paid to a few individuals.

The other basis for justifying bonuses is sheer force, or power, sometimes disguised as a special talent, and sometimes not. In his investigation of how bonuses are legitimated, Olivier Godechot highlights two justificatory mechanisms: the discursive exaltation of total freedom and the definition of profit as a "good without a master," appropriable by sheer will (Godechot 2007, pp. 79, 103). At least as interesting are public reactions to this argument, some of which are to be found on the blog of the French daily *Libération*: "it is the critics' fear to confront their own mediocrity, which moves these pathetic guys to criticize those who succeed and earn much more than them." And, "not everybody can be a trader, [which is being] like star soccer players!"[25] These anonymous readers' reactions are indicative of the justification of bonuses by virtue of a special talent, or force, similar to stardom and not shared by the envious, mediocre, and critical masses.

Another facet of the financial übermensch is that of the person who in the end works for society, and who uses his or her force to a higher aim; if excess of greed is fascination with the "dark side of the force" (to keep within this world), excess of care is fascination with the "good side." When Warren Buffett announced his decision to leave 85% of his fortune to charity, parts of the public reacted by enthusiastically embracing financial markets, at least in their declarations if not in practice. Here's another blog sample:

> If Warren Buffett and Bill Gates had volunteered every day of their lives work-ing at a soup kitchen, how many people could they have helped? And how many people can they help with $85bn? Go get rich everybody. (*Guardian* 2006)

Some others tried to distinguish between "generosity" and "the system" in a way which actually replicates the force-based hierarchy of speculators:

> The uber-rich try to do good once they have done their damage. Anyone who accumulates and generates that much cash has a lot of blood on their hands. The engines of international finance ultimately crush many people in their cogs. I admire Gates and Buffett for their generosity, but I also loathe the system that put them at the top of the food chain. (*Guardian* 2006)

This acknowledgment of hierarchies, of a "food chain" which may ulti-mately end in "generosity," radically undermines the promise of freedom through investment and speculation, of opportunity and prosperity.

Perhaps nowhere has this promise been formulated more forcefully, and has come to crash more bitterly, than in the mortgage and credit mar-kets. Freedom through ownership, the quintessential family dream, has depended, among other things, upon slicing up, standardizing, and pack-aging mortgage debt together with other forms of debt. These packages, called CDO (or collateralized debt obligations) have been traded in the market,[26] allowing lenders to loosen the ties between mortgage offers and the clients' capacity to pay them back.[27]

This process of standardization and repackaging is contingent upon mathematical models (for calculating the risk of default), expert groups (who gather and analyze data), and computing technologies (for data storing and processing). In other words, the transformation of material

savings (like a home) into capital depends on the very observational instruments constituting the boundaries of finance and the groups associated
with them. Taking up a mortgage, maybe even stretching it a bit beyond
one's means is tied to a series of trust assumptions which go well beyond
the office of the local bank, involving actors other than just the mortgage
applicants: trust in the accuracy of risk assessing models, trust in the cor-
rectness and comprehensiveness of data, in the expertise of the analysts,
in the institutions trading debt obligations. At bottom, this trust (and the
authority associated with it) is based on nothing else but the legitimacy
of finance as a form of scientific knowledge, on the accuracy and robustness of its observational instruments, and on the capacity of the experts
running them. This is the basis on which facts are created, to use Donald
MacKenzie's (2008) recent formulation. And when this trust unravels,
everything comes to a halt. Freedom through home ownership becomes
again a far away promise.

The realization of this promise of freedom, of universal opportunity
and prosperity through speculation, is problematic in itself; abstracting
from this, however, its only legitimacy is given by the appeal to knowledge. If this appeal is taken away, what remains is folly, of the kind commented upon by eighteenth-century observers. The appeal to knowledge,
however, is constantly hollowed out by the lack of a proper, public system
of financial education, a system independent from (and objective with
respect to) specific market players, as well as by the entrenched notion
of überspeculators embodying a vital force other mortals simply do not
possess. It should be the task of a public educational system in finance to
dismantle it, among other things. Such a system should properly teach the
public not only about the risks related to financial transactions, but also
the institutional and cultural underpinnings of global financial markets.
Unless this happens, what we are stuck with is the kind of hope expressed
by Dostoevsky's narrator:

> I've now got fifteen louis d'or, and it was fifteen gulden that I started off with!
> If I start carefully . . . but surely, surely I can't be such a child! Surely I'm not
> forgetting that I'm a ruined man. But why can't I rise up again? Yes! All I need
> to do is to be careful and prudent, just once in my life, and—that's all! All I have
> to do is to keep control of myself for once, and I can change my whole destiny
> in just one hour! The most important thing is strength of character. [. . .] But
> what if I had lost heart, if I had not dared to make that decision? . . . Tomorrow,
> tomorrow it will be all over! (Dostoevsky [1866] 1991, pp. 274–75)

Notes

Introduction

1. See, for example, Richard W. Stevenson and David E. Sanger, "In Speech, Bush Sketches a Bold Domestic and Foreign Agenda," *New York Times*, front page, February 3, 2005. The reshaping of individual economic identities around financial activities has been accompanied by reconfiguring many institutional identities, as illustrated not only in the proliferation of investment funds, but also in the increased institutional involvement with financial markets. Educational institutions, counties and cities, and all sorts of corporations have become market players and/or investors. And even if the project of "reinventing Social Security" as financial speculation has not been realized (for the time being), it still exists as a perfectly legitimate option.

2. The definitional status of carbon allowances is a contested area: several institutional actors push for their recognition as financial entities, a move which would firmly situate them in the sphere of financial markets.

3. See http://www.attac.org/indexen/index.html (accessed March 19, 2005).

4. ATTAC does not protest against financial markets as such, but merely asks for the introduction of a tax on international capital movements (the so-called Tobin tax). At the end of the 1990s, there were some short-lived protests staged at the London Stock Exchange. They did not develop into any organized, national or international mass movement against financial markets. See also "Protesters 'paid' to riot in the City," *The Sunday Times*, June 20, 1999.

5. I have heard several times finance professionals say that day traders just hit computer keys very quickly. Having conducted extensive participant observation of day traders, I find this notion completely puzzling. It is, however, relevant for what is popularly perceived to be "recklessness" vs. "prudence."

6. It is one of my aims to investigate how this distinction is constituted in the nineteenth century and to what consequences. Therefore, in the following, I talk about the investor as a general social position with respect to financial transactions, and not as one characterized by mere passivity.

7. It should be also stressed here that public participation in financial investments has not been equal across all social, income, and ethnic groups; large gaps still persist (Keister 2000, pp. 177–89).

8. Journalistic accounts of the financial crises which convulsed the 1990s, for instance, see this orientation as fairly recent and as initiated by the options reward schemes adopted in some sectors (e.g., the software industry) in the late 1980s and early 1990s (e.g., Lowenstein 2004; Mahar 2004). While factors like options schemes, corporate tax legislation, or pension plans certainly play an important role, they alone cannot explain either the ubiquity of this orientation nor its persuasiveness.

9. While financial markets were acknowledged as "the nucleus of one of the most complex institutions the history of man has produced" (Polanyi 1957, p. 11), and while they have received intermittent sociological attention, we still lack a comprehensive theoretical account of them as instrinsic to the modern capitalist order.

10. Both Marx and Weber were aware of the importance of financial markets and addressed them in some of their writings. It is more accurate, therefore, to say that the canonization of these authors did not always include their analyses of finance. I discuss Marx's and Weber's views on financial markets in chapter 1.

11. The main characteristics of the first globalization wave are price convergence and market integration (O'Rourke and Williamson 1999, pp. 2, 4; O'Rourke 2000, 2001; Rousseau and Sylla 2001, p. 7). While price convergence means a historically narrowing gap in real wages and cost of capital between the two sides of the Atlantic, integration designates the increasing interdependence (and reciprocal influence) of capital, production factors, and labor markets. This means that, in part, events in one market influence prices in other markets, and that this process gains in speed, so that the time gap between price changes in different markets narrows too. The first globalization wave is also characterized by social and economic transformations which led to the territorial diffusion of investment activities, their broader social outreach, and a considerable increase in the number of investors. These transformations, which cannot be detailed here, include the consolidation of the nation-state (Neal 1990), economic policy favoring joint-stock companies (Dobbin 1994; Alborn 1998), international migration (Wilkins 1999), and urbanization and the rise of the news industry (Blondheim 1994; Leyshon and Thrift 1997; Winseck and Pike 2007). Economic historians, however, have been quick to notice that factors like urbanization, international migration, the electric telegraph, or economic policy, while important, are not enough. As Jonathan Baskin and Paul Miranti (1997, p. 134) put it, market integration and the attraction of capital from wide geographic areas presuppose "procedures enabling investors to evaluate the underlying worth of traded securities" in the same or similar ways. These procedures imply a knowledge framework mutually recognized and accepted over such an area: in other words, one with global features and a potential for expansion. In

this framework, financial investments are acknowledged as socially legitimate and even desirable. Moral doubts are, for all practical purposes, suspended. Social actors can make sense of investing with respect to their personal and social lives. The cultural framework which legitimates financial markets (with stock exchanges at their core) cannot be mechanically deducted from economic growth, urbanization, or industrialization, but implies a series of transformations which are more focused and at the same time complement general changes in social and economic life.

12. Max Weber (1948, pp. 183, 185) revisits Marx's notion of class struggle as the only instance where communal action is driven by economic interests. Class struggle, however, requires the orientation of class members not toward each other, but toward an external category perceived as the opponent. Struggle is not market exchange; in order for it to emerge, a divisive boundary has to be erected (e.g., proletariat v. bourgeoisie).

13. It should be noted here that the notion of collectively held beliefs is not without challenges either. How can dispersed individuals acquire sets of very similar beliefs and, more importantly perhaps, how can we explain (even individual) beliefs without recourse to the (sociologically inaccessible) concept of mind? We could easily choose to postulate something like a "collective mind," thus falling back into a long-discredited version of idealism.

14. The uncertain coordination of action is different from the mass coordination discussed by Michel Foucault (1977). While this latter aims to ensure preset outcomes through technologies of the self, the uncertain coordination of action does not necessarily include the projection of normative goals. Financial markets do not discipline in the same way as prisons, armies, or schools. The goal of speculation is not the same as the normative goals of the "good citizen" or the "diligent student." Moreover, while financial speculation may involve bodily discipline (e.g., Zaloom 2005), its concrete paths are neither preset nor constrained by a panopticon. Speculators do not coordinate with each other under the gaze of a warden or teacher.

15. In a different context, this point is made by Harrison White (2002, p. 2) and by Niklas Luhmann (1994, p. 49), who conceive economic action as self-reflexive and economic systems as closed systems.

16. Faced with the problem of uncertain coordination, a tempting solution would be to see markets as a field (Bourdieu 1980)—understood as a system of structural differences in which actors occupy various positions with respect to each other, while publicly seeking to maximize individual, material profits (Bourdieu 1997, p. 51). A set of specific (bodily and cognitive) routines corresponds to each position, thus enabling a variety of actions. If we were to adopt this concept, financial actors would appear as positions in a general and self-supporting system of classifications (i.e., the market), characterized by power relationships and by strategic games among actors vying to maintain their position or challenging the competition (Fligstein 2001, pp. 68–69). A first major difficulty encountered when working with this concept is that each position in a field seems to possess a sort

of force (Martin 2003) which keeps it on a certain, fixed orbit with respect to the other figures. The highbrow writer will never write cheap mass-market novels and the mystery writer will never make it into the literary canon. But grand speculators can fall from grace and become small, insignificant ones (not to mention that they can go to jail, or die in utter poverty). Conversely, some small speculators dream of becoming grand financiers one day. A second difficulty is that we cannot account for agency anymore. How do structural positions project paths of action without predetermining them? How is access to financial activities shaped? A further difficulty is that we have to account for forms of financial behavior which are not mere habits.

17. In fact, some of the online traders I have observed even refuse to participate in online forums and chat rooms, which they regard as infested with manipulators.

18. It is often assumed in economic sociology that market signals are independent of the signaling procedures or techniques, or that information is independent of the prisms; this, however, is a problematic assumption. Communication procedures impact not only the form of communication, but also the recipients' understanding, interpretations, and reactions.

19. This speaks against reducing observation to intranetwork forms. If relationships act as internal prisms through which market actors observe each other, and use these observations in order to process uncertainties about price, quality, and quantity, it follows that the boundaries of market transactions are regarded as already set and unproblematic. Otherwise, market actors would have to think about them instead of worrying about quality and price. (Is this a legitimate exchange? Are the procedures valid and reliable?)

20. See, for instance, http://www.fin.edu/~mizrachs/oldnew.html (accessed October 6, 2006), for more information on computer hackers.

21. This means that the legitimacy of investment activities is ensured with respect to individual well-being, but also with respect to ethical, political, or cultural aspects.

22. Lamination is related to keying—that is, to interactional exchanges which can add new layers of meaning. In this sense, in the interaction order lamination has a temporal dimension which is not present in my argument. A triply laminated boundary does not necessarily mean that feature (b) has to be added after (a), and (c) after (b).

23. There are limited similarities between this notion and Niklas Luhmann's (e.g., 1990, p. 103) thesis that social systems operate by codes which allow them to absorb and manage contestations. However, I do not adopt Luhmann's notion of binary communication codes as instrumental in the process of managing social clashes.

24. As will become clearer, I do not argue that boundaries are made solely of discursive representations. Boundaries are complex observational arrangements

integrating heterogeneous tools. An appropriate analogy here would be a scientific laboratory, which does not use a single tool to keep phenomena under observation but an array of heterogeneous, reciprocally calibrated devices.

25. This does not mean at all that paths of action are determined and controlled by the groups which set in place boundaries. They allow for uncertain coordination, leaving room for contingencies, resistances, and variety. Moreover, such groups may know internal debates, conflicts, or resistances related to certain features of their boundaries. I deal with such resistances in chapters 4 and 5. It would follow then that the social closure of a domain of action would entrain the emergence of a boundary legitimating it as accessible. This can happen in relationship to the domain's closure by a profession, but is not necessarily restricted to this kind of closure. Many professions put in place boundaries for those who want to access it without necessarily becoming members themselves. The medical and legal professions, for instance, have put in place elaborate observational boundaries for the lay public, for recruiting new members, for influencing regulatory measures, and so on.

26. What happens when closure does not take place? We could then be confronted with a situation not only dominated by the importance of physical copresence (I tell others what I saw), but also with fragmented, heterogeneous, and idiosyncratic observational arrangements. It would be then more difficult to regard the respective domain of action as socially palatable or as legitimate. Such a situation would increase uncertainties. Think of what would happen if no observational boundaries existed for legal or medical professions. It would be much harder to evaluate legitimacy claims and to establish legitimate ways of access, and we would need to rely much more on gossip and personal checks.

27. These entities may include, for instance, indicators generated elsewhere and transferred into the kaleidoscope of finance. Conversely, entities generated at the boundaries of finance may be transferred elsewhere too. Think here of the economic indicators used to justify the economic functions of financial markets, or of indicators like the Dow or NASDAQ indices transferred into political discourses, for instance.

Chapter One

1. The continuous preoccupation with building and testing social indicators helping the scientist to see otherwise hidden phenomena, for instance, a preoccupation which can be traced back at least to Auguste Comte and Émile Durkheim, bears witness to the early constitution of sociology as an observational system.

2. While it could certainly be argued that Adam Smith does not directly belong to the canon of classical sociology, examining his arguments appears necessary in this context, both because he was an observer of the eighteenth century and because of his influence on nineteenth-century sociological thinking.

3. Smith refers here to public debt, which dominated the financial markets of the eighteenth century. See also Neal 1990; Carruthers 1996.

4. We could trace in this way the intellectual roots of Durkheim's notion of collective representation.

5. The following episode reveals that this distinction has a relevance which goes beyond the sphere of philosophy. In the 2005 debates over Social Security, the Bush administration decided to change the name of the planned investment accounts from "private" to "personal" accounts. The shift was justified by a Republican consultant, who said, " 'Personal' is encompassing. It's individual. It's ownership. In the end, you need the combination of 'personal' and 'security' " (Robin Toner, "It's 'Private' vs. 'Personal' in Social Security Debate," *New York Times*, March 22, 2005, http://www.nytimes.com [accessed March 22, 2005]). To put it with Pierre Bourdieu (1994, p. 80), the rhetoric of financial speculation is revealed here as having a chiastic structure: the speculation of ownership ("I will have a pension, if financial markets do well") is the ownership of speculation ("What I own are uncertain promises"). Uncertainty is thus laid as the cornerstone of a secure future.

6. Absolute free will cannot be exercised in the ethical sphere, where the self is subjected to norms (but neither can it be exercised in economic life, which is subjected to civic norms). Thus, to put it very roughly, Hegel sees the self as characterized by freedom (as the manifestation of the will) and norm assimilation at the same time. Economic life is the locus of freedom, while family, public, and state life is the locus of norms. This is not to say that, according to Hegel, economic life is not governed by any (ethical) norms. Quite the contrary; Hegel sees economic life as subordinated to civil society (e.g., Muller 2002, p. 159).

7. I shall hasten to add here (and will discuss in detail later) that Weber's position is more complex than a reduction to ethical norms.

8. Hegel never saw ownership as pertaining only to inanimate objects but acknowledged that skills and knowledge, for instance, can be treated as objects which the self alienates ([1821] 1986, p. 104).

9. Most probably, Marx had in mind here the financial speculations of the eighteenth century, like the South Sea and the Mississippi Bubbles from England and France, respectively.

10. According to Marx, the subject is determined by the person—that is, ownership relations determine which norms of behavior we follow. Let me stress here again that person, in this context, does not refer to any particular individual, but is defined by the freedom to own and alienate ownership.

11. This transformation concerns not individuals, but persons; therefore, institutions, which are juridical persons, are attracted into this cycle too, being transformed into capitalist institutions. Examples here are universities, which both invest *and* borrow money in the capital market.

12. These articles are "Aim and External Organisation of Stock Exchanges" (Zweck und äußere Organisation der Börsen) and "Transactions on the Stock Ex-

change" (Der Börsenverkehr). They have been only recently translated into English by Steven Lestition (Weber 2000a, b) and published in the journal *Theory and Society* (2000) 29, no. 3, pp. 305–38 and 339–71, respectively; Friedrich Naumann (1860–1919) was a Protestant preacher, politician, and trade union activist who had close ties to Max Weber.

13. This Weberian insight is supported, among others, by the recurrent debates about whether the state should intervene and rescue private financial institutions which fail due to unsound trading decisions. We should not think that such debates are confined to "statist" continental Europe. The March 2008 intervention of the Federal Reserve in the rescue of the investment bank Bear Stearns, as well as the October 2007 intervention of the Bank of England in rescuing the mortgage lender Northern Rock, and the subsequent bailouts, indicate that Weber's insight has a broader validity.

14. Without going into great detail, we can note here a major difference between Max Weber's and Georg Simmel's position. For Simmel, who also works within the Hegelian distinction between person and subject, the central economic figure of modern life is the consumer (e.g., [1901] 1989, pp. 601–8). In complex and individualized societies, the actors' orientation toward objects is mediated by money and defined as consumption. This brings about egoism and superficiality in intersubjective relationships. For Weber, the social fabric of complex, individualized societies isn't torn into pieces, but held together by reciprocal tributary obligations, which are mediated by the stock exchange. The investor, not the consumer, is the central economic figure here. While Simmel's position has received a great deal of attention in sociology and cultural studies, Weber's analysis of the stock exchange went largely unnoticed, although it has far-reaching consequences (and, I dare say, far more so than Simmel's).

15. I will not discuss here whether Weber's is a realistic view. In any case, a large number of historical episodes and accounts point to the fact that the honor system did not always work.

16. It should not be inferred from this sentence that Weber associated financial investments with gambling. For him, the main problem of the small investor was lack of access to the sort of knowledge and information in which decisions should be anchored. The relationship between financial knowledge and gambling is discussed in detail in chapter 3.

17. Readers shouldn't necessarily believe that project making was something only the eighteenth century knew. Enron is a quite recent example of how the public, including the own employees, were persuaded to part with their money on the basis of promises about broadband capacity trading, movies on demand, and much more.

18. Since the sociological literature, as well as the writings which I am going to analyze in the next chapters, overwhelmingly represents the investor as a male figure, I am using here the masculine pronoun.

19. Hirokazu Miyazaki (2006) highlights the role of hope in the self-presentation of financial markets as engines of social transformation.

Chapter Two

1. White's position bears a striking resemblance to Niklas Luhmann's (1994) systems theory, which conceptualizes markets as closed, self-referential communication systems. From a more general perspective, we find here a variety of the differentiation theory—i.e., the thesis that forms of social order differentiate and subdifferentiate into autonomous, relationship cum communications systems.

2. We can find many examples of networks transacting in human and nonhuman beings, as well as in various substances and artifacts, but which lack legitimacy. This lack contributes to justifying their illegal status, and makes it rather difficult to regard them as markets. Can we really talk about a "market" in sex slaves or in child laborers? While such networks (usually grouped together under the umbrella of the "informal economy") may be hierarchically structured and have an internal organization, they do not enjoy a positive social status. Moreover, such networks operate on the basis of erecting barriers to public observation: they set in place arrangements which make them (and their transactions) opaque and inaccessible to external observers. We do not find, for instance, an index of tiger penis prices published daily in the Wall Street Journal. Rather than having boundaries with the rest of society, these networks encounter barriers. However, we can also have situations in which transactions operate in a legal limbo or are simply tolerated. Being tolerated or in a limbo increases uncertainty and makes transactions rather unstable in the long run.

3. This approach is echoed in Mary Douglas's (1987, p. 46) definition of legitimate social institutions as groupings claiming to fit the order of the universe (which can be natural or social).

4. Military rituals of public expulsion and humiliation of dishonored members are a case in point. Party expulsions (think of the Stalinist purges of the 1930s and 1940s) are another example. This also explains why members of the group voluntarily participate, and often initiate the humiliation and expulsion of "deviant" or "dishonored" members.

5. Patrik Aspers (2006, p. 146) makes the argument that markets actually are status-generating arrangements, set in place by actors who are uncertain about their relative positions. Markets appear thus primarily as allocation-based stratification mechanisms. Allocation, in its turn, emerges as a means toward but not as the ultimate market end, which is prestige. While Aspers primarily means uncertainties about the actors' positions with respect to each other, uncertainties can arise about the actors' general position in society as well.

6. The legal ban on short selling and options trading was lifted in 1885 on the Paris Bourse. These operations, however, had been informally acknowledged

already in 1860 (Jovanovic 2006c, p. 539). At the same time, the coulisse—the informal, yet tolerated Parisian stock exchange—practiced short selling on a wide scale (Preda 2004, p. 375). In the state of New York, short selling was prohibited in 1812, but the ban was lifted in 1858 (Campbell [1914] 1922, p. 35; Meeker 1922, p. 547). In Britain, Sir John Barnard's Act of 1733 (in force until 1860) rendered illegal contracts for the payment of differences only, as well as contracts in the nature of options, but its enforcement was circumvented with the help of courts of law, which declared that the act was meant to protect only the English funds. Legal cases from the eighteenth and nineteenth centuries show that Barnard's Act was largely ignored (Brodhurst 1897, pp. 10, 171).

7. The legal character of unwritten broker-client transactions and their status as contracts are recognized in Britain only at the end of the nineteenth century. Legal treatises cite about twenty-seven landmark legal cases from the nineteenth century as laying the basis for the argument that an oral broker-client transaction has the character of a commercial contract, on the grounds of the customs of the stock exchange (Brodhurst 1897, pp. 88–89). On the New York Stock Exchange, the legality of the broker's obligation to obey definite orders is established only toward the end of the nineteenth century, and only after several court cases (Goldman 1914, p. 77).

8. The New York State Personal Property Law of 1909 defines financial securities as "instruments [. . .] evidencing, representing or embodying a chose in action or a right with respect to property or a share, participation or other interest in property or in an enterprise" (New York State Personal Property Law 1909, 7-B, Sections 251–52). Financial securities were thus understood not as commodities, but as representations of ownership.

9. There were some exceptions here. In mid-nineteenth-century Germany, the official brokers of the Frankfurter Börse were bound to write down securities prices. In Germany, as in France, official brokers were assimilated to civil servants; they were nominated by the stock exchange corporations and confirmed by the government. The German Stock Exchange Law of 1896 had rules for establishing prices; official brokers were bound to act according to them (Kurth 1999, pp. 1–2).

10. An important exception here is the Paris Bourse, which was very early organized as a state institution. The transactions of its official brokers were recognized as binding commercial contracts. Yet, the French state tolerated (if not encouraged) throughout the eighteenth and nineteenth centuries the coulisse, an unofficial stock exchange with a much greater volume of trade.

11. The official stockbrokers of the Paris Bourse actually were all well-to-do noblemen and merchants. The Savoyards (from Southeast France's border with Italy) were perceived as dishonest and treacherous.

12. Stockjobbers were analogous to the market makers who emerge later on the New York Stock Exchange. In the nineteenth century, this role is kept by the London Stock Exchange.

13. Economic historians agree that, at least until the turn of the twentieth century, government regulation of financial transactions, when attempted, was largely ineffectual (e.g., Harrison 2004, p. 679). Stock exchanges successfully fought off attempts to regulate or open them to public scrutiny (Banner 1998, p. 129), and the honor system was presented as *the* guarantor of transactions.

14. Similarly, in mid-nineteenth-century Chicago, the Chicago Board of Trade (CBOT) had control over space, time, and membership. Although the CBOT was from the beginning a corporation, and not a private association like the New York Stock Exchange, it was granted very broad power in 1859 by the Illinois legislature. Above all, the CBOT had complete control over the acceptance of new members and over the conditions under which a person might transact business. While the Board made considerable efforts to restrict grain trading to its indoor location, a street market outside its jurisdiction quickly developed (Lurie 1979, pp. 27, 40, 49).

15. While the New York Stock Exchange was a private association, commodities exchanges emerging later in the nineteenth century in Manhattan were incorporated (Van Antwerp 1913, pp. 415, 438).

16. A glimpse in the spatial organization of financial markets in nineteenth-century Paris is provided by Émile Zola's novel *L'Argent* (money). At the time of its publication in 1891, *L'Argent* was savaged by literary critics for being too realistic and too much based on empirical observations—in other words, for being too much of an ethnographic description instead of fiction. Zola writes of the "wet feet" exchange where securities fallen from grace are traded in the street by sordid speculators who specialized in these kinds of transactions (Zola [1891] 1897, pp. 26–27). These securities are then resold to capitalists eager to pump up the asset side of their books, a practice which strongly reverberates today in the subprime mortgage markets, among others.

17. In 1963, the chairman of the Securities Exchange Commission characterized the New York Stock Exchange as still having the characteristics of a private club (Sobel 1975, p. 283).

18. Richard Sennett (1974, p. 218) notices that by the end of the nineteenth century the general terms of the audience have changed, with authoritative voices being fenced off from the public realm. The public's task was seen as listening and observing.

19. While Pierre Bourdieu (1996, p. 186) sees nineteenth-century intellectuals as distinguishing themselves from politics and claiming cultural autonomy, financial writers of the same period claim that their honesty, experience, and knowledge provides them with a unique authority in addressing the public.

Chapter Three

1. This lithograph had an extensive commentary upon the folly of financial speculation. It was circulated at least in English and in French throughout Europe.

2. While the beneficial effects of trade upon human character and upon social relationships are acknowledged and discussed by eighteenth-century observers (e.g., Hirschman 1977, pp. 60–61), the incompatibility between commerce and financial markets precludes that these effects are triggered by speculation.

3. While Sir John Barnard's Act of 1733, for instance, prohibited all short sales in London, it was neither enforced nor respected (Harrison 2004, p. 677). Lack of legal boundaries contributed to the general perception of uncertainty about the nature of financial knowledge. At the same time, the legal boundaries emerging at the turn of the twentieth century incorporate and rely on definitions of financial knowledge present in brokers' writings.

4. In Great Britain as well as in the US, public opinion turned against gambling in the early nineteenth century. Gambling and betting were considered to pervert work ethic and encourage the cruel inclinations of the poorer classes. Gambling was also attacked as antithetical to production and as leading citizens into the temptations of idleness and luxury (Fabian 1990, pp. 66–67). Legislation adopted in Great Britain in 1845 (the Gaming Act) had different attitudes to rich and poor. In the US, by the end of the nineteenth century, horse racing remained the only gambling medium in most federal states (Munting 1996, pp. 21–29). The working classes, however, could have hardly been perceived as being tempted by financial speculation. This, in part, is indicative of the fact that the roost of the opposition to speculation must be sought elsewhere. At the same time, legislation prohibiting options trading associated it with gambling. In France (see Guillard 1875), as well as in the US and Great Britain, trading in derivatives or short selling was banned (in a completely ineffective manner) several times during the nineteenth century. In 1863, Abraham Lincoln prohibited gold futures (Phillips 2002, p. 298). The Illinois legislature also prohibited options trading as gambling contracts. These bans left unofficial markets unaffected. Their transactions (which were not enforced by internal board rules) continued in a legal limbo until the turn of the twentieth century, when legal treatises assimilated financial transactions with commercial contracts and distinguished them from gambling. These legal distinctions, in their turn, used arguments formulated in publications associated with and justifying the stock exchange.

5. This is not to say that moral questions disappeared altogether; but, to a considerable extent, they were now debated in works of fiction, being thus relegated to the domain of disbelief. This, in part, is why we witness such a preoccupation with the ethics of finance in Victorian fiction, for example (Reed 1984; Holway 1992).

6. Investor manuals showed in detail how to compute interest rates on state, city, and corporate bonds, since their modalities of payment and maturities could differ considerably. French state bonds, for example, had annual payments; some city and corporate bonds were redeemed according to a lottery principle. This required continuous recalculations of interest rates, and manuals had to explain the procedures for each type of bond.

7. Terms like "speculation" and "investing" have multiple meanings in the financial literature of the nineteenth century. They are used to designate the distinction

between long- and short-term commitment, but also the distinction between short-selling, together with futures and options trading, on the one hand, and trading in more orthodox instruments, on the other. In some cases, there is an additional distinction between "speculation" and "gambling," with the latter designating transactions in futures and options. Partly, this distinction overlaps with legal distinctions, like that made by the French law, which until 1885 forbade options trading.

8. Since Louis Bachelier, the random walk hypothesis has treated securities prices similar to gas molecules, moving independently of each other, with future movements being independent of past movements. This tenet grounds models for computing the probability of future price movements, such as the Black-Merton-Scholes formula (Mehrling 2005; MacKenzie 2006).

9. The *Chance Calculus* is the only book published by Jules Regnault (at the age of twenty-nine). At the same time, he had a successful career as a financial investor, if not a speculator. While he arrived in Paris with very modest financial means, he died a millionaire, with the bulk of his fortune consisting in bonds and stocks (for more biographical details, see Jovanovic 2004, pp. 220–22).

10. Regnault was strongly influenced by the "social physics" of Adolphe Quételet, who expanded the program of Laplace and Condorcet to the study of social phenomena (see also Jovanovic and Le Gall 2001). Accordingly, his aim was to uncover the general laws governing financial investments, by applying the probabilistic calculus to the study of price movements.

11. The standardization of price data is discussed in detail in chapter 4, which deals with price-recording technologies. It suffices to mention here that the Paris Bourse introduced a price-recording technology, the pantelegraph, in 1865, which was abandoned after two years. Afterward, in stark contrast with the New York and the London Stock Exchanges, the Paris Bourse continued to use paper slips and pencils for price recording until well into the twentieth century.

12. During the nineteenth century, French actuaries and engineers were involved in the formal treatment of markets and prices, while economists had almost exclusively a literary and legal education (Breton 1992, p. 32). The preoccupation with formal models of price movements can be understood against the background of a wider distrust in the accuracy of statistics, of the lack of standardized price data in financial markets, and a perceived inferiority of statistics compared to formal modeling (Ménard 1980, pp. 532, 534). In the period 1872–80, the *Journal des Actuaires Français* published articles like Léon Pochet's "La géometrie des jeux de Bourse" (The geometry of stock exchange games) (1873), which aimed at modeling the phenomena of the stock exchange by assimilating them to a game (Zylberberg 1990, p. 92). Another author, Eugène Fontaneau, treated the problem of securities prices as determined by supply and demand (Zylberberg 1990, p. 97). In 1913, Marcel Lenoir published a largely unnoticed thesis, "Studies on the Formation and the Movement of Prices," in which he combined modeling with statistical analysis. All this shows a constant preoccupation with treating the stock

NOTES TO PAGES 104–105

exchange as an object of systematic inquiry, anchored in abstract principles, not in the observation of idiosyncratic behavior. The specificity of the French intellectual milieu, combined with the lack of price-recording technologies, also helps us better understand why certain developments (like formal models of price behavior) occur in France, while others (like the emergence of financial chartists) occur primarily in the US. Overall, while there are commonalities, the legitimate relationship of the stock exchange to society at large is filtered through intellectual activities (such as writing) which cannot be separated either from specific intellectual milieus or from the technological architecture of financial transactions.

13. The *auto-compteur* was a device for computing the relative chances of bets on horse races. It consisted in a wooden board divided by horizontal and vertical lines. The horizontal lines represented fractions, from 1/1 to 1/100. The vertical lines were numbered from 0 to 55 at the lower end of the board, and from 55 to 110 at the upper end. Each cross of a vertical and a horizontal line represented a bet at the fraction on the left and at the corresponding stake above or below, respectively. Several wires were anchored at the squares 0, 55, and 110, and could be moved diagonally across the board, with the help of five wooden pieces mounted on rails on the four sides. The wooden pieces were lettered B, B', C, A, A'. Each piece had a hook which held the wire. There were two permanently attached wires. One of them went to A and from there to B', so that moving B' would also mean moving A. The other one went to A', from there to C and from C to B, so that moving C would mean also moving A' and B. Another line was permanently anchored at 0 and 55 (Lefevre 1871, p. 30).

14. Bachelier offered the first mathematical formulation of the random walk hypothesis, which was to play a decisive role in the development of mathematical finance (more specifically, of the options pricing theory) fifty years later. The main tenet of the random walk hypothesis is that securities prices move independently of each other, and that future movements do not depend on past movements. One of the most important implications of this hypothesis is that in the long run, the market cannot be controlled by any group or person. For the history of the random walk hypothesis, see, among others, LeRoy 1989; Courtault et al. 2000; Sullivan and Weithers 1991; Harrison 1997; Jovanovic 2000, 2001. In 1908, Vincenz Bronzin, a professor at the Commercial Academy in Trieste (then part of the Austro-Hungarian empire) published the *Theory of Premium Contracts*, laying out "every element of modern option pricing" (Zimmermann and Hafner 2006, p. 238).

15. Franck Jovanovic (2008) argues that formal modeling of the random character of stock prices took off in the US in the 1960s against the background of institutional changes taking place in prominent economics departments. While some 1930s economists were interested in financial markets, but paid more attention to econometrics than to modeling, in the 1960s a network of academics based at the University of Chicago managed to link the random walk model to key concepts from economics. This explains the unclear academic status of financial economics

until the 1960s, as well as its tensioned relationship with alternative explanations of price variations, such as financial chartism. Nevertheless, the much earlier shift to price behavior as an explanatory variable (superseding individual behavior) supports the idea that prices incorporate information.

16. The term used by Proudhon here is "marchés à terme," which can be "au comptant" (for delivery) or "à découvert" (without delivery). Therefore, the term used by Proudhon can be taken to include both futures and options markets.

17. The distinction between speculating and gambling was both a legal one and a strategy used by investment manuals with respect to the legitimacy of financial operations.

18. This shift did not imply that ethical doubts entirely disappeared. Some pamphlets continued to question options contracts as adequate transactions for the middle classes. Nevertheless, morality did not constitute anymore the exclusive (or dominant) frame for conceptualizing these transactions. As in the case of gambling, what was perceived as appropriate for the upper classes was thought less so for the middle and working classes. This strongly contrasted with the drive to attract more and more participants into financial speculation, both in official and in unofficial markets.

19. During the French Revolution, *agiotage* (initially a premium fee levied in currency exchange) meant not only financial speculation, but speculation in (badly needed) agricultural produce and other commodities (including hoarding them in order to create artificial scarcity). Therefore, the word had particularly negative connotations afterward.

20. Broadly speaking, bucket shops were unofficial brokerage offices. There were, however, considerable differences among bucket shops, with regard to their financial standing, their reputation, and the financial securities they dealt in.

21. See, for instance, *Pearce v. Rice*, 142 US 28.

22. Stephen Turner (2003) regards this as a fundamental contradiction embedded in the notion of democratic expertise.

23. I examine these aspects in chapter 6.

Chapter Four

1. The pantelegraph had a convex copper surface on which a paper sheet (about 4x6 inches) was placed. The message was written in very thick ink. A stylus placed on a mechanical arm scanned the paper and transmitted an electrical signal, interrupted by the thick ink. At the receiving end, another stylus scanned a paper sheet imbibed with potassium cyanide, leaving traces in the places where the electric current was interrupted.

2. I can only speculate here about the reasons for which the Paris Bourse did not adopt the pantelegraph, nor any other price-recording technology until well

into the twentieth century. Among the reasons might have well been the desire for maintaining a monopoly over price information, a monopoly guaranteed by the French state. At the time of the pantelegraph, the Bourse was in acerbic competition with (and constantly trying to undermine) the coulisse, its unofficial yet tolerated counterpart. Since its price data had a state guarantee on it, the Bourse was not interested in introducing any technology which might be copied or used by the competition, weakening thus the already existing authority of its own data.

3. This aspect is also emphasized by organization sociologists (e.g., Perrow 1967; Blau et al. 1976; Carruthers and Stinchcombe 2001), historians (e.g., Porter 1995), accountants (Miller 2001, p. 385), and sociologists of technology (e.g., Hughes, Rouncefield, and Toulmie 2002) who show that financial technologies standardize informational outputs and make them transferable across various contexts.

4. In my analysis, I rely on the distinction between the price-recording and the price-transmitting features of technology, on the premise that the two will not necessarily overlap. For instance, the rules and technology for writing letters do not overlap with those of the postal system that distributes those letters.

5. I am examining here only the organization of trading on the New York Stock Exchange. For reasons of space, the other stock and commodities exchanges which existed in Lower Manhattan in the second half of the nineteenth century will not be discussed here.

6. Until the end of the nineteenth century, business data collection and management relied exclusively on pen, ink, and paper technologies. It is only in the 1880s and the 1890s that data recording and compiling became mechanized, with the spread of typewriters, the adoption of card files, and the introduction of Hollerith machines (Yates 1994, pp. 34–35).

7. As I have shown in chapter 1, the Paris Bourse was organized in a similar way. There was a status group of sixty stockbrokers who were practically civil servants. They operated indoors and inherited seats. A much larger group of unofficial stockbrokers dealt in the street. Paris also had multiple prices and several quotation lists for the same securities (Vidal 1910). There were at least three official daily quotations, plus a number of unofficial ones (Maddison 1877, p. 17).

8. In the 1840s and 1850s, the Regular Board traded behind closed doors and under a veil of secrecy. Quotations were not disclosed during trade (Warshow 1929, p. 70). Agents would listen at the keyhole and sell the price information in the street.

9. At least some of the New York City restaurants had tickers in the dining rooms. At Miller's and Delmonico's, investors could follow the price variations in real time, ordering a meal and some stocks at the same time (Babson 1908, p. 47). Private stock auctioneers also installed tickers on the exchange floor. Not only was the ticker present in places where the upper middle classes congregated, it was also present on the fringes of the marketplace, in the cramped, badly lit bucket shops where poorer people came to invest their few dollars. So strong was the influence

of the ticker and the prestige associated with it that some bucket shop operators felt compelled to install fake tickers and wires going only to the edge of the rug, together with additional paraphernalia like mock quotation tables and fake news-letters (Fabian 1990, p. 191; Cowing 1965, p. 103). The ticker was praised by some contemporaries as "the only God" of the market (Lefevre 1901, p. 115) and as a wonder of the outgoing nineteenth century (King 1897, p. 108). Successful stock operators were fictionalized as "Von Moltke of the ticker" and as "masters of the ticker" (Lefevre 1907, pp. 83, 122). It became a prized possession, to be kept until a speculator's last breath: when Daniel Drew, the famed speculator of the 1850s and early 1860s died in 1879, his only possessions were a Bible, a sealskin coat, a watch, and a ticker (Wyckoff 1972, p. 28).

10. It should be noted here that in the US and in Britain, at the time of the ticker's invention, several efforts were under way to develop machines for making speech visible. On the one hand, there were attempts at developing technical de-vices for the deaf, connected to the method of lip reading. The people involved in these attempts were also involved in the development of better telegraphic devices and tried their hand (though unsuccessfully) at a telegraphic machine fitted for financial transactions. Alexander Graham Bell's father was among those making such efforts (Siegert 1998, p. 81). On the other hand, there were attempts at devel-oping machines whose aim was to automate speech and writing, turning these into standardized activities (Gitelman 1999, pp. 94, 188). More generally, in late nine-teenth century phonology was devising transcription systems and machines which were meant to make speech sounds visible (Robins 1990, p. 223). These experi-ments were at the forefront of the revolution in linguistics, which took place around 1900, when historical-etymological approaches were replaced by descriptive-structuralist ones.

11. I discuss the emergence of technical analysis (or chartism) and of analyst groups in chapter 5.

12. The technique of pasting newspaper clippings alongside one's own observa-tions (with the latter being checked against the former) appears as an observa-tional instrument for monitoring the market. One's idiosyncratic observations in a particular brokerage office do not appear as sufficient, and the speculator has to use several instruments at once.

13. See also Nelson (1900, pp. 27–28), and Anonymous (1893). For period pho-tographs of brokerage offices see, for example, *Guide to Investors* (Anonymous 1898, pp. 62, 78).

14. This corroborates arguments formulated in economic sociology, as well as in the sociology of knowledge, according to which economic transactions are em-bedded in processes of knowledge production (Knorr Cetina and Bruegger 2002b; Preda 2002).

15. During the 1880s and the 1890s, there were several moments when seat prices fell dramatically. This was due partly to the ticker, partly to economic

slumps. The NYSE fought hard for control of the ticker and price information; after each series of fights, prices rose again. Between 1858 and 1870, there was a fivefold increase in NYSE's seat prices; between 1871 and 1901, this increase (unadjusted for inflation) was thirtyfold (Warshow 1929, p. 341). The Committee of Arrangements of the New York Stock Exchange had to approve all the phone and telegraph connections within the building; it had the right to disconnect phones and cut wires if they considered their monopoly on data to be in jeopardy (Goldman 1914, pp. 28, 187, 189).

16. A contemporary observer estimated that in 1898 there were about seven thousand bucket shops and ten to fifteen thousand brokerage houses in the United States (Hoyle 1898, p. 17). The difference between bucket shops and brokerage houses was not only a matter of financial muscle. Some bucket shops were very prosperous and up market, while others were quite modest. Some bucket shops specialized mainly in derivatives, while brokerage houses did more "classical" securities trading. Bucket shops were prohibited in 1905 in North Dakota and Minnesota, and in 1907 in Arkansas and Nebraska (Cowing 1965, p. 30). In 1908, the state of New York adopted a bucket shop law (modified in 1909) requiring licenses from grain dealers and made manipulation of securities a felony (Goldman 1914, pp. 199–201; Cowing 1965, p. 65n63).

17. Brokerage firms also circumvented controls by having memberships on several exchanges at once (Wyckoff 1930, p. 102). While the New York Stock Exchange forbade its members to deal with members of other stock exchanges, or to provide them with ticker price data, nobody could prevent a broker from giving price information to a colleague from the same firm who also happened to hold a membership on a different exchange.

18. A comparison with the Paris Bourse can best show the knowledge-organizational changes induced by the ticker. In the 1860s, the NYSE and the Paris Bourse had a similar organization of knowledge: both were multiple (discontinuous *and* continuous) markets with multiple prices (Vidal 1910; Walker 2001). For specific reasons, the Paris Bourse did not introduce the ticker at all and continued to work without a price-recording technology until at least the 1920s. There continued to be two classes of stockbrokers: one was a high-status group; the other an illegal, yet tolerated, class that greatly outnumbered the first. Multiple prices and parallel price lists were the rule until 1920 (Parker 1920, p. 37), and even later. Thus, around 1910 there was an official list (*Cote officielle*), a list of curb-traded securities (*Cote du syndicat des banquiers en valeurs au comptant*), and at least two free lists (*Cote Desfossés* and *Cote Vidal*), which published different prices. Opening, lowest, highest, and closing prices were published only by Desfossés and Vidal. The official quotation list was decided every day by a committee of bankers and official stockbrokers (Vidal 1910, pp. 38, 83). In New York, by contrast, after the two boards of brokers merged and worked in the same room, multiple quotations disappeared and price data became both continuous and standardized.

Instead of adopting a price-recording technology, some Paris stockbrokers developed an interest in abstract models of price variations (as discussed in chapter 3), seen as a corrective to inaccurate price information. In Germany, by contrast, where state control over the stock exchange seems to have been much more intense than in France, the Stock Exchange law of 1896 compelled brokers to adopt a single price for one and the same security. The law stipulated that "quotations should reflect the local business situation and not simply transmit prices realized in transactions" (Kurth 1999, p. 2). The law of 1896 made a large part of the brokerage business migrate to Paris and London, and was perceived in the US as having very negative consequences, which spoke against the attempted incorporation of the New York Stock Exchange (Van Antwerp 1913, p. 444).

19. Caitlin Zaloom (2003, p. 261) argues that trading screens shift the traders' social orientation from local sources of information to imagining and identifying competitors according to the numbers on the screen.

Chapter Five

1. Financial chartism is not the only form of expertise present in financial markets. Fundamental analysis, accounting expertise, risk analysis, and credit analysis are among the established forms of expertise underlying contemporary financial transactions. Additionally, several types of traders can be distinguished, according to the form of expertise they mainly rely upon (e.g., Smith 1999; Fenton-O'Creevy et al. 2005). Nevertheless, for the present purposes, I focus on the emergence of chartism as a specific form of expertise.

2. A breaking gap, for example, is a gap in the price chart which indicates the start of a new level of action in the market. A bottom is an event where the price reaches a low and remains there, or a low, then another lower low, then another higher low. A saucer is a gradual change in the trend line. A falling flag is a bearish continuation chart pattern which lasts less than three weeks and slopes against the prevailing trend. A symmetrical coil is made by two trend lines which intersect in rising and declining, respectively. (A more comprehensive overview of technical terms is provided by numerous publications, as well as by Web sites such as stockcharts.com, for instance.)

3. Research in financial economics suggests that stock prices are influenced by analysts' recommendations; investors look at these recommendations for information on returns. Since the cost of the information search is greater than zero, these costs are reflected in commissions for trading. They appear as an indirect product of financial analysis (e.g., Womack 1996, pp. 138, 164).

4. US Market Technicians Association, http://www.mta.org/eweb/Dynamic Page.aspx?Site=MTA&WebKey=9263a439–9ca6–46a8-aa49-a0d3e6b5d139 (accessed April 11, 2005).

5. Technical Securities Analysts Association, http://www.tsaasf.org (accessed September 7, 2004).

6. Banks lacked centralized information about bonds sold on smaller exchanges or over the counter; many had to compile this information time and again from sheets distributed by brokerage houses, and each bank did this for its own use, but did not distribute this information to other banks. In this situation, some brokers saw an opportunity for establishing a centralized information service. This service involved gathering data about the bonds being offered for sale rather than statistical analysis.

7. Richard Wyckoff is seen nowadays as the founder of the "Wyckoff Method of Technical Analysis and Stock Speculation" and as one of the "five titans of technical analysis" (Pruden and Belletante n.d., p. 1).

8. Booker T. Washington was the first principal of the Tuskegee Normal and Industrial Institute (1881), where he created a curriculum combining practical skills with academic education, and emphasizing economic independence as a means of emancipating African Americans.

9. The US Constitution allowed the federal regulation of interstate commerce and of mail services. In order to avoid being subjected to regulation, the management of the New York Stock Exchange prohibited members from advertising their services (Goldman 1914, p. 175). By contrast, unofficial brokerage houses (bucket shops) could advertise, since they were not registered as members of the New York Stock Exchange.

10. Charles Dow (1851–1902), the editor of the *Wall Street Journal*, had not published anything but these articles. During his editorship of the *Wall Street Journal*, he had initiated the publications of industrial averages (1896). Dow's articles did not use charts, but rather enunciated general principles of reasoning when observing the market. Contemporary observers consider that the Dow index was actually elaborated by S. A. Nelson and the other analysts associated with him rather than by Dow himself (see, for instance, http://www.stockcharts.com/education/Market Analysis/dowtheory1.html [accessed March 13, 2006]).

11. In 1927, Babson announced that a major market crash was bound to happen, a warning which he repeated in September 1929 (Vines 2005, p. 145). He attracted ridicule first, but afterward he was held responsible for the Great Crash of October 1929.

12. The notion that prices move in great waves, or cycles, was already presented in the financial advice literature of the 1870s as an "established doctrine in political economy" (Giffen 1877, pp. 102–3).

13. Henry Hall took over Benner's notion of cycles and reworked it as cycles of prosperity and depression, distinguishing between five-, ten-, and twenty-year cycles. He considered that the prices of stocks and bonds are related to "the prevalence of good or bad times" (Hall 1908, p. 55).

14. The tape reader designated both the clerk compiling price data from the ticker tape and the speculator analyzing price data variations.

15. In the 1950s and 1960s, chart users evolved into two distinct categories with respect to the knowledge claims they made, based on interpretations of price variations. The first category (the "true chartists") concentrated on forecasting the emergence of patterns of price variations, based on their incipient traits. The second category (the "technicians") used patterns of price variations as a means of diagnosing economic situations, and of inferring conclusions from this diagnosis. In other words, while the first category concentrated on pattern identification starting from unclear incipient traits, the second category used these patterns as a means of diagnosing broader situations. This differentiation was reflected in a professional divide as well: while "true chartists" found their audience in nonprofessional market participants, technicians addressed mainly a professional audience.

16. Formulations can be understood as definitions of practical accomplishments which are intrinsic to the accomplishment itself (see also Garfinkel and Sacks [1970] 1990, p. 71). The intelligibility of formulations consists in their "use as a maxim or reminder—a kind of litany—to be rehearsed *for* the game and recalled *in* game-specific situations" (Bogen and Lynch 1993, p. 89).

17. It is relevant here that contemporary online traders, who derive their information almost exclusively from on-screen observation, rely heavily (and almost exclusively) on technical analysis.

Chapter Six

1. We can see how these four major arguments formulated in the eighteenth century resonate in the nineteenth-century social sciences, not only in the work of Thorstein Veblen ([1899] 1949) about conspicuous waste, but also in Marx's notion that the reproduction of representations of capital becomes its dominant form of expansion. Werner Sombart, in his turn, stresses adventurism as lying at the roots of the capitalist expansion. On a more contemporary note, the current discussion in the Western European media about whether the high salaries of traders and hedge fund managers are justified or not can be seen as a continuation of this criticism. In sociology, it is the topic of Olivier Godechot's (2007) recent work on the "working rich."

2. For the view on speculation as an ordinary business see, among others, Clews 1888, p. 23; *Les écueils* 1865, pp. 34–35; Van Antwerp 1913, p. 74; Giffen 1877, p. 41. The notion that speculation is the expression of an unbounded spirit of adventure can also be found in Horace Greeley's writings, among others (1850, p. 255).

3. The hero of a moralizing novel from the era of British railway speculation gives his wife the following rationale for abandoning his job and becoming a financial speculator: "I think Ellen, he said at last—I think it is nearly time for me to change my occupation, and seek something different to the drudgery I follow,

day by day. It fairly fags me out, and I dislike it more and more every day. Other persons enjoy life, and their employment brings it what makes life a pleasure" (Macfarlane 1856, p. 18).

4. Proudhon was a leading Socialist figure of the nineteenth century and the author of a revolutionary political program based not on the abolition of private ownership, but on preserving and expanding it through the creation of workers' associations, a program which attracted Marx's scorn. Usually seen as influenced by Hegel's philosophy (which, Marx argued, Proudhon distorted and misunderstood), Proudhon's position on financial speculation contains an important biologistic strain, which I will detail in the following.

5. Regnault uses here the term *spéculateur à découvert*, which includes, but is not necessarily restricted to, short-selling.

6. Proudhon also saw society as "living from circulation" and social ills as being mostly "troubles of the circulatory function" ([1848] 1938, p. 305).

7. The public treatment of the stock exchange as a natural force continues today, becoming visible in crisis situations, when disruptions have to be justified. Media treatment of the 1987 crash, for instance, made copious use of biologic and naturalistic metaphors in representing what had happened (Warner and Molotch 1993, pp. 178–79).

8. Nevertheless, as I shall argue in more detail below, speculation as a vital force supports not only a picture of social closure and inequality, but also a utopian one, of class cooperation and common interests.

9. Caitlin Zaloom (2006, pp. 25–30) highlights the importance of the buildings of the Chicago Board of Trade as symbols of local and national power.

10. Talmage was against speculating on margin rather than against financial investments per se (Talmage 1879, p. 299), which shows that he was operating within the distinction between "good" and "bad" speculation.

11. This transformation appears against the background of a more general metamorphosis of merchants, industrialists, and bankers into a self-conscious class claiming to represent the nation as a whole. The struggles over the control of cultural life and the eagerness to become integrated into society, if not to represent "society" as a whole, are part and parcel of the social transformations marking the late nineteenth century (Beckert 2001, p. 247).

12. In France, debates (often populist) about the supposed negative influence of trading foreign securities instead of French ones continued well into the first decade of the twentieth century and can be seen as echoing an intraclass struggle between financial and industrial capitalists (Freedeman 1993, p. 65).

13. We can find echoes of this organicist notion both in Émile Durkheim's insistence on "totalizing social facts," on the irreducibility of society to the sum of individual relationships, and in Marcel Mauss's stress on systems of exchange as crucial for the constitution of societies and as always involving collectivities rather than individuals (e.g., Mauss [1950] 1999, p. 150).

14. The liberalization argued by the author is set in the context of debates about the relationships between the bourse and the coulisse, which have marked the 1860s in France. The coulisse represented the unofficial securities market, tolerated by the French state and commanding a much higher volume than the bourse. Trading in futures and options was illegal and prohibited on the bourse, yet tolerated on the coulisse. While official brokers were practically civil servants, unofficial ones (the coulissiers) had a much lower status. The call for liberalization appears thus as a protest against this discriminatory system, a protest which nevertheless does not contradict the utopian project of the stock exchange as a source of social reform (see also *La Bourse* 1860, p. 31; Tétreau 1994). Another significant factor here is that before the law of March 28, 1885, which recognized all markets for future delivery as legal, persons entering an options contract could decline to pay their differences by presenting the plea of gambling (Vidal 1910, p. 199). Time bargains were not recognized as contracts upon merchandise and therefore not enforceable in a court of law. Moreover, only transactions concluded through an official stockbroker of the Paris Bourse were automatically valid as commercial contracts. Hence the argument that financial securities are indistinguishable from any other commodity, which makes transactions in them generally similar with commercial contracts.

Chapter Seven

1. Following Bennett Harrison, Richard Sennett (2006, p. 40) calls this mode "impatient capital" and argues that it puts pressure on more "patient" forms of capital (i.e., on corporations) to shorten their time horizon and to operate with a view to quarterly profit statements. This statement is echoed by organizational sociologists (e.g., Zorn et al. 2005) who show how corporations have changed their modus operandi under the pressure of financial markets.

2. While this gallery contains almost exclusively white male figures, this does not mean that women speculators, or even women brokers, or non-Caucasian investors, did not exist. Arguments have been made that during the nineteenth century financial investments weren't confined to men (e.g., Rutterford and Maltby 2006), and Wall Street has perpetuated the myth of Hettie Green as an example of a woman's success in the harsh male world of speculation. By 1878, US newspapers also published articles about African Americans who had amassed money from speculation; they were living in New York City and some of them were women (see "People of African Blood. Something about the Wealthy or Well-to-Do Negroes of New York and Brooklyn," newspaper clipping in the diary of Edward Neufville Tailer, December 13, 1878, New York Historical Society).

3. See, for instance, Nelson D. Schwartz, "A Spiral of Losses by a 'Plain Vanilla' Trader," *New York Times*, January 25, 2008; Nicola Clark and David Jolly, "French

Bank Says Rogue Trader Lost $7 Billion," *New York Times*, January 25, 2008; James Kanter, "Charges Are Sought Against French Trader," *New York Times*, January 28, 2008; Doreen Carvajal and James Kanter, "A Quest for Glory and Bonus End in Disgrace," *New York Times*, January 29, 2008; Nelson D. Schwartz and Katrin Bennhold, "A Trader's Secrets, a Bank's Missteps," *New York Times*, February 5, 2008.

4. This phenomenon is by far not restricted to US literature or to the nineteenth century. In Western Europe, writers like Anthony Trollope ([1875] 1982) or Émile Zola ([1891] 1897), among others, have dealt critically with financial speculation in their novels. Among those perpetuating the notion (if not the myth) of speculation as freeing the individual is Ayn Rand, who seems to exercise some influence on the contemporary, general philosophy of speculation. Several investors and traders I have interviewed mentioned Ayn Rand as a formative influence, in the same breath with names like Nassim Taleb.

Chapter Eight

1. I did not encounter the word panic in the eighteenth-century documents I examined; this notion seems to have been first introduced into the financial vocabulary in the nineteenth century.

2. Platzschwindel is loosely translated as dizziness caused by presence in a particular space.

3. The notion that panic attacks are triggered by location is contested in contemporary psychiatry.

4. Robert Shiller, who has investigated the emotional reactions of investors during the crash of 1987, reports that 23% of the individual investors and 42% of the institutional investors in his sample reported anxiety-related bodily changes, like rapid pulse, tightness in chest, sweaty palms, and difficulties of concentration (Shiller 1993, p. 496). While anxiety symptoms do not automatically mean panic, it becomes even more challenging to explain how panic can spread without direct, reciprocal observations of anxiety.

5. This is a major problem for the conceptualization of panics as collective behavior (e.g., Adler and Adler 1984, p. 86): how can dispersed participants "copy opinion leaders" and "shadow" the beliefs of others without an adequate observational system? This issue is related to the second conceptual problem, namely that financial transactions (or, more generally, economic actions) have an imminently individualistic orientation: their ultimate goal is individual profit, not collective benefits (although cooperation or conflicts are not excluded as means toward attaining this ultimate goal).

6. Peter Garber (2000, pp. 124–26) argues against the notion of crowd psychology on the grounds that this is an ill-defined and unmeasured phenomenon. In

his view, panics as well as bubbles are thoroughly rational economic phenomena, which should be rather grasped in terms of economic experiments. The distinction to be made here is that between "crowd psychology" as an essential (if not the sole) causal factor explaining liquidity crises and asset depreciation, on the one hand, and imitation as a form of behavior requiring sociological investigation, on the other. More recently, Deirdre McCloskey, in an effort to argue that markets are not devoid of ethics, makes the point that financial bubbles are made possible by trust and friendship, without which strangers could not be attracted into speculative activities (McCloskey 2006, p. 159). This kind of psychological volatility (wide sudden swings from trust to distrust) would require then an explanation.

7. These observations are second order because institutional closure prevents direct observations of transactions. Accessible to external observers are representations of transactions as observable, representations which involve the tools of the financial imaginary.

8. They represent financial transactions and make them available to direct perception at the same time. The more appropriate term here is Husserl's notion of appresentation, which I have used in chapter 4.

9. This does not mean that, generally, traders and investors do not panic at all, or that lay traders display more hysterical behavior than professional traders. Such questions cannot be answered within the frame of the present investigation. What is of interest here is how representations of panic serve to justify the notion of vital force intrinsic to the understanding of modern finance.

10. Even in situations of considerable financial strain, Tailer continued to project an alternative, counterfactual course of action and to keep an overview of his actual and potential losses. He makes occasional mentions of "small crowds" during the panic of 1873, as well as of rumors about speculators like John Stewart and James H. Banker, and, while depressed, did not seem to succumb to hysteria.

11. Next to this article, Tailer wrote: "The article on panics and their power is well worth reading in these panicky times, when gold rises and falls from five to ten points in a day."

12. We can observe this not only in the case of Orson Welles's broadcast, but also in some actual situations in contemporary financial markets, where apparently irrational behavior spreads through a dispersed crowd, in spite of the fact that each actor taken apart behaves rationally. For instance, Donald MacKenzie (2005) makes the argument that the collapse of Long Term Capital Management (LTCM) in 1998, followed by a market panic, was due to the formation of an unraveling superportfolio. Investors imitated the LTCM's trades, which could work only on the assumption of uniqueness. Through imitation, the arbitrage advantages which such trades might have had at the start were eliminated, which in turn led to eliminating the advantages of the copy traders. Such an imitation could not have been one based on direct observation, since other traders and hedge funds did not

have direct access to LTCM's traders; they could not sit next to them and observe every move. Rather, this imitation was grounded in the observation of the imagined behavior of LTCM traders, a behavior induced from the observation of price movements, gossip, and post hoc rationalizations.

13. In 1877, Tailer recorded in his diary: "Feb 14 1877: The Central New Jersey Railroad went into the hands of a receiver today, and this sad event will entail loss and suffering upon . . . [illegible]. Mrs. Tailer, the children and myself are holders of 330 shares—besides some bonds. This is one of the severest losses, which I have ever sustained at one blow. In the panic of '57,' Winzer and I lost $27,000, in 1861 $100,000." (Diary of Edward Neufville Tailer, from July 1876 to Feb 1878, New York Historical Society). This shows that panics also work as memory props—that is, they help correlate present events to past ones.

Conclusion

1. Accessing the market does not automatically mean here actively participating in financial transactions. Markets can and are accessed primarily in an observational fashion, both individually and collectively, in private as well as in public places.

2. This is the case with, for instance, Luc Boltanski's and Eve Chiapello's (Chiapello 2003) "new spirit of capitalism," but also with statistical analyses which purport to show how the rhetoric of finance has affected the structure of the corporation (e.g., Davis and Robbins 2005).

3. Generally speaking, we can identify here at least two patterns of technological development: a centralized one, characteristic for exchanges like the Paris Bourse, which has adopted and implemented a preexisting model of automated trading. There is also a decentralized model, according to which some serious technological innovations come from brokerage houses. This, for instance, has happened on the New York Stock Exchange, where developments in trading software have been initiated by brokerage houses. The emergence of electronic brokerages in the 1990s has also blurred some professional distinctions, with software engineers entering into and transforming brokerage services.

4. Interviews I had with brokers active on the NYSE since the late 1950s point out that, from the practitioner's perspective, price recording and trading remained largely nonintegrated during the 1980s. It was only since the mid-1990s that trading software integrated these two aspects.

5. The widespread belief (not necessarily true) is that day traders are nonprofessionals who trade on the whims of the moment, getting in and out of the market within the same day. The Securities Exchange Commission had difficulties in establishing the boundaries between professional and day traders. In 1999, Arthur Levitt, the then SEC chairman, considered that the main differences between day

traders and professional traders consisted in the kind of broker-dealer through which transactions were conducted (SEC 1999). In the year 2000, the SEC estimated in a *Special Study* that there were less than seven thousand full-time day traders in the US, but acknowledged that the number of part-time traders was difficult to estimate. This study considered the "mind set" as a distinguishing characteristic of day traders (SEC 2000).

6. Ethnographic observations also indicate that online trading generates new forms of sociality, characterized by interactions with virtual experts and trading partners. Traditional networks seem to be replaced here by imagined partners and communities (see also Pollner 2002, p. 237).

7. While finishing this book, I had the occasion to conduct ethnographic observations and interviews with several day traders (who prefer to call themselves independent traders), as well as with more traditional ones. It appears that electronic traders spend about 95% of their total trading time on price observation. Placing a transaction on an electronic platform is a matter of seconds. It also appears that the widespread perception of independent traders as frantically getting in and out of the market is inadequate. In fact, the number of daily transactions appears to be relatively small. Compared with traditional traders, electronic ones spend decidedly less time on gathering information from networks of friends and acquaintances. Some independent traders I have observed actually do not spend any time on network-based information gathering.

8. While global trading platforms declare that they strive to ensure best order placement by using routing optimization algorithms, such procedures remain opaque to participants and may not always be matched by hardware configurations. Needless to say, there are also questions about fairness and justice which, in a global allocation system, cannot be reduced to routing optimization.

9. Both online and off-line traders I have interviewed consider that online trading platforms actually increase volatility, since traders have to act on the basis on a narrow range of information (price data and volume being the most important), have to conduct more trades, and trade more often. They also claim that an increased number of participants have reduced margins, and that they were forced to trade more on narrower margins.

10. Many of the electronic traders I have observed have told me that they were not greatly interested (if at all) in other types of data about the companies the shares of which they were trading. While they had a general knowledge of what the said companies dealt with, they made minimal efforts to obtain fundamental financial data about these companies. By contrast, they constantly used the technical charts embedded in their trading software programs. In fact, most of their trading sessions consisted in constantly flipping back-and-forth between observing columns of price and volume data, and observing charts.

11. Especially in the case of electronic trading, the traders I have observed needed an instrument for "seeing" the flickering price columns in a meaningful

way, as well as for making meaningful assumptions about what other traders were doing. Since in electronic trading social networks seem to play a diminished role (compared with the more traditional trading), traders cannot rely much on gossip for getting a picture of what others are doing. They need therefore a tool for generating an imagined sociality out of the price movements they see on their computer screens, and charts are here an invaluable tool. Their predictive power—that is, the capacity to assume broadly that a price will move in a certain direction and within a certain range—appears more as an epiphenomenon of this imagined sociality. In other words, electronic traders use the charts to make up suppositions about what other traders are doing and then, based on these suppositions, they try to infer broader price movements. The suppositions about other traders' actions are the trader's "me" as opposed to the "I" of his own screen trades (Mead [1934] 1952, pp. 175–76).

12. TradeStation, which is a major electronic brokerage, provides this possibility. Alerts and automated trades can be embedded in the chart (see http://www .tradestation.com/aboutts/default.shtm [accessed June 18, 2006]). Some of the electronic traders I have interviewed saw automated trading as providing them with more time for observing the market.

13. In this respect, we have to do with a populist trend different from the closure of expertise analyzed by Stephen P. Turner (2003).

14. See, for instance, http://www.shaeffersresearch.com as just one example of hybrid online financial expertise combining personal charisma with the authority of technical systems.

15. This view is echoed by, among others, Max Weber, who saw the stock exchange as an instrument of political power, never to be abandoned.

16. The 1990s belief that the stock market will continue to rise almost infinitely can be also seen as an expression of this religious trust. Articles like James K. Glassman and Kevin A. Hassett's "Dow 36,000" (the *Atlantic*, September 1999), while derided today, scorned experts who warned that stocks are risky; in the authors' view, these experts performed "a terrible disservice" to millions of investors by frightening them away from the market (p. 37).

17. Euronext was initially formed by the merged stock exchanges of Paris, Amsterdam, and Brussels, joined later by LIFFE and the Lisbon stock exchange.

18. See, for instance, "Chirac takes a Swipe at Advance of NYSE into Europe," the *Guardian*, June 7, 2006, p. 23. Even the expression "advance into Europe" suggests a state of confrontation reminiscent of Max Weber's observation about the stock exchange as a political weapon. Needless to say, had Euronext tried to buy the New York Stock Exchange, the US media would not have reacted differently. It is also to be remarked that neither the Sarbanes-Oxley Act nor the authority of the SEC will apply to the European part of this merged entity. This raises the question whether the regulation set in place in the US after the financial scandals of the late 1990s will not be bypassed within this newly created entity.

19. See, for instance, "Stock Exchange Faces Foreign takeover after German Bid," the *Guardian*, December 14, 2004, p. 1; "The Eagle Is Landing," the *Scotsman*, December 19, 2004, p. 5. This latter article was accompanied by a picture superimposing the large shadow of the German eagle emblem over the entrance of the London Stock Exchange.

20. The German media speculated on this occasion that the aim of Anglo-Saxon investment funds' plan was actually to acquire and then sell the Deutsche Börse piecemeal.

21. He was president of Merrill Lynch's Private Client Group at the time of this speech. SIA's motto is "the voice of the industry representing nearly 93 million investors."

22. Resistance to public economic education comes not only from vested interest groups. Deirdre McCloskey (2006, p. 483) notices that it also comes from the left of the political spectrum, though on entirely different grounds.

23. The investor rights movement, of the kind exemplified by John Bogle, purports to revert from "managerial capitalism" back to "ownership capitalism" by combating the excesses and the greed of big corporations. Yet this movement does not advocate widespread, public financial education (in spite of being engaged in a public campaign of "enlightening" small investors), but advocates rather paying more attention to fundamental economic data and cutting down corporate excesses like compensation packages (see, for instance, Bogle 2006).

24. Ashley Seager, "City Bonuses Hit Record High with £14bn Payout," the *Guardian*, August 28, 2007, p. 1.

25. *Libération*, May 28, 2007, http://www.liberation.fr/php/pages/page ReactionsList.php?rubId=7288docId=256461 (accessed May 28, 2007).

26. Donald MacKenzie (2008) provides an accessible overview of how CDOs have been created and traded, as well as of the collapse of this process.

27. The expansion of mortgages in conjunction with their trading into financial instruments can be seen as pertaining to the transformations of savings into capital (as analyzed by Marx). These transformations expand the web of tributary relationships (Weber's argument), so that the availability of mortgages depends at least in part upon them being seen and trusted as financial products by institutions which are not mortgage providers at all (for instance, hedge funds).

References

Abbott, Andrew. 1988. *The System of Professions: An Essay on the Division of Expert Labor*. Chicago: University of Chicago Press.

——. 1995. "Things of Boundaries." *Social Research* 62 (4): 857–82.

Abolafia, Mitchel Y. 1996. *Making Markets: Opportunism and Restraint on Wall Street*. Cambridge, MA: Harvard University Press.

Adler, Patricia A., and Peter Adler. 1984. "The Market as Collective Behavior." In *The Social Dynamics of Financial Markets*, ed. Patricia A. Adler and Peter Adler, 85–105. Greenwich CT: JAI Press.

Agnew, Jean-Christophe. 1986. *Worlds Apart: The Market and the Theater in Anglo-American Thought, 1550–1750*. Cambridge: Cambridge University Press.

Alborn, Timothy L. 1994. "Economic Man, Economic Machine: Images of Circulation in the Victorian Money Market." In *Natural Images in Economic Thought: "Markets Read in Tooth and Claw,"* ed. Philip Mirowski, 173–95. Cambridge: Cambridge University Press.

——. 1998. *Conceiving Companies: Joint-Stock Politics in Victorian England*. London: Routledge.

Alexander, Jeffrey C. 2006. *The Civil Sphere*. Oxford: Oxford University Press.

The Anatomy of Exchange-Alley: Or, A System of Stock-Jobbing. 1719. London: E. Smith.

Andreassen, Paul. 1990. "Judgmental Extrapolation and Market Overreaction: On the Use and Disuse of News." *Journal of Behavioral Decision Making* 3:153–74.

Anonymous. 1721. *Some Considerations with Respect to the Bill for Preventing the Infamous Practice of Stock-Jobbing*. London.

——. 1736. *Reasons Humbly Offered to the Members of the Honourable House of Commons, against a Bill now depending to render more effectual, an Act made in the Seventh Year of His Majesty's Reign, intitled, An Act to Prevent the infamous Practice of Stock-Jobbing*. London.

——. 1748. *A Winter Evening's Conversation In a Club of Jews, Dutchmen, French Refugees, and English Stock-Jobbers*. London: G. Smith.

——. 1750. *The Villainy of Stock-Jobbers detected, and the Causes of the Late Run upon the Bank and Bankers Discovered and Considered*. London.

———. 1848. *Stocks and Stock-Jobbing in Wall Street*. New York: New York Publishing Co.

———. 1854. *The Bulls and Bears or, Wall Street Squib No. I*. New York: published at Nassau Street, Nr. 128.

———. 1875. *Secret of Success in Wall Street*. New York: Tumbridge & Co.

———. 1876. *The Rationale of Market Fluctuations*. London: Effingham Wilson.

———. 1893. *The Boston Stock Exchange*. Boston: Hunt & Bell.

———. 1898. *Guide to Investors', Haight & Freese's Information to Investors and Operators in Stocks, Grain and Cotton*. New York: Haight & Freese.

———. 1908. "Modern Brokerage Establishments: Organization and Machinery of the House of J. S. Bache & Company." *The Ticker* 1 (4) (February): 7.

———. 1927. *The Magazine of Wall Street* 40 (9) (August 25): 753.

———. 1983. "Quote Vending from Edison to Scantlin to Intelligent Work Stations." *Wall Street Computer Review* 3 (1): 60.

Aspers, Patrik. 2006. *Markets in Fashion. A Phenomenological Approach*. London: Routledge.

Austin, J. L. [1962] 1976. *How to Do Things With Words*. Oxford: Oxford University Press.

Avis rélatif à la construction d'un édifice pour la Bourse de commerce de Paris. 1807 (August 1). Section de l'intérieur, M. Regnaud rapporteur. Paris: Bibliothèque Nationale de France.

Babson, Roger Ward. 1908. "The Theory of Financial Statistics." The *Ticker* 1 (3).

———. 1914. *The Future Method of Investing Money: Economic Facts for Corporations and Investors*. Boston: Babson's Statistical Organization.

———. 1935. *Actions and Reactions: An Autobiography of Roger W. Babson*. New York: Harper & Brothers.

Bachelier, Louis. [1900] 1964. "Theory of Speculation." In *The Random Character of Stock Market Prices*, ed. Paul H. Cootner, 17–78. Cambridge MA: The MIT Press.

Baker, Wayne. 1984. "The Social Structure of a National Securities Market." *American Journal of Sociology* 89 (4): 775–811.

Bakke, John. 1996. "Technologies and Interpretations: The Case of the Telephone." *Knowledge and Society* 10:87–107.

Banner, Stuart. 1998. "The Origin of the New York Stock Exchange, 1791–1860." *Journal of Legal Studies* 27 (1): 113–40.

Barlow, David Harrison. 1991. "Disorders of Emotion." *Psychological Inquiry* 2 (1): 58–71.

Barnes, Barry. 1992. "Status Groups and Collective Action." *Sociology* 26 (2): 259–70.

———. 1995. *The Elements of Social Theory*. London: UCL Press.

———. 2000. *Understanding Agency: Social Theory and Responsible Action*. London: Sage.

Barnes, Barry, David Bloor, and John Henry. 1996. *Scientific Knowledge: A Sociological Analysis*. Chicago: The University of Chicago Press.

Barry, Andrew, and Don Slater. 2002a. "Introduction: the Technological Economy." *Economy & Society* 31 (2): 175–93.

————. 2002b. "Technology, Politics, and the Market: An Interview with Michel Callon." *Economy and Society* 31 (2): 285–306.

Baskin, Jonathan Barron, and Paul Miranti. 1997. *A History of Corporate Finance.* Cambridge: Cambridge University Press.

Baxter, Vern, and A.V. Margavio. 2000. "Honour, Status, and Aggression in Economic Exchange." *Sociological Theory* 18 (3): 399–416.

Beckert, Jens. 1996. "What is Sociological about Economic Sociology? Uncertainty and the Embeddedness of Economic Action." *Theory & Society* 25 (2): 125–46.

Beckert, Sven. 2001. *The Monied Metropolis: New York City and the Consolidation of the American Bourgeoisie.* Cambridge: Cambridge University Press.

Beeton's Guide Book to the Stock Exchange and Money Market: With Hints to Investors, and the Chances of Speculators. 1870. London: Ward, Lock, and Tyler.

Benjamin, Walter. [1972] 1999. *The Arcades Project.* Cambridge MA: The Belknap Press.

Benner, Samuel. 1876. *Benner's Prophecies of Future Ups and Downs in Prices: What Years to Make Money on Pig Iron, Hops, Corn, and Provisions.* Cincinnati, OH: published by the author.

Berezin, Mabel. 2005. "Emotions and the Economy." In *The Handbook of Economic Sociology,* 2nd ed., ed. Neil Smelser and Richard Swedberg, 109–27. Princeton, NJ: Princeton University Press and Russell Sage Foundation.

Berk, Gerald. 1994. *Alternative Tracks: The Constitution of American Industrial Order 1865–1917.* Baltimore: Johns Hopkins University Press.

Bernstein, Peter L. 1996. *Against the Gods: The Remarkable Story of Risk.* New York: Wiley.

Bertinotti, Dominique. 1985. "Carrières féminines et carrières masculines dans l'administration des postes et télégraphes à la fin du XIXe siècle." *Annales ESC* 3:625–40.

Beunza, Daniel, and Raghu Garud. 2007. "Calculators, Lemmings, or Frame Makers? The Intermediary Role of Securities Analysts." In *Market Devices,* ed. Michel Callon, Yuval Millo, and Fabian Muniesa, 13–40. Oxford: Blackwell.

Bijker, Wiebe E., Thomas P. Hughes, and Trevor Pinch, eds. 1987. *The Social Construction of Technological Systems: New Directions in the Sociology and History of Technology.* Cambridge, MA: MIT Press.

Blanc, M. François. 1861. *Des valeurs étrangères et de leur négociation en France.* 2nd ed. Paris: Dentu.

Blanchard, Ch. 1861. *De la valeur des actions du chemin de fer du Dauphiné à l'époque de la fusion.* Paris: Castel.

Blau, Peter M., Cecilia McHugh Falbe, William McKinley, and Phelps K. Tracy. 1976. "Technology and Organization in Manufacturing." *Administrative Science Quarterly* 21:20–40.

Blondheim, Menahem. 1994. *News Over the Wires: The Telegraph and the Flow of Public Information in America, 1844–1897.* Cambridge, MA: Harvard University Press.

Bloor, David. 1992. "Left and Right Wittgensteinians." In *Science as Practice and Culture,* ed. by Andrew Pickering, 266–83. Chicago: University of Chicago Press.

Bogen, David, and Michael Lynch. 1993. "Do We Need a General Theory of Social Problems?" In *Constructionist Controversies: Issues in Social Problems Theory*, ed. G. Miller and J. A. Holstein, 83–108. New York: Aldine De Gruyter.

Bogle, John. 2006. "Investor Wisdoms and Human Values." Speech at the United States Military Academy, April 6. http://www.vanguard.com/bogle_site/sp20060406.htm (accessed June 29, 2006).

Boltanski, Luc, and Eve Chiapello. 1999. *Le nouvel esprit du capitalisme*. Paris: Gallimard.

Borel, L. 1835. *Traité de la Bourse et de la spéculation*. Paris.

Bouchary, Jean. 1939. *Les manieurs d'argent à Paris à la fin du XVIIIe siècle*. Paris: Marcel Rivière & Cie.

———. 1940. *Les compagnies financières à Paris à la fin du XVIIIe siècle*. Paris: Marcel Rivière & Cie.

Bourdieu, Jérôme, Johan Heilbron, and Bénédicte Reynaud. 2003. "Les structures sociales de la finance" [The social structures of finance]. *Actes de la Recherche en Sciences Sociales* 146–47:3–70.

Bourdieu, Pierre. 1979. *La distinction: Critique sociale du jugement*. Paris: Minuit.

———. 1980. *Le sens pratique*. Paris: Minuit.

———. 1994. *Raisons pratiques: Sur la théorie de l'action*. Paris: Seuil.

———. 1996. *The Rules of Art: Genesis and Structure of the Literary Field*. Cambridge: Polity Press.

———. 1997. "Le champ économique." *Actes de la Recherche en Sciences Sociales* 119:48–66.

Bowen, H. V. 1986. " 'The Pests of Human Society': Stockbrokers, Jobbers and Speculators in Mid-eighteenth-century Britain." *History* 78:38–53.

Bowker, Geoffrey C. 2005. *Memory Practices in the Sciences*. Cambridge, MA: The MIT Press.

Brenner, Reuven, and Gabrielle A. Brenner. 1990. *Gambling and Speculation: A Theory, a History, and a Future of Some Human Decisions*. Cambridge, MA: Cambridge University Press.

Breton, Yves. 1992. "L'économie politique et les mathématiques en France 1800–1940." *Histoire et Mesure* 7 (1–2): 25–52.

Brodhurst, B. E. Spencer. 1897. *The Law and Practice of the Stock Exchange*. London: William Clowes.

Bruce, Brian. 2002. "Stock Analysts: Experts on Whose Behalf?" *The Journal of Psychology and Financial Markets* 3 (4): 198–201.

Burnley, James. 1901. *Millionaires and Kings of Enterprise*. London: Harmsworth Brothers.

Burton, Jack. 1929. *The Story of the Trans-Lux*. New York: Trans-Lux Daylight Picture Screen Corporation.

The Business Methods and Customs of Wall Street; Or, How Stocks and Bonds are Dealt In for Investment or on a Margin. 1888. New York: John H. Davis & Co.

Caine, Stanley P. 1974. "The Origins of Progressivism." In *The Progressive Era*, ed. Lewis L. Gould, 11–34. Syracuse, NY: Syracuse University Press.

Calahan, Edward A. 1901. "The Evolution of the Stock Ticker." *The Electrical World and Engineer* 37 (6): 236–38.

Callon, Michel, ed. 1998. Introd. to *The Laws of the Markets*, 1–50. Oxford: Blackwell.

———. 2004. "Europe Wrestling with Technology." *Economy & Society* 33 (1): 121–34.

———. 2007. "What Does It Mean to Say that Economics Is Performative?" In *Do Economists Make Markets? The Performativity of Economics*, ed. Donald MacKenzie, Lucia Siu, and Fabian Muniesa, 311–57. Princeton, NJ: Princeton University Press.

Callon, Michel, and Fabian Muniesa. 2003. "Les marchés économiques comme dispositifs collectifs de calcul" [Markets as collective computing dispositives]. *Réseaux* 21 (122): 189–234.

Calomiris, Charles W., and Joseph R. Mason. 1997. "Contagion and Banking Failures during the Great Depression: The June 1932 Chicago Banking Panic." *American Economic Review* 87 (5): 863–83.

Campbell, Douglas. [1914] 1922. *The Law of Stockbrokers, including the Law relating to Transactions for Customers of the New York Stock Exchange*. 2nd ed. New York: Baker, Voorhis & Co.

Carroll, Patrick. 2006. *Science, Culture, and Modern State Formation*. Berkeley, CA: University of California Press.

Carruthers, Bruce G. 1996. *City of Capital: Politics and Markets in the English Financial Revolution*. Princeton, NJ: Princeton University Press.

Carruthers, Bruce G., and Arthur L. Stinchcombe. 2001. "The Social Structure of Liquidity: Flexibility in Markets, States, and Organizations." In *When Formality Works: Authority and Abstraction in Law and Organizations*, 100–139. Chicago: University of Chicago Press.

Castelli, Charles. 1877. *The Theory of "Options" in Stocks and Shares*. London: Fred. C. Mathieson.

Caygill, Howard. 2007. "Life and Energy." *Theory, Culture & Society* 24 (6): 19–27.

Chancellor, Edward. 1999. *Devil Take the Hindmost: A History of Financial Speculation*. New York: Farrar, Straus & Giroux.

Charaudeau, Patrick, and Dominique Maingueneau. 2002. *Dictionnaire d'analyse du discours*. Paris: Seuil.

Charlemagne, Armand. 1796. *L'Agioteur, comedie en un acte*. Paris: Barba.

Chen, Ychning. 1999. "Banking Panics: The Role of First-Come, First-Served Rule and Information Externalities." *Journal of Political Economy* 107 (5): 946–68.

Chiapello, Eve. 2003. "Reconciling the Two Principal Meanings of the Notion of Ideology: The Example of the Concept of the 'Spirit of Capitalism.'" *European Journal of Social Theory* 6 (2): 155–71.

Chiswell, Francis. 1902. *Key to the Rules of the Stock Exchange*. London: Effingham Wilson.

Clews, Henry. 1888. *Twenty-Eight Years in Wall Street*. New York: Irving Publishing Co.

Coleman, James. 1990. *Foundations of Social Theory*. Cambridge, MA: Belknap Press of Harvard University Press.

Colling, Alfred. 1949. *La prodigieuse histoire de la Bourse*. Paris: SEF.

Collins, Harry M., and Robert Evans. 2002. "The Third Wave of Science Studies: Studies of Expertise and Experience." *Social Studies of Science* 32 (2): 235–96.

Collins, Harry M., and Martin Kusch. 1998. *The Shape of Actions: What Humans and Machines Can Do*. Cambridge, MA: The MIT Press.

Collins, Randall. 1986. *Weberian Sociological Theory*. Cambridge, MA: Cambridge University Press.

———. 2004. *Interaction Ritual Chains*. Princeton, NJ: Princeton University Press.

———. 2008. *Violence: A Micro-sociological Approach*. Princeton, NJ: Princeton University Press.

Colquhoun, P. 1814. *A Treatise on the Wealth, Power, and Resources of the British Empire*. London: Joseph Mawman.

A Complete Narrative of the Life, Adventures, Frauds, and Forgeries, of Thomas Tyler, the Celebrated Swindler, Who Was Executed November 24, 1790. 1790. London.

Cope, S. R. 1978. "The Stock Exchange Revisited: A New Look at the Market in Securities in London in the Eighteenth Century." *Economica* 45 (177): 1–21.

Cordingley, W. G. 1901. *Cordingley's Guide to the Stock Exchange*. London: Effingham Wilson.

Cornwallis, Kinahan. 1879. *The Gold Room and the New York Stock Exchange and Clearing House*. New York: A. S. Barnes.

Courtault, Jean-Michel, Yuri Kabanov, Bernard Bru, Pierre Crépel, Isabelle Lebon, and Arnauld Le Marchand. 2000. "Louis Bachelier on the Centenary of *Théorie de la Spéculation*." *Mathematical Finance* 10 (3): 341–53.

Courtois, Alphonse. 1862. *Tableau des cours des principales valeurs: Du 17 janvier 1797 (28 Nivose an V) à nos jours*. Paris: Garnier-frères.

Cowing, Cedric. 1965. *Populists, Plungers, and Progressives: A Social History of Stock and Commodity Speculation*. Princeton, NJ: Princeton University Press.

Cowles, Alfred 3rd. 1933. "Can Stock Market Forecasters Forecast?" *Econometrica* 1 (3): 309–24.

Cox, Harvey. 1999. "The Market as God." The *Atlantic*, March 1999. www.theatlantic.com/issues/99mar/marketgod.htm.

Crampon, A. 1863. *La Bourse: Guide pratique à l'usage des gens du monde*. Paris: H. Durandin.

Crary, Jonathan. 1990. *Techniques of the Observer: On Vision and Modernity in the Nineteenth Century*. Cambridge, MA: MIT Press.

Davis, Gerald, and Gregory Robbins. 2005. "Nothing but Net? Networks and Status in Corporate Governance." In *The Sociology of Financial Markets*, ed. Karin Knorr Cetina and Alex Preda, 290–311. Oxford: Oxford University Press.

De Bondt, Werner. 2005. "The Values and Beliefs of European Investors." In *The Sociology of Financial Markets*, ed. Karin Knorr Cetina and Alex Preda, 163–86. Oxford: Oxford University Press.

Defoe, Daniel [signed anonymous]. 1701. *The Villainy of Stock-Jobbers Detected*. London: n.p.

De Goede, Marieke. 2005. *Virtue, Fortune, and Faith: A Genealogy of Finance*. Minneapolis, MN: Minnesota University Press.

DeMark, Thomas. 1994. *The New Science of Technical Analysis*. New York: John Wiley & Sons.

De Mériclet, A. 1854. *La Bourse de Paris: Moeurs, anecdotes, spéculations et conseils*. Paris: D. Giraud.

Desrosières, Alain. 1998. *The Politics of Large Numbers: A History of Statistical Reasoning*. Cambridge, MA: Harvard University Press.

Deutsches Aktieninstitut. 2007. *DAI-Factbook*. Frankfurt/Main: DAI.

Deux Arrests du Conseil du Roy, des 24 Septembre et 14 Octobre 1724. Paris: Bibliothèque Nationale de France.

Dobbin, Frank. 1994. *Forging Industrial Policy: The United States, Britain, and France in the Railway Age*. Cambridge: Cambridge University Press.

Dostoevsky, Fyodor. [1866] 1991. *Notes from the Underground and The Gambler*, trans. Jane Kentish. Oxford: Oxford University Press.

Douglas, Mary. 1987. *How Institutions Think*. London: Routledge & Kegan Paul.

Downey, Greg. 2000. "Running Somewhere between Men and Women: Gender in the Construction of the Telegraph Messenger Boy." *Knowledge and Society* 12:129–52.

Du Camp, Maxime. 1869. *Paris: Ses organes, ses fonctions, et sa vie dans la seconde moitié du XIXe siècle*. Paris: Librairie Hachette.

Duguid, Charles. 1901. *The Story of the Stock Exchange: Its History and Position*. London: Grant Richards.

DuPlessis, Robert. 2002. "Capital Formations." In *The Culture of Capital: Property, Cities, and Knowledge in Early Modern England*, ed. Henry S. Turner, 27–50. New York: Routledge.

Durkheim, Émile. [1915] 1965. *The Elementary Forms of the Religious Life*. New York: The Free Press.

Eadie, John. 1873. *Panics in the Money Market and Recovery from Their Effect*. New York: John W. Amerman.

Eames, Francis L. 1894. *The New York Stock Exchange*. New York: Thomas G. Hall.

Eggleston, George Cary. 1875. *How to Make a Living: Suggestions upon the Art of Making Saving, and Using Money*. New York: G. P. Putnam's Sons.

Eichenwald, Kurt. 2005. *Conspiracy of Fools: A True Story*. New York: Broadway Books.

Emery, Henry Crosby. 1896. *Speculation on the Stock and Produce Exchanges of the United States*. PhD thesis, Columbia University, New York.

Emirbayer, Mustafa, and Ann Mische. 1998. "What Is Agency?" *American Journal of Sociology* 103 (4): 962–1023.

An Essay Towards Preventing the Ruine of Great Britain. 1721. London: J. Roberts.

Fabian, Ann. 1990. *Card Sharps, Dream Books, & Bucket Shops: Gambling in 19th-Century America*. Ithaca, NY: Cornell University Press.

Fama, Eugene. 1965. "The Behavior of Stock Market Prices." *Journal of Business* 38 (1): 34–105.

The Fatal Consequences of Gaming and Stock-Jobbing: A Sermon Preach'd in the City of London, on Sunday, November 6, 1720. 1720. London: printed for T. Jauncy.

Fearn, Henry Noel. 1866. *The Money Market*. London: Warne & Co.

Fenn's Compendium of English and Foreign Funds. 1854. London: Effingham Wilson.

Fenton-O'Creevy, Mark, Nigel Nicholson, Emma Sloane, Paul Willman. 2005. *Traders: Risks, Decisions, and Management in Financial Markets*. Oxford: Oxford University Press.

Fischer, Claude S. 1992. *America Calling: A Social History of the Telephone to 1940*. Berkeley, CA: University of California Press.

Fleischmann, Kenneth R. 2006. "Boundary Objects with Agency: A Method for Studying the Design-Use Interface." *The Information Society* 22:77–87.

Flichy, Patrice. 1995. *Dynamics of Modern Communication: The Shaping and Impact of New Communication Technologies*. London: Sage.

Fligstein, Neil. 1990. *The Transformation of Corporate Control*. Cambridge, MA: Harvard University Press.

———. 2001. *The Architecture of Markets: An Economic Sociology of the Twenty-First Century Capitalist Societies*. Princeton, NJ: Princeton University Press.

Fogarty, Timothy J., and Rodney K. Rogers. 2005. "Financial Analysts' Reports: An Extended Institutional Theory Evaluation." *Accounting, Organizations and Society* 30:331–56.

Foray, Dominique. 2004. *The Economics of Knowledge*. Cambridge, MA: The MIT Press.

Foreman, Paul B. 1953. "Panic Theory." *Sociology and Social Research* 37 (5): 295–304.

Forman, Robert E. 1963. "Resignation as a Collective Behavior Response." *American Journal of Sociology* 69 (3): 285–90.

Fortune, Thomas. 1810. *An Epithome of the Stocks & Public Funds*. London: T. Boosey.

Foucault, Michel. 1977. *Discipline and Punish: The Birth of the Prison*. London: Allen Lane.

Fowler, William Worthington. 1870. *Ten Years in Wall Street*. New York: Burt Franklin.

Francis, John. 1849. *Chronicles and Characters of the Stock Exchange*. London: Willoughby.

Frank, Thomas. 2000. *One Market under God: Extreme Capitalism, Market Populism, and the End of Economic Democracy*. New York: Anchor Books.

Franklin, Benjamin. [1774] 1777. *The Way to Wealth; as Clearly Shewn in the Preface of an Old Pennsylvania Almanack, Intitled Poor Richard Improved*. Philadelphia: printed by the author.

Fraser, Steve. 2005. *Wall Street: A Cultural History*. London: Faber and Faber.

———. 2008. *Wall Street: America's Dream Palace*. New Haven, CT: Yale University Press.

Freedeman, Charles E. 1993. *The Triumph of Corporate Capitalism in France 1867–1914*. Rochester, NY: University of Rochester Press.

Freedley, Edwin T. 1852. *A Practical Treatise on Business: Or How to Get, Save, Spend, Give, Lend, and Bequeath Money*. Philadelphia: Lippincott, Grambo and Co.

Gal, Susan, and Judith T. Irvine. 1995. "The Boundaries of Language and Disciplines: How Ideologies Construct Difference." *Social Research* 62 (4): 967–1001.

Gann, William D. 1923. *Truth of the Stock Tape*. New York: Financial Guardian Publishing Co.

Garber, Peter M. 2000. *Famous First Bubbles: The Fundamentals of Early Manias*. Cambridge, MA: MIT Press.

Garfinkel, Harold. 2002. *Ethnomethodology's Program*. Lanham, MD: Rowman and Littlefield.

Garfinkel, Harold, and Harvey Sacks. [1970] 1990. "On Formal Structures of Practical Actions." In *Ethnomethodological Sociology*, ed. Jeff Coulter, 55–84. Brookfield, VT: Edward Elgar.

Gassiot, John P. 1867. *Monetary Panics and Their Remedy*. London: Effingham Wilson.

A Genuine Narrative of the Life and Actions of John Rice, Broker. 1763. London: printed for the author.

George, Henry. [1880] 1971. *Progress and Poverty*. New York: Robert Schalkenbach Foundation.

Gibson, George Rutledge. 1889. *The Stock Exchanges of London, Paris, and New York: A Comparison*. New York and London: G. P. Putnam's Sons.

———. 1891. *Wall Street: The Utilities and Ethics of Speculation—The Stock Exchange as an Economic Factor—International Finance*. New York: Lockwood Press.

Giddens, Anthony. 1987. *Social Theory and Modern Sociology*. Cambridge: Polity.

Gieryn, Thomas. 1999. *Cultural Boundaries of Science: Credibility on the Line*. Chicago: University of Chicago Press.

Giffen, Robert. 1877. *Stock Exchange Securities: An Essay on the General Causes of Fluctuations in Their Price*. London: George Bell & Sons.

Gitelman, Lisa. 1999. *Scripts, Grooves, and Writing Machines: Representing Technology in the Edison Era*. Stanford, CA: Stanford University Press.

Godechot, Olivier. 2007. *Working rich: Salaires, bonus et appropriation du profit dans l'industrie financière* [Working rich. Salaries, bonuses, and profit appropriation in the financial industry]. Paris: La Découverte.

Goffman, Erving. 1959. *The Presentation of Self in Everyday Life*. New York: Doubleday.

———. 1974. *Frame Analysis: An Essay on the Organization of Experience*. New York: Harper.

Goldman, Samuel P. 1914. *A Handbook of Stock Exchange Laws*. New York: Doubleday.

Goldstein, Matthew. 2005. "Citigroup Eliminates Stock Technical Analysis Group." TheStreet.com, February 17. http://www.thestreet.com/stocks/brokerages/10209532.html (accessed June 28, 2006).

Gorman, James P. 2004. "Will the New Rules Make a Difference?" Speech accessed at http://www.ml.com/media/42462.pdf (accessed June 28, 2006).

———. 2005. "Collision at the Corner of Wall Street and Main Street: Remarks of James P. Gorman 2006 Chairman, Securities Industry Association." SIA

Annual Meeting, November 11. http://www.sia.com/speeches/html/gorman11–11–05.html (accessed June 28, 2006).

Granovetter, Mark. 1985. "Economic Action and Social Structure. The Problem of Embeddedness." *American Journal of Sociology* 91 (3): 481–510.

Greeley, Horace. 1850. *Labor's Political Economy: An Essay in Hints toward Reforms, in Lectures, Addresses, and Other Writings.* New York: Harper & Brothers.

Grint, Keith, and Steve Woolgar. 1995. "On Some Failures of Nerve in Constructivist and Feminist Analyses of Technology." *Science, Technology & Human Values* 20 (3): 286–310.

Gross, Samuel R., and Jennifer L. Mnookin. 2003. "Expert Information and Expert Evidence: A Preliminary Taxonomy." *Seton Hall Law Review* 34:141–89.

Guardians Over-Reached in Their Own Humour, The: Or, the Lover Metamorphos'd. 1741. London: printed for A. Jackson.

Guillard, Edouard. 1875. *Les opérations de Bourse: Histoire—pratique—législation—jurisprudence—reformes—morale—economie politique.* Paris: Guillaumin & Cie.

Hacking, Ian. 1990. *The Taming of Chance.* Cambridge: Cambridge University Press.

Hall, Henry. 1908. *How Money Is Made in Security Investments, or a Fortune at Forty Five.* 3rd ed. New York: The De Vinne Press.

Hamilton, Alexander, James Madison, and Jay John. [1788] 1961. *The Federalist Papers.* New York: New American Library.

Hamon, Henry. 1865. *New York Stock Exchange Manual.* New York: John F. Trow.

Hannerz, Ulf. 1997. "Flows, Boundaries, and Hybrids. Keywords in Transantional Anthropology." Working paper WPTC-2K-02, Dept. of Social Anthropology, Stockholm University.

Harrison, Paul. 1997. "A History of Intellectual Arbitrage: The Evolution of Financial Economics." *History of Political Economy.* Suppl. no. 29: 172–87.

———. 2004. "What Can We Learn for Today from 300-Year-Old Writings about Stock Markets?" *History of Political Economy* 36 (4): 667–88.

Hartfield's Wall Street Code. 1905. New York: Hartfield Telegraphic Code Publishing Company.

Hautcoeur, Pierre-Cyrille. 1997. "Le marché financier entre 1870 et 1900." In *La longue stagnation en France,* ed. Yves Breton, Albert Broder, and Michel Lutfalla, 235–65. Paris: Economica.

Hegel, Georg Friedrich Wilhelm. [1807] 1986. *Phänomenologie des Geistes* [Phenomenology of spirit]. Frankfurt: Suhrkamp.

———. [1821] 1986. *Grundlinien der Philosophie des Rechts* [Philosophy of right]. Frankfurt: Suhrkamp.

Heidegger, Martin. [1962] 1977. *The Question Concerning Technology and Other Essays,* trans. William Lovitt. New York: Harper Torchbooks.

Henderson, Kathryn. 1999. *On Line and On Paper: Visual Representations, Visual Culture, and Computer Graphics in Design Engineering.* Cambridge, MA: The MIT Press.

Hennessy, Elisabeth. 2001. *Coffee House to Cyber Market: 200 Years of the London Stock Exchange*. London: Ebury Press.

Herrick, Myron T. 1907. *The Panic of 1907 and Some of Its Lessons*. Philadelphia: Publications of the American Academy of Political and Social Science (550).

Hickling, John. 1875. *Men and Idioms of Wall Street: Explaining the Daily Operations in Stocks, Bonds, and Gold*. New York: John Hickling & Co.

Hilkey, Judith. 1997. *Character Is Capital: Success Manuals and Manhood in Gilded Age America*. Chapel Hill: University of North Carolina Press.

Hinton, Devon, Michael Nathan, Bruce Bird, and Lawrence Park. 2002. "Panic Probes and the Identification of Panic: A Historical and Cross-Cultural Perspective." *Culture, Medicine and Psychiatry* 26:137–53.

Hirschman, Alfred O. 1977. *The Passions and the Interests: Political Arguments for Capitalism before Its Triumph*. Princeton, NJ: Princeton University Press.

Hirst, Francis W. 1911. *The Stock Exchange*. London: Williams & Norgate.

History of the New York Stock Exchange. 1887. New York: The Financier Company.

The History of the United States for 1796. 1797. Philadelphia: Snowden & McCorkle.

Hochfelder, David. 2006. "'Where the Common People Could Speculate': The Ticker, Bucket Shops, and the Origins of Popular Participation in Financial Markets, 1880–1920." *Journal of American History* 93 (2): 335–58.

Holloway, Laura C. 1884. *Famous American Fortunes and the Men Who Made Them*. Philadelphia: Bradley & Co.

Holway, Tatiana. 1992. "The Game of Speculation: Economics and Representation." *Dickens Quarterly* 9 (3): 103–14.

Hopkinson, Francis. 1780. *A Tory Medley*. Philadelphia: n.p..

Hoyle [pseud.]. 1898. *The Game in Wall Street, and How to Play It Successfully*. New York: J. S. Ogilvie.

Huebner, S. S. [1922] 1934. *The Stock Market*, rev. ed. New York: D. Appleton-Century.

Hughes, John A., Mark Rouncefield, and Pete Toulmie. 2002. "The Day-to-Day Work of Standardization: A Sceptical Note on the Reliance on IT in a Retail Bank." In *Virtual Society? Technology, Cyberbole, Reality*, ed. Steve Woolgar, 246–63. Oxford: Oxford University Press.

Husserl, Edmund. [1912] 1977. *Cartesianische Meditationen* [Cartesian meditations]. Hamburg: Felix Meiner.

The Imperial Magazine, Or Complete Monthly Intelligencer for the Year 1760. 1760. London: printed for J. Scott in Paternoster-Row.

Jenkins, Alan. 1973. *The Stock Exchange Story*. London: Heinemann.

Jenkins, Reese V., et al., eds. 1989. *The Papers of Thomas Alva Edison: The Making of an Inventor, February 1847–June 1873*. Baltimore: The Johns Hopkins University Press.

Jevons, William Stanley. 1886. *Letters and Journal*. London: Macmillan.

Jones, Malcolm. 1991. Introd. to *Notes from the Underground and The Gambler*, trans. by Jane Kentish, vii–xxviii. Oxford: Oxford University Press.

Josephson, Matthew. [1934] 1962. *The Robber Barons*. San Diego: Harcourt.

Jovanovic, Franck. 2000. "The Origin of Financial Theory: A Reevaluation of the Contribution of Louis Bachelier." *Revue d'Économie Politique* 110 (3): 396–418.

———. 2001. "Pourquoi l'hypothèse de marché aléatoire en théorie financière? Les raisons historiques d'un choix éthique." [Why the random walk hypothesis in financial theory? The historical reasons of an ethical choice]. *Revue d'Économie financière* 61:203–11.

———. 2002. "Instruments et théorie économique dans la construction de la 'science de la Bourse' d'Henri Lefevre." *Revue d'Histoire des Sciences Humaines* 7:41–68.

———. 2004. "Éléments biographiques inédits sur Jules Regnault (1834–1894), inventeur du modèle du marché aléatoire pour représenter les variations boursières." *Revue d'Histoire des Sciences Humaines* 11:215–30.

———. 2006a. "Economic Instruments and Theory in the Construction of Henri Lefevre's Science of the Stock Market." In *Pioneers of Financial Economics*, vol. 1, ed. Geoffrey Poitras, 169–90. Cheltenham: Edward Elgar.

———. 2006b. "A Nineteenth Century Random Walk: Jules Regnault and the Origins of Scientific Financial Economics." In *Pioneers of Financial Economics*, vol. 1, ed. Geoffrey Poitras, 191–222. Cheltenham: Edward Elgar.

———. 2006c. "Was There a 'Vernacular' Science of Financial Markets in France During the Late Nineteenth Century? A Comment on Preda's 'Informative Prices, Rational Investors.'" *History of Political Economy* 38 (3): 531–45.

———. 2008. "The Construction of the Canonical History of Financial Economics." *History of Political Economy* 40 (2): 213–42.

Jovanovic, Franck, and Philippe Le Gall. 2001. "Does God Practice a Random Walk? The "Financial Physics" of a Nineteenth-Century Forerunner, Jules Regnault." *European Journal of the History of Economic Thought* 8 (3): 332–62.

Judt, Tony. 2007. "The Wrecking Ball of Innovation." *New York Review of Books* 54 (19): 22–27.

Kahn, Otto Hermann. 1917. *The New York Stock Exchange and Public Opinion*. New York: The New York Stock Exchange.

Keister, Lisa. 2000. *Wealth in America: Trends in Wealth Inequality*. Cambridge and New York: Cambridge University Press.

Kelly, Morgan, and Cormac O Grada. 2000. "Market Contagion: Evidence from the Panics of 1854 and 1857." *American Economic Review* 90 (5): 1110–24.

Khurana, Rakesh. 2002. *Searching for a Corporate Savior: The Irrational Quest for Charismatic CEOs*. Princeton, NJ: Princeton University Press.

Kindleberger, Charles, and Robert Z. Aliber. 2005. *Manias, Panics, and Crashes: A History of Financial Crises*. Houndmills, Basingstoke: Palgrave.

King, Moses, ed. 1897. *King's Views of the New York Stock Exchange: A History and Description with Articles on Financial Topics*. New York: King's Handbooks.

Knight, Frank. [1921] 1985. *Risk, Uncertainty, and Profit*. Chicago: The University of Chicago Press.

Knorr Cetina, Karin. 1992. "The Couch, the Cathedral, and the Laboratory: On the Relationship between Experiment and Laboratory in Science." In *Science as Practice and Culture*, ed. Andrew Pickering, 113–38. Chicago: University of Chicago Press.

————. 1997. "Sociality with Objects: Social Relations in Postsocial Knowledge Societies." *Theory, Culture & Society* 14 (4): 1–30.

————. 2005. "How Are Global Markets Global? The Architecture of a Flow World." In *The Sociology of Financial Markets*, ed. Karin Knorr Cetina and Alex Preda, 38–61. Oxford: Oxford University Press.

Knorr Cetina, Karin, and Urs Bruegger. 2000. "The Market as an Object of Attachment: Exploring Postsocial Relations in Financial Markets." *Canadian Journal of Sociology* 25 (2): 141–68.

————. 2002a. "Global Microstructures: The Virtual Societies of Financial Markets." *American Journal of Sociology* 107 (4): 905–50.

————. 2002b. "Traders' Engagement with Markets: A Postsocial Relationship." *Theory, Culture & Society* 19 (5–6): 161–87.

Knorr Cetina, Karin, and Alex Preda. 2007. "The Temporalization of Financial Markets: From Network to Flow." *Theory, Culture & Society* 24 (7–8): 123–45.

Kocka, Juergen. 1995. "The Middle Classes in Europe." *Journal of Modern History* 67 (4): 783–806.

————. 2004. "The Middle Classes." In *The European Way: European Societies during the Nineteenth and Twentieth Centuries*, ed. Hartmut Kaeble, 15–43. New York: Berghahn.

Krippner, Greta. 2001. "The Elusive Market Embeddedness and the Paradigm of Economic Sociology." *Theory & Society* 25 (2): 125–46.

————. 2004. The Fictitious Economy: Financialization, the State, and Contemporary Capitalism. Dissertation Abstracts International, A, 64/11, 4228-A.

Kurth, Ekkelhard. 1999. "Die historische Entwicklung des Kursmakleramtes" [The historical development of the office of the stockbroker]. *Amtliches Kursblatt der Frankfurter Wertpapierbörse 253*. http://www.boersenaufsicht.de/text_k.htm (accessed April 9, 2001).

Kurze Remarques über den jetziger Zeit welberuffener Mississippischer Aktien-Handel in Paris, entworfen von P.J.M. 1720. Leipzig: im Durchgange des Rathhauses.

La Bourse. 1866. Paris: Michel Levy Frères.

La Bourse est un marché libre. 1860. Paris: L. Dentu.

La Bourse et les emprunts etrangers. 1868. Paris: L'Indépendant Français.

La Bourse. Réponse à ses detracteurs. Moralité de son marché. 1854. Lyon: Méra.

L'agio, ou traité de l'agiotage, à l'usage des agents de change, courtiers, marons et agioteurs; D'apres le plan d'education de MM. Les Lionnois & Genevois. 1789. Paris: n.p.

Lamont, Michèle, and Virag Molnar. 2002. "The Study of Boundaries in the Social Sciences." *Annual Review of Sociology* 28:167–95.

Laporte. 1789. *Essai sur la legislation et les finances de la France.* Bergerac: J. B. Puynesge.

————. 1790. *Organisation et administration des finances pour un peuple libre.* Paris: Gastelier.

Lardner, Dionysius. 1850. *The Steam Engine Familiarly Explained and Illustrated.* 5th American ed. Philadelphia: A. Hart.

———. 1880. *Die elektrischen Telegraphen, das Telephon und Mikrophon: populäre Darstellung ihrer Geschichte, ihrer Einrichtung und ihres Betriebes*, ed. F. Binder. Weimar: Voigt.

Latour, Bruno. 1999. *Pandora's Hope: Essays on the Reality of Science Studies*. Cambridge, MA: Harvard University Press.

Lazega, Emmanuel. 1992. *The Micropolitics of Knowledge: Communication and Indirect Control in Workgroups*. New York: Aldine De Gruyter.

Le Bon, Gustave. [1895] 1917. *The Crowd: A Study of the Popular Mind*. London: T. Fisher Unwin.

Le Bon-Homme, no. 20. 1795. Geneva: n.p.

Lefevre, Edwin. 1901. *Wall Street Stories*. London: McClure, Phillips & Co.

———. 1907. *Sampson Rock of Wall Street*. New York: Harper & Brothers.

Lefevre, Henri. 1870. *Traité des valeurs mobilières et des opérations de Bourse, placement et spéculation*. Paris: E. Lachaud.

———. 1871. *Le jeu sur les courses des chevaux*. Paris: Chez l'auteur.

———. 1874. *Principes de la science de la Bourse: Méthode approuvée par la chambre syndicale des agents de change de la Bourse*. Paris: Publications de l'Institut Polytechnique.

LeRoy, Stephen. 1989. "Efficient Capital Markets and Martingales." *Journal of Economic Literature* 27:1583–1621.

*Les écueils de la Bourse.*1865. Paris: Librairie du Petit Journal.

Levecq, Hugues, and Bruce W. Weber. 2002. "Electronic Trading Systems: Strategic Implications of Market Design Choices." *Journal of Organizational Computing and Electronic Commerce* 12 (1): 85–103.

Lewis-Fernandez, Roberto, Peter J. Guarnaccia, Igda E. Martinez, Ester Salman, Andrew Schmidt, and Michael Liebowitz. 2002. "Comparative Phenomenology of *Ataques de Nervios*, Panic Attacks, and Panic Disorder." *Culture, Medicine and Psychiatry* 26:199–223.

Leyshon, Andrew, and Nigel Thrift. 1997. *Money/Space: Geographies of Monetary Transformation*. London: Routledge.

The Life of Jonathan Wild, from His Birth to His Death; Containing His Rise and Progress in Roguery. 1725. London: T. Warner.

Limoges, Camille, and Claude Ménard. 1994. "Organization and the Division of Labor: Biological Metaphors at Work in Alfred Marshall's *Principles of Economics*." In *Natural Images in Economic Thought: "Markets Read in Tooth and Claw,"* ed. Philip Mirowski, 336–59. Cambridge and New York: Cambridge University Press.

Liste générale des noms et qualités des coquins, des fournisseurs infidels, des dilapidateurs du trésor public, des agioteurs. n.d. Extract of Postillion of Calais, Genthon. Paris: Bibliothèque Nationale de France.

Louchet, L. 1793. *Motion d'ordre faite dans la séance du 26 Vendemiaire (1), quatrième année de la Republique Française*. Paris: Bibliothèque Nationale de France.

Lowenstein, Roger. 2004. *Origins of the Crash: The Great Bubble and Its Undoing*. New York: Penguin.

Lowry, Ritchie. 1984. "Structural Changes in the Market: The Rise of Professional Investing." In *The Social Dynamics of Financial Markets*, ed. Patricia A. Adler and Peter Adler, 19–38. Greenwich, CT: JAI Press.

Luhmann, Niklas. 1990. *Essays on Self-Reference*. New York: Columbia University Press.

———. 1994. *Die Wirtschaft der Gesellschaft* [The economy of society]. Frankfurt: Suhrkamp.

Lurie, Jonathan. 1979. *The Chicago Board of Trade 1859–1905: The Dynamics of Self-Regulation*. Urbana, IL: University of Illinois Press.

Lynch, Michael. 1992. "Extending Wittgenstein: The Pivotal Move from Epistemology to the Sociology of Science." In *Science as Practice and Culture*, ed. A. Pickering, 215–65. Chicago: University of Chicago Press.

Macfarlane, A. 1856. *Railway Scrip; or, the Evils of Speculation: A Tale of the Railway Mania*. London: Ward & Lock.

MacKenzie, Donald. 2005. "How a Superportfolio Emerges: Long-Term Capital Management and the Sociology of Arbitrage." In *The Sociology of Financial Markets*, ed. Karin Knorr Cetina and Alex Preda, 62–83. Oxford: Oxford University Press.

———. 2006. *An Engine, Not a Camera: Finance Theory and the Making of Markets*. Cambridge, MA: MIT Press.

———. 2008. "End-of-the-World Trade." *London Review of Books*, May 8, 2008: 24–26.

MacKenzie, Donald, and Yuval Millo. 2003. "Constructing a Market, Performing Theory: the Historical Sociology of a Financial Derivatives Exchange." *American Journal of Sociology* 109 (1): 107–46.

MacKenzie, Donald, and Judy Wajcman. 1985. "Introductory Essay: The Social Shaping of Technology." In *The Social Shaping of Technology: How the Refrigerator Got Its Hum*, ed. D. MacKenzie and J. Wajcman, 2–26. Milton Keynes: Open University Press.

Maddison, E. C. 1877. *The Paris Bourse and the London Stock Exchange*. London: Effingham Wilson.

Mahar, Maggie. 2004. *Bull: A History of the Boom and Bust 1982–2004*. New York: Collins.

Mandelbrot, Benoit, and Richard Hudson. 2004. *The (Mis)Behavior of Markets: A Fractal View of Risk, Ruin & Reward*. New York: Basic Books.

Mann, Leon, Trevor Nagel, and Peter Dowling. 1976. "A Study of Economic Panic: The 'Run' on the Hindmarsh Building Society." *Sociometry* 39 (3): 223–35.

Markham, Jerry W. 2002. *From Christopher Columbus to the Robber Barons (1492–1900)*. Vol. 1 of *A Financial History of the United States*. Armonk, NY: M. E. Sharpe.

Martin, John Levi. 2003. "What Is Field Theory?" *American Journal of Sociology* 109 (1): 1–49.

Martin, Joseph G. 1886. *Martin's Boston Stock Market: Eighty-eight years, from January, 1798, to January, 1886*. Boston: published by the author.

Marx, Karl. [1867] 1996. *Capital*. Vol. 1. London: Lawrence & Wishart.

———. [1872] 2002. *Das Kapital. Kritik der politischen Ökonomie, 2nd ed*. Köln: Parkland.

———. [1894] 1964. *Das Kapital. Kritik der politischen Ökonomie. Dritter Band, Buch III: Der Gesamtprozeß der kapitalistichen Produktion*. Berlin: Dietz.

Marx, Karl, and Friedrich Engels. 1964. *Werke*. Vol. 30. Berlin: Dietz.

Mauss, Marcel. [1950] 1999. *Sociologie et anthropologie*. Paris: Quadrige/Presses Universitaires de France.

Mayr, Ernst. 1982. *The Growth of Biological Thought: Diversity, Evolution, and Inheritance*. Cambridge, MA: The Belknap Press of Harvard University Press.

McCloskey, Deirdre. 2006. *Bourgeois Virtues: Ethics for an Age of Commerce*. Chicago: Chicago University Press.

Mead, George Herbert. [1934] 1952. *Mind, Self and Society from the Standpoint of A Social Behaviourist*. Chicago: The University of Chicago Press.

Medbery, James K. 1870. *Men and Mysteries of Wall Street*. Boston: Fields, Osgood & Co.

Meeker, J. Edward. 1922. *The Work of the Stock Exchange*. New York: The Ronald Press Company.

Mehrling, Perry. 2005. *Fischer Black and the Revolutionary Idea of Finance*. Hoboken, NJ: Wiley.

Ménard, Claude 1980. "Three Forms of Resistance to Statistics: Say, Cournot, Walras." *History of Political Economy* 12 (4): 524–41.

Michie, Ranald. 1999. *The London Stock Exchange: A History*. Oxford: Oxford University Press.

Miller, Peter. 2001. "Governing by Numbers: Why Calculative Practices Matter." *Social Research* 68 (2): 379–95.

Mirabeau, Honoré Gabriel de. 1785. Lettre à M. Le Coulteux de la Noraye, sur la Banque de Saint Charles et sur la Caisse d'Escompte. Brussels: n.p.

———. 1787. Dénonciation de l'Agiotage au Roi et à l'Assemblée des Notables. Paris: n.p.

Mirowski, Philip. 1989. *More Heat than Light: Economics as Social Physics, Physics as Nature's Economics.* Cambridge: Cambridge University Press.

———, ed. 1994. *Natural Images in Economic Thought: "Markets Read in Tooth and Claw."* Cambridge: Cambridge University Press.

———. 2002. *Machine Dreams: Economics Becomes a Cyborg Science.* Cambridge: Cambridge University Press.

———. 2007. "Markets Come To Bits: Evolution, Computation and Markomata in Economic Science." *Journal of Economic Behavior and Organization* 63:209–42.

Miyazaki, Hirokazu. 2006. "Economy of Dreams: Hope in Global Capitalism and Its Critiques." *Cultural Anthropology* 21 (2): 147–72.

Moede, Walther. 1920. *Experimentelle Massenspychologie. Beitraege zur Experimentalpsychologie der Gruppe*. Leipzig: S. Hirzel.

A Monument Dedicated to Posterity in Commemoration of the Incredible Folly Transacted in the Year 1720. 1720. Paris: Bibliothèque Nationale de France.

Morford, Janet. 2001. "Modern Manners: The 'New' Middle Classes and the Emergence of an Informal Civility in France." *Journal of the Society for the Anthropology of Europe* 1 (1): 23–32.

Morgan, V. A. 1898. *The "House" on Sport: By Members of the London Stock Exchange*. London: Gale and Polden.

Mortimer, Thomas. [1761] 1782. *Every Man His Own Broker: Or, A Guide to Exchange-Alley*. London: printed for G. Robinson.

————. 1801. *Lectures on the Elements of Commerce, Politics, and Finances*. London: A. Strahan.

Muller, Jerry Z. 2002. *The Mind and the Market: Capitalism in Western Thought*. New York: Anchor Books.

Mumford, Lewis. 1967. *The Myth of the Machine*. London: Secker & Warburg.

Muniesa, Fabian. 2003. Des marchés comme algorithmes: Sociologie de la cotation éléctronique à la Bourse de Paris. Unpublished dissertation, École des Mines, Paris.

Munting, Roger. 1996. *An Economic and Social History of Gambling in Britain and the USA*. Manchester: Manchester University Press.

Neal, Larry. 1990. *The Rise of Financial Capitalism: International Capital Markets in the Age of Reason*. Cambridge: Cambridge University Press.

Nelson, Samuel Armstrong, ed. 1900. *The ABC of Wall Street*. New York: S. A. Nelson.

————. 1902. *The ABC of Stock Speculation*. New York: S. A. Nelson.

————. 1904. *The ABC of Options and Arbitrage*. New York: S. A. Nelson.

A New Edition, Being a More Minute and Particular Account of That Consummate Adept in Deception, Charles Price, Otherwise Patch, Many Years a Stock-Broker and Lottery-Office Keeper in London and Westminster. 1786. London: printed for the editor.

New York Curb Exchange History. 1931. New York: New York Curb Exchange Committee on Publicity.

The New York Curb Exchange: Silver Anniversary. 1946. New York: New York Curb Exchange.

New York Institute of Finance. 1989. *Technical Analysis: A Personal Seminar*. New York: New York Institute of Finance.

New York State Personal Property Law. 1909. http://caselaw.lp.findlaw.com/nycodes/c83/a1.html (accessed August 30, 2005).

The New York Stock Exchange. 1887. New York: Historical Publishing Co.

Noel-Fearn, Henry. 1866. *The Money Market: What It Is, What It Does, and How It Is Managed*. London: Frederick Warne & Co.

Norris, Frank. [1903] 1956. *The Pit: A Story of Chicago*. New York: Grove Press.

Notions générales de Bourse, de banque & de change. 1877. Paris: le Moniteur des Fonds Publics.

Office for National Statistics. 2007. *Share Ownership: A Report on Ownership of UK Shares as of 31 December 2006*. London: Office for National Statistics.

O'Rourke, Kevin. 2000. *When Did Globalization Begin?* NBER Working Paper no. 7632. Cambridge, MA.

————. 2001. *Globalization and Inequality*. NBER Working Paper no. 2685. Cambridge, MA.

O'Rourke, Kevin, and Jeffrey Williamson. 1999. *Globalization and History: The Evolution of a Nineteenth-Century Atlantic Economy*. Cambridge, MA: The MIT Press.

Orr, Jackie. 2006. *Panic Diaries: A Genealogy of Panic Disorder*. Durham, NC: Duke University Press.

Paine, Thomas. 1796. *The Decline and Fall of the English System of Finance*. New York: printed by William A. Davis.

Paoli. 1864. *La Bourse et ses tripots*. Paris: Arnauld de Vresse.

Parker, William. 1920. *The Paris Bourse and French Finance: With Reference to Organized Speculation in New York*. New York: Columbia University.

Perrow, Charles. 1967. "A Framework for the Comparative Analysis of Organizations." *American Sociological Review* 32 (2): 194–208.

Peterffy, Thomas. 2005. Speech before the International Options Market Association, April 12, Chicago, IL. http://www.interactivebrokers.com/en/general/about/commentLetters.php?ib_entity=uk (accessed June 28, 2006).

Phillips, Kevin. 2002. *Wealth and Democracy: A Political History of the American Rich*. New York: Broadway Books.

Phillips, Richard. 1826. *Golden Rules for Bankers; With a Postscript on the Present Panic, and on the Destruction of Commercial Credit*. London: Effingham Wilson.

Pickering, Andrew. 1995. *The Mangle of Practice: Time, Agency, and Science*. Chicago: University of Chicago Press.

———. 2001. "Practice and Posthumanism: Social Theory and a History of Agency." In *The Practice Turn in Contemporary Theory*, ed. Theodore R. Schatzki, Karin Knorr Cetina, and Eike von Savigny, 163–74. London: Routledge.

Pinch, Trevor. 2003. "Giving Birth to New Users: How the Minimoog Was Sold to Rock and Roll." In *How Users Matter: The Co-Construction of Users and Technologies*, ed. Nelly Oudshoorn and Trevor Pinch, 247–70. Cambridge, MA: The MIT Press.

Pinto, Erasmus. 1877. *Ye Outside Fools! Glimpses into the London Stock Exchange*. New York: Lovell, Adam, Wesson & Company.

Pixley, Jocelyn. 2004. *Emotions in Finance: Distrust and Uncertainty in Global Markets*. Cambridge: Cambridge University Press.

Playford, Francis. 1855. *Practical Hints for Investing Money: With an Explanation of the Mode of Transacting Business on the Stock Exchange*. London: Smith, Elder & Co.

Podolny, Joel. 1993. "A Status-Based Model of Market Competition." *American Journal of Sociology* 98 (4): 829–72.

———. 1994. "Market Uncertainties and the Social Character of Economic Exchange." *Administration Science Quarterly* 39: 458–83.

———. 2001. "Networks as the Pipes and Prisms of the Market." *American Journal of Sociology* 107 (1): 33–60.

Poitras, Geoffrey. 2000. *The Early History of Financial Economics, 1478–1776: From Commercial Arithmetic to Life Annuities and Joint Stocks*. Cheltenham: Edward Elgar.

Polanyi, Karl. [1944] 1957. *The Great Transformation*. Boston: Beacon Press.

Pole, Jack Richon, ed. 1987. *The American Constitution For and Against: The Federalist and Anti-Federalist Papers*. New York: Hill and Wang.

Poley, A. D. 1926. *The History, Law, and Practice of the Stock Exchange*. London: Sir Isaac Pitman and Sons.

Pollner, Melvin. 2002. "Inside the Bubble: Communion, Cognition, and Deep Play at the Intersection of Wall Street and Cyberspace." In *Virtual Society? Technology, Cyberbole, Reality*, ed. Steve Woolgar, 230–46. Oxford: Oxford University Press.

Poovey, Mary. 2008. *Genres of the Credit Economy: Mediating Value in Eighteenth- and Nineteenth-Century Britain*. Chicago: University of Chicago Press.

Porter, Theodore. 1995. *Trust in Numbers: The Pursuit of Objectivity in Science and Public Life*. Princeton, NJ: Princeton University Press.

Pratt, Sereno S. 1903. *The Work of Wall Street*. New York: D. Appleton & Co.

———. [1903] 1912. *The Work of Wall Street: An Account of the Functions, Methods and History of the New York Money and Stock Markets*. Rev. and enlarged ed. New York: D. Appleton & Co.

Preda, Alex. 2000. "Financial Knowledge and the 'Science of the Market' in England and France in the 19th Century." In *Facts and Figures: Economic Representations and Practices*, ed. Herbert Kalthoff, Richard Rottenburg, and Hans-Jürgen Wagener, 205–28. Marburg: Metropolis.

———. 2001a. "In the Enchanted Grove: Financial Conversations and the Marketplace in England and France in the 18th Century." *Journal of Historical Sociology* 14 (3): 276–307.

———. 2001b. "The Rise of the Popular Investor: Financial Knowledge and Investing in England and France, 1840–1880." *The Sociological Quarterly* 42 (2): 205–32.

———. 2002. "Financial Knowledge, Documents, and the Structures of Financial Activities." *Journal of Contemporary Ethnography* 31 (2): 207–39.

———. 2004. "Informative Prices, Rational Investors: The Emergence of the Random Walk Hypothesis and the Nineteenth Century 'Science of Financial Investments.'" *History of Political Economy* 36 (2): 351–86.

———. 2007. "STS and Social Studies of Finance." In *Handbook of Science and Technology Studies*, 2nd ed., ed. Ed Hackett, Olga Amsterdamska, Michael Lynch, and Judy Wajcman, 901–20. Cambridge, MA: The MIT Press.

Proudhon, Pierre-Joseph. [1840] 1926. "Qu'est-ce que la propriété? Recherches sur le principe du droit et du gouvernement: Premier mémoire." Vol. 1 of *Oeuvres complètes*, ed. C. Bouglé and H. Moysset, 97–363. Paris: Marcel Rivière & Cie.

———. [1841] 1938. "Qu'est-ce que la propriété? Deuxième mémoire: Lettre à M. Blanqui sur la propriété." Vol. 9 of *Oeuvres Complètes*, ed. C. Bouglé and H. Moysset, 3–153. Paris: Marcel Rivière & Cie.

———. [1847] 1923. *Système des contradictions économiques ou philosophie de la misère I*. Paris: Marcel Rivière.

———. [1848] 1938. "Programme révolutionaire." Vol. 9 of *Oeuvres Complètes*, ed. C. Bouglé and H. Moysset, 287–333. Paris: Marcel Rivière & Cie.

Proudhon, Pierre-Joseph [published anonymously]. 1854. *Manuel du spéculateur à la Bourse* [Manual of the stock exchange speculator]. Paris: Garnier Frères.

Pruden, Hank, and Bernard Belletante. n.d.. "Wyckoff Laws and Tests." http://www.hankpruden.com/Law+test.pdf (accessed April 11, 2008).

Quarantelli, E. R. 1954. "The Nature and Conditions of Panic." *American Journal of Sociology* 60 (3): 267–75.

Radcliffe-Brown, Arthur Reginald. [1910] 1984. "Comparative Sociology." In *Functionalism Historicized: Essays on British Social Anthropology*, ed. George W. Stocking Jr., 113–15. Madison, WI: The University of Wisconsin Press.

The Rationale of Market Fluctuations. 1876. London: Effingham Wilson.

Reed, John. 1984. "A Friend to Mammon: Speculation in Victorian Literature."
    Victorian Studies 27 (2): 179–202.
Regnault, Jules. 1863. *Calcul des chances et philosophie de la Bourse*. Paris:
    Mallet-Bachelier.
Reith, Gerda. 1999. *The Age of Chance: Gambling and Western Culture*. London:
    Routledge.
Rhee-Piening, Daniel. 2006. "Das Geld der Anderen" [Other people's money]. *Der
    Tagesspiegel*, May 24. http://archiv.tagesspiegel.de/drucken.php?link=archiv/24
    .05.2006/2552575.asp (accessed May 24, 2006).
Roberts, Harry V. 1959. "Stock Market 'Patterns' and Financial Analysis: Method-
    ological Suggestions." *Journal of Finance* 14 (1): 1–10.
Robins, Robert Henry. 1990. *A Short History of Linguistics*. London: Longman.
Rosenberg, Nathan. 2000. *Schumpeter and the Endogeneity of Technology: Some
    American Perspectives*. London: Routledge.
Rougemont, Henri. 1857. *Guide-manuel du placement et de la spéculation à la
    Bourse*. Paris: Passard.
Rousseau, Peter, and Richard Sylla. 2001. *Financial Systems, Economic Growth,
    and Globalization*. NBER Working Paper no. 8323. Cambridge, MA.
Roussel, Etienne. 1904. *Manuel du spéculateur et du capitaliste*. Paris: Guillemin.
Rutterford, Janette, and Josephine Maltby. 2006. " 'The Widow, the Clergyman and
    the Reckless': Women Investors in England, 1830–1914." *Feminist Economics*
    12 (1–2): 111–38.
Schabas, Margaret. 1994. "The Greyhound and the Mastiff: Darwinian Themes in
    Mill and Marshall." In *Natural Images in Economic Thought: "Markets Read
    in Tooth and Claw,"* ed. Philip Mirowski, 322–35. Cambridge and New York:
    Cambridge University Press.
Scharfstein, David S., and Jeremy C. Stein. 1990. "Herd Behavior and Investment."
    American Economic Review 80 (3): 465–79.
Schatzki, Theodore. 2002. *The Site of the Social: A Philosophical Account of the
    Constitution of Social Life and Change*. University Park, PA: The Pennsylvania
    State University Press.
Schumpeter, Joseph. 1934. *The Theory of Economic Development*. Cambridge,
    MA: Harvard University Press.
———. 1943. *Capitalism, Socialism, and Democracy*. London: George Allen &
    Unwin.
———. [1954] 1994. *History of Economic Analysis*. New York: Oxford University
    Press.
———. 1991. *The Economics and Sociology of Capitalism*, ed. Richard Swedberg.
    Princeton, NJ: Princeton University Press.
Schutz, Alfred. [1945] 2003. "Teiresias oder unser Wissen von zukünftigen Eriegnis-
    sen" [Teiresias, or our knowledge about future events]. In *Theorie der Lebens-
    welt. Die pragmatische Schichtung der Lebenswelt*, 251–75. Konstanz: UVK.
———. 1967. *Collected Papers I: The Problem of Social Reality*. The Hague:
    Nijhoff.
Schutz, Alfred, and Thomas Luckmann. 1974. *The Structures of the Life-World*.
    Trans. Richard M. Zaner and H. Tristram Engelhardt, Jr. London: Heinemann.

Schwalbe, Walter S., and G. A. H. Branson. 1905. *A Treatise on the Laws of the Stock Exchange*. London: Stevens and Sons.

SEC. 1963. *Report of the Special Study of Securities Markets of the Securities and Exchange Commission*. Washington, DC: Government Printing Office.

———. 1999. Testimony of Arthur Levitt, Chairman of the U.S. Securities and Exchange Commission, before the Senate Permanent Subcommittee on Investigations, Committee on Governmental Affairs, Concerning Day Trading, September 16. http://www.sec.gov/news/testimony/testarchive/1999/tsty2199 .htm (accessed June 27, 2006).

———. 2000. Special Study: Report of Examinations of Day-Trading Broker-Dealers, February 25. http://www.sec.gov/news/studies/daytrading.htm (accessed June 27, 2006).

Secret of Success in Wall Street. 1875. New York: Tumbridge & Co.

Selden, George C. 1917. *The Machinery of Wall Street*. New York: The Magazine of Wall Street.

———. 1922. *Scientific Investing and Trading*. New York and Philadelphia: W. H. McKenna & Co.

Selwyn-Brown, Arthur. 1910. "Economic Crises and Stock Security Values." *Annals of the American Academy of Political and Social Science* 35 (3): 154–63.

Sennett, Richard. 1974. *The Fall of Public Man*. Cambridge: Cambridge University Press.

———. 2006. *The Culture of the New Capitalism*. New Haven, CT: Yale University Press.

Shapin, Steven. 1994. *A Social History of Truth: Civility and Science in Seventeenth Century England*. Chicago: University of Chicago Press.

Shefrin, Hersh. 1999. *Beyond Greed and Fear: Understanding Behavioral Finance and the Psychology of Investing*. Boston, MA: Harvard Business School Press.

Sherwood, Rufus. 1720. *South-Sea; Or, the Biters Bit: A Tragi-Comi-Pastoral Farce*. London: J. Roberts.

Shields, Rob. 2006. "Boundary-Thinking in Theories of the Present: The Virtuality of Reflexive Modernization." *European Journal of Social Theory* 9 (2): 223–37.

Shiller, Robert. 1993. "Speculative Prices and Popular Models." In *Advances in Behavioral Finance*, ed. Richard H. Thaler, 493–505. New York: Russell Sage Foundation.

———. 2003. *The New Financial Order: Risk in the 21st Century*. Princeton: Princeton University Press.

Siegert, Bernhard. 1998. "Switchboards and Sex: The Nut(t) Case." In *Inscribing Science: Scientific Texts and the Materiality of Communication*, ed. T. Lenoir, 78–90. Stanford, CA: Stanford University Press.

Simmel, Georg. [1901] 1989. *Philosophie des Geldes*. Frankfurt: Suhrkamp.

Smelser, Neil. 1962. *Theory of Collective Behavior*. London: Routledge & Kegan Paul.

Smith, Adam. [1759] 1966. *The Theory of Moral Sentiments*. New York: Augustus M. Kelley.

———. [1776] 1991. *The Wealth of Nations*. Amherst, NY: Prometheus Books.

Smith, Charles. 1999. *Success and Survival on Wall Street: Understanding the Mind of the Market*. Rev. ed. Lanham, MD: Rowman & Littlefield.

Smith, Matthew Hale. 1871. *Twenty Years Among the Bulls and Bears of Wall Street*. Hartford: J. B. Burr & Hyde.

Sobel, Robert. [1972] 1999. *Panic on Wall Street: A History of America's Financial Disasters*. Rev. ed. Frederick, MD: Beard Books.

———. 1975. *N.Y.S.E.: A History of the New York Stock Exchange 1935–1975*. New York: Weybright and Talley.

Sombart, Werner. 1920. *Der Bourgeois. Zur Geistesgeschichte des modernen Wirtschaftsmenschen* [The bourgeois: The intellectual history of the modern economic man]. München and Leipzig: Duncker & Humblot.

Some Seasonable Considerations for Those Who Are Desirous, By Subscription, Or Purchase, to Become Proprietors of South-Sea Stock. 1720. London: J. Morphew.

Sourigues, M. 1861. *De la valeur des actions de la Cie du Chemin de Fer de Lyon à Genève*. Paris: Castel.

———. 1862. *De la valeur des actions du Credit Foncier de France*. Paris: Castel.

Staeheli, Urs. 2002. "Fatal Attraction? Popular Modes of Inclusion in the Economic System." *Soziale Systeme* 8 (1): 110–23.

Star, Susan Leigh, and Geoffrey Bowker. 1999. *Sorting Things Out: Classification and Its Consequences*. Cambridge, MA: MIT Press.

Star, Susan Leigh, and Jean R Griesemer. 1989. "Institutional Ecology, 'Translations' and Boundary Objects: Amateurs and Professionals in Berkeley's Museum of Vertebrate Zoology, 1907–39." *Social Studies of Science* 19:387–420.

Statistical Abstract for the US. 1913. Washington: Govt. Printing Office.

Stedman, Edmund Clarence, ed. 1905. *The New York Stock Exchange: Its History, Its Contribution to the National Prosperity, and Its Relation to American Finance at the Outset of the Twentieth Century*. New York: New York Stock Exchange Historical Company.

Stein, Jeremy. 2001. "Reflections on Time, Time-Space Compression and Technology in the Nineteenth-Century." In *Timespace: Geographies of Temporality*, ed. J. May and N. Thrift, 106–19. London: Routledge.

Stinchcombe, Arthur L. 1990. *Information and Organizations*. Berkeley, CA: University of California Press.

Stocks and Stock-Jobbing in Wall-Street, with Sketches of the Brokers, and Fancy Stocks. 1848. New York: New York Publishing Company.

"Stocks: And the Big Operators of the Streets; The Science of Speculation as Studied by a Leading Operator." 1881. *Cincinnati Enquirer*, April 13.

Stock Speculation: A Daily Market Report. 1875. New York: L. W. Hamilton & Co.

Suchman, Mark C. 1995. "Managing Legitimacy: Strategic and Institutional Approaches." *The Academy of Management Review* 20 (3): 571–610.

Sullivan, Edward J., and Timothy M. Weithers. 1991. "Louis Bachelier: The Father of the Modern Options Pricing Theory." *Journal of Economic Education* 22 (2): 165–71.

Sur la proposition du premier ministre des finances, relative à la Caisse d'escompte. 1789. Paris: Baudouin.

Swedberg, Richard. 2005. "Conflicts of Interests in the US Brokerage Industry." In *The Sociology of Financial Markets*, ed. Karin Knorr Cetina and Alex Preda, 187–203. Oxford: Oxford University Press.

Sylla, Richard. 2005. "Origins of the New York Stock Exchange." In *The Origins of Value: The Financial Innovations That Created Modern Capital Markets*, ed. William N. Goetzmann and K. Geert Rouwenhorst, 299–312. Oxford: Oxford University Press.

Talmage, Thomas DeWitt. 1866. *Behind the Counter: A Sermon to Our Clerks*. Philadelphia: George T. Hartman.

———. 1879. *The Masque Torn Off*. Chicago: J. Fairbanks.

———. 1888. *Social Dynamite: Or, the Wickedness of Modern Society*, ed. Frances P. Van Nostrand. Oakland, CA: Arthur Whitney.

Taylor, Charles. 2004. *Modern Social Imaginaries*. Durham, NC: Duke University Press.

Tétreau, François. 1994. *Le développement et les usages de la coulisse aux XIXe et XXe siècles*. PhD diss., University of Paris II.

Thévenot, Laurent. 1993. "Agir avec d'autres: Conventions et objets dans l'action coordonnée" [Acting with others: Conventions and objects in the coordinated action]. In *La théorie de l'action: Le sujet pratique en débat*, ed. Paul Ladrière, Patrick Pharo, and Louis Quéré, 275–90. Paris: CNRS Éditions.

———. 2002. "Conventions of Co-ordination and the Framing of Uncertainty." In *Intersubjectivity in Economics: Agents and Structures*, ed. E. Fullbrook, 181–97. London: Routledge.

Tillman, Robert H., and Michael L. Indergaard. 2005. *Pump and Dump: The Rancid Rules of the New Economy*. New Brunswick, NJ: Rutgers University Press.

Tilly, Charles. 1998. *Durable Inequality*. Berkeley, CA: University of California Press.

Tiryakian, Edward. 1959. "Aftermath of a Thermonuclear Attack on the United States: Some Sociological Considerations." *Social Problems* 6 (4): 291–304.

Todhunter, I. 1965. *A History of the Mathematical Theory of Probability from the Time of Pascal to that of Laplace*. New York: Chelsea Publishing Co.

Train, George Francis. 1857. *Young America in Wall Street*. New York: Derby and Jackson.

Trollope, Anthony. [1875] 1982. *The Way We Live Now*. Oxford: Oxford University Press.

Truth: A Letter to the Gentlemen of Exchange Alley. 1733. London: T. Cooper.

Turner, Stephen P. 2003. *Liberal Democracy 3.0.: Civil Society in an Age of Experts*. London: Sage.

US Bureau of Census. 2008. Securities Industry—Financial Summary: 1990 to 2005, table 1208. http://www.census.gov/compendia/statab/tables/08s1192.pdf (accessed April 23, 2008).

Van Antwerp, W. C. 1913. *The Stock Exchange from Within*. New York: Doubleday.

Veblen, Thorstein. [1899] 1949. *The Theory of the Leisure Class*. London: George Allen & Unwin.

Vidal, E. 1910. *The History and Methods of the Paris Bourse*. Washington: Government Printing Office.

Vines, Stephen. 2005. *Market Panic: Wild Gyrations, Risks and Opportunities in Stock Markets*. Singapore: John Wiley & Sons.

Wachtel, Howard M. 2003. *Street of Dreams—Boulevard of Broken Hearts: Wall Street's First Century*. London: Pluto Press.

Walker, Donald. 2001. "A Factual Account of the Functioning of the 19th Century Paris Bourse." *European Journal for the History of Economic Thought* 8 (2): 186–207.

Warner, Kee, and Harvey Molotch. 1993. "Information in the Marketplace: Media Explanations of the '87 Crash." *Social Problems* 40 (2): 167–88.

Warner, Michael. 2002. *Publics and Counterpublics*. New York: Zone Books.

Warren, Pete. 2008. "City Business Races the Games for Power." The *Guardian*, TechnologyGuardian, May 29, p. 3.

Warshow, Robert Irving. 1929. *The Story of Wall Street*. New York: Greenberg.

Waterloo Directory of English Newspapers and Periodicals. 1997. Waterloo, Canada: North Waterloo Academic Press.

Wayland, Francis. 1837. *Elements of Political Economy*. New York: Leavitt, Lord & Co.

Wealth and Biography of the Wealthy Citizens of New York City. 1845. New York: Sun.

Weber, Max. [1894] 1924. "Die Börse." In *Gesammelte Aufsätze zur Soziologie und Sozialpolitik*, 256–322. Tübingen: J. C. B. Mohr.

———. [1894] 2000a. "Stock and Commodity Exchanges." *Theory and Society* 29:305–38.

———. [1894] 2000b. "Commerce on the Stock and Commodity Exchanges." *Theory & Society* 29:339–71.

———. [1920] 1988. *Gesammelte Aufsätze zur Religionssoziologie*. Tübingen: Mohr Siebeck.

———. [1921] 1972. *Wirtschaft und Gesellschaft* [Economy and society]. Tübingen: Mohr.

———. 1948. *From Max Weber: Essays in Sociology*, ed. H. H. Gerth and C. Wright Mills. London: Routledge and Kegan Paul.

Webster, Peletiah. 1785. *A Seventh Essay on Free Trade and Finance*. Philadelphia: Eleazed Oswald.

———. 1791. *To the Stock-Holders of the Bank of North America, on the Subject of Old and New Banks*. Philadelphia.

Weidenfeld, Ursula. 2005. "Heuschrecken im Depot" [Locusts in the portfolio]. *Der Tagesspiegel*, May 10.

Wells, H. G. 1938. *The War of the Worlds* as performed by Orson Welles and the Mercury Theatre on the Air, October 30. http://members.aol.com/jeff1070/script.html (accessed June 8, 2006).

Wheeler, J. F. 1913. *The Stock Exchange*. London: T. C. & E. C. Jack.

White, Harrison. 2000. "Modeling Discourse In and Around Markets." *Poetics* 27:117–33.

———. 2002. *Markets from Networks: Socioeconomic Models of Production*. Princeton, NJ: Princeton University Press.

Wiebe, Robert H. 1962. *Businessmen and Reform: A Study of the Progressive Movement*. Cambridge, MA: Harvard University Press.

Wilkins, Mira. 1999. "Cosmopolitan Finance in the 1920s: New York's Emergence as an International Financial Centre." In *The State, the Financial System and Economic Modernization*, ed. by Richard Sylla, Richard Tilly, and Gabriel Tortella, 271–91. Cambridge, MA: Cambridge University Press.

Winseck, Dwayne R., and Robert M. Pike. 2007. *Communication and Empire: Media, Markets, and Globalization, 1860–1930*. Durham, NC: Duke University Press.

Womack, Kent L. 1996. "Do Brokerage Analysts' Recommendations Have Investment Value?" *The Journal of Finance* 51 (1): 137–67.

Woolgar, Steve. 1991. "The Turn to Technology in Social Studies of Science." *Science, Technology & Human Values* 16 (1): 20–50.

Wright, G. S. 1842. *A Letter to British Capitalists, upon the Present and Prospective Advantages of Investing Capital in Railway Stock*. London: James Baker.

Wyckoff, Peter. 1972. *Wall Street and the Stock Markets: A Chronology (1644–1971)*. Philadelphia: Chilton.

Wyckoff, Richard D. 1930. *Wall Street Ventures and Adventures*. New York: Harper & Brothers.

———. 1933. "1901: Inside Information." *Stock Market Technique* 2 (5): 24–26.

———. 1934a. "It's Not the *Kind* of a Chart But Your Ability to Interpret That Counts." *Stock Market Technique* 3 (2): 10.

———. 1934b. "1905: Studying the Big Fellows." *Stock Market Technique* 3 (2): 37–39.

———. 1934c. "1902–1903 Experiences in the Brokerage Business" *Stock Market Technique* 2 (6): 23–25.

———. 1934d. "The Tape Is the Best Guide." *Stock Market Technique* 3 (2): 12.

———. 1934e. "Why the Dots on the Tape?" *Stock Market Technique* 3 (2): 20.

———. 1934f. "Why You Should Use Charts." *Stock Market Techniques* 2 (6): 16.

Wyckoff, Richard D. [Rollo Tape, pseud.]. 1908. "Market Lecture: Manipulation—Tape Readings—Charts." The *Ticker* 1 (4) (February): 33–35.

———. 1910. *Studies in Tape Reading*. New York: The Ticker Publishing Company.

Wyckoff, Richard D. [signed anonymous]. 1907. "A Method of Forecasting the Stock Market." The *Ticker* 1 (1): 2–4.

———. 1908. "Why Not Investment Experts? Demand for Advice and Opinions on Investments, Suggests the Establishment of a New Profession." The *Ticker* 1 (6) (April): 35.

Yates, JoAnne. 1994. "Evolving Information Use in Firms, 1850–1920: Ideology and Information Techniques and Technologies." In *Information Acumen: The Understanding and Use of Knowledge in Modern Business*, ed. Lisa Bud-Frierman, 26–51. London: Routledge.

Zaloom, Caitlin. 2003. "Ambiguous Numbers: Trading Technologies and Interpretation in Financial Markets." *American Ethnologist* 30 (2): 258–72.

———. 2005. "The Discipline of Speculators." In *Global Assemblages: Technology, Politics, and Ethics as Anthropological Problems*, ed. Aihwa Ong and Stephen Collier, 253–69. Oxford: Blackwell.

———. 2006. *Out of the Pits: Traders and Technology from Chicago to London*. Chicago: The University of Chicago Press.

Zimmerman, David. 2003. "Frank Norris, Market Panic, and the Mesmeric Sub-
    lime." *American Literature* 75 (1): 61–90.
Zimmermann, Heinz, and Wolfgang Hafner. 2006. "Vincenz Bronzin's Option Pric-
    ing Theory: Contents, Contribution and Background." In vol. 1, *Contributions
    Prior to Irving Fisher*, of *Pioneers of Financial Economics*, ed. Geoffrey Poitras,
    238–64. Cheltenham, UK: Edward Elgar.
Zola, Émile. [1891] 1897. *L'argent*. Paris: Charpentier.
Zorn, Dirk, Frank Dobbin, Julian Dierkes, and Man-Shan Kwok. 2005. "Managing
    Investors: How Financial Markets Reshaped the American Firm." In *The So-
    ciology of Financial Markets*, ed. Karin Knorr Cetina and Alex Preda, 269–89.
    Oxford: Oxford University Press.
Zuckermann, Ezra. 1999. "The Categorical Imperative: Securities Analysts and the
    Illegitimacy Discount." *American Journal of Sociology* 104 (5): 1398–1438.
Zylberberg, André. 1990. *L'économie mathématique en France 1870–1914*. Paris:
    Economica.

Index

abacus of the speculator, 104. *See also*
  Lefevre, Henri
access: control and, 152; information and,
  75; knowledge and, 133, 136, 148, 162,
  172, 183, 189, 212; membership and,
  65; observations and, 9, 12, 13, 242–43,
  248, 256, 277; price data and, 109, 116,
  120, 125, 127, 138, 171; public, 18; space
  and, 66–67; status groups and, 56, 58;
  the ticker and, 138, 139; tools of, 16;
  transactions and, 15, 17, 19, 21, 24,
  43–45, 141, 144, 170, 173, 195, 204
accumulating capitalist, 29, 33, 35, 38, 44, 49
accumulation, 26, 32, 35–38, 40–41, 45,
  49, 85–86, 200–201. *See also* capital;
  capitalist
action: agency and, 116; collective, 7,
  255n12; coordination of, 6, 8, 10–11,
  13, 15–16, 28, 34–35; dispersed, 6, 8,
  13, 15, 18, 196, 222; economic, 7–8, 33,
  41, 46, 51, 117–18, 169, 255n15, 275n5;
  financial, 53, 64; group action, 57; honor
  and, 57; intentional, 116; observation
  and, 137, 150, 155, 161, 169, 196, 236,
  256n16, 257n25; rational, 41; rules of, 87,
  90; technology and, 119, 120, 128, 132;
  uncertain coordination of, 8, 11, 18, 234,
  255n14, 255n16, 257n25. *See also* actors;
  agency; behavior: collective
actors: behavior of, 101, 104, 108, 114, 118,
  28, 132, 137, 142; brokers as, 94; calculations and, 143, 145, 150, 153–54, 168–70,
  172, 180, 196, 204, 211; categories of, 60;
  dispersed actions and, 9, 11–17, 19, 25,

27, 217–19, 223, 232, 234, 236, 255n16,
  256n19, 259n14, 260n5, 276n12; economic, 5–6, 8, 31, 33, 43, 44, 117; expectations and, 100; financial, 45, 50–56,
  63–64, 76–77, 80, 82–83, 90, 111, 113;
  honor and, 91; knowledge and, 98. *See
  also* action; agency
admission criteria on the stock exchange,
  56, 58, 68, 70–71, 75. *See also* access
agency: action and, 116; boundaries and, 22,
  116; financial, 16; panic and, 220, 256n16
agential capacity, 120, 173
agiotage, 108, 266n19
allegory, 84, 204
American Stock Exchange, 141
analogy: gambling and speculation, 85;
  investing and the natural sciences, 90;
  society and living organisms, 185; stock
  exchange and nature, 91, 101, 102, 202
analysts: chart, 162, 164, 167, 170, 244;
  classifications and, 150; culture of star,
  163; data and, 21, 25, 27, 53, 54, 120;
  market, 143, 145; profession of, 149;
  technical, 147–48, 245, 251, 270n3,
  271n5n10; technical and fundamental,
  146; witnessing and, 153. *See also*
  analytical techniques; expert knowledge;
  information; professions; technology
analytical techniques: charts and, 147; examination of markets and, 101; language
  and, 54, 90, 166. *See also* expert
  knowledge; information; technology
appresentation, 20, 129, 276n8
arbitrage, 140, 276n12

gambling: capital accumulation and, 201,
206; court cases and, 109; fury, 46–47,
49; modeling of, 98–99, 102; options
and, 105, 182–83, 199–200, 274n14; panic
and, 233; public opinion and, 263n4;
redefinition of, 107; speculation and, 20,
64, 85–86, 89, 108, 175–77, 181, 259n16,
264n7, 266n17n18
game, 23, 27, 133, 179, 201, 255n16, 264n12,
272n16
Gaming Act, 105, 263n4
general system of exchange, 191
genre, 20, 77, 80, 88, 90, 111, 195, 203. See
also figure
gentlemanly conduct, 72. See also honor;
witnessing
globalization, 7, 22, 246, 254n11
groups: analysts and, 143–45, 148, 153–58,
160, 170; boundaries and, 10–11, 15, 17,
19, 21, 52, 58, 60–61, 63, 80, 274n25; of
brokers, 26, 162; conformity and, 47;
control and, 25; of experts, 146, 151, 250;
hierarchy of, 76; intermediary, 53–55,
58; jurisdiction and, 120, 150; knowledge
and, 28; legitimacy and, 12–13, 16, 67;
monopolies and, 45; networks and, 53–
54; observation and, 55, 59; panic and,
215, 218, 220; small, 5; social position
and, 7; ticker and, 142. See also status
growth, 47, 88, 183, 241, 255n11

Hegel, Georg Friedrich Wilhelm, 33–35, 38,
258n6, 258n8, 273n4
hierarchy: of brokerage houses, 154; force
and, 231; of groups, 65, 236; observation
and, 223; of speculators, 26, 31, 58,
205–7, 209, 214, 246, 250; of transaction
places, 76
honor: behavior and, 43–45; brokers and, 59,
62–63, 73–75, 78–80, 125, 187; codes of,
62–63; hierarchies and, 76; lack of, 64;
social indicators of, 195, 259n15, 262n3;
and status, 50–51, 56–58. See also
groups
hysteria, 92, 215, 218–19, 276n10. See also
panic

identity, 1, 5, 11, 56, 253n1
imaginary, 37, 39, 105, 276n7
individualization, 31, 46, 200, 216, 237

industry: cycles and, 159; economic action
and, 30; panic and, 227; securities and, 4,
238; as source of wealth, 175; speculation
and, 186, 190, 210–11
information: analysts and, 149; behavior
and, 92, 94, 100; communication and,
256n18; groups and, 75; narrative, 95,
122; networks and, 9, 53, 278n7; panics
and, 222; prices and, 25, 95, 97, 112–13,
121–22, 140, 239–40, 266n15, 267n2,
267n8, 269n15, 269n17, 270n18; private,
95–96; public, 100; statistics and, 156,
271n6; stock exchanges and, 42, 50;
technology and, 54, 153, 272n17
innovation, 46–47
institution: boundaries and, 39, 52, 207;
economic life and, 35, 202, 254n9; honor
and, 57; knowledge and, 88; legitimacy
and, 19, 260n3; persons and, 258n11;
politics and, 196; professions and, 150; of
the stock exchange, 4, 16, 21, 24, 42, 59,
75, 77, 151, 177, 184, 188, 193, 237, 239,
241, 261n10; trading and, 249
institutionalization, of the stock exchange,
67. See also institution
interface: financial markets as, 38; between
regulators and markets, 239; rhetoric
as, 50. See also device: mediating; lens;
observation: system
invention, 114, 116, 268n10. See also
institution; stock exchange; technology
investor: behavior, 25, 92, 90, 93, 97–98, 112,
114, 118, 134, 224; brokers and, 132–33,
135–36; classes of, 167–68; education
and, 247; gender and race, 274n2; information and, 95, 97, 100; institutional, 5;
observation and, 92; panic and, 275n4;
religion and, 190; rights movement,
280n23; as a scientist, 26; small, 8, 16, 45,
107, 206, 259n16, 280n23; speculators
and, 3, 253n6; spirit of capitalism and,
6–7, 44, 259n14; status and, 58; technology and, 267n9; transactions and,
130; tributary rights and, 42

journalism, financial, 77
judgment, 161–62, 163, 214
jurisdiction: control and, 67; expertise and,
149, 150, 153; markets and, 262n14;
status and, 56–57; technology and, 118